HEAVY HANDS

An Introduction to the Crimes of Family Violence

Third Edition

Denise Kindschi Gosselin

Western New England College

PEARSON

Prentice
Hall

Upper Saddle River, New Jersey 07458

Library of Congress Cataloging-in-Publication Data

Gosselin, Denise Kindschi
  Heavy hands : an introduction to the crimes of family violence / Denise Kindschi Gosselin.— 3rd ed.
    p.   cm.
  Includes bibliographical references.
  ISBN 0-13-118885-2
1. Family violence—Philosophy.   2. Family violence—Government policy.   3. Victims of family violence—Services for.   I. Title.

HV6626.G67 2005
362.82′92—dc22

2004020561

Executive Editor: Frank Mortimer, Jr.
Associate Editor: Sarah Holle
Production Editor: Karen Berry, Pine Tree Composition
Production Liaison: Barbara Marttine Cappuccio
Director of Manufacturing and Production: Bruce Johnson
Managing Editor: Mary Carnis
Manufacturing Buyer: Cathleen Pertersen
Creative Director: Cheryl Asherman
Cover Design Coordinator: Miguel Ortiz
Cover Designer: Anthony Gemmellaro
Cover Image: Digital Vision
Marketing Manager: Tim Peyton
Formatting and Interior Design: Pine Tree Composition
Printing and Binding: Phoenix Book Technology Park

Pearson Prentice Hall™ is a trademark of Pearson Education, Inc.
Pearson® is a registered trademark of Pearson plc
Prentice Hall® is a registered trademark of Pearson Education, Inc.

Pearson Education LTD.
Pearson Education Singapore, Pte. Ltd
Pearson Education, Canada, Ltd
Pearson Education–Japan
Pearson Education Australia PTY, Limited
Pearson Education North Asia Ltd
Pearson Educación de Mexico, S.A. de C.V.
Pearson Education Malaysia, Pte. Ltd
Pearson Education Upper Saddle River, New Jersey

10 9 8 7 6 5 4 3 2 1
ISBN 0-13-118885-2

To my parents, Elizabeth and Gerald Feldmann.
My gratitude for your unconditional and unwavering
love and support throughout the years.

From your example I have learned many things:
Respect is the foundation of a good relationship;
hard work is the key to successful living;
and continued learning brings lifelong fulfillment!

Contents

Part Five

Preface

Thousands of police officers across the country routinely come face to face with domestic violence. With little direction they face the challenges that researchers and academics ponder. Rarely are they part of the intellectual discourse on abuse and neglect. This book is a small step toward bringing us all together. This third edition includes current information on numerous topics of interest in the field of family violence. Each chapter begins with a practical scenario that poses a question for students to consider. The answers will be provided within that chapter. This will allow students to anticipate some information as they read the text and then apply that information to a real-life situation. There are new sections throughout the text that address the crimes committed against adults and children with disabilities, as well as the police role in these domestic situations. New also are sections on elder battering and elder abuse treatment for perpetrators. In the legal section of the text is new information on domestic violence courts and on the full faith and credit provisions of the Violence Against Women Act. Primary and dominant aggressor determination is the newest response to the difficult problem of dual arrest situations; this is new for the third edition. New and expanded information on death review teams and on stalking are included also. I hope that this current information will be helpful for instruction with your students. All Internet links have been tested throughout the text to make every effort toward currency.

My first domestic call came shortly after graduation from the Massachusetts State Police Academy in 1980. Impressed with my accomplishments, the call was a rude awakening. To this day I remember the gut-wrenching feeling when going through the front door of that home. I did not have a clue about what should be done.

More surprisingly, the victim was a man, over six feet tall. He had just announced that he was moving out and his girlfriend didn't want him to leave. When he was on the phone with the police, she had grabbed the phone and struck him over the head with it. Blood was everywhere and he required numerous stitches. Afterward I returned him to the house and counseled them both. The resolution never seemed quite right!

Fortunately, the movement to intervene in family violence had begun and I became a part of that change. W. Michael Ryan, the Northwestern District Attorney, was instrumental toward developing my interest in domestic abuse. I owe him a debt of gratitude for the training and support that this office supplied while I was a detective assigned to his organization. We developed the first multidisciplinary team in Massachusetts to screen and investigate child abuse allegations. Struggling through the new legislation on mandated reporting, the office was inundated with complaints of sexual and physical abuse. Working together with the Department of Social Services, prosecutors, physicians, victim witnesses, and mental health agencies, an increase in successful prosecution was accomplished.

Our success was due in part to the aggressive investigation of family violence. It was treated like any other major crime. Child victim statements were routinely videotaped to assure the defense of their accuracy. Adult victims were treated equally and with respect regardless of their sexual orientation, gender, race, or the make-up of the offender. Evidence to corroborate the statement was collected through search warrants whenever possible. Perpetrators were arrested and prosecuted only after a thorough investigation. Interviews and interrogations were the norm in every case.

After 12 years on the state police force I became an educator at Western New England College in Springfield, Massachusetts. My passion to understand the dynamics of family violence and the role of criminal justice led me to develop a course on the topic in 1992. It has been offered numerous times since then, with minor revisions each time. My approach is sociolegal, with a leaning toward the criminal justice perspective. It is now a permanent course offering at our institution and has been cross referenced and may be taken at the undergraduate level as a criminal justice or sociology course. There is so much to learn that this book can provide only a comprehensive beginning. It includes information on all forms of family violence.

The book is designed to follow in content the course that I have offered over the years. It is meant to assist both educators with no field experience and those with professional backgrounds to meld the theory and practice of domestic violence for students of the social sciences. It is meant to tear down myths about both victims and offenders. Women and men have been victimized. Elderly and children are present as both perpetrators and victims as well. Heterosexuals and homosexuals can both be violent; dating relationships can be dangerous. To leave anyone out is to ignore the pain and suffering that domestic violence brings.

Students of criminal justice tire quickly when hearing about the mistakes of the profession. Therefore, I wrote this book with an eye toward the future, without dwelling on the past. It is my desire that crimes of domestic violence be identified and the consequences understood. As much as possible, the perpetrators are characterized and victimization is illustrated. My purpose is to provide a positive and instructive book from the criminal justice perspective, bringing together the causes and consequences of domestic violence and law enforcement response. The text addresses the following questions: What is domestic violence? Why does it happen, and what are the consequences? Who are the offenders, and who are the victims? What legislation exists relative to family violence? How does the criminal justice community respond? How do you get help? What resources are available?

More human misery has been caused by domestic relationships than all of the wars in history combined. The very nature of these relationships dictates that they will be imperfect, fluctuate, and perhaps end. Yet it is not the unhappiness caused by a failed or flawed relationship that we find egregious. What is unacceptable is when one human being purposely inflicts pain upon another and does so by design. This is when the inevitable human discord crosses the line into abuse and one party chooses to apply a heavy hand to the other. It does not matter one bit whether the abuse takes the form of physical, emotional, or sexual violence. This type of act is such that it can and is being regulated by recently enacted laws in countries that are advanced in areas of public policy and criminal law enforcement. It is the wave of the future. More laws will follow; more countries will follow; more of us will agree. Heavy hands are wrong!

Acknowledgments

Thank you to the many victims who have confided in me about atrocities too horrible to recount. I *still* remember you. You taught me the value of dignity and the importance of equal enforcement of the law. To the women, men, boys, and girls who have suffered from domestic crimes, I marvel at your resilience and applaud your survival.

I owe a debt of gratitude to Kathy Arenstam, whose contribution in the first edition provided consistency. Thank you, Danielle D. McIntosh, for the research on elder law. Cynthia Kindschi, always there when I needed your support! A very deep appreciation to my parents, Elizabeth and Gerald Feldmann, whose love and guidance have provided a positive basis for comparison. To Robert Gosselin, without whom this book would not have been possible, my love.

To my friends and colleagues at Western New England College, who encouraged my efforts, thank you. In particular, Professor Janet Bowdan, whose reading and editing on the first edition was invaluable, and to Professor Larry Field, who offered great insight and shared his expertise on the historical account, which was included in the second edition. Thank you to the reviewers who spent so much time and effort in reviewing the third edition: Yvonne Downes, Hilbert College, Hamburg, NY; Dennis McCarty, SUNY Albany, Albany, NY; and Bernadette Muscat, California State University–Fresno, Fresno, CA. Your comments and suggestions added significantly to this third edition.

About the Author

A pioneer in law enforcement, the author became the first uniformed female officer for her hometown, Lunenburg, Massachusetts, and the first female campus police officer at the Community College she had attended. The Massachusetts Senate honored her in 1978 as the first woman appointed constable for the City of Fitchburg. In 1979 she was named an Outstanding Young Woman of America.

Trooper Gosselin graduated in the 61st Recruit Training Troop of the Massachusetts State Police in January, 1980. During the 12 years that followed she served as a uniformed officer performing route patrol activities; as an instructor at the Massachusetts State Police Academy; and as a major crime detective. Recognized as a local expert in Child Abuse Investigation, she spoke on cable television and on radio. She and Trooper Gibbons appeared on *America's Most Wanted* when John Walsh presented their fugitive case on the show. Additionally, she has made many presentations at professional meetings with the Department of Social Services, Department of Mental Health, and for the Office of the District Attorney. Trooper Gosselin has testified on numerous major crime cases, both in Criminal Court and in Civil Hearings.

Like many police officers, her education was fragmented, interrupted over the years by demanding work and family responsibilities. Denise holds an Associate

Degree in Science in Law Enforcement from Mt. Wachusett Community College; her Bachelor and Masters Degrees in Criminal Justice were awarded from Westfield State College. At the University of Massachusetts she studied at the doctoral level in the Political Science department. She was awarded a scholarship to attend the first Child Abuse and Exploitation Investigative Techniques Training Program at the Federal Law Enforcement Training Center. Denise has additional training in homicide investigation, rape, search and seizure, and stalking. In 1995 she studied at the International Institute for the Sociology of Law in Onati, Spain. Denise is a doctoral candidate at Capella University.

From 1991 to the present the author has lectured at Greenfield Community College, Holyoke Community College, and Westfield State College as an adjunct. Presently she serves on the faculty of the Criminal Justice and Sociology Department at Western New England College in Springfield, Massachusetts. Her research efforts have concentrated on domestic violence, juvenile law, and interviewing/interrogation. She developed the curriculum for courses in Domestic Violence and Interviewing/ Interrogation that have been made permanent course offerings at Western New England College. Mrs. Gosselin taught Domestic Abuse for the 74th Massachusetts State Police Recruit Training Troop.

Part One

Domestic Violence Crime:
Definition, Prevalence, and History

Domestic violence is a familiar phrase to most people today, but what does it really mean? How often does it occur? Is domestic violence a new phenomenon? Do any countries other than the United States view domestic abuse as problematic? These and many other questions are answered in Part One.

In Chapter 1, "Violence in the Family," we provide a base for future chapters to build upon. This is where you learn the meaning of common terms and look at the prevalence rates for the various forms of domestic violence. What are the recognized illegal acts? How are the relationships defined? Are all forms of domestic violence criminal behavior? Are there separate laws that forbid violence between people that are related by blood or marriage? Every discipline has a unique vocabulary so those professionals can communicate within the field; familiarization of the terminology allows students to join in the dialogue.

In Chapter 2, "A Global View of Family, Social, and Legal Relations," we broaden the foundation for future chapters. Domestic violence is recognized as a current social problem of epidemic proportions affecting millions of women, men, and children. Here domestic violence is put into perspective both historically and globally. How widespread is family violence? Beyond the people who are victimized and those who perpetuate the violence, a larger picture emerges. Has society only recently begun to legislate against violence committed within the family? Have laws that were poorly designed and sporadically enforced actually encouraged and contributed to the problems that we face today? Have we discovered something new, or are we looking at unresolved issues of the past? Additionally, we examine the concerns of foreign nations on the issues of family violence. Is domestic violence particular to our society? We look from the past to the present without being confined to our own society.

CHAPTER 1

VIOLENCE IN THE FAMILY

SIMPLY SCENARIO

Man Tries to Burn Down House

Charles had been drinking heavily and had an argument with his ex-girlfriend. He threatened to burn down her house. A short time later he set fire to some cardboard boxes on the porch, causing charring to the wood before she could put it out. Charles then tried to light a door on fire with a lighter before running to his truck. Charles started up his truck and starting ramming the vehicle owned by his ex-girlfriend. The ex-girlfriend indicated that she feared for her life.

Question: Is there any indication that this scenario represented a domestic violence situation? Explain your answer.

KEY TERMS

Abuse prevention acts
Battered child syndrome
Battering
Child abuse
Dating violence
Domestic abuse acts
Domestic violence
Elder abuse
Emotional abuse
Financial exploitation

Neglect
Parent abuse
Partner battering
Physical abuse
Psychological abuse
Rape
Sexual abuse
Spouse abuse
Wife abuse

INTRODUCTION

This book is about terror, fear, confusion, and despair: a hopelessness that characterizes the victims caught in a web of **domestic violence**. Consider this: The person you love is your tormentor. You walk through the door of your home wondering what is going to happen to you today. Will it be a good day, or a bad day? The unpredictability heightens your fear. Domestic violence is a reality. Domestic violence is a crime. The victims are from every walk of life, rich and poor, of every race. The majority of victims are women, but men are terrorized in their homes as well. Intimate dating partners are battered and raped, setting the stage for a life of anguish. Lesbian and homosexual domestic partners may be threatened and beaten as well. Children and spouses victimize the elderly, who thought they knew their abusers. As if that were not bleak enough, adults are not the only victims. Children are physically abused and sexually molested by the adults who "care" for them. Victims are being stalked, and some are being killed. Who is doing these horrible things? Loved ones, parents, and children are the perpetrators. For example,

- A biological father on numerous occasions during visitations raped his 14-year-old daughter. Her 22-year-old sister was also his victim; she had been impregnated by her father when she was 15. The family never talked about it, but the resulting baby was a constant reminder of the physical and emotional pain caused by the rapes.

- A 6-year-old girl complained that her stepbrother who lived with her was hurting her. Physical examination of the child confirmed that she had been raped. The 13-year-old boy was found guilty of rape and sodomy, which had occurred over a two-year period.

- An 11-year-old boy told his social worker that his mother's boyfriend had hit him over the head with the handle of a machete, and that he was having headaches. His mother insisted that her son was not telling the truth. An investigation by the police determined that the boyfriend had repeatedly beaten the boy with a belt on at least one occasion. Another time the man forced the child to stand in front of a door that had a poster picture of Mickey Mouse on it. He fired numerous shots from a handgun at the child, both above his head and at his feet, yelling "you're dead, you're dead!" Afterward, the man took a razor blade and cut him on the little finger, telling him, "When you die, I am going to be the one to kill you." When a search warrant was executed on the home, the poster of Mickey Mouse was found under a mattress, and 11 bullet holes were located on the floor and in the wall.

- An old woman was reluctant to report that her grown son was stealing her money. She was afraid because of his drug habit and believed that he might take what little she had left in her life. At 70 years old, she knew there was no other way to keep from having to go into a nursing home; she had to remain self-sufficient. That meant turning her son in for larceny.

- An investigation into multiple sexual assaults on one young woman was difficult. She came forward as an adult because it had taken time for her to get away from her stepfather, who physically assaulted her as well. Unfortunately, it took her too long to break free. The assaults against her were beyond the statute of limitations; the stepfather could not be prosecuted! The case prompted the local prosecutor to submit a proposal to change the law, extending the statute of limitations in Massachusetts. Future sexual assault victims will now have ten years after reaching majority to come forward with complaints.

- Lying in the hospital was a woman whose face was so swollen that it was barely recognizable. Her eyes were blackened, her nose was swollen twice its size, and her lips were grotesque. It would be years after this particular incident before the woman could bring herself to testify against her abuser in court for the years of battering. During her marriage she had suffered broken bones, broken teeth, and a detached retina, among other injuries too numerous to mention. Due to the many times that he kicked her on the ground and twisted her legs around the kitchen table until they snapped, she walks with a cane. Even worse, she had suffered psychological abuse that ranged from cruel to bizarre. Coming home to find the bloody head of her horse on the walkway was just another way he intimidated and kept control of her.

- A 15-year-old girl pushed her father down the stairs yet another time. She had injured her mother in the past, also. It was not that the parents were elderly, just older than most parents. They were tired from fighting with their growing child and embarrassed that anyone would find out. She was the child of their dreams who turned into a nightmare.

- A 14-year gay relationship ended in the death of the abuser from multiple stab wounds. The victim had endured several years of physical, sexual, and emotional abuse prior to committing the killing. This case became the first successful use of the battered spouse defense where the relationship involved a gay couple.

These are just a sample of the cases that come to mind when domestic violence is discussed. For victims of domestic violence, life is lived in hell, with the perception that there is no way out. Their home is a prison.

Yes, we have noticed the problem. We talk about it. Most people know, or think they know, what domestic violence is. Daily newspapers, magazines, and television report on domestic violence. Stories about famous people in sports, politics, and Hollywood are linked with whispers and screams of family violence. Articles appear on the Internet and in academic journals. Researchers are examining the signs and symptoms of domestic violence. Sitting in coffee shops or in boardrooms, people are talking about it. Still, people laugh and tell jokes about domestic violence! People say that if it is so bad, the victim ought to leave. Plain and simple: Just leave. If they don't leave, it can't really be that bad. Or can it?

On the other hand, *domestic violence* is a term frequently used to describe acts that are not violent, such as mental and verbal abuse. By themselves, these forms of abuse are not illegal. It is difficult to separate mental and verbal abuse from the portrayal of a domestic violence victim. The power and control exercised in a relationship are part of the **battering** syndrome. They warn of the potential for a violent relationship or the existence of one. Mental and verbal indignities are the signs and symptoms of an abusive relationship. They are the tools used to break the spirit and overcome the will. Noncriminal acts of violence must be documented because they increase the creditability of the victim, particularly in cases where the greater injuries may not be visible. Professionals with the duty to respond must understand the crime and make the distinction between criminal and noncriminal domestic violence.

Domestic violence is a crime. Still, some people think that domestic violence legislation is just one more way for the government to interfere in a citizen's private life. A person once asked if he needed to get written permission from his wife to have sexual relations. The man was afraid of being accused of rape! He felt that laws designed to prevent domestic violence were akin to having a police officer in every bedroom.

Whether the perpetrator is a stranger, husband, lover, or parent, **rape** is a criminal act. It is the act that determines the crime, not the relationship. An act is defined as illegal through legislative statutes or through case law. It is the relationship between the offender and the victim that determines if the crime is domestic. Legislation to prevent domestic violence is a social as well as a legal statement. It is a commitment to enforcement of existing statutes for all persons, regardless of their relationship to the offender. Some states have created special court orders designed to protect victims of domestic abuse. Looking closely, one would find similar orders of protection from strangers when the need occurs. Recognizing a domestic relationship does not excuse an otherwise illegal act. It empowers the victim and in turn empowers society. Misinformation and misunderstanding of the issue have become problems, which must be corrected.

Recognition of all victims of domestic violence is not meant to undermine the immensity of the problem faced by millions of female victims. All forms of domestic violence will be addressed fully in this book to examine the dynamics of family battering. Assaults against men by their female partners are not infrequent. However, women who are victimized in domestic violence usually suffer more severe injuries than do male victims. Females batter other females in lesbian relationships. Men victimize other men in homosexual and bisexual relationships. Violence is present in many intimate relationships in the United States. **Sexual abuse** against men and boys is more common than we want to admit. Fear and embarrassment often inhibit a victim from coming forward. Women batter partners in both lesbian and heterosexual relationships, although the exact amount of female perpetrated abuse is unknown.

An arrest is not routinely made when the perpetrator of abuse is a woman. Why? Police officers occasionally suggest a range of excuses for not taking action when probable cause exists to do so. These run the gamut from "he would be embarrassed" to "she didn't hurt him that badly." If domestic violence is to be taken seriously, gender cannot be the determining factor for law enforcement action. There is no law enforcement documentation of the numerous abuse calls where the male is the victim and no action is taken. Domestic violence intervention offers legal protection for all victims, regardless of their relationship to the perpetrator or their gender.

Feminist organizations are responsible for having brought the issue to the forefront, where it can no longer be ignored. Credit must be given to the dedicated women and men who pioneered efforts to understand the dynamics of spousal battering and to protect those victims of abuse. Domestic violence is now recognized as a major social problem. Having identified the problem, people seek ways to do away with it. Federal and state funding has been established for research, protection, and education on domestic violence. Legislation was passed to provide necessary protection for the victims. Criminology, victimology, and family violence courses are offered in colleges and universities to address the issues and discuss solutions. We have taken enormous strides toward understanding the various ways in which we hurt the ones that we "love."

Where has all the media hype, research, and dialogue brought us? Quite frankly, back to the beginning. What we know about domestic violence is anything but complete. There is no easy way to abolish it, no pill to take to make it better. Experts debate implications of this festering illness that breeds among us and weakens family structure. Theorists discuss possible explanations: cultural, social, psychological, biological, and learned. In the recent past, people routinely did not want to acknowledge that incest and **physical abuse** to children existed. It was difficult to accept that the elderly were being battered and neglected by their own children. Spousal abuse was also readily denied. Now that these forms of domestic abuse have been identified, the dialogue will continue.

The criminal justice community has been identified as the most logical source of protection and empowerment for the domestic violence victim. New legislation and public policy, which now mandate a law enforcement response, are in effect. Police officers are delineated as the primary first responder in the war to eradicate and control this disease, at least until another option is discovered. Simultaneously, researchers and policy makers must remain concerned by the pitfalls of an inadequate response by the criminal justice system to domestic violence. The law enforcement community is charged with dealing with this serious problem. Educational avenues must be explored that may assist us to meet the formidable task.

This book is about meeting that challenge. It will be rewarding for every person who is interested in the factors involving domestic violence in the United States. What do we know about it? What has been done to control domestic violence? How do we recognize battering, and what action should be taken? The purpose of this book is to bring a detailed explanation of domestic violence and prevention efforts to those who have been tasked by society to intervene and to those who want to become involved.

WHAT IS DOMESTIC VIOLENCE?

There is no one definition of domestic violence that totally explains the complex dynamics of family violence. Diverse perspectives are provided here. The *Roxbury Dictionary of Criminal Justice* (Champion, 1997) offers a good definition for the criminal justice professional:

> Domestic violence: any spousal altercation or interfamilial conflicts of sufficient nature to justify law enforcement intervention; spousal abuse is most frequently cited. May involve parent–child conflict, either physical or psychological.

Police action is not the only way to identify whether or not domestic violence has occurred since most domestic violence is never reported to the police. Federal and state laws recognize that domestic relationships include partnerships where people live together but are not legally married. Any definition that is furthered to explain domestic violence is necessarily general in nature. Same-sex relationships and roommates may also constitute domestic partners. Persons in same-sex and transgender relationships define domestic violence in ways that are similar to heterosexual abuses. Island and Letellier (1991) define gay male domestic violence as

> Any unwanted physical force, psychological abuse, material or property damage inflicted by one man on another.

Within the context of lesbian battering Hart (1986) provides a definition that addresses the dynamics of battering that is applicable to all relationships:

> Lesbian battering is a pattern of violent or coercive behaviors whereby a lesbian seeks to control the thoughts, beliefs, or conduct of her intimate partner or to punish the intimate for resisting the perpetrator's control. Individual acts of physical violence, by this definition, do not constitute lesbian battering. Physical violence is not battering unless it results in the enhanced control of the batterer over the recipient.

The California Family Code defines domestic violence as abuse or violence that is perpetrated against any person in a legally recognized domestic relationship. It is important to note that many forms of abuse are socially unacceptable and are part of the violent relationship but do not rise to the level of criminal violations. Other domestic abuse situations clearly constitute crimes and require law enforcement intervention. Domestic violence situations are often not easy to interpret legally and are always unpleasant. Sometimes it is difficult to determine exactly who has done what. The response role is not limited to law enforcement, however. Noncriminal abuse and **neglect** will also often come to the attention of law enforcement officers. In these situations, police officers can play an important role by referring the apparent victim to appropriate health or social service agencies. There may be children involved who desperately need someone to intervene on their behalf.

In many cases, the law requires that the first responder take action when he or she is a service provider or law enforcement officer. When police, medical, and educational professionals become aware of **child abuse**, all states require them to report the matter to a designated agency, whether it be an appropriate child welfare agency or law enforcement agency.

Crimes Against the Person

Domestic abuse is a classification containing many crimes that are committed against the person, where that person has an intimate or a familial type of relationship with the offender (Figure 1–1). Examples of crimes committed against the person include the following:

- Assault
- Assault and battery
- Assault with a dangerous weapon
- Aggravated assault
- Murder
- Rape
- Stalking

Figure 1–1 Any crime of violence committed against an intimate or family member is domestic violence.

As stated earlier, these acts are illegal if committed against a stranger; therefore, it is the relationship of the perpetrator to the victim that often characterizes these crimes as domestic violence. Individual states have outlined which relationships will be considered as "domestic" through legislation. When domestic abuse situations that do not constitute criminal activity come to the attention of criminal justice practitioners, they should take proper alternative action. It is essential that criminal justice personnel recognize signs and symptoms of abuse so that the response might be appropriate.

Forms of Domestic Violence

Domestic violence comes in many different forms. The severity of an act or the extent of harm is routinely the measuring tool used by the police to determine whether the act is criminal. The author suggests that this approach is outdated and should be changed to reflect contemporary knowledge of domestic violence: It is meant to hurt, intimidate, control, or place the victim in fear of the abuser. With this understanding, the physical extent of harm becomes moot. Probable cause that a crime has been committed is the standard of every other law enforcement action and therefore must continue to be applied equally when domestic crimes are being investigated.

Arrest of the perpetrator should not be viewed as the punishment for domestic crimes; it is simply the legal intervention when a crime has been committed. This form of intervention should be taken whenever the law of the state determines it to be appropriate. The courts will ultimately resolve the matter. The following examples suggest some types of violence that might be considered criminal conduct that is prohibited by law. Fredrica Lehrman suggested the following list of domestic violence forms (Lehrman, 1997):

- Beating
- Pulling hair
- Shoving
- Striking
- Pulling
- Punching
- Slapping
- Kicking
- Hitting
- Choking
- Biting
- Pointing weapons
- Throwing things
- Threatening

- Harassing
- Sexual abuse
- Stalking
- Homicide

ABUSE PREVENTION ACTS

Legislation to prevent domestic violence attempts to address problems specific to intimate and familial relationships and provide additional protections to the victims of abuse. These laws represent a strong statement of public policy: that domestic violence is a serious crime and cannot be dismissed as merely family business. Legislation varies slightly from state to state, but its content is similar, defining domestic violence or abuse relationships recognized by the particular state and including general descriptions of criminal conduct that is domestic in nature. Of particular importance are the remedies provided to protect the victim, in addition to criminal sanctions. Court-issued protection orders are now commonly issued in accordance with **abuse prevention acts**. Violation of protection orders is a criminal act. **Domestic abuse acts** (as they are sometimes called) also provide clear instructions to law enforcement on the intent of the law, outlining the responsibility of police officers. Mandated arrest and preferred arrest policies are routine for domestic violence–related crime and are covered in depth later in the book.

RELATIONSHIPS

There is no uniform understanding of what constitutes a domestic relationship. Legal definitions vary slightly from state to state. Some common ground exists, and generally the domestic relationships are defined via marriage. These include

Figure 1–2   The legal domestic relationship is independent of gender, age, or marital status of the individuals. All persons in a legally recognized relationship are protected from abuse.

- Persons who are or were legally married: a spouse or former spouse
- Persons who reside together without marriage: a cohabitant or former cohabitant
- Persons related through marriage: any person related by consanguinity or affinity within the second degree, related by blood or through marriage
- Persons who share a child in common: where the presumption applies that the male is the biological father of the child and the female is the biological mother (whether they were ever legally married or not)
- A woman who is pregnant and the man who is presumed to be the father
- Persons who are having or have had a substantial dating or engagement relationship
- Biological children or stepchildren
- Biological parents or stepparents

The category of persons who simply reside together is controversial. This may be interpreted to include apartment dwellers and students who share dorm accommodations, depending on the jurisdiction. It definitely includes persons who share a house or apartment, regardless of whether they are married. Some, but not all, states include substantial dating relationships as a category where violence would be viewed as domestic violence. Same-sex relationships where the persons reside as if they were married are considered to be domestic. Remember that it is not the gender of the victim or the relationship of the people that determines the crime; it is the act committed.

DEFINITIONS OF COMMON TERMS

The following definitions are provided as guidelines for identifying the problems associated with abuse. They provide insight into the various types of abuse that criminal justice professionals encounter. Each specific type of abuse is defined by federal and state law and varies from jurisdiction to jurisdiction. Researchers and practitioners may use different definitions for the following types of abuse.

Physical abuse: Use of force or threat of force that may result in bodily injury, physical pain, or impairment. The signs of physical abuse may be external, internal, or both. Physical injuries that are untreated in various stages of healing might indicate an approximate time of injury. External signs of physical abuse include, but are not limited to, bruises, welts, marks, burns, bleeding, missing or pulled hair, ripped clothing, crying, wincing, and the appearance of a drug-induced state. Broken blood vessels or unequal pupil dilation in the eyes may indicate physical child abuse. Additional signs of physical abuse may be human bites, strangulation, immersion in scalding water, and poisoning. Internal signs of physical abuse include, but are not limited to, internal tissue or organ injuries, bone fractures, broken bones, bleeding, sprains, and dislocations.

Sexual abuse: Nonconsensual sexual contact of any kind. Sexual contact with a person incapable of giving consent is also considered sexual abuse. A minor is presumed unable to give informed consent; therefore, any sexual contact with a minor is sexual abuse. Sexual conduct includes, but is not limited to, unwanted touching, rape, sodomy, coerced nudity, and sexually explicit photographing. Force, threat of force, or implied force may accomplish sexual abuse. Physical signs of abuse and the use of force are not always present in relationships where one person is dominant and the power is inherent in the position rather than the person. Physical signs of sexual abuse are the exception rather than the rule. They include bruises around the breasts or genital area, venereal disease or genital infections, vaginal or anal bleeding, and clothing that is torn, stained, or bloody.

Emotional or **psychological abuse:** Intentional infliction of anguish, pain, or distress designed to control the victim. The verbal or nonverbal forms of emotional/psychological abuse include, but are not limited to, verbal assaults, insults, threats, frightening, intimidation, humiliation, and harassment. With the exception of threats, this category of abuse is rarely illegal. It is often evidenced along with other forms of abuse. Over extended periods of time, emotional/psychological abuse may be the "force" by which other forms of abuse occur. Emotional or psychological abuse can be more damaging than physical violence.

Neglect: Failure or refusal to provide care or services for a person when there is an obligation to do so. This form of abuse carries with it a resulting harm due to the action or inaction of the caregiver. Examples of neglect are failure to provide to a minor or elder life necessities such as food, water, clothing, or shelter. Leaving a young child unattended or unsupervised may also be considered neglect. Signs of neglect include, but are not limited to, dehydration, malnutrition, untreated bedsores, untreated health problems or conditions, unsanitary living conditions, a failure to thrive, or abandonment.

Financial exploitation: Illegal or improper use of an elder's funds, property, or assets. Theft, fraud, and unfulfilled promises of care in exchange for assets are examples of financial exploitation. Substantial monetary or property gain to another person is considered exploitation when the elderly victim consented to enrich that person as a result of misrepresentation, undue influence, coercion, or threat of force.

Wife abuse: Physical, sexual, mental, and emotional abuse to a married woman at the hands of her husband. Use of the term should be restricted to research as a way to limit and narrowly define the population of study.

Spouse abuse: Common substitute for wife abuse. The term is gender neutral and refers to wife or husband battering. Use of the term without definition is problematic because it excludes partners who live together and are not legally married.

Partner battering: Most comprehensive designation that refers to violence between intimates. It includes all adult intimate relationships between people regardless of sexual preference, marital status, or age of the intimates. Additionally, the term *battering* suggests an ongoing complex pattern of violent behavior.

Battering: Initially used to describe a form of domestic abuse, hitting; now commonly used to refer to the pattern of violent and coercive behavior used to gain control in an intimate relationship. The control may be accomplished through economic forms, such as withholding or denying access to money or other basic resources, or sabotaging employment, housing, or educational opportunities. Social isolation is quite common, including the denial of communication with friends and relatives or making communication so difficult that the victim chooses to avoid it; prohibiting access to the telephone or transportation; and denying access to needed health care. Verbal and emotional forms of assault and control include intimidation, coercion, threats, or degradation. Physical and sexual assaults may occur. Individual acts do not constitute battering; it is the violence in general, regardless of the form, relationship, living arrangement, marital status, or age of the intimates.

Parent abuse: The abuse of parents by their adolescent. Conflict becomes abusive when one person uses threats, force, or manipulation to gain power over the other. It is any act of a child that is intended to cause physical, psychological, or financial damage to gain power and control over a parent.

Dating violence: A term that includes physical, sexual, financial, or emotional abuses committed by a nonstranger. The relationship that exists between the victim and offender may be intimate or casual. It excludes persons that are living together or married and typically refers to persons that are courting.

Rape: Sexual intercourse forced by violence or threat of violence. Forced sexual penetration is not excused by martial or dating relationships and is independent of sexual orientation.

Child abuse: Includes nonaccidental physical injury, sexual abuse or exploitation, emotional or psychological injury, and neglect or maltreatment to a person under the age of 18 (or the age specified by the law of the state). It is a general term that includes all abuses involving minors. *Child abuse* is frequently the term used to describe abuse by caregivers (e.g., legal guardians, teachers) and abuse by family members. Incest is the sexual abuse of children by a family member.

Elder abuse: May be physical, sexual, or emotional/psychological and involve neglect, abandonment, or financial exploitation. Most researchers agree on two general categories of elder abuse: domestic and institutional. Domestic elder abuse refers to any of several forms of maltreatment of an older person by someone who has a special relationship with the elder, such as a spouse, a sibling, a child, a friend, or a caregiver in the older person's home. A caregiver is one who is responsible for the elder due to a legal or contractual arrangement. Institutional abuse is any form of abuse that occurs in residential facilities for older persons, such as nursing, foster, or group homes. Perpetrators of institutional abuse are usually persons who have a legal or contractual obligation to provide elder care and protection. A significant amount of elder abuse is believed to be in the category of self-neglect. Further, elder abuse may involve both the purposeful or active abuse and passive abuse that results in negligence due to ignorance or an inability to provide care. It is important that professionals who respond to elder abuse understand the legal definitions in their state. Classifications of elder abuse as criminal, civil, or requiring social service intervention vary greatly from state to state.

PREVALENCE OF DOMESTIC VIOLENCE

Battering

Family violence is the most frequent violence that police officers encounter. At one time it was considered the most dangerous police call; now it is generally accepted as the most frequent form of violence in the United States.

The battered woman is by far the most frequent victim of domestic violence. She is typical of any woman that you encounter in public, but the danger for her is in her own home. She comes from every walk of life, age, race, ethnicity, and social class.

Figure 1–3   Police respond to domestic violence calls with alarming frequency.

Figure I–4 When a pregnant woman is injured other than in a car accident, the most likely cause is domestic violence.

Women's battering has reached epidemic proportions in the United States and is considered a major social problem. Domestic violence is the leading cause of injury and death to American women, causing more harm than vehicular accidents, rapes, and muggings combined. Although lower income levels is one predicator of domestic violence, the picturing of domestic victims as poor and uneducated women is inaccurate. Their partners victimize many professional women. Working women, including those who serve in the military and those earning more money than their abusers, are all at risk. In the United States, approximately 1.5 million women are raped and/or physically assaulted each year by an intimate partner according to the National Violence Against Women Survey (Tjaden & Thoennes, 2000).

Female murder victims are substantially more likely than male murder victims to have been killed by an intimate. In 1999 women were three out of four of the murder victims attributed to intimate partners (Rennison, 2001). Many people fault the battered woman who does not leave her abuser. Yet women do leave abusive relationships. It is at the time of separation that the women are most vulnerable to being beaten and even killed. When separated from their husbands, women are victimized more frequently by intimates than other categories of women (Tjaden & Thoennes, 2000). Violence against women is estimated to occur against 6 percent of pregnant women (Martin et al., 2001). Findings indicate that pregnancy increases the risk of minor assaults against Hispanic-American women while increasing the risk of severe assaults among Anglo-American women (Jasinski & Kaufman Kantor, 2001).

Determining the extent of marital rape is complicated by the fact that while it is prohibited by law in all states, 33 states still provide exemptions to husbands for prosecution (VAWnet, 1999). Studies have indicated that marital rape has long-term and severe consequences for women and that it is usually accompanied by other forms of violence. As many as one in ten wives may have been sexually assaulted by their spouses at least once.

Some researchers suggest that the incidence of male battering may be as high as female battering, a highly contentious position. Most experts accept the incidence rate of male battering by females to be approximately 15 percent of domestic violence. The full extent of violence by women against men is not known and some males do experience significant injury as a result of victimization. Recent reports of an increase in the arrest rate of females for domestic violence is explained as an unintended effect of police training and new legislation that seeks to identify the "primary aggressor" in cases of family violence. No scientific studies have examined the claim made by the Associated Press that the rate of women arrested in California has risen from 5 percent in 1987 to 16 percent in 1998 (Clifford, 1999).

Often cited as precursors to spouse abuse, dating violence and acquaintance rape have received considerable national attention lately. The sexual climate on college campuses has been identified as nothing less than treacherous for women. As reported by the U.S. Department of Justice, a recent study found (Fisher et al., 2000)

- The victimization rate was 27.7 rapes per 1,000 female students.
- Nearly 5 percent (4.9%) of college women are victimized in any given calendar year. Over the course of a college career—which now lasts an average of five years—the percentage of completed or attempted rape victimization among women in higher educational institutions might climb to between one-fifth and one-quarter.
- For a campus with 10,000 women, this would mean the number of rapes could exceed 350 in a given academic year.

In a recent study, Harned states that women and men reported comparable amounts of overall aggression from dating partners but differed in the types of violence experienced (Harned, 2001). She found that the rates of physical violence were similar for men and women and that contrary to contemporary theses, women were not more likely to use physical violence in self-defense, a finding that has been confirmed in numerous earlier studies. Although both genders experienced similar amounts of aggressive acts from dating partners, the impact of such violence was more severe for women, Harned reports.

Nancy Knauer has demonstrated that lesbian violence is a significant problem, noting the reluctance by both lesbians and mainstream society to recognize violence between women for fear of validating negative sterotypes of same-sex relationships (Knauer, 2001). No significant differences in prevalence rates were found in cases of lesbian, gay, bisexual, and transgender domestic violence by the National Coalition of

Anti-Violence Programs (NCAVP, 2003). Violence in these communities are esti-mated to be similar to the estimates found in heterosexual communities, 25 to 30 per-cent. Gay, lesbian, bisexual, and transgender violence is difficult to reconcile due to societal preconceptions about a battered victim. We expect that the perpetrator will be larger and stronger than the victim. Frequently, we view battering between men as normal aggressive behavior, violence between women as nonexistent. Issues in alterna-tive relationships are forcing us to reconceptualize domestic violence. Battered gay and bisexual victims often respond to battering by striking back, which also occurs in male–female relationships. Typically, this attempt at self-protection is viewed as mutual physical aggression. When the perpetrator and victim are roughly of the same physical size and strength, the violence is misperceived as "mutual" (Duthu, 2001).

Of all forms of domestic violence, this one is the least known of all: children bat-tering their parents. How much battering goes on can be left to one's imagination. Parents who are physically, sexually, or financially victimized will rarely report their child abuser. It is a source of shame and confusion. We do know that relatives, inti-mates, and other persons well known to the victim committed about one-fifth of the violence against people 65 years old or older (Klaus, 2000). Approximately 2 percent of murders annually are termed parricide, the killing of parents by a child. The majority of these perpetrators are white middle-class youths without a history or prior criminal conviction (Hillbrand et al., 1999). Research indicates that the perpetrators are fre-quently suffering from major mental disorders or suffer from abuse at the hands of their victim. In 1999, 234 murders were committed against mothers and fathers by their son or daughter (Sourcebook of Criminal Justice Statistics, 2000).

Child Abuse

Historical accounts tell us that children have always been abused and neglected by one or both parents; it is not uncommon or newly revealed. Rarely is child abuse a single physical attack or a single act of deprivation or molestation. For a child, emotional abuse includes excessive, aggressive, or unreasonable parental behavior that places demands on a child to perform beyond his or her capabilities. Sometimes emotional abuse is not what a parent does, but what a parent fails to do. Children who receive no love, no care, no support, and no guidance will carry the scars into adulthood.

Until recently, few considered the treatment of children in the United States to be a matter of public concern. Awareness came with the coining of the phrase **battered child syndrome** in 1962 by C. Henry Kempe. Although we don't know the exact numbers of children abused or neglected, private- and government-sponsored research has given us some insight into the extent of the problem. Upward of 3 million child victims are reported annually and that number does not represent all cases of abuse. For those cases that are reported, approximately 33 percent are substantiated. Physical abuse is the most common cause of death to children, often committed by their own parents. By anyone's standard, this is a significant problem. An estimated 2,000 children in the United States die of child abuse and neglect each year; approxi-

Figure 1–5 Children are particularly vulnerable to abuse and neglect from either a mother or father.

mately 40 percent of them are younger than a year old, and the majority are younger than 5 years (Langstaff & Sleeper, 2001). The criminal justice community is at the center of efforts to combat what used to be considered a parent's prerogative. No longer is child abuse considered a family affair. Specialized units have been developed for investigating reports of child abuse in the courts, police departments, and social service agencies across the country.

Sexual abuse of children is an area of great controversy. Experts disagree on the prevalence of child sexual abuse, yet it was at one time the fastest-growing form of reported child abuse. Sexual abuse of children is an issue of power and control, not love and intimacy. Between 1980 and 1986 the rate of sexual abuse to children more than tripled, according to the Study of National Incidence and Prevalence of Child Abuse and Neglect—now it is considered less of a concern than physical abuse. Unfortunately, indications are that the average age of the sexually abused child has been on a downward trend since the 1970s. Preschool-aged children are being victimized more frequently than 20 years ago, which may account for fewer reported cases, since cases of sexual abuse to preschool children are extremely difficult to investigate and confirm. Seldom is there physical evidence, and young children have difficulty in explaining the nature of their abuse. Only the most serious cases involving young children, where significant physical injury is documented, can go forward for prosecution.

The harm caused to children from exposure to domestic violence is a recent research effort. According to the National Clearinghouse on Child Abuse Information, the co-occurrence of child abuse and woman battering is estimated to take place in 30 to 60 percent of cases (2003). Confirming the need to protect victims of domestic violence to ensure the safety of children, the effects to children who witness domestic violence may be more devastating than direct victimization. These victims experience multiple psychological problems with below average social and cognitive development.

Adolescents who had witnessed family violence as young children and those who had been directly victimized may be at greater risk of abusing their mother, other vulnerable household members, or pets (Cottrell, 2001). The use of corporal punishment in child rearing and exposure to family violence leads to increased parent abuse by adolescents against his or her mother (Ulman & Straus, 2003).

Elder Abuse

In this book we focus on "domestic" elder abuse, perpetrated by family members or others who are known through a caregiving role in the victim's home. Abuse may have relatively little impact on the elderly, or it may threaten their lives. Physical abuse ranges from a slap that knocks off an elder's glasses, to kicking and punching that might result in death. Financial exploitation may be as simple as theft from the elder's wallet, to the appropriation of one's home.

Crimes against the elderly include sexual assault, domestic violence, physical assault, homicide, burglary, and fraud. The first National Elder Abuse Incidence Study estimated that, during 1996, at least 500,000 older persons in domestic settings were abused and/or neglected or experienced self-neglect, and that for every reported incident approximately 5 went unreported. Of the nearly 71,000 incident reports that were substantiated by Adult Protective Services (APS), nearly one in two (49%) are cases of neglect (Phillipson, 2000). The vast majority of self-abusing elders are age 80 and older and may also be suffering from depression. In what was a surprising result, an early study found that in cases of spousal abuse among the elderly, perpetrators were equally likely to be either male or female, giving rise to the existence of a battered husband syndrome among the elderly (Pillemer & Finkelhor, 1988). More research is needed to confirm or deny the syndrome. It is suspected that some elderly spouse abuse begins with the strains of caregiving for a partner who is deteriorating physically or mentally. A majority of abuse victims are female.

The elder population is extremely vulnerable to domestic abuse because of lifestyle and infirmity. According to the Administration on Aging (1998), The National Incidence Study conducted in 1996 found the following:

- In the age bracket of 60 and over, 551,011 persons experienced abuse, neglect, and/or self-neglect in a 1-year period;
- Almost four times as many new incidents of abuse, neglect, and/or self-neglect were not reported as those that were reported to and substantiated by adult protective services agencies;
- Persons aged 80 years and older suffered abuse and neglect 2 to 3 times their proportion of the older population; and

Figure 1-6 Elder men and women are equally likely to be victimized in spousal abuse. *(Photo courtesy of the Administration on Aging.)*

- Among known perpetrators of abuse and neglect, the perpetrator was a family member in 90 percent of cases. Two-thirds of the perpetrators were adult children or spouses.

Elders are susceptible to substantial injury during the performance of routine tasks such as cooking, or even walking when their eyesight is impaired. When injuries do occur, they tend to be more serious: Bones break more easily and bruising is more likely to occur. Elders' fear of crime victimization is greater than that of any other group in society and they do experience disproportionate amount of property crime when compared with other age groups. More than 9 in 10 crimes against the elderly were property crimes, compared to fewer than 4 in 10 crimes against persons age 12 to 24 (Klaus, 2000). On average, however, for every 1,000 persons at their age level, persons age 65 or older experienced about 5 violent crimes and those younger than age 25 experienced over 100. Often, older Americans will attempt to limit their potential for victimization by altering their lifestyles. They sometimes withdraw from society by staying at home and not participating in activities after dark. Fear of being victimized may provide the catalyst for elders to isolate themselves more than is medically necessary, thereby increasing the possibility of domestic elder abuse. It is no wonder that the elderly fear victimization. Further complicating the issue is that some elders require restraint because of dementia; such restraint will often leave marks and bruises. When restraints cause suffering, pain, or are used for punitive reasons, the use is considered abusive.

The increase in domestic reporting is probably the result of recently legislated mandated reporting laws. All states have legislation that in some way addresses elder abuse; some are mandatory reporting laws, adult protective services laws, domestic violence laws, or specific elder abuse and neglect laws. As of 1994, all states but eight designated certain types of professionals as mandatory reporters of domestic elder abuse. They are required by law to report suspected cases of abuse, neglect, and exploitation. An agency is designated by law to investigate the reports. The investigating agency differs from state to state and may be a law enforcement or social service agency. In some states the reported victim may refuse further investigation into the report. The majority of elder abuse reports are substantiated after investigations.

Perpetrators of domestic abuse are equally likely to be male or female. This equity is explained by the Administration on Aging; since the majority of neglect offenders are female and males account for most of all other abuse, the numbers average out to being almost equal (AOA, 1998). What we don't know is the percentage of perpetrators who were abused as children by the elders to whom they are giving care. Are the victims acting out the consummate role reversal, treating their parents as they had been treated? The most frequent elder abuser is the elder's adult child. Adult children may be responsible for providing care for their parent(s) regardless of the quality of relationship they enjoyed in earlier years. Caring for an elderly person is made even more difficult with the added strains of a poor relationship. Additionally, codependence develops when the adult child receives room and board in exchange for caregiving to an elderly parent. The adult child may be reluctant or unable to provide the level of care necessary but dependent on the elder for living arrangements. Conversely, the elder victims are often reluctant to report domestic abuse from a family member for fear of retaliation or isolation.

The majority of elders aged 65 and above who are not institutionalized are living in a family setting, according to U.S. Census reports. This population is most vulnerable to abuse that is domestic. The situation will become more desperate as demographics on aging change. The Administration on Aging reports that approximately 30 percent (9.7 million) of all noninstitutionalized older persons in 2000 lived alone (7.4 million women, 2.4 million men). They represented 40 percent of older women and 17 percent of older men. The proportion living alone increases with advanced age. Among women aged 75 and over, for example, half (49.4%) lived alone (AOA, 2001).

Figure 1–7 Physicians and other health care professionals play an important role in the identification of elder abuse. *(Photo courtesy of the Administration on Aging.)*

With an increase in the older population, police can anticipate more domestic elder abuse cases, and we must be prepared to respond.

CONCLUSIONS

Domestic violence includes every imaginable form of violence that can occur as long as there is a domestic relationship between perpetrator and victim. Thinking of domestic violence as a group of crimes linked together into a general category is helpful for remembering just what domestic violence is. The individual crimes that we refer to as domestic violence are usually crimes without being placed into the category of domestic. Defining the crimes as domestic in a legislative act allows each state to encourage law enforcement officers to enforce the laws regardless of the relationship between the people. Sometimes mandatory arrest or preferred arrest policies are included, spelling out the expectations that the state has with regard to police action. Some states include inducements for full enforcement. These topics are addressed later in the book.

Once in a while, a particular crime, such as the violation of a civil domestic restraining order, becomes a crime that is specific only to domestic violence. An "Act to Prevent Domestic Violence" is one way that the legislation in each state defines the specific crimes that will be placed into the domestic category. Further, such acts define what relationships will be considered. The relationships generally include all intimate partners, regardless of gender or marriage. Additionally, people who are related through marriage or blood are considered domestic partners.

The scope of domestic violence seems overwhelming when reading the statistics. It is important to note that not all statistics are what they appear to be. There are many reasons why a particular study or research project concludes with figures that are less than perfect. It really doesn't matter for the purposes of studying the issues. It is clear that we do not know exactly the extent of domestic violence! Experts agree that domestic violence crimes are largely underreported. Skeptics suggest that the numbers are inflated. So we should expect that the figures might not be exact. What they tell us, more importantly, is that there is a problem of violence in the United States. The violence has invaded many homes. There are many children who are sexually and physically abused and neglected every day. We know that people are killing their children, partners, and elders. In adult intimate relationships, many people are being dominated or controlled, physically, emotionally, or sexually, and even harmed financially. We have to face the horrible truth, even if we don't know the exact numbers. If you look around, you will see it.

QUESTIONS FOR REVIEW

1. Define *domestic violence*.

2. Domestic abuse is a classification containing many crimes that are committed against the person. List examples of these crimes.

3. What are abuse prevention acts?

4. What relationships constitute a domestic relationship?

5. List the various types of domestic abuse.

6. When is a woman at the greatest threat of being beaten or abused?

7. Who are the most frequent victims of domestic violence?

8. What is the main cause of death among children? Name one significant risk factor for child abuse.

9. How serious is partner violence within gay, lesbian, and transgender relationships?

10. Who are the most likely perpetrators of elder abuse?

INTERNET-BASED EXERCISES

1. Visit the Web site for the National Incident-Based Reporting System (NIBRS) (http://www.search.org/nibrs/default.asp). Can you identify states that are currently using this system and examples of those that are not? What is the effect of NIBRS on crime statistics?

2. At the Bureau of Justice Statistics site (http://www.ojp.usdoj.gov/bjs/welcome .html), you will find information on victim characteristics and offender relationships. Go there and find examples of this category.

REFERENCES

Administration on Aging. 1998. *The National Incidence Study; Final Report.* Washington, DC: The National Center on Elder Abuse.

Administration on Aging. 2001. *A Profile of Older Americans: 2001.* Washington, DC: AOA.

Champion, Dean J. 1997. *The Roxbury Dictionary of Criminal Justice: Key Terms and Major Court Cases.* Los Angeles: Roxbury Publishing Company.

Clifford, James O. 1999. Spouse Abuse Crackdown, Surprisingly, Nets Many Women. Associated Press, November 23. *http://www.fact.on.ca/newpaper/ap99112a.htm.* 2002.

Cottrell, B. 2001. *Parent Abuse: The Abuse of Parents by Their Teenage Children.* Ottawa, Canada: Health Canada.

Duthu, Katheen Finley. 2001. "Why Doesn't Anyone Talk About Gay and Lesbian Domestic Violence?" Pp. 191–203 in *Domestic Violence Law,* Nancy K. D. Lemon (ed.). St. Paul, MN: West Group.

Fisher, Bonnie S., Francis T. Cullen, and Michael G. Turner. 2000. *The Sexual Victimization of College Women.* The U.S. Department of Justice NCJ 182369. Washington, DC: National Institute of Justice.

Harned, Melanie S. 2001. "Abused Women or Abused Men? An Examination of the Context and Outcomes of Dating Violence." *Violence and Victims* 16(3):269–285.

Hart, B. 1986. "Lesbian Battering. An Examination." In K. Lobel (ed.), *Naming the Violence*. Thousand Oaks, CA: Sage.

Hilbrand, Marc, Jason W. Alexandre, John L. Young, and Reuben T. Spitz. 1999. "Parricides: Characteristics of Offenders and Victims, Legal Factors, and Treatment Issues." *Aggression and Violent Behavior* 4(2):179–190.

Island, D., and Letellier, P. 1991. *Men Who Beat the Men Who Love Them: Battered Gay Men and Domestic Violence*. Binghamton, NY: Harrington Park Press.

Jasinski, Jana L., and Glenda Kaufman Kantor. 2001. "Pregnancy, Stress and Wife Assault: Ethnic Differences in Prevalence, Severity, and Onset in a National Sample." *Violence and Victims* 16(3):219–233.

Klaus, Patsy. 2000. *Crimes Against Persons Age 65 or Older, 1992–97*. NCJ 176352. Washington, DC: Bureau of Justice Statistics.

Knauer, Nancy J. 2001. "Same-Sex Domestic Violence: Claiming a Domestic Sphere While Risking Negative Stereotypes." Pp. 203–212 in *Domestic Violence Law*, Nancy K. D. Lemon (ed.). St. Paul, MN: West Group.

Langstaff, John, and Tish Sleeper. 2001. *The National Center on Child Fatality Review*. FS–200112. Washington, DC: Office of Juvenile Justice and Delinquency.

Lehrman, Fredrica. 1997. *Domestic Violence Practice and Procedure*. Washington, DC: West Group.

MacFarlane, Kee, Jill Waterman, Shawn Conerly, Linda Damon, Michael Durfee, and Suzanne Long. 1986. *Sexual Abuse of Young Children: Evaluation and Treatment*. New York: Guilford Press.

Martin, Sandra L., Linda Mackie, Lawrence L. Kupper, Paul A. Buescher, and Kathryn E. Moracco. March 2001. "Physical Abuse of Women Before, During, and After Pregnancy." *Journal of the American Medical Association* 285(12):1581.

National Clearinghouse on Child Abuse and Neglect Information. 2003. *In Harm's Way: Domestic Violence and Child Maltreatment. www.acf.org*.

National Coalition of Anti-Violence Programs (NCAVP). 2003. *Annual Report on Lesbian, Gay, Bisexual, Transgender Domestic Violence, 2002*. New York: NCAVP.

Phillipson, Chris. 2000. "National Elder Abuse Incidence Study." *Journal of Elder Abuse and Neglect* 12(1):29–32.

Pillemer, Karl, and David Finkelhor. 1988. "The Prevalence of Elder Abuse: A Random Sample Survey." *Gerontologist* 28(1):51.

Rennison, Callie M. 2001. *Intimate Partner Violence and Age of Victim, 1993–99*. NCJ 187635. Washington, DC: U.S. Department of Justice.

Sherman, Lawrence W., and Richard A. Berk. 1994. "The Specific Deterrent Effects of Arrest for Domestic Assault." *American Sociological Review* 49:261–72.

Sourcebook of Criminal Justice Statistics. 2000. *Murders and Non-Negligent Homicide Known to Police*. Washington, DC: U.S. Department of Justice. Table 3.141: p. 310.

Tjaden, P., and N. Thoennes. 2000. *Extent, Nature, and Consequences of Intimate Partner Violence*. NCJ 181867. Washington, DC: U.S. Department of Justice.

Ulman, A., and M. A. Straus. 2003. "Violence by Children Against Mothers in Relation to Violence Between Parents and Corporal Punishment by Parents." *Journal of Comparative Family Studies* 34(1):41–61.

U.S. Department of Justice. 1994. *National Crime Victimization Survey: Elderly Crime Victims*. NCJ 147186. Washington, DC: DOJ.

VAWnet. 1999, "Marital Rape." *http://www.vaw.umn.edu/Vawnet/mrape.pdf*.

CHAPTER 2

A GLOBAL VIEW OF FAMILY, SOCIAL, AND LEGAL RELATIONS

S I M P L Y   S C E N A R I O

Life in Uganda

After her first husband died, Sules was forced to remarry by her father. Her new husband had 3 wives and 15 children, aside from hers. He beat her and raped her persistently. She is now HIV positive. "I was commonly the one who was beaten. He would beat me to the point that he was too ashamed to take me to the doctor. He forced me to have sex with him and beat me if I refused. This went for every woman [wife]. Even when he was HIV+ he still wanted sex. He refused to use a condom. He said he 'cannot eat sweets with the paper [wrapper] on'" (Karanja, 2003).

Question: In Uganda. what is the crime(s) described here? Explain your answer.

K E Y   T E R M S

Curtain rule

Dowries

Entail

Incest

Infanticide

Lobola

Parens patriae

Patria potestas

Patriarchy

Primogeniture

Rule of thumb

Social–legal historal perspective

Stitch rule

INTRODUCTION

> For too long, the collective consciousness of contemporary Western society has promoted an idyllic image of the family as a safe haven in an otherwise turbulent, violent, and unsafe world. Closer examination of the nuclear family, however, provides considerable evidence that this unit of social organization is actually a fertile environment for deadly aggression. (Struve, 1990)

Family violence is seen in numerous forms. Although they are often discussed separately, it must be remembered that all forms of domestic violence are interrelated. They occur within the family unit. Violence within families is a pervasive and long-standing problem, although it was not considered as such until quite recently. Even without an exact count of the numbers of victims, it certainly can be said that it affects millions of women, men, and children across the United States and around the world. It is not simply a family problem; the effects of the fight go beyond the individual family experiencing the hostility.

The contemporary field of domestic violence is the study of a social problem. Society is a collection of many groups. Patterns of behavior guide our interactions and reflect the goal of the group. We study human social behavior and interaction in sociology, psychology, and anthropology: the social sciences. They are the branches of learning that deal with the institutions and functions of human society. Family

Figure 2–1   Family violence negatively affects millions of women, men, and children across the world.

violence is studied through all of these perspectives, each using different approaches to examining human behavior.

In addition to the groups that make up a society are the institutions that interact. These institutions of government, families, and education are concerned with accomplishing goals within the society. The family is an important institution within the scheme of human stability. Its members follow rules and are bound by acceptable standards of behavior. Codified into a body of law are the principles of the past and of the present. Reflecting changes in human behavior are changing laws that document rights and responsibilities in marital relations. Examining these guideposts of human behavior is one way to understand the positioning of people today.

The social sciences use various approaches to examine social events, and often they consider the same circumstance from different points of view. Historians, for example, trace the development of families over time. Economists look at the labor pool, major lines of communication, and easily accessible consumer markets that would influence households. Both approaches have netted interesting information for the modern family. In this chapter, the status of gender relationships is presented through legal definitions of the roles within the family.

There is very little social historical work available that will shed light on the condition of the family in ancient and medieval times, nor is this historical account complete. The legal sanctions on wife assault inform us about the expected code of behavior by husbands. Some evidence of the expectations of wives is also evidenced in legal history. This brief historical account, while not necessarily sequential, will show that family structures and social status of these members have dictated the manner in which people are treated and how the expectations of family have evolved.

Like people themselves, social relationships change. Awareness of the problems associated with family violence today has brought us to a point where it is a recognized indicator of a dysfunctional family. That was hardly the case throughout history. In the past, violence against intimates has been tolerated as accepted social conduct and alternatively condemned as deviant behavior. There is often a difference between the law and social practice. Isolated initiatives to control interpersonal violence can be traced back as far as the Roman era, when **patriarchy** defined the relationships between the husband and his wife and children (Belknap, 1992). Even today, social mores will keep private the abuses that are legally prohibited.

Wife battering and child abuse are the oldest forms of what we currently refer to as domestic violence. Looking at these historical examples of legally defined social relations may seem like comparing oranges and apples. Socially accepted views on property in ancient times are very different from those of today. Women were considered inferior to men, intellectually and physically. Punishment of errant wives was in the best interest of the husband, whose status has developed from a property owner to a life partner. The purpose of this chapter is to provide insight into the legal developments of family relationships. A kernel of truth may be found in all explanations for crime, and the **social–legal historical perspective** is only one of many factors in a larger picture.

EARLY SOCIAL–LEGAL HISTORY

Domination of men over women and children has a strong historical foundation. Some experts suggest that this inequality of the sexes is the foundation for the assumption of male superiority and the foundation for domestic violence. By providing husbands with the right to punish wayward wives, the system gives a rationale to male brutality against women. Others advise that the social order was just that, an order to life's relations for purposes of survival. The term *patriarchy* is used today to describe this inequity of power. It comes from the Greek for patriarch, or "father as ruler."

The Ancient World of Greece

The first written laws appeared in Athens around 621 B.C. (Rhodes, 1984). They were attributed to Dracon, a lawgiver. Regardless of how small or serious the infraction the punishment was the same, death. Dracon felt that people guilty of small infractions of the law deserved the death penalty and that there was, after all, no greater penalty for those that had committed the more serious infractions. As a result, laws today that are cruel and harsh are sometimes referred to as Draconian. His Codes of Law, along with the Solonian Codes, had great influence on the courts in Athens, since rulings were based on interpretation of the law (Rhodes, 1984).

Solon, the Athenian law reformer who mitigated the Draconian laws, was appointed lawgiver in Athens around 594 B.C. When he replaced Dracon, Solon threw out all of the old laws except for the homicide law, and he created many new laws, especially in the categories of tort and family laws. Solon introduced the concept that all citizens should have access to justice in the courts, redefining the nature of citizenship. Where formerly an individual's status had been largely a matter of birth, now it would seem that all citizens were defined according to their economic class. This change did not affect the status of women at that time, yet it can be recognized as an important step toward attaining political equality.

Solon's family laws were laws that regulated the behavior of men and women. He wrote laws on allowances in marriage and adoption, as well as laws concerning inheritances and supporting roles of parents. Penalties for these laws were not set but were enforced by the head of the particular family. Linked to family laws were laws concerning women, whose role in Greek law was extremely small. Women were controlled by

---

Back Then . . .

In 753 B.C., Romulus, who is credited with the founding of Rome, formalized the first law of marriage. In part, this law "obligated both the married women, as having no other refuge, to conform themselves entirely to the temper of their husbands and the husbands to rule their wives as necessary and inseparable possessions" (O'Faolain & Martines, 1973).

men at nearly every stage of their lives. This is because they were under constant supervision by their *kyrios*, or "official guardian." Most often the *kyrios* was a girl's father, or if she were married it was her husband. Because of this supervision, women's role in law was limited to rare court appearances, where they were either presenting evidence in a homicide case or were being displayed along with their family to try to evoke pity from the jury. The most important duties for a city-dwelling woman were to bear children—preferably male—and to run the household (Romano & White, 2000). In ancient Athens, the birthplace of democracy, not only were children denied the vote but also were women, foreigners, and slaves.

THE ROMAN EMPIRE

According to the civil law of Rome, the male head of the family had full rights and powers over his wife, children, and any descendants who sprang from him through male lineage only. This power was at one time exercised over the lives and deaths of both women and children. Women, children, and slaves were property that could be sold or bought. Any harm committed against a woman was viewed as an offense against the father if she was unmarried, or as an offense to the husband, but not to the victim.

The husband originally had the right to kill his wife if she engaged in adultery; this right was later limited to the father. Consequently, it was the male "owner" who sought vengeance or compensation for his loss. A female could not be an aggrieved party, nor was she held responsible for her actions. It was therefore the responsibility of the husband or father to punish the woman whose actions were injurious to others. This lack of legal standing prohibited women from appealing to the courts for relief when their punishment was excessive or without cause.

Illustrations of acceptable physical punishment by husbands against their wives are evidenced in the early Roman Empire. Although the law sometimes placed obligations on both the husband and wife, the purpose was clearly to assure that the husband had control over his property. Early Roman law treated women and children as the property of the husband.

Under the laws of Romulus, the wife could not divorce her husband (Lefkowitz & Fant, 1992). He was granted rights of divorce when the woman had used drugs or magic, and for adultery. Other reasons were stipulated as acceptable motives for the male seeking divorce, but he would forfeit part of his estate for doing so.

The legitimate punishment of errant Roman wives during the first and second centuries A.D. is recorded through the following accounts (Lefkowitz & Fant, 1992):

- Egnatius Metellus took a cudgel and beat his wife to death because she had drunk some wine. He was not charged with a crime as she had violated the laws of sobriety.
- Quintus Angistius Vetus divorced his wife after he had seen her having a private conversation with a common freedwoman in public.

THE CHRISTIAN ERA

Christianity embraced the subordination of wives over their husbands, and scriptures commanded women to be silent, obedient, and accepting of their husbands' authority. A passage from the New Testament, Ephesians 5:22–24, specifically states the role of a married woman according to the Church: "Wives should regard their husbands as they regard the Lord, since as Christ is head of the Church and saves the whole body, so is a husband the head of his wife; and as the Church submits to Christ, so should wives to their husbands, in everything" (Jerusalem Bible, 1996).

The notion that male supremacy was supported unconditionally by the Christian faith is further supported by the actions of Constantine the Great, the first Christian Roman emperor, later canonized as a saint. Constantine was the first emperor to order the execution of his own wife in A.D. 298.

BRITISH COMMON LAW

Patriarchy is not the only social arrangement between married people, but it has been the dominant one in Western civilizations. Under common law, women and children were no longer viewed as property, but the results were the same. The order was based on the belief that when two are joined in marriage, they become one, socially and legally. The rights of the woman are then subordinate to those of the male, unlike the woman who remained single.

Historian Laurel Thatcher Ulrich offers this comment on the legal status of women under common law. It was authored by William Blackstone in Commentaries on the Laws of England (Ulrich, 1991) and explains the concept of this patriarchal order: "By marriage, the husband and wife are one person in law; that is, the very being or legal existence of the women is suspended during the marriage, or at least is incorporated and consolidated into that of the husband; under whose wing, protection, and cover, she performs everything."

> **Back Then . . .**
>
> Corporal punishment of an errant wife was a widely accepted practice. A Christian scholar generated the Rules of Marriage in the late fifteenth century. They specified: "When you see your wife commit an offense, don't rush at her with insults and violent blows . . . Scold her sharply, bully and terrify her. And if this doesn't work . . . take up a stick and beat her soundly, for it is better to punish the body and correct the soul than to damage the soul and spare the body. . . . Then readily beat her, not in rage but out of charity and concern for her soul, so that the beating will redound to your merit and her good" (Davidson, 1978).

Back Then . . .

According to Lunn, the earliest case of domestic violence heard in the British court was in 1395. Margaret Neffield and witnesses testified that her husband attacked her with a dagger, causing several wounds and broken bones. The court was not satisfied that this constituted grounds for a judicial separation, and Mrs. Neffield was ordered to return to living with her husband (Lunn, 1991).

The **rule of thumb** is believed to have originated from an English case with a resulting influence on common law. This rule asserted that a husband had the right to beat his wife as long as the stick was no thicker than his thumb. Husbands had the right and even a duty to chastise their wives (Pagelow, 1984). While the rule is considered harsh by most standards, it is thought to be a compassionate replacement for the law that allowed a husband to beat his wife "with any reasonable instrument" (Dutton, 1998).

FRENCH LAW

It was a dangerous thing to question the inferiority of women presumed by the Declaration of the Rights of Man. Olympe de Gouges wrote a Declaration of the Rights of Women in 1791 and was quickly arrested and tried for treason. On November 3, 1793, she was executed by the guillotine (Levy et al., 1979). In the early nineteenth century Napoleon Bonaparte formalized the civil code in France, subjugating women as legal minors for their entire lives. Under the Napoleonic Code wives could be beaten, punched, and permanently disfigured for minor disobedience or for "scolding" (Pagelow, 1984). The French code of chivalry allowed the husband to knock her to the earth, strike her in the face with his fist, and break her nose so that she would always be blemished and ashamed (Dobash & Dobash, 1978).

The Napoleonic Code influenced French, Swiss, Italian, and German law (Dutton, 1998). Court relief in the form of divorce was a rare intervention for battered victims. It came only when the beatings reached the level of attempted murder.

MARITAL RELATIONS IN EARLY AMERICA

Patriarchy continued in the colonies as the ideal family structure. The British immigrants reestablished their customs of inheritance by the eldest son, called **primogeniture**. Land was retained within the family through a legal proscription against the sale or grant of land outside the lineage, which is referred to as **entail**.

Figure 2–2   Here is a statue of the great Napoleon. His code was introduced into a number of European countries. It also became the model for the civil codes of Québec Province, Canada, the Netherlands, Italy, Spain, some Latin American Republics, and the state of Louisiana.

Physical force and chastisement of one's wife was clearly accepted under English common law, the legal foundation in the colonies. The rule of thumb is thought to have influenced the American system. Although there is no evidence that the rule was ever evoked in America (Pleck, 1989), it existed as a common law restriction on the size of the weapon to be used in wife chastisement.

Puritan Restrictions

As early as 1599, Puritan ministers in England spoke out against wife beating. Bringing this objection to America, the Puritans were the first to prohibit domestic violence through legislation. Puritan laws provided penalties for wife beating, consisting of fines, whipping, or both. Since wife beating was considered a social problem that involved the community, enforcement included "holy watching" by neighbors.

The Next 100 Years

After 1776 and the American Revolution, Americans formed their own laws that tolerated wife beating (Davidson, 1977). In instances when the practice exceeded restrictions that were set down by law, wife beating was rarely brought before the courts. Between 1633 and 1802, only 12 cases of domestic violence were prosecuted in the Plymouth Colony (Pleck, 1989).

Some early American legislation on domestic violence control included corporal punishment and fines as penalties for wife beating. Some courts exacted promissory notes from perpetrators who beat their wives, with the understanding that the

---

Back Then . . .

In 1642 the American Puritan legal criminal code provided the following: "Everie marryed woman shall be free from bodilie correction or stripes by her husband, unlesse it be in his own defense upon her assault" (Sherman & Rogan, 1992).

---

offender would forfeit the money if reconvicted. In 1824 the Supreme Court of Mississippi upheld the husband's right of chastisement in cases of "great emergency," saying that husbands should not be subjected to "vexatious" prosecutions for assault and battery (Dobash & Dobash, 1979). This period of nonprotection for victims of domestic violence lasted from the late 1770s to the 1850s.

Not coincidentally, at this time in history women were fighting for equitable laws including the right to vote. The first women's rights convention took place in New York in 1848. Elizabeth Cady Stanton drafted the 1848 Seneca Falls declaration, in which she proclaimed that all men and women were created equal. Citizenship was granted to blacks in the Fourteenth Amendment to the U.S. Constitution in 1868, and the right to vote was granted by the Fifteenth Amendment in 1870, but women were not included. Not until 1920 and the passage of the Nineteenth Amendment to the Constitution were women afforded the rights of citizenship.

African American Families

The West African peoples were stripped of family ties and kinship connections under slavery in Colonial America. Additionally, black women lacked the paternalist protection of the domestic sphere and were subjected to the sexual and economic desires of their owners. There was no legal recourse for the violence against black women during slavery. Any stability attained by kinship was transitory since neither church nor law sanctioned slave marriage. Slaves could be bought and sold, families separated at the whim of the master.

Interracial marriage was also forbidden. Early colonial statutes made it a criminal act to marry outside one's race or to conduct such a marriage ceremony. The Virginia Statute on Racial Intermarriage (1705) stated, "Be it enacted, . . . That whatsoever English or other white man or woman, being free, shall intermarry with a Negro or mulatto man or woman, bond or free, shall by judgment of the county court be committed to prison and there remain during the space of six months, without bail . . ." (Wortman, 1985).

Sharon Angella Allard maintains that the historical legal view of women ignores the significant differences that exist between white and black victims of domestic violence (Balos & Fellows, 1994). In her view, the women of color are excluded from legal protections due to perceptions that they are stronger than other victims of patriarchy. They have been characterized as immoral and undeserving of refuge from the sexual

---

Back Then . . .

"Whoever is ruled by his wife, may he be the worst damned! Such men become soft, shameless, silly, unfree, and inarticulate." Further, the Church warned that to give a woman freedom was like committing suicide for a man. Disorder and destruction would be the inevitable results (Pushkareva, 1997).

---

predators who have stalked them. Since colonial times the black slave woman was a contradiction to the stereotypical passive white victim.

During the reconstruction period following the Civil War, the African American couple slowly was afforded the legal right to marry. South Carolina was among the first states to regulate and recognize the marriage between persons of color (1866). In part, the statute provided the following permissions (Wortman, 1985):

1. The relation of husband and wife amongst persons of color is established.

2. Those who now live as such, are declared to be husband and wife.

Native American Families

Gender roles and marital customs among Native Americans were different from those in the English patriarchal system. Family membership and descent were traced through the mother's side in most Native American cultures (Williamsburg Foundation, 1998). The matriarchal system allowed for divorce. The traditional Navajo society was matriarchal, matrilocal, and matrilineal (Feinman, 1992). Indian children,

Figure 2–3 Slavery in Colonial America stripped the West African people of family ties and kinship connections. Neither church nor law sanctioned slave marriage. *(Photo courtesy of the Administration on Aging.)*

however, were later required to attend boarding schools, where they were taught Anglo values. The matriarchal system eroded and was replaced with colonists' views of patriarchy. As the women's traditional roles were devalued, abuse of children and women became prevalent.

A Brief Change

By 1870, wife beating had taken on an aura of social unacceptability and was once again declared illegal in most states of the United States. This change coincided with a growing concern over child maltreatment. Women were given legal standing in some isolated cases. Judges in Alabama were the first to recognize that white women should be afforded the same legal protections as other victims.

One Hundred Years of Secrecy

Not long after Fulgham, the Supreme Court considered whether females could be prohibited from practicing law. In 1873 the Court decided in *Bradwell v. Illinois* that the laws of Illinois did not abridge any of the privileges and immunities of citizens of the United States by legislating what offices and positions should be filled by men only. The legal and social positioning of women for that time period was evidenced in the concurring opinion. Concurring with the opinion of the Court, Justice Bradley said, in part, "The constitution of the family organization, which is founded in the divine ordinance, as well as the nature of things, indicates the domestic sphere as that which properly belongs to the domain and functions of womanhood. . . . So firmly fixed was this sentiment in the founders of common law that it became a maxim of that system of jurisprudence that a woman had no legal existence separate from her husband, who was regarded as her head and representative in the social state" (*Bradwell v. Illinois*, 1873).

Court denials of a husband's "right" to batter his wife continued slowly. Responses differed between the states, and women had little success in prosecutions for wife beating (Gordon, 1989). Although wife battering had become socially repugnant in the United States, it continued behind closed doors. States created innovative

---

Back Then . . .

"The privilege, ancient though it be, to beat [one's wife] with a stick, to pull her hair, choke her, spit in her face or kick her about the floor, or to inflict upon her like indignities, is not now acknowledged by our law. . . . [I]n person, the wife is entitled to the same protection of the law that the husband can invoke for himself. . . . All stand upon the same footing before the law as citizens of Alabama, possessing equal civil and political rights and public privileges" (*Fulgham v. State*, 1871).

> **Back Then . . .**
>
> Acknowledging the secretive practice and justifying a husband's right to batter, the North Carolina Supreme Court held, "If no permanent injury has been inflicted, nor malice, cruelty nor dangerous violence shown by the husband, it is better to draw the curtain, shut out the public gaze, and leave the parties to forget and forgive" (*State v. Oliver*, 1874).

laws to allow the practice of battering. Until recently, some states allowed arrest of a husband only if he inflicted injury that required stitches, the **stitch rule**. In North Carolina, the **curtain rule** allowed police to "interfere" with a husband's actions toward his wife only after permanent injury had been inflicted on her (Belknap, 1992).

In 1882 Maryland became the first state to pass a law that made wife beating a crime, punishable by 40 lashes or a year in jail (Davidson, 1977). Oregon passed similar legislation in 1906. By the beginning of the twentieth century, domestic violence as a legally sanctioned crime disappeared. Unfortunately, the brief reform period ended around 1914. By World War I, the concern for wife beating had faded again. Over the next half-century, the courts rarely intervened in domestic affairs, even when laws existed to prohibit the behavior. Social attention fluctuated, and no significant changes occurred with respect to domestic abuse. It was not until the 1960s that violence toward intimates again became a subject of concern and an object of government interference. By this time, effective legal remedies to prevent domestic violence ran from seriously lacking to nonexistent.

WOMAN BATTERING

Wife battering reemerged along with child abuse as a social issue in the 1960s. The dominant view held that marital violence was a "private affair." Domestic violence continued behind closed doors, although not sanctioned by law. Intervention was rare, occurring in cases where the victim had been killed or severely maimed. Forms of spousal violence prohibited by criminal law usually amounted to misdemeanors; unless police witnessed the violence, they had no powers of arrest. Most domestic violence assaults fell within this category. Police officers were trained to respond to the crisis of domestic violence by separating the parties for a "cooling-down period." It was a common practice for officers to "counsel" the parties. In extreme cases the victim would be referred to the court to file a private complaint. The complaints were not taken seriously, however, and resulted in fewer prosecutions than for any other crime.

The lack of effective legal remedies for the victim hindered progress, including police action. New legislation was needed to address the contemporary concerns of domestic violence that began to surface. A major complaint focused on the ineffective law enforcement response. The critique of the system is well founded, given that law enforcement could not legally intervene in family disputes. Isolated attempts to protect victims of abuse were contrary to the prevailing legal and social atmosphere.

Although a few examples of effective law enforcement intervention did occur, police noncompliance was a far more frequent occurrence. Faced with domestic violence situations, police officers often failed to effect an arrest, even when the law demanded it. During the 1970s, reformers sought changes that might ensure effective intervention. The debates centered on what type of intervention would be most appropriate, as well as the form that it might take. Civil actions against police departments and mandatory arrest of the perpetrator were tactics devised to force compliance.

Deterrence of future battering was a major impetus for the swift arrest of the perpetrator. Still, problems surfaced regarding victims' reluctance to follow through with complaints of domestic violence. Was law enforcement the appropriate agency to control domestic violence? If not, what other measures could be taken to protect victims of abuse? With many questions and few answers, the critics debated these issues. The first national study of domestic violence, *Behind Closed Doors*, reported that spouses strike partners in one out of every six households (Straus et al., 1980). That now-famous study on family violence found that there was little difference in the rate of violence between husbands and wives.

The first controlled, randomized test of the effectiveness of arrest for domestic violence occurred in Minneapolis in 1980, with the results published in 1984 (Sherman & Schmidt, 1993). The findings of the study to assess the effects of various police responses, including arrest, suggested that the arrest of the perpetrator produced the least amount of repeat violence for the same victims within a six-month period. Subsequent domestic violence was reduced by nearly 50 percent when the suspect was arrested, as opposed to other interventions, such as ordering one of the parties out of the residence or counseling the couple. Richard Berk and Lawrence Sherman, who conducted the research, made three recommendations regarding the study: first, that police should probably employ arrest in most cases of minor domestic violence; second, that the experiment should be replicated to see whether it would hold up in other cities with many different kinds of people; and third, that mandatory arrest laws not be adopted, if only because they would put an end to further research and replications (Sherman & Rogan, 1992).

However, it was only a matter of months after the results emerged before mandatory arrest procedures in instances of domestic assault were adopted across the nation. The move has been called "unusual, if not unprecedented in the social sciences," and was cheered by feminists and battered women's advocacy groups (Gelles, 1993). The Minneapolis domestic violence experiment paved the way for six replications and extensions of the experiment. Known collectively as the Spouse Assault Replication Program, the research was undertaken in a variety of U.S. police departments. The results of the replications were inconsistent; in some instances, there was no deterrent effect due to arrest of the perpetrator. Only certain types of offenders were deterred by arrest, and in some cases, the arrest escalated violence (Garner et al.,

1995). Lawrence Sherman and others involved in the Minneapolis experiment now advocate repeal of mandatory arrest policies in favor of varied responses based on the individual cases (Sherman & Rogan, 1992). Others are suggesting that law enforcement alone is insufficient to combat the problems of domestic violence (Buzawa & Buzawa, 1996), necessitating a more systemwide approach. The coordinated approach includes implementation of policies that train personnel and develop guidelines and protocols for enforcing laws related to domestic violence as well as accountability measures that ensure enforcement of the law by all officers in the department. Adding to the law enforcement component are strategies to coordinate with other criminal justice agencies and victim service providers. Probation departments have instituted enhanced victim safety measurements and vigorously enforced protection orders. Prosecutors and advocates seek to keep victims better informed about their cases and the whereabouts of the perpetrators.

A recent review of the Spouse Assault Replication Program suggests that the results were flawed, indicating that arrest generally is the superior method of deterring future violence—all of the studies do in fact indicate that arresting deters batterers better than other police responses (Maxwell, Garner, & Fagan, 2003). The National Center on Women and Family Law conducted a study on mandatory arrest laws and policies. It concluded that these policies do result in an increase in arrests, enable more victims to be put in contact with helping agencies, and communicate to the entire community that domestic violence is a crime. The National Institute of Justice is sponsoring new research to evaluate the effects of an integrated response to domestic violence. Through grants funded by Title IV, the Violence Against Women Act, the

---

Case in Point: No Provision for an Arrest

In 1971 a Massachusetts state trooper was sent to a domestic call at a home in his patrol area. The trooper had responded to the same house many times before. Each time the wife had accused the husband of beating her. This time she let the trooper in the door crying that her husband had hit her. Wearing only his underwear and drinking a beer, the husband yelled at his wife, "You called the police!! You called the police!! Just wait till he leaves; I'll get you good this time." To the officer he said, "I know my rights: You can't do anything to me—now get out of my house!"

In the 1970s, there was no provision to arrest a man on an allegation of domestic violence when the officer did not see the beating occur, even though it appeared as though the woman had been beaten. The officer had no power of arrest. Knowing that the woman would be beaten for having made the call to the police, the trooper took action that he should not have had to take. He threw the husband out of the door into the snow on his front steps. There he was promptly arrested for public drunkenness, a misdemeanor that amounted to a breach of the peace, for which the officer did have the power of arrest.

need for research to assess the effectiveness of arrest in the context of a systemwide, coordinated approach to domestic violence will be conducted in the near future.

WHAT ABOUT THE CHILDREN?

Experts agree that children have always been abused and neglected (Sagatun & Edwards, 1995). *Patria potestas,* the Roman civil law espousing patriarchy, denied legal standing to children as well as women. Generally, children have been regarded as second-class citizens, and their treatment has historically been harsh. Physical abuse, neglect, and sexual abuse were considered socially acceptable behavior in ancient times (Sagatun & Edwards, 1995). Therefore, there is an absence of legal challenges to the status of children as property.

Ancient Times

Infants were the property of their fathers and had no rights of their own. Their fathers could even kill them for a number of "practical" reasons. Physical deformity, questionable health, and illegitimacy were rationales for **infanticide**, since destroying children who were bound to be a burden was viewed as promoting the general welfare of society (Iverson & Segal, 1990). Female children were a strain on the financial resources of a father, another justification for infanticide. Early Greek philosophers condoned infanticide, the killing of a newborn. Aristotle even recommended a law prohibiting crippled children to be raised.

The Code of Hammurabi provided that the father had full control of his children until they married. This right transferred to the mother in the absence of the father and included the right even to sell the children (King, 1998). Only **incest** was forbidden. The male perpetrator of incest with his daughter was exiled.

The Christian Era

Under Judaism and Christianity the children's right to live was protected, regardless of the quality of life. During the fourth century, the right to live for a child was established through the Christian faith. The commandment "Thou shalt not kill" was linked with the practice of infanticide. A similar trend is evidenced in the experience of the Russian Orthodox Church. Bearing children was the major task of women during the tenth century, defining the woman's role. Severe penalties were prescribed for committing infanticide, terminating pregnancies, or practicing birth control. Abortion was considered similar to that of murder—and the punishment varied with the stage of pregnancy. Aborting an embryo brought five years of fasting as punishment, seven years if it was completely formed (Pushkareva, 1997).

Social restrictions against sexual relations with children differed from today's standards also. With the exception of incest, it was permissible to loan children to guests or to hire them out for sexual use (Radbill, 1987). Pushkareva offers evidence that father–daughter incest continued to be practiced well into seventeenth-century Russia. She states that fathers had absolute authority over their daughters. Overall, child rearing was strict, and parents were encouraged to beat children frequently. Young boys and girls were also forbidden to complain about family beatings and would be flogged publicly if they brought family business out into the open.

Marriage in Russia could legally take place at age 12 for girls and 15 for boys. Since people often died very young during the seventeenth century, the restriction was not enforced. Only 7 percent of urban Muscovites during that period were over the age of 25 (Pushkareva, 1997).

English Law

Chancery courts in medieval Britain were granted control over the property rights of children, extending to their general welfare. These courts utilized the concept of *parens patriae,* which referred to the right of the king to act in the best interests of the child. There is little evidence that the courts used this power to protect children from abuse or neglect. As early as 1535, the English Poor Laws allowed for children who were identified as neglected or delinquent to be put to work or be placed in poor-houses (Sanders, 1945). The provisions are not considered by history as protections, but rather as attempts to maintain strict control over children who were resistant to parental punishment.

Apprenticeship was another form used to remove children from their homes and place them into the care of adults who would train them in various skills. Some apprenticeships were forced until the child was 21 years old. Child labor practices included long hours, with physical punishment often leading to deformities. English records as late as 1829 cite the cause of death for infants as including babies drowned in pits full of water, cisterns, wells, ponds, and even pans of water (Radbill, 1987).

Figure 2–4 It was not until the 1870s that child abuse was revealed. While we have made great strides since then, it is still a serious problem.

Babies were also starved by their nurses, or killed by burning or scalding. A common form of death for children was overlaying or lying upon a child. This form of suffocation by carelessness accounted for 20 deaths in one English city in 1920, according to Samuel Radbill.

CHILDREN IN EARLY AMERICA

Early attempts to protect children are questionable by contemporary standards of justice. Often, the methods of government intervention amounted to control rather than opportunities for relief for the child. The colonists brought the English notions of juvenile protection to the United States. Here they instituted poor laws (Bremmer, 1970) and continued to practice forced apprenticeship. The range of acceptable punishment for errant children stopped with permanent disfigurement; laws against physical child abuse were nonexistent. Early law actually held parents responsible for the actions of their children, giving them the authority to punish harshly. Historian and psychoanalyst Lloyd de Mause wrote an article in 1975 in which he clearly describes the unfortunate role of the child: "A child's life prior to modern times was uniformly bleak. . . . A search of historical sources shows that until the last century children were . . . offered beatings and whippings, with instruments usually associated with torture chambers. In fact, the history of childhood is a nightmare from which we have only recently begun to awaken. . . . The further back in history we went, the lower the level of childcare we found, and the more likely children were to have been killed, abandoned, whipped, sexually abused and terrorized by their caretakers" (Pagelow, 1984).

During the Victorian era, infanticide was the most covered-up crime, according to Marlene Stein Wortman. In Philadelphia alone, between 1861 and 1901, an annual average of 55 dead infants were found on the streets (Wortman, 1985), their cause of death listed as "unknown." During that same period, only one trial led to a first-degree murder verdict. Changes in the attitudes toward children came about slowly. Two significant reform periods to protect children took place during the first half of the nineteenth century. These were the Refuge Movement and the Child Saver Movement.

The Refuge Movement

The first refuge statute was passed in New York State in 1882, permitting the commitment of neglected and dependent children in a house of refuge (Pfohl, 1977). This led to the New York House of Refuge, which became the first in the country. Other states soon followed New York's lead, however. With strict prison-type organization, the houses were not meant to be therapeutic. Delinquent and runaway children, as well as those who were neglected or incorrigible, were sent to the same institutions. Discipline was harsh, and the conditions often met with rebellion. Many children who had been removed from their homes eventually returned to society as criminals. Critics soon charged that poverty and a cheap labor source were the reasons for removal of the children and placement in the houses of refuge.

In 1838 juvenile authorities were granted even greater power through the case of *Ex Parte Crouse*. Reaffirming the concept of parens patriae, the right to claim guardianship, a Pennsylvania court ignored the father's plea for custody of his daughter. Her mother had placed the girl in a house of refuge because she was unmanageable. A higher court denied the father's claim that parental control is exclusive, natural, and proper. The decision that was applied only to Pennsylvania was noticed by the other states that followed suit. The state had been given the right to restrain and protect children despite the wishes of parents.

The Child Saver Movement

Linda Gordon, historian and scholar, asserts that policy response to domestic violence emerged in the late 1870s with the "discovery" of family violence (Gordon, 1989). Social service agencies were confronted with problems of wife battering when their child welfare clients cited abuse as a major issue. The incidence of violence was linked to alcohol abuse and poverty. Identified as a problem confined to the low classes, the social service response to family violence was judgmental and prejudicial, with poverty as the common element of its clients. There was a lack of effective legal remedies for the domestic violence victim.

Societies for the Prevention of Cruelty to Children

The late 1870s witnessed a national movement to protect children who were abused or neglected. The child savers of the late nineteenth century established Societies for the Prevention of Cruelty to Children (SPCCs). According to Linda Gordon, the SPCC workers acted as quasi–law enforcement officers: They conducted investigations, home searches and seizures, and threatened families with arrest for noncompliance of their directives. To further their stated mission of enforcement of existing laws against child abuse, they conscripted police officers to make arrests and to act as supervisors in their cases. Both New York and Boston SPCCs acknowledged that sufficient laws existed at the time to protect children, but no one had been held responsible for their enforcement.

Due to their increased professionalism and police reluctance toward enforcement, the problems of child abuse were largely left with the social service agencies after 1920. Police officers did not perceive child abuse enforcement as part of their role or were simply too busy with other duties to enforce child abuse statutes. The Social Security Act of 1930 somewhat improved intervention on behalf of children in need, because it mandated child welfare services for neglected or dependent children. Today, legal intervention has improved through specialized child abuse investigation units within police departments. Unfortunately, enforcement of child abuse protections is still not a priority with many police agencies.

DOMESTIC VIOLENCE: A GLOBAL CONCERN

The legal history presented on domestic relations develops from early European examples based on patriarchal social relations. Have things changed elsewhere in the world? Is domestic violence an international social problem? Are the concerns for social equality confined to the United States? The resounding answer is that America is not alone, either in its problem or in the search for change.

No comprehensive summary records the magnitude of family violence internationally. Piecemeal information is available; it documents concerns about the extent of family violence that has prompted action on a global basis. According to the Report from Committee on Equal Opportunities for Women and Men Violence, it is estimated that domestic violence affects one in five women across Europe, with the vast majority of incidents committed by a member of the family or a close acquaintance (Keltosova, 2002). The Report cites three factors that make it difficult to know the true extent of domestic violence in European countries: the hidden nature of the problem, underreporting, and the rare identification of domestic violence as a separate crime that, therefore, does not appear in statistical data. Few national surveys are committed to examining the problem. The 2001 national survey in France has shown that 1.35 million women had been victims of domestic violence that year. For a half of them, it was the first time that they had revealed the fact of violence. In Norway, with its population of 4 million people, each year 10,000 women seek medical treatment because of physical damage due to domestic violence.

In the News: Women and the United Nations

In June 1998, approximately 250 representatives of 150 nongovernmental organizations, social movements, and indigenous peoples groups met in Ottawa, Canada, to review and affirm the commitment to the principles of the Vienna Human Rights Conference of 1993. Among the key issues were these:

- The human rights of women and of the girl-child are an inalienable, integral, and indivisible part of universal human rights.

- The promotion and protection of all human rights and fundamental freedoms must be considered as a primary objective of the United Nations in accordance with its purposes and principles.

- All human rights—civil, cultural, economic, political, and social—are universal, indivisible, interdependent, and interrelated.

Source: Women's International Network News (1998).

It appears as though the movement to protect women and children from family violence has occurred internationally at roughly the same time as our own feminist movement in the United States. Comparisons between the United States and some countries are possible due to limited reports of research efforts on wife abuse. With few exceptions, violence to women has been legislated against with no mention of the other forms of domestic violence that were presented in Chapter 1.

The United Nations

The United Nations (UN) General Assembly adopted the Declaration on the Elimination of Violence against Women in 1993. It emphasizes violence against women as a violation of human rights and recommends strategies to be employed by member states and specialized agencies to eliminate it. The fourth UN World Conference on Women then took place in Beijing, China, in 1995. Highlighting the problems of violence against women, the conference signified a worldwide effort toward ending domestic violence.

The United Nations' active movement toward eliminating female violence has prompted action toward that goal. The United Nations Development Fund for Women (UNIFEM) was created to provide financial and technical assistance to innovative programs and strategies that promote women's human rights, political participation, and economic security. UNIFEM promotes gender equality and links women's issues and concerns to national, regional, and global agendas by fostering collaboration and providing technical expertise on gender mainstreaming and women's empowerment strategies. As a result of UNIFEM-supported training, police throughout Cambodia are now working more closely with village chiefs, and men who exhibit violence toward their wives are required to sign a contract stating they will discontinue their threatening behavior (UN Publication, 2000). The contract is used as evidence against the man in court if violent behavior continues. "With an end in Sight" illustrates how a Kenyan group developed an alternative rites of passage ritual, offering new coming-of-age ceremonies for girls as a way of discouraging female genital mutilation (FGM). More than 1,500 village elders, parents, circumcisers, youth, and families participated in alternative rituals, replacing FGM with education on self-esteem, health, and women's empowerment. As a result, one community has abolished FGM and alternative traditions are now being expanded throughout Kenya. In the West Bank and Gaza, women's organizations are working to end "honor killings." In communities where male family members would kill female relatives suspected of alleged sexual misconduct, women advocates are now saving lives working with families to develop signed agreements where the family pledges its opposition to "honor killings."

One initiative that resulted was the forming of WAVE (Women Against Violence Europe). National membership of WAVE now stands at 15 organizations. By 1997, laws against domestic violence had been enacted in at least 44 countries around the world, including the United States (UNICEF, 1997). Of these, 17 have made marital rape a criminal offense, and 27 have passed sexual harassment laws.

Prevalence Rates in Selected Countries

Albania.   UNICEF (2000) recently reported on the state of domestic violence in Albania. Without benefit of law enforcement protection, poverty and excessive drinking contribute to the high rates of abuse. The right to beat one's wife and publicly humiliate her are encoded in the Kanun (code of law) and supported through patriarchy. Citing the research of S. Miria, the first data on the plight of Albanian women indicates that 64 percent (out of 849 females) of surveyed women revealed that they experienced physical, emotional, and sexual abuse (Miria, 1996).

Afghanistan.   The rights and status of women became a global concern prior to the U.S.-led coalition that led to the end of the Taleban regime in November 2001. Colin Powell, U.S. Secretary of State, declared that the "recovery of Afghanistan must entail the restoration of the rights of Afghan women." Amnesty International reports that violence against women by husbands, male family members, and on occasion by female family members has been widely reported (2003). Broken arms, broken legs, and other injuries are normal practice indications of the domestic and physical violence women experience. No formal reporting on domestic violence occurs in Afghanistan; therefore, prevalence rates are nonexistent. Amnesty International's research indicates that country custom or tradition is used to legitimize the violent deaths of women by family members.

Armenia.   Domestic violence is a serious problem in Armenia, according to the report from the Minnesota Advocates for Human Rights (Cooper et al., 2000). The advocates report on surveys documenting that many instances of domestic violence are never reported to legal authorities. When women did report, the cases were insufficiently prosecuted or perpetrators were penalized in ways that were detrimental to the victims. In many cases, women in Armenia suffer serious injury or even death at the hands of their husbands. In a comprehensive study of murder committed in the home, Sergey Vaganovich Arakelyan, a criminologist at Yerevan State University, found that over 30 percent of all murders between 1988 and 1998 were committed within the family. He also determined that 81 percent of domestic murders were committed by men, and in 35 percent of all cases, the victims were wives or girlfriends (Arakelyan, 1999).

Australia.   Domestic violence is the most common form of assault in Australia, according to the Women's Resource Information and Support Centre, WAVE (Women's Resource Information and Research Centre, 1998). Based on regional research, the Centre estimates that each year in Victoria, between 30 and 40 women and children are killed by their husbands, boyfriends, ex-partners, fathers, and sons. One of seven married women is subjected to domestic violence.

Austria.   In 1997 the first law was enacted to protect women from domestic violence. It empowers police to expel abusers from their home for a period of seven days; during that time the victim may apply for a court order (WAVE Database, 2001).

Britain.   Erin Pizzey founded the first refuge for victims of domestic violence in 1971. She first published *Scream Quietly or the Neighbors Will Hear* in 1974 (Pizzey, 1977). It is the earliest book about domestic violence from the battered women's perspective. Her clients in Chiswick, England, grew to over 200 by the end of the decade. Her conclusion that some people actually choose violent relationships has been met with hostility (Pizzey, 1982). She noticed that some women seemed to be using the shelter when the level of violence got too much; afterward they returned to their violent men for another few weeks, returning to the shelter when the violence escalated. In her subsequent book, *Prone to Violence*, she talks about why people are violent and her experiences working with problem families. Research indicates that violence against women in Great Britain occurs at roughly the same rate as in the United States. Every minute in the U.K., the police receive a call from the public for assistance for domestic violence. This leads to police receiving an estimated 1,300 calls each day or over 570,000 each year (Stanko, 2000). In December 2003 a free 24-hour national domestic violence hotline became available in Britain for the first time (Women's Aid Federation, 2004). An Internet Fact Sheet posted by the Women's Aid Federation Web site (2004) reported the following information on the status of domestic violence in Britain:

- An analysis of 10 separate domestic violence prevalence studies by the Council of Europe showed consistent findings: 1 in 4 women experience domestic violence over their lifetimes and between 6 and 10 percent of women suffer domestic violence in a given year (Council of Europe, 2002).

In the News: Vatican City

Although Christianity was once the catalyst for social injustices against women, the Roman Catholic Church has taken a stand of family peace. In contrast to the scripture of the Bible, Pope John Paul II condemned violence against women and children in 1998 and made a plea for justice during a special New Year's Mass to mark the Roman Catholic Church's World Day of Peace (CNN Interactive, 1998). The news report quotes the Pope as saying, "The abuse of women and children is one of the most widespread violations of human rights, which has become an instrument of terror: Women taken hostage and children savagely massacred . . . Practical steps are needed to put an end to the increase in these forms of violence."

- The 2001/02 British Crime Survey (BCS) found that there were an estimated 635,000 incidents of domestic violence in England and Wales. Eighty-one percent of the victims were women and 19 percent were men. Domestic violence incidents also made up nearly 22 percent of all violent incidents reported by participants in the BCS (Myhill & Allen, 2002).
- Repeat victimization is common. The results of the British Crime Survey found that more than half (57 percent) of victims of domestic violence are involved in more than one incident. No other type of crime has a rate of repeat victimization as high (Home Office, July 2002).

Canada.   Canadian authorities have concluded that the most dangerous place for a disabled girl or woman is in her own home (Webb, 1998). A 1987 survey of women with disabilities, carried out by DAWN Toronto and funded by the Ministry of Community and Social Services, discovered that

- Sixty-seven percent of those surveyed had been physically or sexually assaulted as children, compared with 44 percent of nondisabled women.
- Almost half of disabled women surveyed reported that they had been sexually abused as children, compared with 34 percent of nondisabled women.
- Thirty percent of disabled women reported that they were assaulted during their adult years, mostly by husbands; 22 percent of nondisabled women reported similar abuse.
- Thirty-one percent of disabled women reported being sexually assaulted as adults, compared with 23 percent of nondisabled women.

The Kennedy and Dutton survey (1989) in Alberta discovered that the Canadian incidence rates for minor wife assault were almost identical with the United States (Dutton, 1998). Dutton further reported that as the acts became more violent, the rates of incidence fell sharply below that of the United States. Still, he suggests that approximately 1,550,000 men in Canada are assaultive to women in any given year, presenting an incredible problem for law enforcement.

An Internet fact sheet on the prevalence of domestic violence in Canada reveals these statistics (*The Daily*, 2002): Released by Statistics Canada on July 25, 2000, the 1999 General Social Survey (GSS) on spousal violence measures the prevalence of violence in intimate relationships across the country. The GSS findings reveal that the rates of spousal violence experienced by men and women were only slightly different—8 percent for women and 7 percent for men in relationships five-years prior, and 4 percent for both women and men in their current relationships.

- More than twice as many women as men reported being beaten;
- Five times as many women as men reported being choked;

- Almost twice as many women as men reported having a gun or knife used against them;
- More than six times as many women as men reported being sexually assaulted;
- Four out of ten women are afraid for their lives, as compared to one out of ten men;
- Four times as many women as men reported being threatened or harmed, or having someone close to them being threatened or harmed;
- More than twice as many women reported having their property damaged or their possessions destroyed as compared to men; and
- Four times as many women as men reported being denied access to family income.

China.   No legal protection from domestic violence exists in China's southern Fujian Province, where family violence occurs in more than one-fourth of households, according to a recently released survey (Family Violence Prevention Fund, 1998). In the Chinese province, incidents of domestic violence are considered "family quarrels," and neither the court nor police tend to interfere. Parental battering of children in Chinese families in Hong Kong was found to be a common occurrence according to a recent study (So-Kum-Tang, 1998). The author cites the prevalence rate of 526 per 1,000 children for minor violence and 461 per 1,000 children for severe violence. A comparative report on sexual abuse in Taiwan found that victimization was more common in preadolescence and adolescence, as in the United States (Chen, 1996). At least one-third of the abusers were known to the victims in this study. The rate of victimization for females was found to be 34.6 percent and 2.6 percent for males.

India.   Violence against women in this country takes on an added twist with commerce due to the customs of India. More than 5,000 women are killed each year

Figure 2–5 In China, family violence is still considered personal, and the authorities tend not to interfere. Rates of child abuse are extremely high when compared to the United States.

because their in-laws consider their **dowries** inadequate (UNICEF, 1997), often setting the women afire. In a country where hundreds and perhaps thousands of newborn girls are murdered each year simply because they are female, little value is given to adult women (Anderson & Moore, 1993). Of 1,250 women questioned, one survey concluded that more than half had killed baby daughters. Women are often sold to the highest bidder or given into marriage through dowries. Those who survive their husbands are so stigmatized that they seldom remarry. One out of every three Indian women has experienced domestic violence in her lifetime (PROWID, 2003).

Indonesia.   Until recently, domestic violence by men against women members of their families was considered in Indonesia, as in many other countries, to be a purely private matter in which the police and courts would not interfere. Domestic violence was not a crime under the Indonesian Criminal Code. The issue of male violence against women (VAW) rose to public prominence following Indonesia's political turmoil, escalating in May 1998 when women were particularly targeted during the ethnic violence in Jakarta. Information about violence against women in other provinces, particularly in Aceh, Papua, and the then province of East Timor also began to emerge. With communal violence continuing in Indonesia and evidence that the economic crisis has contributed to an increase in domestic violence in general, the situation for women is increasingly urgent (UNIFEM East and South East Asia, 1999).

Ireland.   Domestic violence affects one in five Irish women, according to Women's Aid (2004). Since the end of 1996 there have been 89 women murdered; a

Figure 2–6 The violence against women in India may include female infanticide; dowry payments (bridal gifts, compulsory marriage); *sati* (widow immolation); wife battery; dowry harassment; sexual abuse and incest; witch burning; physical violence; and the emotional and mental abuse of girls and women.

significant number were killed by a current or ex-partner. More than 11,000 women contacted the Women's Aid Helpline in 2002, which represents a 12.5 percent increase on the 2001 figures. In 2001, 9,983 callouts were responded to by *An Garda Siochana* (Irish police). In 2001, the police recorded that sexual assault increased by 91 percent while aggravated sexual assault increased by 50 percent.

Korea.   The rate of family violence is believed to be much higher in Korean society than in the United States (Dutton, 1998). Dutton reports that a 1992 study by Kim and Cho estimated the rate of wife assault to be 37.5 percent compared to 12.4 percent in the United States at that time.

Pakistan.   In the last eight years, more than 4,000 women in Pakistan have been doused in kerosene and burned alive by family members in the area surrounding the capital Islamabad, according to an article by freelance journalist Juliette Terziell (2002). Reasons for these burning attacks predominantly by husbands or in-laws vary, but most cases center on failure to give birth to a son, a husband's desire to marry a second wife without having the financial means to support the first, and animosities with mothers-in-law. There are no reliable numbers for the rest of the country, but human rights campaigners estimate that three women a day die as a result of "choola," or stove death—a term invented by Pakistani human rights campaigners in response to the claim of perpetrators that the deaths are attempted suicides or the result of exploding stoves.

Poland.   The movement to protect battered women in Poland is fairly new. The Women's Rights Center in Warsaw was founded in 1994 (Nowakovska, 1997). This is an organization that addresses violence against women within a broad context of gender equality and discrimination. The majority, 98 percent, of perpetrators of domestic violence are male (Polish Ministry of Justice, 1996). According to the same report, 81 percent of the victims are married to their abusers. Although 78 percent of perpetrators (12,087) in 1996 were found guilty and given jail sentences, none of them actually served time! As in the United States, there are options for community service and suspended sentences in lieu of jail.

The 1998 Penal Code in Poland prohibiting domestic violence is gender neutral, and it includes violence against children. Article 184-1 states, "Whoever abuses physically or psychologically a member of a family, an intimate relation, a physically or mentally disabled person, or a juvenile may be found guilty and sentenced from 3 months to 5 years in jail. If the abuser acts with cruelty, the penalty is from 1 to 10 years."

The Women's Rights Center reported that research conducted by the Public Opinion Research Center in 1993 and 1996 suggests that more than half of Polish women personally know someone who is a victim of domestic violence (Polish Ministry of Justice, 1996). One in twenty Polish women is believed to live in an abusive environment.

Romania.   In January of 2003 the first campaign against domestic violence was launched in this country, where aggressive relationship behavior is considered normal (NEWW Polska, 2003). Over the previous year 800,000 women in Romania had suffered from violence in their home. According to research conducted by the Partnership for Equality Center, an incredible 80 percent of the victims failed to report the violence to authorities, in part because of the belief that the police will not protect them. Almost half of the victims interviewed did not know that domestic violence was illegal, stating that women deserve to be beaten from time to time! Poverty and alcoholism were found as contributing factors to this violence.

Russia.   In October of 1997, Sinelnikov writes, the Russian Department of Internal Affairs under Ministry of the Interior (GUVD) admitted that a woman is beaten in Russia every two seconds (Sinelnikov, 1998). Currently, from 20 to 30 percent of all murders committed in Russia take place in the family. And the numbers only increase with each passing year. Still very few services exist for victims of violence in Russia. The Russian police force likewise treats incidence of family violence to be funny accidents, second-class crimes committed against second-class citizens. The general reaction to complaints is best described by the experience of one battered woman, who, upon calling the local precinct for help, was told, "You're still alive. When we get a corpse, then we'll investigate."

In Russia 13,000 women are killed each year, mostly by husbands or boyfriends. As a comparison, 14,000 Russians were killed during the war in Afghanistan, which lasted for 10 years (Keltosova, 2002).

South Africa.   Violence against women in South Africa is similar to international complaints of patriarchal social inequality. Compounded with the issues of apartheid and community instability, resources to confront the problems are scarce (Dangor et al., 1998). The authors report that the violence is often underreported and unrecognized. Without national studies, they report prevalence estimated from various sources:

- In Cape Town, the Rape Crisis Centre estimated that their partners beat one out of six women regularly.
- Preliminary studies reveal that 50 percent to 60 percent of marital relationships involve violence and abuse.
- In the Dangor study, 46 percent of respondents reported that they were personal victims of physical or sexual abuse.

A dowry system, *lobola,* is used among some African groups, further complicating the status of women whose customs involve payment for their marriage. The practice is seen to devalue the woman who has been "bought" and forced into arranged marriages by tradition and custom.

In the News: Spain

A 60-year-old Spanish woman was doused with petrol and burned alive by her husband after she had spoken on television about his repeatedly abusing her, according to news reports (BBC News Online: World, 1998). BBC News reported that the killing sparked widespread protests about the level of domestic violence in Spain, where their partners in 1997 killed more than 60 women. Husbands or boyfriends attacked at least 1,900 other women during the same period. The Spanish government announced new measures to combat domestic violence following the protests. The initiatives included greater police powers and heavier penalties against the perpetrators.

According to previous estimates (Richter, 1988), there are over 9,000 street children in South Africa (Dangor et al., 1998). These are children between the ages of 7 and 16 who have been abandoned by their families, schools, and immediate communities and who live on the streets. Incest and battering of children are emerging as recent concerns.

Sweden.   Since the late 1970s, Swedish activists have raised the issue of male violence against women. Their first battered women's shelters were opened in Stockholm and Gothenburg in 1978 (Beausang, 2004). One study indicated that police were reluctant to proceed with any action; only 33 percent of victims ever spoke with a prosecutor (Elman & Eduards, 1991). That same study suggested that Swedish shelters provided the best response to victims.

ROKS is the national organization in Sweden that has coordinated 123 shelters or crisis lines in all parts of the country. The organization reports that in 1998, 20,447 cases of women battering were reported to the police, equal to 35 percent of all cases of physical abuse in that country. Approximately 35 to 50 women are beaten to death every year, and most acts of violence against women are committed at home by men they know (National Organization of Battered Women's Shelters in Sweden, 2004).

Thailand.   There has been growing concern about the problem of domestic violence and the recognition that women are subject to domestic violence, including physical, sexual, and mental abuse by their husbands. Other problems include husbands' irresponsibility for their families, infidelity, and multiple marriage registration (UNIFEM East and South East Asia, 2000).

Turkey.   Until January 1998, Turkish victims of domestic violence were required to document complaints of abuse by a physician who could confirm that the physical damage lasted at least ten days. Under new legislation, any person witnessing a domestic violence incident can file a complaint, and judges can forbid batterers from contacting their victims (Family Violence Prevention Fund, 1998).

Third World Countries.   The Fourth UN World Conference on Women keynotes documented epidemic proportions of domestic victims in third world countries (UN publication: Note for Speakers, 1995): "In Bangladesh, the killing of women by their husbands accounts for 50 percent of all murders. In a study of 80 battered women in San José, Costa Rica, 49 percent reported being beaten during pregnancy. In Papua New Guinea, 67 percent of rural women and 56 percent of urban women have been victims of spousal abuse, according to a national survey conducted by the Papua New Guinea Law Reform Commission."

Uganda.   There are no laws that specifically protect Ugandan women from domestic violence (Karanja, 2003). It is estimated that 41 percent of Ugandan women have suffered from domestic violence. In a country where a payment is made to the parents of the bride prior to marriage, the husband assumes to own his wife as his

Figure 2–7   This woman from New Guinea has approximately a 50/50 chance of living without being victimized by spousal abuse.

property. Polygamy, the marriage of a man to more than one wife, is practiced. Additionally, men inherit the wife of a brother who has died. Marital rape is not a legal concept in Uganda; there is a common-law presumption of consent within marriage. Complicating the issues of domestic violence, including forced marital sex, is the high incidence of AIDS/HIV that is passed to women from their husbands. These wives report fear of being beaten if they suggest that a condom be used during intercourse (Karanja, 2003).

CONCLUSIONS

In this chapter, the social–legal historical perspective does not consider the existence of violence perpetrated against males, or within same-sex relationships. The predominant explanation for domestic violence is the evidence of female inferiority created by the patriarchal system of oppression against women throughout the ages. Women and children have been legally subordinated to men, first as property and, in the cases of females, as inferior partners in marriage.

In the United States, the changes in social and legal standing of women are documented. We do not, however, live in a vacuum! There is a larger world around us with many similar problems of legislated and social inequality. Our histories may be lineal in many respects. The patriarchal social system remains today as the primary explanation for violence against women in countries around the world. The United Nations, a collective group whose interest is in humane treatment for all human beings, has recently acted as one in this case, coming forth with a stand against female oppression. Other organizations have emerged that seek legislative changes to assure equal rights and treatment of women in their countries. Education on family violence and increased resources for its victims are international concerns.

Still, Erin Pizzey, renowned author and a pioneer in the field, cautions against the view that men are the only perpetrators of domestic violence (Pizzey, 1998). She suggests that a "gender war" has been declared against men based on mistaken beliefs about family assaults. The suffering of men who are physically and sexually abused and stripped of their right to have access to their children goes unnoticed, she maintains. In 1971, men, women, and children came to her door, the first shelter for victims of domestic violence in the world. Pizzey maintains that the female victims were often as violent as the men from whom they sought refuge. Other explanations for the violence that invades so many homes will be put forth in future chapters.

Violence against children is illustrated in this view with similar explanations. The presumed superiority of men over children due to the patriarchal system is at the root of current problems. Children, to an even larger extent than adult females, are viewed as the property of parents, most notably the father. Discipline can take any form and is usually viewed to be within the acceptable limitations of parental authority. Only recently has the idea been introduced into society that children should be protected against abuse from their families.

QUESTIONS FOR REVIEW

1. Describe the inequity of power termed patriarchy.

2. Explain *Fulgham v. State* (1871).

3. What did the First National Study of Domestic Violence conclude?

4. Through what case was the government given the right to act in the best interest of children, effectively overriding the right of parents?

5. What were the Societies for the Prevention of Cruelty to Children (SPCCs), and what did they do to protect children?

6. Throughout the chapter, various countries and time periods are discussed. Compare the prevalence rate of any one (perhaps your own ethnicity?) to that of the United States.

7. Compare the treatment of children between two time periods. Have things changed in today's approach?

8. Explain the significance of the Minneapolis experiment conducted in 1980. How did it impact the policing approach to domestic violence?

INTERNET-BASED EXERCISES

1. Go to the Internet and find the meaning and extent of Gender Apartheid—The Elimination of Women's Rights Under Taliban Rule. The following is a good place to start: http://www.feminist.org/afghan/facts.html#2.

2. Update your knowledge on the Global Response to Woman Abuse at http://endabuse.org/.

REFERENCES

Amnesty International. 2003. *Afghanistan: No one listens to us and no one treats us as human beings: Justice denied to women* (Report No. ASA 11/023/2003). London, England: Amnesty International.

Anderson, John W., and Molly Moore. 1993. "The Burden of Womanhood: Third World, Second Class." *Washington Post*, February 14, p. A01.

Arakelyan, S. V. 1999. "Murder in the Sphere of Domestic Relations and its Prevention." Unpublished doctoral dissertation, Yerevan, cited in Cooper, Belinda, Elisabeth Duban, and Robin Phillips. 2000. *Domestic Violence in Armenia*. Minneapolis, MN: Minnesota Advocates for Human Rights. *http://www.mnadvocates.org/Publications_by_Date.html*

Balos, Beverly, and Mary L. Fellows. 1994. *Law and Violence against Women: Cases and Materials on Systems of Oppression*. Durham, NC: Carolina Academic Press.

BBC News Online: World. 1998. "Spain Moves to Curb Domestic Violence." January 16. *http://news.bbc.co.uk/1/hi/world/48088.stm*. 2004.

Beausang, Angela. 2004. "Sweden ROKS." *http://www.wave-network.org/Main_frame.html*. 2004.

Belknap, Joanne. 1992. "Perceptions of Woman Battering." Pp. 181–201 in *The Changing Roles of Women in the Criminal Justice System*, 2nd ed., Imogene L. Moyer (ed.). Prospect Heights, IL: Waveland Press.

Bremmer, Robert. 1970. *Children and Youth in America*. Cambridge, MA: Harvard University Press.

Buzawa, Eve S., and Carl G. Buzawa. 1996. *Domestic Violence: The Criminal Justice Response*, 2nd ed. Thousand Oaks, CA: Sage Publications.

Chen, Roda. 1996. "Risk Factors of Sexual Abuse among College Students in Taiwan." *Journal of Interpersonal Violence* 11(1):79–93.

CNN Interactive. 1998. "Pope Targets Plight of Women, Children at New Year's Mass." *http://www.cnn.com/WORLD/9801/01/pope/index.html*. 1998.

Cooper, Belinda, Elisabeth Duban, and Robin Phillips. 2000. Domestic Violence in Armenia. Minneapolis, MN: Minnesota Advocates for Human Rights. *http://www.mnadvocates.org/ Publications_by_Date.html*

Cordova, Luis. 1997. "Rights—Women: Latin American Laws on Domestic Violence." *http://www.ips.fi/koulut/199750/8.htm*. 1998.

Council of Europe. 2002. "Recommendation Rec 2002, 5 of the Committee of Ministers to member States on the protection of women against violence." Adopted on 30 April 2002 in *Explanatory Memorandum. Council of Europe: Strasbourg, France* as cited in Women's Aid Federation. (2004). *Until Women & Children Are Safe*. Retrieved January, 2004, from *http://www.womensaid.org.uk/*

The Daily. 2002. "Family violence: Impacts and consequences of spousal violence." Statistics Canada, Catalogue 11-001E. *http://www.statcan.ca/Daily/English/020626/d020626a.htm*. June 26, 2002.

Dangor, Zubeda, Lee A. Hoff et al. 1998. "Woman Abuse in South Africa: An Exploratory Study." *Violence Against Women* 4(2):125–49.

Davidson, Terry. 1977. "Wife Beating: A Recurring Phenomenon Throughout History." Pp. 19–57 in *Battered Women: A Psychosociolological Study of Domestic Violence*, Maria Roy (ed.). New York. Van Nostrand Reinhold.

———. 1978. *Conjugal Crime*. New York: Hawthorn Books.

Davis, Elizabeth G. 1971. *The First Sex*. New York: Penguin Books.

Dobash, Emerson, and Russell P. Dobash. 1978. "Wives: The 'Appropriate' Victims of Marital Violence." *Victimology* 2:426–39.

———. 1979. *Violence against Wives: A Case against the Patriarchy*. New York: Free Press.

Dutton, Donald G. 1998. *The Domestic Assault of Women: Psychological and Criminal Justice Perspectives*, 3rd ed. Vancouver, British Columbia: UBC Press.

Elman, Amy, and Maud Eduards. 1991. "Unprotected Swedish Welfare State: A Survey of Battered Women and the Assistance They Received." *Women Studies International Forum* 14(5):413–21.

Family Violence Prevention Fund. 1998. "World Round-Up." February. *http://www.igc.org/ materials/speakup/02_13_98.htm*. 1999.

Feinman, C. 1992. "Woman Battering on the Navajo Reservation." *International Review of Victimology* 2(2):137–46.

Garner, J., J. Fagan, and C. Maxwell. 1995. "Published Findings from the Spouse Assault Replication Program: A Critical Review." *Journal of Quantitative Criminology* 11(1):3–28.

Gelles, Richard. 1993. "Constraints against Family Violence: How Well Do They Work?" *American Behavioral Scientist* 36(5):575–86.

Gordon, Linda. 1989. *Heroes of Their Own Lives: The Politics and History of Family Violence.* New York: Penguin Books.

Horne, Charles F. 1915. "Ancient History Sourcebook: Code of Hammurabi." *http://www .fordham.edu/halsall/ancient/hamcode.html.* 1998.

Iverson, Timothy J., and Marilyn Segal. 1990. *Child Abuse and Neglect: An Information and Reference Guide.* New York: Garland Press.

Jerusalem Bible, The. 1996. New York: Doubleday.

Karanja, L. 2003. "Just Die Quietly: Domestic Violence and Women's Vulnerability to HIV in Uganda." *Human Rights Watch* 15(15A)1–80.

Keltosova, Olga. 2002. "Domestic Violence." Accessed 2004. Available at *http://www.roks.se/ english/olga_report_0210.html.*

King, L. W. (transl.) 1998. "Hammurabi's Code of Laws." *http://www.fordham.edu/halsall/ ancient/hamcode.html.* 1998.

Kennedy, L. W., and D. G. Dutton. 1989. "The Incidence of Wife Assault in Alberta." *Canadian Journal of Behavioral Science* 21(1):40–54.

Lefkowitz, Mary R., and Maureen B. Fant. 1992. "Women's Life in Greece and Rome: A Source Book in Translation." *http://www.stoa.org/diotima/anthology/wlgr/wlgr-romanle-gal109.shtml.* 2004.

Levy, Darline, H. Applewhite, and M. Johnson (eds.). 1979. "Declaration of the Rights of Woman and Female Citizen." Pp. 92–96 in *Women in Revolutionary Paris, 1785–1795.* Urbana, IL: University of Illinois Press.

Lunn, T. 1991. "Til Death Do Us Part." *Social Work Today* 29(8):16–17.

Maxwell, C. D., Garner, J. H., and Fagan, J. A. 2003. "The Preventive Effects of Arrest on Intimate Partner Violence: Research, Policy, and Theory." *Domestic Violence Report* 9(1):9–10.

Miria, S. Dhuna. 1996. "ndaj grave dhe tabute psikosociale qe e favorizojne ate, Botim i shoqates Refleksione, Tirane 1996." P. 3 in Mapping of Existing Information on Domestic Violence in Albania. Tirana, Albania: UNICEF. 2000.

Myhill, A., and Allen, J. 2002. "Rape and sexual assault of women: the extent and nature of the problem." *Home Office Research Study 237: London* as cited in Women's Aid Federation. 2004. *Until Women & Children Are Safe.* Retrieved January, 2004, from *http://www.womensaid .org.uk/*

National Organization of Battered Women's Shelters in Sweden. 2004. "About ROKS." *http://www.roks.se/english/beginning.html.* 2004.

NEWW Polska. 2003. "800,000 Romanian Women Victims of Domestic Violence." *http://www.neww.org.pl/1/en.php/news_druk.php?id=1349.*

Nowakovska, Urszula. 1997. "Poland." *http://www.wave-network.org/Main_frame.html.* 1998.

O'Faolain, Julia, and Lauro Martines. 1973. *Not in God's Image.* New York: Harper & Row.

Pagelow, Mildred D. 1984. *Family Violence.* New York: Praeger Publishers.

Pfohl, S. 1977. "The 'Discovery' of Child Abuse." *Social Problems* 24:431–33.

Pizzey, Erin. 1977. *Scream Quietly or the Neighbors Will Hear.* Hillside, NJ: Enslow Publishers.

———. 1982. "Prone to Violence." *http://www.massey.ac.nz/~kbirks/gender/viol/ptv/ptv.htm.* 2004.

———. 1998. "VAWA II Must Be Stopped." *http://www.acfc.us/spokesperson-diannathompson.htm.* 2004.

Pleck, Elizabeth. 1989. "Criminal Approaches to Family Violence, 1640–1980." *Family Violence* 11:19–57.

Polish Ministry of Justice. 1996. "Violence against Women." *http://free.ngo.pl/temida/violstat.htm*. 2004.

PROWID. 2003. Annual Report 2002. Washington, DC: International Center for Research on Women.

Pushkareva, Natalia. 1997. *In Women in Russian History: From the Tenth to the Twentieth Century*, Eve Levin (ed./transl.). Armonk, NY: M. E. Sharpe.

Radbill, Samuel X. 1987. "Children in a World of Violence: A History of Child Abuse." Pp. 3–22 in *The Battered Child*, 4th ed., Ray E. Helfer and Ruth S. Kempe (eds.). Chicago: University of Chicago Press.

Rhodes, Henry A. 1984. "The Athenian Court and the American Court System." Yale-New Haven Teachers Institute. *http://www.yale.edu/ynhti/curriculum/units/1984/2/*. 2004.

Richter, L. 1988. "Street Children: The Nature and Scope of the Problem in Southern Africa." *Child Care Worker* 6:11–14.

Romano, Irene, and Donald White. 2000. "Women's Life." University of Pennsylvania Museum of Archaeology and Anthropology. *http://www.museum.upenn.edu/Greek_World/Index.html*. 2004.

Sagatun, Inger J., and Leonard P. Edwards. 1995. *Child Abuse and the Legal System*. Chicago: Nelson-Hall Publishers.

Sanders, Wiley B. 1945. *Some Early Beginnings of the Children's Court Movement in England*. New York: National Council on Crime and Delinquency.

Sherman, Lawrence, and Dennis Rogan. 1992. P. 46 in *Policing Domestic Violence: Experiments and Dilemmas*. New York: Free Press.

Sherman, Lawrence, and Jannell Schmidt. 1993. "Does Arrest Deter Domestic Violence?" *American Behavioral Scientist* 36(5):601–9.

Sinelnikov, Andrei. 1998. "RUSSIA: Inside the Broken Cell." Family Violence Prevention Fund. *http://endabuse.org/programs/display.php3?DocID=106*. 2002.

So-Kum-Tang, Catherine. 1998. "The Rate of Physical Child Abuse in Chinese Families: A Community Survey in Hong Kong." *Child Abuse and Neglect* 22(5):381–91.

Stanko, E. 2000. "The Day to Count: A Snapshot of the Impact of Domestic Violence in the UK." *Criminal Justice* 1:2.

Straus, Murray A., Richard J. Gelles, and Suzanne K. Steinmetz. 1980. P. 222 in *Behind Closed Doors: Violence in the American Family*. Garden City, NY: Anchor Press/Doubleday.

Struve, Jim. 1990. "Dancing with Patriarchy: The Politics of Sexual Abuse." Pp. 3–45 in *The Sexually Abused Male*, Vol. I, Mic Hunter (ed.). New York: Lexington Books.

Terzieff, J. 2002. Pakistan's Fiery Shame: Women Die in Stove Deaths. *http://www.womensenews.org/article.cfm/dyn/aid/1085/context/archive*

Ulrich, Laurel T. 1991. P. 7 in *Good Wives: Image and Reality in the Lives of Women in Northern New England, 1650–1750*. New York: Vintage Books.

UN publication: Note for speakers. 1995. "The Advancement of women." *http://www.unifem.org/index.php?f_page_pid=48*

UN publication: Progress for the World's Women. 2000. *http://www.UNIFEM.undp.org/arep*. 2000.

UNICEF. 1997. "Outlawing Violence Against Women: A First Step." Women, Progress, and Disparity. *http://www.unicef.org/pon97/p48a.htm*. 2002.

UNICEF. 2000. "Mapping of Existing Information on Domestic Violence in Albania. Tirana, Albania: UNICEF." *http://www.unicef.org/albania/publications/domviol.pdf*. 2004.

UNIFEM East and South East Asia. 2000. Gender and Development in Thailand, UNIFEM East and South East Asia *http://www.unifem.org/global_spanner/index.php?f_loc=e_se_asia*. 2004.

UNIFEM East and South East Asia. 1999. A Commitment by the Government of Indonesia to a National Plan of Action to Eliminate Violence Against Women. *http://www.UNIFEM-eseasia.org/news/newsNOV99-MAR2000.html#commitment*. 1999.

Violence Against Women, Services E.C. 1998. "Statistics to Consider . . ." *www.info.london.on.ca/vawsec/stats.html*. 1998.

WAVE Database. 2001. *http://www.wave-network.org/Database.asp*. 2001.

Webb, Tracy. 1998. "Abuse of the Disabled." *http://dawn.thot.net/fact.html*. 1998.

Williamsburg Foundation. 1998. "Redefining Family." *http://www.history.org/Almanack/life/family/essay.cfm*. 2004.

Women's Aid. 2004. *http://www.womensaid.ie/ 2004*.

Women's Aid Federation. 2004. Until Women & Children Are Safe. *http://www.womensaid.org.uk/*.

Women's International Network News. 1998. "Vienna Human Rights Conference Five Years Later: Declaration and Programme of Action." *Women's International Network* 24(4):13.

Women's Resource Information and Support Centre. 1998. "Women's Resource Information and Support Centre." *http://wrisc.ballarat.net.au*. 2004.

Wortman, Marlene S. (ed.). 1985. Discussion of the Virginia Statute on Racial Intermarriage. Pp. 70, 136, 269 in *Women in American Law: From Colonial Times to the New Deal*, Vol. 1. New York: Holmes & Meier Publishers.

C ASES

Fulgham v. State, 46 AL 146–47 (1871).
State v. Oliver, 70 NC 60 (1874).
Ex Parte Crouse, 4 Wharton 9, PA 11 (1838).
Bradwell v. Illinois, 16 Wallace 130 (1873).

Part Two

Theories on Causation and Victimization

It is not enough to know that domestic violence occurs in numerous forms and that various populations are victimized. Why does it happen? What is being done to stop the perpetrators and to help the victims? Who are the perpetrators of these crimes? What happens to the victims? These are among the questions that are answered in Part Two.

In Chapter 3, "Theories on Family Violence," we examine the development of contemporary criminological theories and argue for the recognition that domestic violence crimes appropriately are studied from within similar theoretical perspectives. Why do people beat and sometimes kill the people they are intimate with or related to? Why do parents and dating partners commit rape? The questions are too complex to answer using any one theory alone. We consider the issues from biological, sociological, and psychological perspectives. Contemporary theoretical models have emerged that involve a combination of the older theories that guide us toward the need for future research.

Chapter 4, "Survivors and the Consequences of Victimization," is an essential component in any discussion of domestic violence. For too long the victim has been ignored by the criminal justice system. What movement brought victimization to the forefront of today's examination? What is the children's rights movement? Have we learned anything about childhood abuse and its consequences? Do child victims grow up to become offenders? What has the battered women's movement contributed? Can theories on victimization help us to understand why victims sometimes stay in an abusive relationship? Since victims often do leave, however, what effects of long-term victimization must they overcome to be termed survivors? To reflect growing concern over the numbers of children and women who have disabilities and are being abused or neglected by family members, new sections have been added to Chapter 4. They are entitled "Maltreatment of Children with Disabilities" and "Women with Disabilities." The section "Violence Against Same-Sex Partners" has been expanded to include new and important information on this population.

CHAPTER 3

THEORIES ON FAMILY VIOLENCE

SIMPLY SCENARIO

Why Some Women Choose to Stay . . . for a While

Cindy fell deeply in love with Jim and they married; it was her second marriage. She had two children by her first husband and one more since she and Jim have married. They own their own home and both hold professional jobs. Shortly after the birth of their daughter, things started getting tense. Cindy felt like she was walking on eggshells because Jim would get angry about the most insignificant things. One day he flew into a rage and hit her; he pulled her across the room by her hair. Afterward he was so sorry, he promised to change. He bought her a gift. Things got really good, like when they had first met—it was great! About ten months later he started getting cranky again . . .

Question: What theory best describes this scenario? What will likely happen next?

KEY TERMS

Biological theory
Classical school
Culture theory
Deterrence theory
Ecological theory
Eugenics
Family systems theory
Gender-role theory
Hedonistic

Multidimensional theories
Patriarchal theory
Positive school
Psychological theory
Rational choice theory
Resiliency theory
Social–psychological model
Social structure and cultural theories

INTRODUCTION

> To try to deny to ourselves and others that we feel anger is a distortion of reality that is likely to cause trouble; and to suppress issues precludes the possibility of resolving them. (Straus et al., 1980, p. 171)

Anger is not the cause of domestic violence. You can see it, though—it is there. Anger is brought out by a real or supposed injury to others or to us. When the back of your neck feels red and hot with anger, what do you do? The outward manifestation of that feeling is violence; it is evidenced due to a lack of self-control. Do you clench your teeth? Do you yell? Do you walk away? Do you punch a wall? Do you punch the one you love? Are all of these options allowed for the release of that anger—that monster inside us all? When feeling vulnerable and powerless, just how far are you willing to go?

All people are faced with situations that cause them to be angry, many times over the course of our lives. A teacher, our boss, a friend, or a motorist who cuts you off on the highway: All can arouse anger, that is, a passion or emotion. Love is also a passion or emotion. Few people will hit their teacher, yell at the boss, or rape a friend. Why do so many people feel free to abuse their lover, their child, or their parent? A simple answer is that we do it because we can. But can we get away with it? Most believe that the answer is not so straightforward.

No one really knows why people commit domestic crimes. We try to understand for many reasons. As a society, we don't want to be helpless or hopeless. As individuals, the more we find out about others and the world around us, the better we know ourselves. For every form of crime that is committed, there are many possible explanations; some of them make sense, some less so. Since we began to view domestic violence as criminal behavior, old theories were applied and new ones developed. There is a lack of consensus on the causes of family violence. The older theories often provide the cornerstone for new perspectives. For that reason, we focus first on the classical, biological, psychological, and sociological explanations.

Abuse within the family is not a simple matter, and we cannot expect simple solutions. Criminology, the study of crime causation, has long accepted that there is no single explanation for law breaking. Since the 1970s, there has been an incredible amount of research into domestic violence, resulting in theories too numerous to include in this introductory text. The most popular theories are multidimensional and draw from the old "schools" of thought, forming a new school. Some of the more contemporary ideas are included in the latter part of the chapter.

The social–legal historical viewpoint outlined in Chapter 2 is often placed under a broader umbrella as a political–historical approach. As stated earlier, it is useful as a description of the cause of wife and child abuse. Its limitation is that it excludes other theoretical explanations and other forms of violence. Still, this sociocultural anthropology view fits well within the broader understanding of family violence as one of the multidisciplinary descriptions within the social sciences. Theories that consider the family, social system, and others focus on individual characteristics. These theories generally define the other major categories under which familial violence occurs.

Society Viewed at the Macro or Micro Level

There are two ways to study society: on a macro or a micro level. These terms do not refer to a particular theory, just the general approach that is used by theorists. As you proceed through this theoretical chapter, try to determine the level that describes the concept.

The social sciences approach acknowledges that social interactions are not random acts. Members of the family unit act purposefully to accomplish the goals of society. The learned patterns of behavior that are passed down from generation to generation are based on shared values and are shaped by the accepted rules of the group. This larger view of society and the influences that determine behavior is considered an examination on the macro level of society.

When inferences are made from individuals and applied to society at large, the study is being done on the micro level. From this perspective, an act that occurs between individuals is applied to the whole of society to form a theory. Typically, these involve psychological or individualist theories that are examined on the micro level of society. Most, although certainly not all, domestic abuse theory comes from this view. It allows generalizations to be made about groups of people while understanding that the individual results may be different. What happens in domestic violence is considered predictable, yet the result varies from one person to another based on intervening circumstances.

Figure 3–1   "Why—why me?" or "What did I do to deserve this?" These questions are particularly relevant for those affected by family violence. The victim is not responsible for the hurtful actions, yet self-blame is common. This chapter examines theories that attempt to reason why these criminal behaviors occur.

Think of each theoretical school described in this chapter as your own school. Although you can make a general statement about your college or university, you know that there are individuals within your institution that make it unique. Your generalization will not fit to describe each person but could be a fairly accurate statement about your institution.

THE CLASSICAL SCHOOL

Classical criminology is based on the idea that individuals choose to engage in crime. Cesare Beccaria (1738–1794) is called the father of classical criminology. He suggested that people possess a will that is free and therefore have the ability to reason. He suggested that to control behavior it would be necessary to spell out specifically through written law what was considered criminal behavior as well as the punishment associated with the act. Since people are **hedonistic** or pleasure seeking, the threat of humiliation, pain, or disgrace would influence the will of the person, according to Beccaria.

To be effective, the punishment must fit the crime and be administered in a swift manner. It cannot be excessive or arbitrary in order to influence offenders into conformity.

Jeremy Bentham (1748–1833) popularized Beccaria's ideas through a "moral calculus" theory. He determined the extent of punishment necessary to deter the criminal. Believing that deterrence was the only acceptable reason for government punishment to be administered, he suggested that only minimal force could be used to encourage lesser crimes.

Since control and punishment are central to this theory, it is sometimes called the *legalistic* approach. You will note in upcoming chapters that the recent trend to criminalize domestic violence is often justified by the need to control family offenders. Arresting family lawbreakers is considered a form of punishment and a deterrent to future domestic violent acts. Applying penalties for family violence brings into the public forum acts that have traditionally been considered private. This is a huge departure from the way that society has conceived crime. In one generation, we have tried to change the perception that private violence is a public wrong. This was not possible until domestic violence was established as a social problem, and is still highly controversial.

Since the time of Beccaria and Bentham, government interference into the actions of individuals has been justified by the overriding needs of society. Recent research into the consequences of domestic violence has suggested that it is a pattern of behavior detrimental to a large number of citizens. Without regulation, family violence victims would be without the protection of the government.

The *classical school* was the dominant perspective in crime control for approximately 100 years. It established criminal procedures that continued in existence and sustained law enforcement practices after the theory was no longer debated. Neoclassical theory is a more current application of the principles contained in classical

Figure 3-2 Is arrest an excessive response to domestic violence? It appears that there is a risk of escalating future domestic violence when the offender is arrested. "I'll get you later!" is an expression that some victims are familiar with.

thought. It includes an economic perspective and an updated view of the behavioral sciences within the context of deterrence.

It is fair to say that contemporary classical thought is a restatement of the classical theories suggested by Beccaria and Bentham. They reaffirm the concept of punishment and have been categorized as separate approaches to combat domestic violence as well as other crimes. Social influences are believed to have an effect on the ability of the individual to exercise free will in the updated awareness of control and punishment.

Rational Choice Theory

Free or **rational choice theory** states that criminal behavior is more than just a response to social pressures or upbringing—it is also a choice (National Institute of Justice, 1994). Under this perspective, offenders calculate the relative costs and benefits of behavior and choose to commit domestic crimes. The National Institute of Justice report points out that offender choices are not necessarily rational but draw on previously established beliefs about their opportunities to commit personal violence and the likelihood of benefiting from their actions. The focus in this theory is to determine the effectiveness of interventions in order to decide how best to reduce the benefits of crime and increase the cost of criminal action.

Deterrence Theory

As with earlier statements, today's **deterrence theory** is based on the idea that punishment must be swift and certain in order to deter crime. The deterrent effect of punishment can be specific or general in nature. Theorists suggest that we don't understand how effective deterrence is, and why it works or fails. They seek to update the concept with a greater understanding of community reinforcements and the role of official sanctions (National Institute of Justice, 1994).

When people are targeted in prevention efforts for a particular crime, the deterrence is considered specific. Larry Siegel suggests that efforts to reduce domestic violence through mandatory arrest policies exemplify specific deterrence (Siegel, 1995). Recidivism is reduced in some instances of domestic violence; the reduction appears greatest for those who have a greater stake in conformity. When nonoffenders are affected by the punishment of offenders and choose not to risk apprehension, deterrence is general. If during an argument a person walks away muttering "you're not worth it" and holds himself or herself back when he or she might otherwise have swung out in his or her anger, that is an example of the general deterrence effect. One way that experts measure the deterrent effect of legislation is to examine the level of domestic crime to determine if the rate has gone down or risen. Only recently have studies attempted to determine the effects of legal sanctions, both criminal and civil, on the recurrence of domestic violence. We still do not know whether legal sanctions can control it effectively.

Critique of the Classical School

Classicism is a clear statement of law and punishment. All people are presumed equal and have the same opportunities to avoid crime. The assumption that all are equal is a target of criticisms of the legalist approach. Opponents claim that the law is unequally applied with bias toward minorities and the disadvantaged.

The **classical school** has often been referred to as simplistic because it does not look to explain why people commit crimes; it seeks to control those who do. Domestic violence policy in the last decade has been based on efforts to control behaviors, and we have not yet determined if this has had the desired impact on recidivism. Classicism is reactive rather than proactive or preventive: It may not adequately protect the victim of abuse. The criminal justice system has a dual responsibility of protection as well as punishment. If deterrence is the goal of punishment, we must find out if legal sanctions deter the violence.

The classical school can also be criticized because strict adherence to the theory leaves no room for mitigating circumstances or defenses. You do the crime, you do the time! Even Beccaria had to admit that some populations were incapable of exercising free will due to age or mental limitations, such as children and the insane! Classical theory was ultimately replaced in popularity with the **positive school**.

THE POSITIVE SCHOOL

Positive theories are located in a broad school of thought where it becomes important to identify the cause of crime through scientific advances. The implication is that once the cause is isolated, a cure can be found to alter the behavior. *Cure* is a broad term in this sense; it could be a physical cure, a change in circumstances, or elimination of poverty. There are many possibilities.

The positive school recognizes that the causes of crime are recognized from biological, psychological, and sociological viewpoints. The theories are not mutually exclusive and often overlap. It is not unusual for theorists to combine ideas to give direction toward solving new problems or merely to take a fresh look at old problems. Where classical thought is legalistic, the positive school is scientific. Continued research and the application of scientific principles are critical in this ever-changing body of thought.

BIOLOGICAL THEORIES

Biological theories are the most controversial and have limited application to family violence. Under this model violent or criminal behavior is beyond the control of the individual and caused by the person's biology. Once believed to result from a constant conflict between good and evil spirits, the triumph of evil was characterized by physical distinctiveness. Evilness was thought to reside in persons with red hair, according

---

Been There . . . Done That

"Why should criminal justice students have to study theory? Criminological theories are only excuses that criminals use to 'get off' after being caught! This has nothing to do with criminal justice!" Statements such as these are typical of those from my criminal justice students over the years. Many would rather take any other three courses if they could escape being subjected to theory.

The question remains: Why should criminal justice students study theory? To recognize the monster among us or inside us, if for no other reason. After having interviewed over 100 abusers, I arrested clergy, professional persons, men, women, and children. They were old and young, educated and illiterate. Most didn't look bad or different. Some would have seemed like nice people if I hadn't known what they had done. What made them criminal was the act that they had committed. In domestic violence, the perpetrators are our neighbors and our friends, some of them "nice" people. "Why" becomes the operative word. When you study theory, it becomes possible to understand—not excuse—this criminal behavior.

to Greek and Roman myth. Being ugly was an indictment of a bad person, one predisposed to commit crime.

Publication of Charles Darwin's theory of evolution in *On the Origin of Species* in 1859 influenced theorists who sought explanations for deviant conduct. An Italian psychiatrist, Cesare Lombroso (1835–1909), was the first to develop a theory based entirely on physical characteristics of the offender. His views on the "born criminal" suggested that offenders were less evolved than noncriminals. He concluded that it was possible to identify them through their atavistic or apelike tendencies. Although the atavistic explanation has repeatedly been refuted since then, it established the process of scientific inquiry that characterizes the positive school.

Early critics introduced social and cultural influences that affect biological tendencies as control mechanisms. The later theories forwarded by Lombroso included a variety of causes in addition to physical factors, many of which considered environmental variables (Vold & Bernard, 1986). At first controversial, U.S. society reacted favorably to biological determination, due to its scientific nature (Hofstadter, 1965).

Eugenics

The **eugenics** movement is an example of the reaction to this theoretical explanation for crime. Known as the "science of good breeding," the term *eugenics* was coined by Darwin's cousin, Francis Galton, in 1883 (Hofstadter, 1965). Most people are aware of the role of eugenics in Hitler's attempts to "cleanse" the races; few realize its influence on the American way of behaving at the turn of the century. Richard Hofstadter wrote that eugenics had reached the dimensions of a fad by 1915 and proved to be the most enduring aspect of social Darwinism in the United States. Proponents of eugenics believed in the "survival of the fittest." Due to concern with the social significance of

---

More About It: Chemical Castration

Jennifer Bund explains chemical castration in a preprint article from the University of Pittsburgh Law Review (Bund, 1997). From her analysis, the following information is provided. Medroxyprogesterone acetate treatment, better known by the trade name Depo-Provera, is a synthetic hormone. It lowers the blood serum testosterone levels in males by restricting the release of luteinizing hormones from the pituitary gland. The reduction of testosterone triggers a corresponding reduction in sexual interest and therefore is believed to reduce recidivism. It is also believed to reduce effectively the frequency of erotic imagery and to cause a temporary form of impotence (interference with erections) that also helps to reduce recidivism. The drug takes effect quickly, and positive results usually appear within six months of treatment. The side effects associated with Depo-Provera include weight gain, muscle weakness, fatigue, and increased blood pressure. Once treatment is discontinued, the side effects disappear.

heredity and the expanding slums that were on the increase, the American Breeders' Association and the Eugenics Record Office were created (Hofstadter, 1965). Persons with mental health problems, immigrants, or those with low IQs were among the populations considered biologically inferior. The eugenics movement has rightly been charged with perpetuating racism due to its including persons of color among the unfit.

The eugenics movement advocated for the forced sterilization of both men and women who were considered socially and biologically inferior. In 1907 Indiana became the first state to adopt a sterilization law, and by 1915, twelve states had passed similar measures (Hofstadter, 1965). This approach became an accepted method of controlling the poor, who it was believed were held down by biological inadequacy. Eugenics reached its pinnacle in the 1927 Supreme Court case *Buck v. Bell*. Considering the constitutionality of forced sterilization laws, Justice Oliver Holmes wrote in the opinion for the Court, "It is better for all the world if, instead of waiting to execute degenerate offspring for crime or to let them starve for their imbecility, society can prevent those who are manifestly unfit from continuing their kind. The principle that sustains compulsory vaccination is broad enough to cover cutting the Fallopian tubes" (*Jacobson v. Massachusetts*, 197 U.S. 11). "Three generations of imbeciles are enough" (*Buck v. Bell*, 1927, p. 208).

The practice of forced sterilization was maintained in the United States well into the 1970s (Lilly et al., 1989). Although it is rarely discussed, criminal justice had

Figure 3-3   In the early 1900s the American Breeders' Association pointed to expanding slums and increased numbers of immigrants, the "unfit" of society, as justification for forced sterilization. The question remains—could there have been reasons, other than biological inferiority, to explain the problems these people faced?

continued to use chemical and physical castration and sterilization as forms of punishment as well as a means to control deviant conduct. Its popularity as an alternative to traditional forms of punishment has been rekindled due to scientific evidence suggestive of a link between violence and biological factors.

> Among other areas, modern biological theories link violence to hormones and to neurological dysfunction. These two areas are considered the most promising of contemporary biological research into the causes of violent conduct. They differ from other biological explanations because the conditions are considered measurable and alterable. Although not broadly accepted, there has been a recent surge of interest in the use of biological influences toward explaining criminal behavior. (Wright & Miller, 1998)

Critics of the application of biological theories point to the eugenics movement and diverge from two perspectives, moral and constitutional, although the two views are closely related. Moral critics refer to the biological intervention strategies as the medicalization of repression (Katz, 1984). It has been noted that the people targeted for these medical procedures are often poor and undereducated. Frequent complaints suggest that black and minority populations have been abused by government practices of coerced sterilization. An example is the acknowledgment of widespread abuse carried out by the Indian Health Services and other health care providers to Native American women. In 1975 alone, 25,000 Native American women were permanently sterilized after being coerced, misinformed, or threatened, according to a study by the Government Accounting Office (Define, 1997). Sterilization of women as a condition of probation has continued with few complaints.

Prior to the 1980s, surgical castration as a method of reducing sex offenders' recidivism was practiced. Since then courts have struck down the measure under both "cruel and unusual" arguments and on "equal protection" grounds (Bund, 1997). In the past few years, five states have enacted legislation that permits chemical castration under certain circumstances. Fred Berlin, founder of the Sexual Disorders Clinic at Johns Hopkins University, fueled the debate by noting that molesters may have a recidivism rate as high as 65 percent (Van Biema, 1996). In response to the alarming rates of child molestation, California was the first to pass the legislation in 1996 to allow chemical castration of paroled sex offenders. Montana, Florida, Georgia, and Louisiana quickly followed the example in 1997. Texas passed a similar law in 1998.

Biochemical Imbalance Theories

A number of *biochemical theories*, including glandular and hormonal imbalances, as well as vitamin and diet deficiencies, have been suggested as possible causes of criminal behavior (Vold & Bernard, 1986). The raging hormones of women and the excess of testosterone in men have alternatively been accepted and rejected during this century. The most pervasive theory is a perceived link between testosterone and male aggressiveness. Vold and Bernard point toward research conducted in the 1980s which found that violent males had a significantly higher level of testosterone in their systems.

Neurological Theories

In the study of brain activity, numerous attempts have been made to link abnormal patterns to violent action. Antisocial behavior that afflicts approximately 5 percent of males has been linked to a brain dysfunction indicated by neuropsychological tests, according to recent research (Moffitt, 1997). This study, which attempted to show the connection between brain abnormalities and criminality, concluded that test scores were not helpful in predicting delinquent behavior. However, dysfunction may influence the personal relationships in a small subgroup of men and may have applicability in explaining some forms of domestic violence.

Chemical compounds that influence brain functions have been studied in relation to aggression as well (Siegel, 1995). Of particular interest are the endogenous opiates the brain produces that are similar to opium and morphine. Some theorists suggest that a "thrill" obtained through crime may cause production of these addictive chemicals, according to Siegel. Alderman suggests that excessive endorphin production may explain in part the reasons for self-inflicted violence (SIV) (Alderman, 1997). She maintains that the majority of SIV patients have histories of abuse as children. Feelings of inadequacy, coupled with an inability to cope with life stresses, may influence people to seek pleasure through the pain of self-abuse.

Critique of the Biological Theories

The danger of early biological explanations for behavior was the tendency to view abnormalities as undesirable and unalterable. Belief that crime was caused by a person's biology and exhibited through physical characteristics, including racial differences, led us to adopt drastic measures in response. We should know about the danger

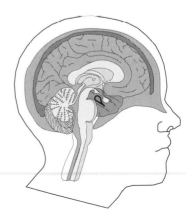

Figure 3–4   Naturally produced chemical compounds that influence brain functions have been studied in relation to aggression. Endogenous opiates are an example that may occur with the "thrill" of crime.

in order to resist the impulse of looking for the easy cure or quick fix to the problems in society. Current controversy on the application of biological theory is aimed at medical procedures that are being used to control the sexual impulses of convicted offenders. Debates on the constitutionality of sterilization and castration as a method of controlling criminal behavior are likely to continue well into the next decade.

SOCIOLOGICAL THEORIES

Adolph Quetelet (1796–1874), a Belgian theorist, is called the "first social criminologist" according to Vold and Bernard (1986). Among the first to establish a relationship between crime and poverty, Quetelet suggested that the great inequality between the wealthy and the poor contributed to lawbreaking. Hundreds of studies on crime and the effects of unemployment have been conducted since that time.

For a short period after the introduction of **biological theory**, some sociological perspectives incorporated biological views. Belief in natural selection was evidenced through the broadly acclaimed works of Herbert Spencer. Between 1870 and 1890, Spencer had a profound influence on arguments within the United States regarding the nature of humankind. Against criticism, he claimed that government aid to the weak was in opposition to the natural order. The unfit should be eliminated, he suggested, and programs to aid the poor were contrary to natural selection of the species. Opposed to compulsory poor laws and other state measures, he did not argue against private charity to the unfit: "If they are not sufficiently complete to live, they die, and it is best that they should die," said Spencer (p. 41) (Hofstadter, 1965).

Despite Spencerism, the sociological explanations have gained credibility in the twentieth century. They provide the bulk of theory on the causes of criminal conduct. This theory is concerned with an interaction between social change and human behavior influenced by economics and culture. Sociological points of view have contributed enormously to the understanding of domestic abuses.

Social Structure and Cultural Theories

Social structure theories attribute domestic violence to the structures and cultural norms that legitimize deviance. Batterer intervention strategies are based on women's experience of these social and cultural factors. They use education and skills building to resocialize battering males, emphasizing equality in intimate relationships (Healey & Smith, 1998).

Culture of Violence Theory.   The *culture of violence theory* looks at the broad acceptance of violence in our society and concludes that its acceptance is the foundation for violence within the family. In this view, theorists point out the perverseness of violence as entertainment and the means for settling disputes at the personal and national levels. The implied approval for violence is acknowledged and legitimizes the use of violence to settle family disputes as well. This theory claims that violence occurs at all levels of society as an accepted means to resolve difficulty, arguing that a restructuring of the cultural variables of society is needed in order to bring change. In other words, to stop wife abuse, it is necessary to alter man's reliance on violence as a means of resolving conflict.

Social Disorganization Theory.   The *disorganization of community life* causes a lack of social control in this theory. Considered in part the result of high mobility, a breakdown in formal and informal controls that might otherwise mitigate family conflict encourages criminal conduct. Poverty in transitional neighborhoods is believed to contribute to the lawlessness that results. People whose emphasis is necessarily on survival lack concern for community matters and fail to benefit from common sources of control such as family, school, and social service agencies.

Strain Theory.   Another type of social structure theory is the one referred to as *strain theory*. This is the struggle between desires and the ability to fulfill them. When social and economic goals are outside the reach due to poverty, strain occurs. The United States is a competitive and property-oriented country. Most people want material possessions, some of which are necessary, such as a car or a home. Beyond the basics are television sets, radios, and computers. For many the opportunity to go to college is outside their economic means. Strain theory suggests that a sense of futility develops when one is unable to achieve financial success or security. In some circumstances, this will lead to crime. As you will note in many of the multidimensional models, it is also believed to contribute to domestic violence crime.

Gamache points out that women of color experience battering in a different context than that of others in society (Gamache, 1998). Her position is in part explained through the strain theory. The "stick by your man" stance is an example of the protective response toward male partners whose dominance and abuse may be tolerated due to a shared sense of mistrust. A perception of a lack of power or ability to have significant impact on the culture has led many black men to make excessive demands on their partners for respect, according to Evelyn White (White, 1998). She suggests that this cause of domestic violence in the black community is based on the reality that black men face bleak futures regardless of how hard they may work to overcome the poverty that embraces them.

Gender-Role Theory

This uncomplicated explanation for domestic violence blames the traditional socialization of children into gender roles conducive to wife battering (Walker, 1979). In this perspective, children are oriented early in life as victims or perpetrators, according to their gender. Girls are taught to be passive and yielding to the "stronger" male sex. Proponents of **gender-role theory** suggest that society dictates the role of women in marriage, in child responsibilities, and toward domestic duties, all of which makes them vulnerable to abuse. Self-reliance or aggressiveness are male attributes that are unbecoming of females in the traditional sense.

According to gender-role theory, the expectation that girls should be physically and sexually pleasing to men makes them susceptible to sexual abuse. In relationships, girls are taught to be submissive while boys are expected to be the sexual aggressors. On the other hand, boys are taught that men must be in control at all times. They must exhibit strength and develop leadership qualities. Men are therefore socialized that their position is to be protected at all costs, including violence.

The tenets of this theory are believed to contribute to sexual violence of young women in dating relationships. Emotionally immature young women socialized in their roles are vulnerable to sexual victimization through aggression and dominance of young men. Py Bateman suggests that reports from adolescent date rape victims are rare in this culture that condones sexual violence toward women (Bateman, 1998). Conversely, young men may respond to peer pressure to be sexually aggressive through the same model. A major source of socialization for this model is the media. Television is blamed for depicting male and female roles in a limited and superficial characterization of male aggression and female passivity.

Critique of the Sociological Theories

Most of the criticism on the sociological theories is that they fail to explain why people who come in contact with crime do not themselves become deviant. The majority of people do not commit domestic violence crime, even though they are socialized through similar media. Not all men are violent, nor all women victims. Nor do sociological theories explain why some victims of sexual or physical violence do not perpetrate violence against others.

PSYCHOLOGICAL THEORIES

Yet another distinct category among the major schools of thought, **psychological theory** is itself diverse in the ways that it looks at people. Under the rubric of psychological theory, many theories examine the influence and impact of individual pathology, culture, socialization, and learning.

Social Learning Theories

According to *social learning theory*, people are not born with violent tendencies. They learn them through their environment and life experiences. Deviance is learned in the same manner as normative behavior. The process of learning is through communication with others and includes motives, drives, attitudes, and rationalizations on the commission of crime. When aggressive action brings desired results, violence becomes an acceptable means to an end. The primary source of learning occurs in intimate personal groups of family and peer, according to this view.

The frequency and duration of the violence in one's environment will influence the learning experience. Since people process life events in different ways, it can be said that your perception is your reality. The manner in which a person perceives a situation from his or her own viewpoint will affect the response. This becomes the reality under which the person will operate in the future and perceive similar events. This perspective provides a popular explanation for many forms of family violence and forms the basis for numerous variations. The continuum of family violence from the social learning perspective is illustrated through the behavior modeling theory and the intergenerational transmission theory.

Behavior Modeling Theory.   Albert Bandura (b. 1925) pioneered the field of *behavior modeling theory.* His studies on family life showed that children who use aggressive tactics have parents who use similar behaviors when dealing with others. Children are most affected by the influence of family members in this view. Bandura is most famous for his modeling therapy, according to George Boeree, who states that the original research involved herpephobics, people with a neurotic fear of snakes (Boeree, 1998). Using real snakes in his original therapy, an actor would go through a slow and painful approach to the snake. Eventually, he picked up the snake and draped it over his neck. The client was then invited to try it him or herself. Many clients were able to grow through the routine and sit with the snake around their neck.

Environmental experiences are another source of influence, according to social learning theory. Children who reside in crime-prone and violent areas are more likely to act out violently. Violent television shows and movies provide a third source of modeling for children. Since violence is often portrayed as acceptable behavior, children begin to view violent acts as normal behavior, which has no consequences for the actors.

Intergenerational Transmission Theory.   A frequently used explanation for domestic violence is the *intergenerational transmission theory.* Abusive behavior is handed down from generation to generation as an appropriate way to deal with conflict: Violence begets violence. This does not suggest that battering tendencies are inherited; rather, they are experienced. People who observe violence in the home as children are more likely to resort to battering in their own relationships later in life. Simply put, if a child is abused, he or she learns that it is an acceptable if not normal way to achieve his or her goal. The child becomes an abusing adult—toward a spouse and often toward his or her own children. A cycle of abuse occurs across generations.

Cycle of Violence Theory.   There is substantial evidence that a generational *cycle of violence* occurs in domestic assaults. The theorist most often cited for application of the transmission of violence theory to domestic abuse is Lenore Walker. In *The Battered Woman,* she described three separate phases of an abuse cycle represented in a pattern that is repeated time and again in a battering relationship (Walker, 1979):

> Phase I, *tension building,* is characterized by poor communication and minor incidents of abuse. In this phase, women are compliant and attempt to minimize problems in

Figure 3–5 Adults form relationships with children based on their own childhood relationships with adults.

the relationship. The male feels increased tension and takes more control through dominance, causing the victim to withdraw. *Acute battering* is referred to as phase II. Here the batterer who is highly abusive evidences a loss of control. The woman suffers stress and injury. Phase III is often referred to as the *honeymoon phase,* when kindness and loving behavior emanate from the contrite batterer. As the tension drops between the perpetrator and victim, a renewed love is experienced. He is often apologetic and attentive to his partner. She at first has mixed feelings, then feels guilty and responsible for the outburst. He continues to manipulate the relationship through promises of change.

It is not unusual during the final phase for the batterer to shower gifts and flowers on the woman. The cycle usually repeats itself, however, and the violence is believed to escalate over time. Being victimized more than once increases the risk of subsequent assault (Straus et al., 1980). Early critics of the theory claimed that the female victim must "like it" or she would leave. It is therefore important to separate the idealized version that the victim has of the relationship from the reality. For many women caught in this repetitive cycle, an early hope for the continuation of kind and loving behavior is reason to hold onto the men with whom they fell in love. Often, the women cling to the idealized version of the men they love, not to the violence that they endure.

The theory was tested regarding children who were raised in violent homes. Would they become more violent in their personal relationships as adults? Research determined that to be the case (Straus et al., 1980).

Social Control Theories

Control theorists suggest that crime and delinquency are likely to occur unless people conform to social demands. *Social constraints* are the mechanisms that control antisocial behavior. When constraints are weakened or absent, delinquent behavior emerges. The three main bonds that link people to socially acceptable behavior are attachment, belief in shared values, and involvement in law-abiding activities (National Institute of Justice, 1994).

Attachment Theory. According to *attachment theory*, the relationship that develops between the infant and his or her primary caregiver affects relationships later in life. Attachment theorists believe that attachment bonds may produce secure, anxious, or disoriented children (Garrett & Libbey, 1997). Children who are secure in their attachments are easily comforted and move freely from caregiver to stranger. The anxious children will resist comfort given to them, or may resist separation from the caregiver, at the same time displaying distrust of the caregiver. A disoriented child displays erratic and confused behavior based on an inability to determine which behaviors gain favorable attention from the caregiver. Garrett and Libbey further explain that whichever attachment patterns develop in childhood will be the type that are expected and re-created in adulthood. Children raised by neglectful parents then develop insecure attachments that they display in their own parenting later in life. Attentive parenting is necessary to develop secure attachments with children.

Individual Pathology and Male Batterers. Some theorists concede that a small number of domestic violence perpetrators exhibit behaviors similar to persons suffering with personality disorders (Tifft, 1993). These people are highly resistant to counseling and other forms of intervention, which is suggestive of psychopathological sickness. Court intervention with supervised therapy is the most likely option for those whose behavior can be dangerous, if not lethal.

Donald Dutton has been working with assaultive men since 1978, both as a clinician and as a researcher. He suggests that approximately 2 percent of the population would qualify as habitual woman batterers (Dutton & Golant, 1995). In addition to that, many of his clients met the criteria for antisocial behavior; he defined them as having shallow emotional responsiveness. They are often violent with others in addition to their partners. Psychopathic batterers are frequently arrested for nonviolent crimes such as forgery, passing bad checks, or confidence rackets.

Dutton points out that his colleague Robert Hare, author of *Without Conscience: The Disturbing World of the Psychopaths among Us (1999)*, found brain abnormalities among psychopaths. Magnetic resonance imaging (MRI) brain scans performed on psychopaths lacked the huge color patterns radiating from the brain stem to the temporal lobes that were present in normal persons. Instead, a small amount of bright color in the stem area toward the back of the brain was the only indication of brain activity. Without evidence that psychopathy is the direct result of social or environmental factors, Hare theorizes that the condition is genetic.

Psychologist Neil Jacobson describes a subgroup of psychopathic men whom he calls *vagal reactors* (Dutton & Golant, 1995). Approximately 20 percent of all batterers and half of all antisocial personalities fall within this category, he maintains. These men become calm internally when engaged in heated arguments with their wives. Subjects actually showed a decline in heart rate during arguments with a spouse. The violence committed against a wife is for the purpose of dominating her; it is both controlling and controlled.

Critique of the Psychological Theories

The different models based on learning are the most frequently cited explanations for domestic violence and its continuation. However, they do not explain why all people do not commit personal violence after witnessing violence or victimization. They also do not adequately address personalities that are extremely successful in other aspects of their lives.

THE CONFLICT SCHOOL

In the *conflict model*, law is seen as the means by which the ruling class maintains its control. The lawmakers are presumed to legitimize their positions of superiority by dominating minorities and the lower classes. Poverty and unemployment resides at the core of crime in this approach. Conflict scholars also question the rule-making process itself and conclude that regulations exist because those in power determine how the rules are made and enforced. Since struggles over power are a normal part of any society, this school does not seek to understand the cause of crime. Rather, it argues that the larger the society, the greater the likelihood that groups will fail to agree on conduct norms.

Within this school, critics have argued for a more substantial role and consideration of gender in theoretical research. John Hagan is one that has called for the development of a research base considering power and dominance in the context of family, work, and criminal justice (Voigt et al., 1994). Feminist scholars agree on this need to examine gender-specific authority relations, charging that violence against women by men has been ignored. The patriarchal theory on woman battering emerged as one challenge to gender assumptions.

Patriarchal Theory

The most widely used perspective on woman battering is **patriarchal theory**, also referred to as the *feminist approach*. As with other radical views that spring from a revolution, the feminist model questions the way that women have been viewed in society and the lack of legal options for those that are victimized. The majority of violence against women occurs in their homes, formally a place of legal sanction for the abusers. This theory has greatly influenced the perception of domestic violence and criminal justice practice.

The major tenets of patriarchal theory are as follows:

- Gender relationships are considered a fundamental component of social life. The experiences of gender are therefore emphasized. Both men and women are part of the analysis, with the greater emphasis placed on the differences within the context of society and viewed from within power relations.

- The power of men by virtue of their privileged status is the means by which women are controlled. Men are the traditional lawmakers and property owners who have excluded female participation and justified abuse in order to maintain power. Therefore, power and control are the key elements that establish and maintain the subordination of women in society, legitimating the positioning of the genders.

- Ending the subordination of women by means of changing the social structure remains the major goal of the movement. This process would include, but is not limited to, equal access and protection through law.

In its most extreme form, the perspective holds that all men will be abusive. Catharine MacKinnon represents this radical feminist position (MacKinnon, 1993). She and colleagues seek to redefine the law from what is considered a male hierarchical system to a gender-equality standpoint. Perceived as initiating a war between the sexes, this is a controversial position that tends to alienate persons due to the hostility it embraces. Critics claim that its confrontational stance is self-defeating.

In a more moderate form, the position is a comparison between men and women within the context of power relations. The theory does not seek to take power away from men, but rather to equalize it and share it between both genders. The status of women in society is related to the frequency of wife beating, according to this view. Wife abuse is explained through the exploration of the social structure of society and the analysis of power that has historically been identified in male dominance.

Research from the feminist perspective looks at the historical evidence of the subordination of women, as was outlined in the social–legal historical perspective from Chapter 2. Inferences are made from the legal status of women and translated into reasons why men batter. Case examples are another source of evidence that illustrates the patriarchal viewpoint.

Gender Inequality

Feminist criminality has also been ignored in criminology. Some authors maintain that female offenders have been considered inferior and their crimes insignificant (Vito & Holmes, 1994). Perhaps that is why there are no concise theoretical explanations that examine why some women abuse their children and lovers. Child abuse advocates point to the devaluation of children in our society. Since women are the primary offenders against children, that may in part explain the absence of research in this area.

The *chivalry hypothesis* holds that women are likely to be protected by the criminal justice system and given more lenient treatment than men when they commit the same crimes (Vito & Holmes, 1994). In communities where mandatory arrest policies on domestic violence have been rigorously applied, the number of female offenders has risen dramatically. Since studies on domestic abuse often originate from law

Example of an Integrated Feminist/Cognitive-Behavioral Strategy

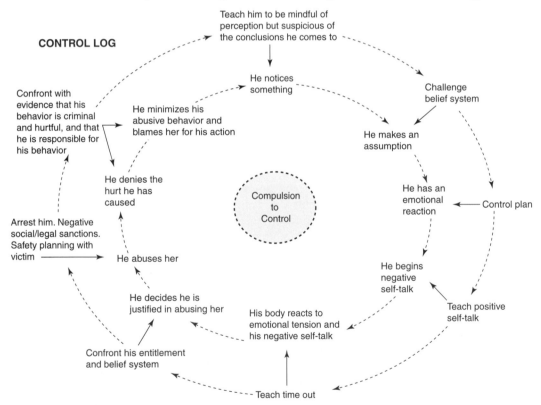

Figure 3–6 This chart depicting the integrated feminist cognitive-behavioral strategy illustrates the dynamics of an abusive relationship. *(Courtesy of The House of Ruth, Baltimore, Maryland.)*

enforcement records, the process would alter the resulting data. Additional research is needed to determine the actual extent and causes of abuse by women.

Critique of the Conflict School

Implicating all men in the crimes of an individual rapist or physical abuser seems extreme to critics. Although the majority of victims of domestic abuse are women, the feminist explanation is considered an extreme indictment against all men. The theory fails to make clear why violence is sometimes perpetrated by women and happens within same-sex relationships. On the other hand, it is impossible to dismiss the value of the perspective. Case examples and the historical analysis point to patterns of behavior that have the effect of dominating women. The good ol' boy network perpetuates the inequality of the sexes while devaluing feminine qualities. Since equal protection is a cornerstone of the U.S. legal philosophy, it is difficult to explain why a group of individuals has been denied access due to gender.

MULTIDIMENSIONAL MODELS

Multidimensional models that combine different theoretical perspectives are among the most popular today to explain why personal violence occurs in specific or newly recognized forms of abuse. Contemporary multidimensional theorists often do not make any distinction among biological, psychological, and sociological views since they interchange frequently in discussions on the causes of domestic violence.

Figure 3–7 One of the strengths seen in the multidimensional models is that they include economic factors, such as poverty and unemployment, as stressors contributing to family violence. Positive community and other social interventions may offset the effects of abuse.

Ecological theories suggest that child abuse and neglect result from multiple factors rather than a parent's personality disorder alone (Garrett & Libbey, 1997). The primary influences are individual, family, community, and culture. Significant influences in these systems are peers, school, workplace, economic factors, childrearing history, child characteristics, parent characteristics, marital relationship, social support, and sociocultural environment.

Ecological theorists include influences on the family such as community violence and isolation from the community, according to Garrett and Libbey. Employment, economic, and relational stressors that may contribute to abuse and neglect are not addressed through community support due to the isolation from the community, and subsequent abuse can lead to further isolation and a code of silence.

Individual-Based Theories

Individual-based theories ascribe domestic violence to psychological problems such as personality disorders, the batterer's childhood experiences, or biological disposition. Early theories on child abuse and neglect presumed a personality disorder of the parent (Garrett & Libbey, 1997). Studies in recent years have refuted that general thesis, since less than 10 percent of abusive parents were found to be emotionally maladjusted. *Multiple factor theories* have sought to determine the causes of abuse and neglect to children. Psychotherapeutic, cognitive–behavioral, and attachment abuse interventions are used to target individual problems and help the batterer control violent behaviors (Healey & Smith, 1998). The underlying psychological cause of the violence is targeted in the psychodynamic approach to therapy. A cognitive-behavioral approach is taken when the batterer is taught new patterns of nonviolent thinking and behavior. If the perpetrator has difficulty in establishing healthy relationships, attempts are made to facilitate secure attachments between batterers and loved ones.

Resiliency Theory.   We know that most children do not grow up to be abusive parents. Many abused and neglected children are not violent toward their own children later in life. Why is this so? The **resiliency theory** examines the learning process and attempts to identify the intervening factors that might overcome the effects of abuse. Resiliency theory explains not why abuse occurs, but why it does not. Its focus on the victims of childhood abuse might offer explanations on ways to interrupt the "cycle of violence" by reinforcement of positive influences (Garrett & Libbey, 1997).

Individual Pathology and Gay Offenders.   David Island and Patrick Letellier suggest that all batterers have a mental disorder, although they may not necessarily be insane or psychotic (Island & Letellier, 1991). In their discussion on gay battering, the authors claim that socialization and cultural theories take the responsibility for battering away from the individual and serve to blame only society for behaviors that are abnormal and criminal. Noting that the research from Hamberger and Hastings (1988) confirmed their position that abusers suffer from a disordered personality, they applied this thesis to men who beat their male lovers (Island & Letellier, 1991). They further assert that accountability through the criminal justice system is the best intervention, an approach that is highly reminiscent of the classical arguments.

Social–Psychological Model of Lesbian and Gay Abuse.   The **social–psychological model** is an integrated theory that brings together three general approaches to crime causation: social learning, unequal power relations, and personal choice theory. The model uses a broad application of social learning theory to explain that people who abuse have learned to do so through direct instruction, modeling, and reinforcement. Unequal power relations (real or perceived) contribute to the likelihood that abusive behaviors will be tolerated, an idea born through the feminist contribution. A third dimension is the recognition that domestic abuse is a personal choice: An abuser acts out with violence instead of using alternative conflict resolution. Social isolation creates an environment where battering in same-sex couples can occur, according to this integrated model (Merrill, 1996). Gregory Merrill draws on the conclusions of Zemsky (Zemsky, 1990) and Gilbert (Gilbert et al., 1990) for his claim that domestic violence must be understood as both a social and a psychological phenomenon. Rather than viewing domestic theories as mutually exclusive of each other, the combination can enhance same-sex theories of violence and apply to heterosexual theory as well.

Munchausen by Proxy.   Within the mental health field, a new and rapidly changing field of study has emerged, Munchausen by proxy. The recognition of this disorder is recent, and prevalence rates have not yet been determined. It is characterized by repeated unnecessary medical tests and procedures, which are demanded by a caretaker and cause physical injury to the child. An individual diagnosed with Munchausen by proxy syndrome intentionally plans and conceals his or her behaviors, which may include suffocating a child or demanding painful medical tests and procedures for the child. To assure hospital admission for the child, case studies indicate that the parent has used a range of intentional behaviors, including an injection of urine or fecal matter into the child and the administering of large amounts of laxative. The medical procedures or inflicted medications may kill the child. An estimated 9 to 31 percent of Munchausen by proxy victims die as a result of the abuse (Parnell & Day, 1997).

The vast majority of Munchausen by proxy perpetrators are women, approximately 98 percent, according to Teresa Parnell. She reports that the victims are equally divided among male and female children. It is a difficult diagnosis to make because the perpetrators believe or have convinced themselves that the child is sick, even though they have caused the ill effects by their own behavior. There is an absence of motivational incentives for the behavior, and it cannot be explained by any other mental disorder (Parnell & Day, 1997).

Family-Based Theories

Violent behaviors are caused by the family structure and family interactions rather than by an individual within the family, according to these theories. **Family systems theory** is one example. Conflict within an intimate relationship is blamed on the lack of communication between the partners. Complicating the issue is the deeply inter-twined mutual dependency that develops in some relationships. Self-imposed social isolation in addition to rigid expectations of loyalty and privacy make this a difficult situation for families when battering is introduced as a means of control (Tifft, 1993).

Family Systems Theory.   *Family systems theory* focuses primarily on the family and seeks to identify the problems that are a consequence of dysfunctional relation-ships among family members. The role that each family member takes in contributing to the abuse or neglect is considered. In situations of incest where the father is the per-petrator, for example, the possibility that the mother's reluctant intervention may appear to be tacit approval would be explored as a contributing factor in the repeated occurrence of abuse (Garrett & Libbey, 1997).

Husband Abuse.   Despite numerous reports that women are equally likely to perpetrate violence against their husbands (Straus, 1996), no specific theory has been forwarded to explain the causes. In *Abused Men: The Hidden Side of Domestic Violence*, Philip Cook reached a similar conclusion (Cook, 1997). Official estimates of husband abuse range from 6 percent to 10 percent of family violence. According to Cook, the National Institute of Health was among those that found an equal or greater rate of offending by women.

Even though a model has not been forthcoming, four factors stand out as leading to husband abuse. The first is ineffective communication between spouses. Straus and colleagues found that husbands are more likely to be beaten in households where spouses do not share major decision making (Straus et al., 1980). A correlation was established between the amount of shared decision making and husband abuse. In families where couples made major decisions together, a lower rate of either husband or wife abuse was evidenced.

Second is a struggle over control and power in the relationship or perception of a lesser power. Although this was not the contention of L. Kevin Hamberger and Theresa Potente, they do suggest that sociopolitically based male offender treatment be applied to female offenders who evidence issues of power and control (Hamberger & Potente, 1996).

Third, husband abuse is evidenced as a form of social disorganization. A lack of adequate financial resources and social bonds leaves a relationship vulnerable to hus-band battering. Wife-to-husband violence was three times greater in households with the lowest family income, according to the Straus survey (Straus et al., 1980). They fur-ther found a relationship between problems reported by the individuals and the level of violence. The greater the family stress, the higher the likelihood of family violence.

Inadequate financial resources do not necessarily suggest poverty; life stresses seem to produce an increase in wife beating and in husband beating in all income brackets.

Finally, wife-to-husband violence is in part explained through social structure theory. The decision to slap, hit, push, or punch a husband or boyfriend is made with the knowledge that the likelihood of apprehension or social censure is slim. These forms of violence against men appear acceptable and are perpetuated by the media. In one national survey, 27.6 percent of the couples felt that slapping a spouse was either necessary, normal, or good (Dibble & Straus, 1980).

Theories on Sibling Abuse.   Social offender theories focus on power and control within the context of social and cultural views. Many explanations look at what the adults do or fail to do in their parental role. Imitation and ineffective parenting are examples. No single explanation has evolved to explain sibling abuse; rather, a combination of conditions has been identified under which a child is born and conditioned into violent behavior.

Power and Control Model.   Rethinking the traditional social and cultural theories in adult maltreatment, Vernon Wiehe maintains that abuse of power generally occurs when a sibling attempts to compensate for a lack or loss of power (Wiehe, 1997). The abusers perceive an imbalance between themselves and younger siblings, who they believe are favored due to academic or social successes or by virtue of their

Figure 3–8   Are these boys engaging in harmless play—or have they already been conditioned to act out violent behavior? While most sibling rivalry is innocent, aggressive child's play may result in someone being hurt.

age or gender. Frequently, the abuse of power occurs along gender lines, with males abusing females. Gender-role socialization that favors male aggressiveness and female passivity contributes to the condition.

One method to assert control over sisters is through the use of physical and verbal force. Left unchecked by parents, the use of force may escalate. The highest level of violence occurs in homes where a boy has only brothers (Wiehe, 1997). What are some of the factors that contribute to rivalry gone awry?

Imitation and Reaction.   Research has indicated when parents are abusive toward each other, there is a high likelihood that they will abuse their children. It is possible that the victims treat younger children as they are themselves treated, in particular during the time they are babysitting their siblings. Erin Pizzey noted that children react differently to abusive situations according to their gender (Pizzey, 1977). Boys tended to become aggressive, and girls often reacted by withdrawal. This lends credibility to the suggestion that boys exposed to parental domestic violence offend violently more often than girls do.

Ineffective Parenting

1. *Overwhelmed parents.* Parents who are coping with problems that are overwhelming lack the ability or energy to intervene in sibling abuse. In this category of causes, Wiehe (1997) considers two major impediments to healthy parenting that can contribute to the problem. The first is drug and alcohol abuse, and the second is stress-related issues. Numerous studies on family violence indicate that abusers are frequently involved in alcohol or drug abuse. The author suggests that a relationship also exists between the parents' abuse of drugs and alcohol and their children's engagement in abusive behaving.

   His second point is more complicated and suggests that sibling incest may occur in homes where parents are absent either physically or psychologically. Fathers who are disinterested in parenting and mothers who are distant to their children promote an atmosphere where children may turn to each other for comfort, nurture, and support with a risk of sexualizing as they enter adolescence. Alternatively, offenders may model their parents' aggressive behavior from what they observe in their parents' relationship.

2. *Inappropriate expectations.* Parents often expect an older sibling to care for younger children in their absence. Some children may not be old enough to handle the responsibility, according to Wiehe (1997), or if old enough, they may lack the skills and knowledge to serve in a parental role. He suggests that parents be sensitive to complaints from children left in this vulnerable position.

3. *Lack of parenting skills.* Sometimes parents are ineffective in controlling sibling abuse because they don't know how or what to do.

Culture Theory

One example of this **culture theory** is suggested by Shawn Sullivan to explain domestic violence against black women by black men (Sullivan, 1996). Some young men are taught by their fathers or older brothers to refer to black women as ho's (whores), she suggests. The lack of respect coupled with the prevalence of violence as an acceptable means of resolving disputes put black women at risk for domestic assault.

The Social Causes of Dating Violence.   According to Denise Gamache, violence in dating relationships is reinforced by cultural beliefs that legitimize power and control over others (Gamache, 1998). She suggests a feminist model where cultural norms make domination appear normal and where challenges are perceived as a threat to the natural order. Although both young women and men report inflicting physical abuse, research has shown females to be the likely recipients of severe physical abuse and of sexual violence. Male battering in dating relationships is also likely to continue into the marriage.

Critique of the Multidimensional Theories

The approach that the **multidimensional theories** have in common is that they do not restrict themselves to any one major school of thought. In this way they retain the flexibility to consider causes and effects of family violence from a broader perspective. Some researchers even question the fact that most people do not commit family crimes—in fact, the majority of children do not grow up to be abusive parents. This positive approach has potential.

With the expansion of theoretical approaches, however, comes confusion. Determining what works and what does not work is more difficult than ever. The lack of consensus on the cause of domestic abuse makes the response vary between jurisdictions. Conflicting approaches to deal with the problems result. Although it is not necessary that all agree, it would be helpful to have a clearer picture of how to combat the violence that is so pervasive.

CONCLUSIONS

There is no excuse for expressing violence against a loved one. Yet it happens frequently. Why does domestic abuse occur? To answer this question, theories examining society from a macro or micro level have been provided in this chapter. Depending on the perspective, either societal norms or individual behaviors are at the core of the explanation.

Traditional criminological theories have been discussed with their application to domestic crime. To the student of criminology, the terms are familiar. The basics from the classical, positive, and critical schools are the foundation for the multidisciplinary models that have emerged in recent times. The classical school with its legalist approach is the one that most criminal justice students find memorable. It is, after all, the model that criminal justice practice depends on. Suggesting that a formula for control is possible with the right combination, it supports punishment as a deterrent to crime. It becomes untenable when the deterrent effect of criminal justice intervention is questioned with respect to domestic violence.

Positive theory contains the most diverse options for examining family abuse. Scientific research questions and reexamines the possibilities from biological, sociological, and psychological viewpoints. Because the early biological explanations rest on racist and sexist foundations, they have been discredited. Modern theories such as the biochemical imbalance and neurological theories are offered from the study of medical conditions rather than physical characteristics.

When first developed, the sociological theories were unique because they explored the idea that a relationship exists between poverty and crime. From there it is possible to conceive that other influences, such as cultural norms and social structures, may have a cause-and-effect relationship to domestic violence. The disorganization of community ties leaves a family vulnerable, according to the social disorganization theory. Finally, socialization into gender roles is at the core of the gender-role theory which maintains that men and women act differently according to expectations from both outside and internal sources.

The psychological theory has developed a number of views that have been applied in the search to understand domestic violence. The collection of social learning theories is most often used to explain family abuse. Its popularity may be due to the intuitive appeal that learning suggests. We are not born violent, it points out. If we can learn to become this way, can't we unlearn the behaviors? Therapeutic practices often focus on education and behavior modification in an attempt to alter behavior.

Attachment theorists claim that our future may be determined from infancy through the early childhood years, depending on the strength or absence of bonds that develop between the child and parent. Neglectful parenting beginning at birth may orient the person into negative patterns of behavior and cause irreparable damage to the psyche. But what about the few people in the population who cannot feel remorse or guilt? Psychopathic theorists claim that there may be a biological indication that these people cannot alter their criminal tendencies. These men are violent both with a spouse and with others. Their detachment to the pain and suffering that they cause is remarkable.

The conflict school contributes the patriarchal and gender inequality theories. While both question the power and control of those in power to make and enforce the laws, they come to opposite conclusions. The feminist model contends that women are subjugated by law that has not protected women as victims of abuse by men. The offenders are protected by a society that seeks to ensure the domination of men. The gender inequality model suggests that women are treated differently in the criminal justice system but that the difference is to their benefit.

After the major schools have been examined, the explanations still seem inadequate to address the problems of family violence for all people at all times. Multidimensional models concede that we need to try new ways to find out why domestic violence is occurring in epidemic proportions in our society. They combine the concepts developed in the major schools and suggest how they apply to situations of abuse. Views from both an individual perspective and the family structure are considered in this body of theory.

No one claims to have the answer—theorists continue to consider the problems and seek to develop ways to address them. Social programs and counseling methods have developed from the ideas covered here. We have gained great insight into the characteristics of batterers from the research that has developed. In the next chapter we look at the practices and applications of these concepts.

QUESTIONS FOR REVIEW

1. Which school of thought do you believe best explains why people commit domestic violence?

2. What role does Cesare Beccaria play in the study of criminology?

3. Explain the advantages and disadvantages of the deterrence theory.

4. Discuss and describe the eugenics movement.

5. What impact did Adolf Quetelet have on criminology?

6. Explain the gender-role theory.

7. Describe the cycle of violence.

8. In your opinion, which theory best explains the reasons that domestic violence occurs?

9. What is Munchausen by proxy?

INTERNET-BASED EXERCISES

1. Prevent Child Abuse America publishes a quarterly newsletter, editions of which you can now read online. Search this site to find the latest copy of the newsletter. Report to the class on at least one prevention initiative aimed at preventing child abuse and neglect. Be sure to identify the criminological basis for the program. http://www.preventchildabuse.org/

2. A recent study indicated that Indian women (Native Americans) are victimized at a rate higher than any other group in the United States, including a rape/sexual assault victimization rate more than twice as high as the rate for black women and more than three and a half times higher than the national rate. Go to the site of the National American Indian Court Judges Association (NAICJA) and identify

the policy changes that attempt to remedy this situation. Can you find any theories in this chapter that would help to explain the problems on the reservations? Go to http://www.naicja.org

REFERENCES

Alderman, Tracy. 1997. *The Scarred Soul.* Oakland, CA: New Harbinger Publications.

Bateman, Py. 1998. "The Context of Date Rape." Pp. 95–99 in *Dating Violence: Young Women in Danger,* 2nd ed., Barrie Levy (ed.). Seattle, WA: Seal Press.

Boeree, George C. 1998. "Albert Bandura." *http://www.ship.edu/~cgboeree/bandura.html.* 2002.

Bund, Jennifer M. University of Pittsburgh Law Review (preprint article). 1997. "Did You Say Chemical Castration?" *http://www.pitt.edu/~lawrev/preprints/bund.htm.* 1998.

Cook, Philip W. 1997. *Abused Men: The Hidden Side of Domestic Violence.* Westport, CT: Praeger Publishers.

Define, Michael S., University of Maine School of Law student. 1997. "Coerced Sterilization of Native American Women." *http://www.geocities.com/CapitolHill/9118/mike2.html.* 2002.

Dibble, U., and M. Straus. 1980. "Some Social Structure Determinants of Inconsistency between Attitudes and Behavior: The Case of Family Violence." *Journal of Marriage and the Family* 42:73–79.

Dutton, Donald G., and Susan K. Golant. 1995. *The Batterer: A Psychological Profile.* New York: Basic Books.

Gamache, Denise. 1998. "Domination and Control: The Social Context of Dating Violence." Pp. 69–83 in *Dating Violence: Young Women in Danger,* 2nd ed., Barrie Levy (ed.). Seattle, WA: Seal Press.

Garrett, Athena, and Heather Libbey. 1997. "Theory and Research on the Outcomes and Consequences of Child Abuse and Neglect." Child Abuse Intervention Strategic Planning Meeting, Washington, DC. Washington, DC: National Institute of Justice.

Gilbert, L., P. B. Poorman, and S. Simmons. 1990. "Guidelines for Mental Health Systems Response to Lesbian Battering." In Confronting Lesbian Battering: A Manual for the Battered Women's Movement. St. Paul, MN: Minnesota Coalition for Battered Women.

Hamberger, L. K., and J. E. Hastings. 1988. "Characteristics of Male Spouse Abusers Consistent with Personality Disorders." *Hospital and Community Psychiatry* 39:763–70.

Hamberger, L. K., and Theresa Potente. 1996. "Counseling Heterosexual Women Arrested for Domestic Violence." Pp. 53–75 in *Domestic Partner Abuse,* L. K. Hamberger and Claire Renzetti (eds.). New York: Springer Publishing Company.

Hare, R. 1999. *Without Conscience: The Disturbing World of the Psychopaths among Us.* New York, NY: The Guilford Press.

Healey, Kerry M., and Christine Smith. 1998. *Batterer Programs: What Criminal Justice Agencies Need to Know.* NCJ 171683. Washington, DC: U.S. Department of Justice.

Hofstadter, Richard. 1965. *Social Darwinism in American Thought,* 11th ed. Boston: Beacon Press.

Island, David, and Patrick Letellier. 1991. *Men Who Beat the Men Who Love Them: Battered Gay Men and Domestic Violence.* Binghamton, NY: Harrington Park Press.

Katz, J. 1984. "Medicalization of Repression: Eugenics and Crime." *Contemporary Crisis* 8(3):227–41.

Lilly, J. R., F. T. Cullen, and R. A. Ball. 1989. "Search for the Criminal 'Man.'" Pp. 17–46 in *Criminological Theory: Context and Consequences.* Newbury Park, CA: Sage Publications.

MacKinnon, Catharine A. 1993. *Only Words.* Cambridge, MA: Harvard University Press.

Merrill, Gregory S. 1996. "Ruling the Exceptions: Same-Sex Battering and Domestic Violence Theory." Pp. 9–33 in *Violence in Gay and Lesbian Domestic Partnerships,* Claire M. Renzetti and Charles H. Miley (eds.). Binghamton, NY: Harrington Park Press.

Moffitt, T. E. 1997. "Neuropsychology, Antisocial Behavior, and Neighborhood Context." Pp. 116–70 in *Violence and Childhood in the Inner City,* Joan McCord (ed.). New York: Cambridge University Press.

National Institute of Justice. 1994. *Breaking the Cycle: Predicting and Preventing Crime.* (Report No. NCJ 140541). Washington, DC: National Institute of Justice.

Parnell, Teresa F., and Deborah O. Day (eds.). 1997. *Munchausen by Proxy Syndrome: Misunderstood Child Abuse.* Thousand Oaks, CA: Sage Publications.

Pizzey, Erin. 1977. *Scream Quietly or the Neighbors Will Hear.* Hillside, NJ: Enslow Publishers.

Siegel, Larry J. 1995. *Criminology,* 5th ed. New York: West Publishing Company.

Straus, Murray A. 1996. "Domestic Violence Is a Problem for Men." Pp. 50–64 in *Domestic Violence,* Bruno Leone (ed.). San Diego, CA: Greenhaven Press.

Straus, Murray A., Richard J. Gelles, and Suzanne K. Steinmetz. 1980. *Behind Closed Doors: Violence in the American Family.* Garden City, NY: Anchor Press/Doubleday.

Sullivan, Shawn. 1996. "Domestic Violence Is a Serious Problem for Black Women." Pp. 37–40 in *Domestic Violence,* Karin L. Swisher (ed.). San Diego, CA: Greenhaven Press.

Tifft, Larry L. 1993. *Battering of Women: The Failure of Intervention and the Case for Prevention.* Boulder, CO: Westview Press.

Van Biema, David. 1996. "A Cheap Shot at Pedophilia?" *Time,* September 6. *http://www.pathfinder.com/time/magazine/archive/1996/dom/960909/crime.html.* 2002.

Vito, Gennaro F., and Ronald M. Holmes. 1994. *Criminology: Theory, Research, and Policy.* Belmont, CA: Wadsworth Publishing Company.

Voigt, Lydia, William E. Thornton, Jr., Leo Barrile, and Jerrol Seaman. 1994. *Criminology and Justice.* New York: McGraw-Hill.

Vold, George B., and Thomas J. Bernard. 1986. *Theoretical Criminology,* 3rd ed. New York: Oxford University Press.

Walker, Lenore E. 1979. *The Battered Woman.* New York: Springer Publishing Company.

White, Evelyn C. 1998. "The Abused Black Woman: Challenging a Legacy of Pain." Pp. 84–93 in *Dating Violence: Young Women in Danger,* 2nd ed., Barrie Levy (ed.). Seattle, WA: Seal Press.

Wiehe, Vernon R. 1997. *Sibling Abuse: Hidden Physical, Emotional, and Sexual Trauma,* 2nd ed. Thousand Oaks, CA: Sage Publications.

Wright, R. A., and J. M. Miller. 1998. "Taboo Until Today? The Coverage of Biological Arguments in Criminology Textbooks, 1961 to 1970 and 1987 to 1996." *Journal of Criminal Justice* 26(1):1–19.

Zemsky, B. 1990. "Lesbian Battering: Considerations for Intervention." In *Confronting Lesbian Battering: A Manual for the Battered Women's Movement.* St. Paul, MN: Minnesota Coalition for Battered Women.

CASES

Buck v. Bell, 274 U.S. 200 (1927).
Jacobson v. Massachusetts, 197 U.S. 11 (1905).

CHAPTER 4

SURVIVORS AND THE CONSEQUENCES OF VICTIMIZATION

SIMPLY SCENARIO

The Relationship Is Over

June knows that the most dangerous time for a survivor of domestic violence is when the relationship is over. After enduring years of abuse, she feels that she must take the chance and go to court for a protection order. When David came in for the court hearing, she could feel his anger and was frightened. The judge issued the order. When June walked out of the courthouse, a chill went up her spine and she thought, "this is only a piece of paper, it's not going to protect me!"

Question: As June's friend, can you advise her on ways to be safer?

KEY TERMS

Battered women's movement
Borderline personality disorder
Children's rights movement
Child witnessing of domestic violence
Direct abuse
Indirect abuse
Learned helplessness

Posttraumatic stress disorder
Restitution
Retribution
Roofies
Stockholm syndrome
Victimology
Victim precipitation

INTRODUCTION

> I make my husband's coffee just the way he likes it—not too hot, not too cold—not too strong, not too weak. I make his coffee just the way that he likes it. It better be…
> (A public service announcement from the Connecticut Public Welfare)

For those who are unfamiliar with the criminal justice process, it is surprising to learn that victims have relatively few rights. Constitutional provisions protect the accused, and crimes are considered to be committed against the state, not against the individual. Victims do not control whether a case is heard in the criminal system. The decision to proceed with a trial is made by the district attorney or prosecutor's office. The severity of the crime against the state and the likelihood that a trial would result in a finding of guilty are among the many factors that go into that decision-making process. Least important of all is whether the victim wants the satisfaction of having the perpetrator punished or compensation arranged for wrongs that were committed.

It was not always like that. Before the modern concept of a criminal justice system the victim and his or her family were responsible for assuring that justice was done. This was accomplished through **retribution** or **restitution**. Retribution is a philosophy that says that offenders should be punished for purposes of revenge. A perpetrator was expected to suffer to the degree of harm that his or her actions caused. Restitution, on the other hand, is a financial compensation arranged to make whole the person who was victimized. The person who suffered loss due to deviant conduct was often responsible for carrying out the punishment and benefiting from any restitution.

In most societies, individual concerns became secondary to the impact of crime and its effect on the public order. Law enforcement developed into a gatekeeper for societal norms rather than a protector against individual injustices. Ultimately, the victim was relegated to the role of a witness to the behaviors committed against society at large. Even retribution and restitution were to compensate a wronged state due to criminal transgressions. The social science approach of conducting research and expanding theory on the causes of criminal behavior ultimately was responsible for bringing the victim back into focus. That criminological specialty concerned with the role of the victim is called **victimology**.

VICTIMOLOGY

In one of the earliest attempts to explain mental illness and symptoms of hysteria in women from the psychological perspective, Sigmund Freud published his seduction theory in 1887 (Adams, 1992). The cause for the majority of these afflictions, he claimed, was that they were victimized through sexual abuse. Freud had found that the majority of his wealthy female clients had been raped by male family members. Faced with professional scorn, Freud recanted the seduction theory in 1890, saying that women were not actual victims of sexual abuse but that they fantasized such abuse. He replaced his seduction theory with the Oedipal complex and notions of penis envy.

Interest into the role of the victim in the commission of crimes was reborn during the 1940s. The first major theorist who contributed to the popularization of this approach was Hans von Hentig. In 1948 he wrote a major study entitled *The Criminal and His Victim*. Hans von Hentig emphasized the victim's vulnerability to crime. Those most likely to be victimized were categorized (von Hentig, 1948):

- The young
- The female
- The old
- The mentally deranged
- Immigrants
- Minorities
- Dull normals
- The depressed
- The acquisitive
- The wanton
- The lonesome and the heartbroken
- The tormentor
- The blocked, exempted, or fighting

The trend to involve victims in the study of crime has continued since von Hentig. Although there are many who have added significantly to the field, a major contribution was made by Benjamin Mendelsohn in the 1940s. He earned the title "father of victimology" with his typologies on victim–offender relationships (Meadows, 1998). Mendelsohn assigned a *victim responsibility* rating, only two of which concern victims whose guilt is less than that of the perpetrator:

- The completely innocent victim (typically children or those who are attacked while unconscious);
- The victim with minor guilt (often victimized because of ignorance);
- The voluntary victim, whose guilt is equal to that of the offender (e.g., a suicide pact);
- The victim who is more guilty than the offender (one who provokes or induces another to commit crime);
- The victim who alone is guilty (the attacker who is killed in self-defense);
- The imaginary victim, who, having suffered nothing, falsely accuses someone.

Victim characteristics and behaviors became a primary focus that was believed to facilitate criminal behavior in the view called **victim precipitation**. It involves the degree to which the victim is responsible for his or her own victimization. Marvin Wolfgang pioneered this approach when he used homicide data to develop a theory on victim involvement in homicide (Wolfgang, 1975). He concluded that victims were more likely to die at the hands of someone they knew rather than those of a complete stranger. The precipitator was the person who had thrown the first blow or otherwise escalated the violence in a personal relationship that lead to his or her being killed. Hence the victim of a spousal homicide was believed to have played a significant part in his or her own demise. The idea that a murder victim may in a way cause his or her own death is controversial.

Wolfgang paved the way to the notorious study of Menachem Amir. In *Patterns in Forcible Rape*, Amir concluded that the victims of forcible rape shared responsibility for their victimization (Amir, 1971). The manner in which a woman dressed, her use of "bad" language, and her alcohol consumption were among the unconscious expressions of her desire to be raped, according to Amir. The reaction to this thesis was anything but positive!

The study of victimology came under harsh criticism from victim advocates and women's groups. The inclusion of women victims did not involve the standpoint of the victim. Critics charged that the opposite was happening. Where crimes involved relationships, the tendency toward victim blaming was evident, particularly crimes where there was an intimate relationship. Theoretical interventions for battered women focused on the pathology of the victim—the "Why doesn't she leave?" question—rather than asking, "Why does he batter?" Changes that have occurred attempt to shift the focus of responsibility from the victim to the offenders.

THE VICTIM MOVEMENT

From the theoretical attempts to understand crime, including the debate on relative responsibility and victim precipitation, sprang genuine concern about the people that were being victimized. More recent avenues of studies in victimology have included how various components of the criminal justice system treat victims; the impact of victimization; and the effectiveness of certain interventions with crime victims.

Practitioners engaging in providing services and treatment began to speak up about what they saw happening. In the middle to late 1960s, several grassroots movements were initiated simultaneously in response to urgent victim needs. The first to gain respect became known as the **children's rights movement**. Another significant effort is the **battered women's movement**. The interest groups have common threads:

1. Identification of the victims through research on the prevalence and severity of the abuse
2. Heightened concerns over the cause of victimization specific to each group
3. The development of intervention strategies, including legal reform
4. Protection and prevention efforts that are sensitive to the identified victims
5. Attempts to reduce future occurrences through services and education

Most of the victim reform effort was concerned with family violence. A model of the "ideal" relationship was conceived, against which relationships were to be judged as healthy or not. The equality wheel (shown in Figure 4–1) illustrates the ultimate relationship goal of equality.

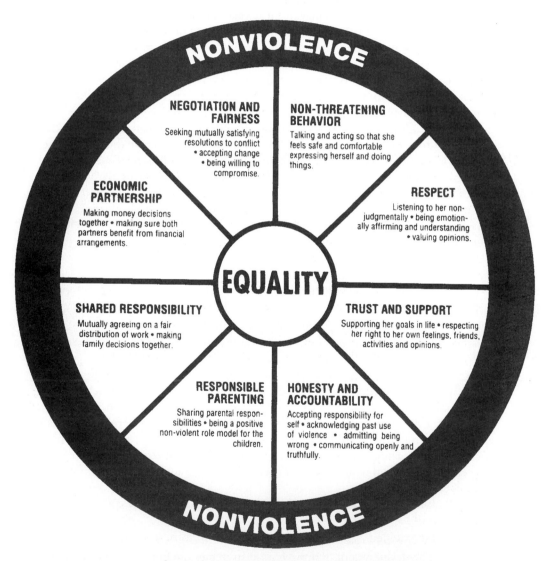

Figure 4–1   Healthy relationships are built on a core of equality as indicated by this equality wheel. *(From* Education Groups for Men Who Batter *[1993, copyrighted], Ellen Pence and Michael Paymar, Springer Publishing Company, Inc., New York 10012. Adapted by permission.)*

THE CHILDREN'S RIGHTS MOVEMENT

Looking back to Chapter 2 and the historical legal status of children, it is not difficult to imagine the need for change. Violence against children in every conceivable form—physical, emotional, through neglect, and by sexual exploitation—had become a normal secret. It was alternately encouraged and tolerated. Beating and abusing children was the privilege of parents. Society did not want to know what was happening under the guise of parenting. Nor did it want to interfere with the legal rights of parents to do what they want with their offspring. As the "chattel property" of parents, a child had no rights whatsoever.

Identifying the victims of child physical abuse is relatively easy: They present visible bruises, broken bones, bite marks, and burns. They are buried in little coffins. Lesser known victimization is committed by poisoning and through neglect. Sexual exploitation from inappropriate touching to intercourse and forced prostitution is not unheard of by the practitioners involved in child advocacy. The professionals who patched the wounds saw what was happening to the future generation; they spoke out about what they were treating behind their closed doors. Raising the public consciousness to the plight of children who were victimized was the first step in the movement. Admitting to the lack of responses to these helpless victims was more difficult. Allocating resources to protect them is still a daunting challenge.

Criminal justice intervention remains inconsistent. When partner domestic violence reports are filed and law enforcement is called, they may not be aware of the need to protect children. Officers seldom consider their authority to intervene in cases of battering when a child is present or realize the harm that can occur through witnessing violence committed against a parent. Indirect harm through witnessing is a criminal justice concern, as well as abuse and neglect where the child is the intended victim. In every domestic violence case, particular attention should be given to the presence of any children in the household. Domestic violence is criminal behavior that affects the children as well as the adult being victimized.

Child Witnessing of Domestic Violence

Perhaps the most pervasive child victimization today is witnessing violence. Recent research tends to consider all forms of violence exposures together along with domestic violence witnessing. According to one report, approximately 8.8 million youths have witnessed someone else being shot, stabbed, sexually assaulted, physically assaulted, or threatened with a weapon (Kilpatrick, Saunders, & Smith, 2003). There is a strong link between partner violence and child abuse. As many as half a million children are encountered by police during domestic violence arrests. The overlap of violence against children and violence against women in the same families is between 30 and 60 percent (Jacobson, 2000). There is the suggestion that violence by husbands against their wives spills over onto daughters in the form of verbal aggression, evidenced by high rates of father–daughter conflict (National Resource Center on

Domestic Violence, 2002). The Center also reports that almost half of women who recount memories of witnessing violence between their parents as children were themselves physically abused during childhood.

Indirect abuse, the child witnessing of intimate violence, places children at greater risk for a numerous psychological, behavioral, social, and educational problems. These children are also at increased risk for physical abuse (Geffner, Ingelman, & Zellner, 2003). Children who are exposed to domestic violence are at increased risk of being murdered (Jacobson, 2000). The numbers of children who witness violence in the home has indirectly been documented by looking at those children who are living with female victims of intimate abuse. It is estimated that between 1993 and 1998, the average number of victims of intimate partner abuse who lived with children under the age of 12 was 459,590 (Rennison & Welchans, 2000).

Although it affects children of different ages in different ways, its impact is noted on children's emotional, social, and cognitive development. Childhood problems that have been linked to the exposure to domestic violence range from increased aggression and hostility to anxiety and depression (NAIC, 2003). The effects of witnessing domestic violence that affects the child's trusting relationships can be especially severe, even in the earliest phases of development for infants and toddlers (Osofsky, 2001). In the past concern about child witnessing of violence was minimal. Studies on child development have indicated this assumption to be false. Experiencing chronic abuse during the first few years of life may cause a persistent state of hyperarousal or dissociation in addition to cognitive impairment (National Information Clearinghouse, 2001).

The effects of indirect abuse are a topic of concern to child advocates. What happens when children reside in a home where parental battering occurs? Reports from battered women show that the majority of children do witness domestic violence; some actually see their mothers being beaten and raped. They hear their parent screaming and crying; they see the effects of blood, bruises, or broken windows and furniture.

Exposing children to violence of one parent against another is one of the most severe forms of psychological abuse that can occur. Childhood exposure to domestic violence has similar detrimental effects to that experienced by children who have been neglected and/or abused physically or sexually (National Resource Center on Domestic Violence, 2002). Hyperactivity and increased tendencies toward argumentative behavior has been noted for both boys and girls.

In addition to the short term, there is evidence of a long-range impact on families and to society when children are exposed to violence in the home. Men who witness their parents physically attack each other are believed to be more likely to hit their own wives and women are more likely to be victims as adults (Whitfield, Anda, Dube, & Felitti, 2003). Approximately 2 million adolescents suffer from **posttraumatic stress disorder** due to their exposure to violence children suffer severe emotional and developmental consequences (Jacobson, 2000). Exposing children to violence may make children more likely to become perpetrators themselves.

Despite the evidence of harm, domestic violence perpetrated in the presence of a child is generally a misdemeanor offense. In 2002 the passage of U.C.A. §76-5-109.1

in Utah made Utah the first state to legislate the act of domestic violence in the presence of a child as a felony. Being in the presence of a child includes if the child is physically present or may hear violence that is likely to produce death or serious bodily harm to a cohabitant.

Childhood Abuse and Criminal Behavior

In addition to the psychological and behavioral effects that children may experience due to their exposure to domestic violence, there is concern about later criminalization due to **direct abuse**. Child victims are at greater risk of becoming offenders themselves. Being abused or neglected as a child increases the likelihood of arrest as a juvenile by 59 percent, as an adult by 28 percent, and of arrest for a violent crime as an adult by 30 percent (Widom & Maxfield, 2001). This "cycle of abuse" suggests strongly that those children who are abused or neglected, either physically or sexually, grow up to engage in criminal activity at a greater rate than those who are not abused or neglected. Both boys and girls are evidenced in the higher rates of criminal activity due to victimization.

The majority of indirect abuse victims do not commit family or other forms of violence as adults; however, many suffer long after the abuse occurs. Victims are at greater risk for many other problems throughout their lives, including participation in violent crime as adults. Due to the added risks of victimization in domestic settings, advocates are seeking additional rights for children in custody and marital torts. Fair consideration of children in the legal system is deemed an important intervention when assessing visitation and custody rights of parents. Children who are exposed to intimate partner violence are more likely to engage in teenage prostitution and to run away from home (Groves, Augustyn, Lee, & Sawires, 2002).

Sexually abused children also run an increased risk of being involved with delinquent behavior. Almost half of the sexually abused boys in one study engaged in delinquent acts compared with only 16 percent of those not victimized (Kilpatrick, Saunders, & Smith, 2003). Girls that had been sexually assaulted engaged in delinquent acts at an increased rate as well.

Figure 4–2   Children with a history of maltreatment experience increased risk factors for delinquency. In addition, maltreatment and victimization can damage self-esteem, demolish families, and destroy futures.

Childhood Abuse and Social Consequences

The closer that violence occurs to children, the more it can affect them. Children may experience similar symptoms to abuse that an adult would when he or she has experienced a traumatic event. What differs is often their ability to verbalize the sadness and fear they feel, thinking they might risk loosing their caregiver (Cohen & Walthall, 2003). For example, an adult might have nightmares or think constantly about a traumatic event; they might loose interest in doing things or avoid activities that remind them of the event. Children may have these same feelings but have not developed skills to understand and deal with these feelings.

Recent reports indicate that victimization of children has grave social consequences. Studying a cohort of children abused as children, Widom (2000) found the victims at age 29 scored significantly lower on intelligence tests and had completed fewer years of school than the control group. The lower levels of IQ were not influenced by sex, race, or criminal history. Unemployment and underemployment were also higher in the cohort of childhood victims. Additional social problems include problems with the quality of personal relationships, evidenced by a higher rate of divorce and separation among the abused and neglected group. These children grow up with violence and learn that it is an acceptable way to handle stress and assert one's views. Higher rates of suicide attempts, diagnosis of antisocial personality disorder, and alcohol abuse regardless of age, sex, race, or criminal history were documented (Widom, 2000). Childhood abuse may make it difficult for the child to concentrate, learn, feel empathy, and develop healthy relationships (Cohen & Walthall, 2003). Sexual assault victims frequently experience a decline in school grades or participation in after-school activities.

Satanic Activities.   Due to recently increasing concerns about satanic beliefs and practices among adolescents, some researchers are looking at a possible connection between child abuse and satanic involvement. In a study involving adolescent boys who admitted to voluntary involvement in group satanic activities, all boys were found to have been physically and/or sexually abused (Belitz & Schacht, 1995). The common

---

Been There . . . Done That

Jay was a willing suspect and confessed during my interrogation of him to having sexually abused his own children and countless others. He knew that what he did was legally wrong, but he professed that he "loved" the children. It was important to him that he not "hurt" the children, and he explained that he thought he did more good for them by showing his love. He was totally unaware of the emotional, physical, and psychological effects on his victims. His actions were not benign, regardless of his claims; he was adjudicated as a sexually dangerous person.

reaction for boys is, however, anger rather than satanic involvement, which is an expression of the rage as well as of pervasive feelings of inadequacy and powerlessness. The harm to a victim does not cause satanic involvement but may be an avenue for some adolescents to gain the power and control that they lack due to victimization. Additionally, cult membership is not illegal; it is the criminal activity that a member may engage in that will bring him or her to the attention of law enforcement.

The Consequences of Abuse to a Child

The majority of children who are victimized through domestic violence do not commit criminal acts as adults (Widom, 2000). What happens is an increased likeliness. The harm to a child who is victimized is not universal and cannot be predicted with any certainty. Many conditions might affect the response, both from the child victim and later in life as an adult. Forms and frequency of abuse, age, and mental condition of the child, as well as his or her personality, will all play a role in how the victim reacts. The consequences of abuse will vary according to multiple factors (Garrett & Libbey, 1997a):

1. *Characteristics of the child.* The age, emotional and cognitive development, gender, race/ethnicity, personality, and strengths or resiliency of the child all play a part in determining the effects of maltreatment.

2. *Type of trauma.* Two types of trauma have to do with the severity and intensity of the abuse. Type I, referred to as acute trauma, is a single event; type II, a chronic or repetitive abuse over time, is usually more difficult for the child to overcome.

3. *Type of abuse or neglect.* All forms of maltreatment to a child—physical, sexual, psychological/emotional abuse, or witnessing domestic violence—carry the

---

Been There . . . Done That

In an otherwise peaceful and quiet neighborhood, shocking facts emerged due to one woman's complaint of childhood abuse. The investigation found that every member of the nuclear and extended family, boys and girls, had been sexually molested: not by neighbors, not by strangers, but by family. The list of victims was long enough that we made charts to keep them clear. A hot curling iron and scissors were among the mutilation tools that rendered at least one woman unable to bear children as an adult. Boys were dressed up and photographed. Little children were made to have sex with one another while an adult watched. Wives said that they were raped by these same men and didn't know the children were being assaulted also. The abuse was traced as high as the oldest living male—he was 72 when I arrested him. The youngest arrested was a 15-year-old boy. Other perpetrators were too young to consider taking them through the criminal justice system as offenders.

possibility of long-term effects on the psychological and social adaptation of the victim.

4. *Co-occurrences of types of abuse and neglect.* When multiple abuses occur simultaneously, the risk of maladaptive behavior is heightened as a result. Frequently, emotional/psychological abuse occurs when any other form of abuse is perpetrated.

5. *Relationship.* Child relationships affect the resiliency of the victim and his or her ability to overcome adverse effects of abuse. All relationships that the child has with the victimizer, the nonoffending parent, other family members, other adults, and peers will affect the consequences of abuse and/or neglect.

Experiencing a physical assault or physically abusive punishment as a child has been associated with a 12 percent increase in the likelihood of posttraumatic stress disorder in boys and 21 percent increase in girls (Kilpatrick, Saunders, & Smith, 2003).

Consequences of Sexual Abuse.   Runaway behavior and prostitution are among the responses by females who are sexually assaulted. Over 70 percent of girls within the juvenile justice system and in shelters report having been sexually abused and assaulted (Jacobson, 2000). Childhood sexual abuse has been found to increase the risk of perpetrating physical abuse on children as adults (DiLillo, Tremblay, & Peterson, 2000).

A child who is being sexually assaulted typically will not report the abuse when it first occurs. Children often do not even realize that it is abusive. There is usually an *engagement phase* before the perpetrator initiates sexual contact. During this time, a relationship is being established between the victim and the offender. By the time any sexual conduct takes place, the child trusts the adult. Next is a *progression phase:* The abuser may begin with common activities that require the child to undress. Swimming is one example. This is done to desensitize the child about removing clothing in the presence of the perpetrator. From then on, a range of sexual abuses may be attempted, ranging from indecent touching to intercourse. The final phase is *suppression.* Somehow the offender must ensure the secrecy of the events that have occurred.

Summit's characterization, referred to as the *sexual abuse accommodation syndrome,* includes five phases common to the experiences of the child who has been sexually victimized: secrecy; helplessness; entrapment and accommodation; delayed, conflicted, and unconvincing disclosure; and retraction (Summit, 1982).

Secrecy.   Child sexual abuse is almost always cloaked in secrecy. Frequently, the perpetrator will threaten the child not to tell anyone. Secrecy is secured in various ways, depending on the age of the child and the relationship to the perpetrator. If a child tries to tell an adult about the behavior, the attempt is usually met with disbelief and minimization. Additionally, the child abuser picks his or her victims carefully; he or she already knows the vulnerability of the child and how to guarantee silence before the abuse occurs.

Rewards and incentives for secrecy are common. For example, a young child may be bribed with toys, a bicycle, or dolls. Affection and attachment for needy youngsters is sometimes enough to win compliance. Adolescents may be given permission to use the family car; buying expensive clothing and jewelry is not uncommon. The fact that the victims are rewarded for incestual secrecy does not mean that they are being "paid" for the act. This becomes confusing when the victim is an adolescent, particularly if the child has been taught manipulative behavior through abuse. In time the victim knows that secrecy has a price, comes to expect gifts and rewards, and may even demand them.

Shame and guilt come as the child begins to realize what is happening to him or her. When the violator is a family member, the child may have been cajoled into the sexual activity, being told "this is normal," "everyone does this," or "this is called love." Although the child probably does not like the activity, he or she has no reason to doubt what he or she has been told. At some point the realization that the activity is not right creeps in, regardless of what the children have been told, and they feel guilt and shame for their participation.

The victim knows that a price is paid for the silence; it takes on importance to a young person. Victims wonder what the cost of breaking that silence would be. Keep in mind that these are children: They don't reason as adults. They might not be able to ride the bike they love or wear that pretty dress. Often, the offender will warn the child that if he or she tells anyone, the offender would go to jail and the child would never see him or her again. To a young child, that idea is devastating. In relatively few cases, the family abuser will threaten to kill the child, other family members, or even pets. Threats do not have to be elaborate or particularly believable to adults to have a severe impact on a child. The perspective of the child is therefore important.

A bond exists in the relationship, even though it is deviant behavior. The child may fear losing his or her parent's love if he or she told anyone. The victim is favored in the family—although others don't know, it is his or her secret.

Helplessness.   Intrusiveness characterizes sexual assaults against children. Frequently, it occurs in their own bedroom, making that place no longer safe for them. The intrusion causes anxiety and insecurity, another part of the victimization process. Children may feign sleep during the assault, even though a sibling may be in the next bed or a parent in the next room. Rarely will a child cry out.

Entrapment and Accommodation.   Self-hate develops over time as the child exaggerates his or her own responsibility in the abuse. "No one will believe you," victims are often told. Older children, frequently adolescents, can be blackmailed through sexually explicit photographs that the abuser states will "prove" that they consented. Remember: Consent is *not* a legal issue when sex occurs between a child and an adult, but children don't know that! In most jurisdictions, a child cannot consent to sexual intercourse.

A promise may be involved not to sexually assault siblings. It is not unusual for a victim to come forward with a complaint of sexual abuse at the time that she or he believes that the offender is breaking that promise. A child who has been victimized over time comes to accommodate his or her abuse yet often will not tolerate it happening to a younger sibling.

Delayed, Conflicted, and Unconvincing Disclosure.   Sexual abuse that is ongoing is frequently kept secret within the family. The victim usually remains silent until he or she enters adolescence. A family fight or punishment that the teenager disagrees with may trigger disclosure. A younger sibling being targeted for abuse may also spark the victim to tell someone. Victims may tell a friend or a teacher. The reaction is usually one of disbelief and denial. If a nonoffending parent is the first told, the reaction will probably affect what happens next.

Retraction.   Whatever a child says about incest, he or she is likely to recant at some point. This is problematic for criminal justice, and it must be anticipated if prosecution is to occur. The victim needs support and reassurance through a prosecution for incest. The investigation needs to seek any form of corroboration available in anticipation that the victim will at some point deny the abuse. If a case for sexual abuse rests solely on the word of a child (without evidence) and the truthfulness of the victim comes into question through a denial, a successful prosecution is impossible.

Maltreatment of Children with Disabilities

Few reports exist that have focused specifically on the abuse of children with disabilities. Concern relative to this population has grown since the early 1990s, when the National Center on Child Abuse and Neglect reported that of all children who are abused, 17 percent had disabilities (Crosse, Kaye, & Ratnofsky, 1993). Of those who had been sexually abused, 15.2 percent were reported to have had disabilities. Consistent with the hypothesis that maltreatment contributes to disabilities, of children that had abuse-related injuries, maltreatment was cited as having led or contributed to the disabilities for 62 percent of the children who experienced sexual abuse and for 48 percent of those who experienced emotional abuse, and for 55 percent of children who experienced neglect.

Contributing to current concerns that children with disabilities are more often targeted and that the abuse occurs more frequently than against nondisabled children, later reports estimate that children with any kind of disability are more than twice as likely to be physically or sexually abused (American Academy of Pediatrics, 2001). The factors that are cited as increasing the risk to the children with disabilities are the higher emotional, physical, economic, and social demands on their family members.

THE BATTERED WOMEN'S MOVEMENT

Battering is a pattern of behavior that is intended to gain power and control over a person. Over 25 years have passed since the beginnings of the alliance to gain equal rights and end oppression against women. The vast majority of survivors of domestic violence are women. Their battering is considered one part of the oppression that patriarchy maintains. The movement seeks social change of the cultural values that enable oppressors to control and maintain the power as it has been in the past. It seeks to empower all women and children and to restructure and redistribute the social power. Ending physical and sexual abuse perpetrated against women and children is a significant effort in the movement, but it is seen in a larger context of economic and sexist oppression.

The movement has accomplished major victories since its inception and it is still strong today:

1. The victims have been identified: They are 85 percent female.

2. Heightened public awareness has been achieved, although the causes and consequences are still hotly debated.

3. Intervention strategies have been established through a range of services: shelter, information services, and hotlines. Complaints of insufficient funds to implement additional needed services and to maintain existing ones are constant. Major organizations, including the American Medical Association and American Bar Association, have acknowledged the high number of instances of domestic violence against women and sought reform to address needs. Legal reform has been accomplished in every state in the United States. Federal legislative reform has brought unprecedented change.

4. Protection and prevention efforts now include civil and criminal actions that were never before available to domestic violence victims.

5. Batterers' programs have become the most frequent response from the courts to domestic battering. Education is occurring at this level on television and in classrooms across the country.

One unintended consequence of the battered women's movement has been increased awareness of violence committed against lesbian and gay partners and males. Violence in dating relationships was discovered as well. The implications of personal violence in these additional populations are included in the discussions that follow.

Woman Battering: Health and Safety Issues

Women who are victimized through domestic violence may suffer emotionally and physically. Financial hardships occur when the victim is forced to seek alternate living arrangements and when caring for her children. Recent studies indicate that as many as one in ten battered women seek professional medical treatment due to their injuries (Greenfeld et al., 1998). Women are the majority of emergency room patients who seek treatment for intentional injuries caused by an intimate. How have professionals sought to address the problems? Some initiatives include emergency hotlines. Another alternative is for the victim to seek emergency shelter.

Injury.   The majority of violence against women consists of pushing, slapping, grabbing, and shoving (Carlson, 2000). Considered less than severe, these forms of violence typically do not require medical attention. Approximately 20 to 30 percent of victims reporting severe forms of violence do require medical attention. Based on a synthesis of research, women's quality of life is severely affected by all forms of domestic violence. The most pervasive health concerns associated with violence against women include gastrointestinal disorders, chronic pain or fatigue, loss of appetite and eating disorders, and gynecologic and urologic disorders (Carlson, 2000). Almost one-million dollars in compensation for medical expenses, mental health counseling, and economic support went to adult victims of domestic violence in 2001 (*Crime Victim Compensation Quarterly*, 2003).

In addition to loss of life, the risk of serious injury due to domestic violence is severe. The National Research Council reports the following (Chalk & King, 1998, p. 206):

> Family violence has been identified as a contributing factor for a broad array of fatal and nonfatal injuries and health disorders, including pregnancy and birth complications, sudden infant death syndrome, brain trauma, fractures, sexually transmitted diseases, HIV infection, depression, dissociation, psychosis, and other stress-related physical and mental disorders.... Estimates on the impact of family violence on the public health and health care system indicate that family violence accounts for 39,000 physician visits each year; 28,700 emergency room visits; 21,000 hospitalizations; and 99,800 hospital days.

The American Medical Association declared in 1992 that physical and sexual violence against women had reached epidemic proportions and recommended that physicians routinely screen all women patients for domestic abuse. Reports indicate that abused women have higher levels of health care use when compared to those with no history of abuse. Family violence victimizations (including those against women, men, and against those in same-sex relationships) result in 1.8 million injuries annually (National Center for Injury Prevention and Control, 2003). The Center reports that 519,031 of these injuries require medical care. Almost 15,000 rape victimizations and more than 240,000 physical assault victimizations result in hospital visits annually. More than one medical care visit is often required for each victimization; therefore, the number of hospital visits resulting from rape and physical assault victimizations is estimated to be 486,151 each year due to family violence. Health care systems continue to be urged toward documenting domestic violence in a patient's medical record, a practice that is not consistently being done (Rudman, 2000). Research on the physical injuries directly caused by abuse continue to be the focus, yet when accurate documentation of family violence takes place the abuse is associated with a wide range of adverse physical health problems. These effects include arthritis, chronic neck or back pain, migraines, stammering, visual impairment, sexually transmitted infections, chronic pelvic pain, peptic ulcers, irritable bowel disease, and other digestive problems.

In addition to the physical effects of victimization is the psychological trauma of family violence, indicated by increased reporting of mental health problems and attempted suicide. Abused women often experience stress-related illnesses, depression, posttraumatic stress disorder, and substance abuse disorders in addition to specific injuries from abuse (Rodrigues et al., 1999).

In a survey of women who were not residents of battered women shelters, McFarlane and colleagues reported that 1 out of every 12 women interviewed reported battering during the current pregnancy (McFarlane, 1998). One-third of the pregnant women had sought medical attention for injuries sustained from the abuse, and 29 percent reported that the abuse had increased with knowledge of present pregnancy. A strong indicator of violence during pregnancy was the pattern of battering beforehand. The majority of pregnant women (87.5 percent) had been battered prior to becoming pregnant. McFarlane cautions that the risks of violence during teen pregnancy are also severe. Twenty-six percent of pregnant teens reported physical battering in one study alone.

Hotlines and Shelters.   The first hotline for battered women started in St. Paul, Minnesota, in 1971. Since then national and local hotlines have been established to provide callers with crisis intervention, details on local resources, and information about domestic violence. Since its inception in 1996, the National Hotline has answered more than 1,014,209 phone calls from victims of domestic violence, family members, and friends from all over the world (National Domestic Hotline, 2003). This number reflects an 18 percent increase in calls from 2001 to 2002, averaging 15,000 phone calls daily.

The first shelter in the United States opened for battered women in St. Paul, Minnesota, in 1974. Over 2,000 shelters and service programs exist today. Due to the magnitude of the problem of domestic violence, however, shelters are inadequate to meet the needs of all survivors. In many areas, shelters turn away four women (and their children) for every woman they can accept (National Coalition Against Domestic Violence, 1998). Women with adolescent male children are frequently denied access to shelters, due to possible disruptions and fear that their presence produces. Lesbians, gay men, and male victims are also denied shelter. Adequate resources for those who qualify are insufficient to meet the demands.

Homelessness.   Battered women who live in poverty are often forced to choose between abusive relationships and homelessness (NCH, 2002). Domestic violence is believed to be the primary cause of homelessness; approximately half of all women and children experiencing homelessness are fleeing domestic violence (NCH, 2002). The policies of response to homeless persons fail to recognize the financial burdens of home management for victims that are homeless due to family violence. Long waiting lists for assisted housing and the lack of affordable housing force many women and their children to choose between abuse at home or life on the streets. The following studies are cited that demonstrate the contribution of domestic violence to homelessness:

- In Missouri, 24 percent of the sheltered homeless population are victims of domestic abuse.
- Shelter providers in Virginia report that 35 percent of their clients are homeless because of family violence, and more than 2,000 women seeking shelter from domestic violence facilities were turned away.
- A 1995 study of homelessness in Nebraska found that victims of domestic violence represent 25 percent of the homeless population.
- In Minnesota, the most common reason for women to enter a shelter is domestic violence. Homeless women surveyed indicated their main reason for leaving housing was to flee abuse.

Safety Planning.   An increased risk of severe and fatal injury to survivors of domestic battering has been linked to the final stage of the relationship, when the batterer knows that the relationship is being ended. Advocates suggest that domestic violence victims take additional precautions to protect themselves during this period. When the batterer has been court-ordered out of the home, the following steps are recommended:

- Consider changing the locks in the house or apartment, even if you have asked the abuser to surrender all keys.
- If you live on the first floor or have an apartment with porch windows, consider ways to secure those windows with metal casement key locks or screw-in window locks.
- If you have no phone, consider having one installed as soon as possible; change your current phone number if you do have one.
- Keep the phone number of the police handy as well as the number of the local shelter.
- Keep all important papers in one place where you can grab them on the way out if you are forced to flee. These include birth certificates, marriage license, social security cards, health cards, checkbooks, and savings accounts.
- Leave extra keys to the apartment and car with a friend or relative who knows the situation.
- Consider talking with your neighbors to ask for their cooperation. A system or code such as lights flicking on and off or banging on the floor or ceiling could indicate that you need the help of the police if they are willing to call. Many neighbors do not want to interfere, so asking them in advance gives them permission to help.

Learned Helplessness Theory

One of the early examples of theory that came from the victim movement was that of **learned helplessness**. In suggesting this alternative, Lenore Walker made clear that the most popular explanation at that time (1978) was that battered women were believed to be masochistic (Walker, 1995). Refuting the assumption that women sought out men who would fill their need to be beaten, she claimed another psychological rationale. Employing the social-learning perspective, Walker theorized that women accept their powerlessness in domestic battering situations due to gender-role socialization that induces a false belief that they cannot escape from the situation. The feeling of powerlessness may be reinforced by the "happy family" cultural stereotype as well, she suggested. Victim isolation from friends, family, and other victims allows the reality of the situation to be minimized while victims accept responsibility for the battering incidents. In this explanation, battering produces a psychological paralysis that maintains the victim status of their victimization. Economic and social factors contribute to their victimization and to its continuance in this view.

The battered woman syndrome describes the cyclical nature of battering over time. Domestic abuse is not a single explosive incident of hitting; it is the building of tensions that contribute to the ever-existing nature of the abusive relationship. Victim denials and accommodation of the batterer add to the victimization, which is psychological and emotional as well as physical and/or sexual.

CONSEQUENCES TO SURVIVORS OF DOMESTIC BATTERING

A recent trend in the study of domestic violence is toward changing the characterization of the battered victim to that of a survivor. Kathleen Ferraro typifies this movement. Citing the Campbell study of 1994, she clarifies the incredible obstacles that are overcome by almost half of battered women who are ultimately successful in leaving their abusers (Ferraro, 1997). Her stages of engagement and disengagement offer insight into the intimacy characteristics of marital relationships and the difficulties of dealing with dependent men who threaten, harass, and often assault women as they try to leave. An adaptation of her theory illustrates that the final desperate attempt to get away may lead to homicide.

Larry Tifft places woman battering in an organization structure consisting of two parts: the initial stages and later stages (Tifft, 1993). He differentiates among pushing, shoving, and slaps that are perceived by others as violent outbursts but are in fact not real violence. Only when both partners understand that the violence is intended does battering occur. Battering in this context steals your soul. It is both physical and spiritual pain that causes the survivor to grieve in the initial stages. Both people will typically pretend that the first real violent episode did not occur. As the violence escalates in frequency or severity, a loss of affection surfaces. For normality to be reestablished, both partners must cooperate; this causes an extension of pain for the woman, according to Tifft. She cannot deny the abuse and will be unable to dismiss the injury. The framework of the family becomes distorted as guilt, ambiguity, and insecurity dominate every interaction. Hostility, anger, depression, and fear increase within the relationship. The continued focus on her pain distorts the survivor's vision, suggests Tifft. Her own strategies for survival narrow as she tries to cope with the

---

Phase I: Physical and emotional attraction brings the partners together. During the first six months of the relationship there is no battering. She enjoys time alone with her partner and does not see his desire for social exclusivity as oppression but as mutual affection.

Phase II: The first act of physical violence is met with disbelief. The woman rationalizes the assault and denies the uncharacteristic victimization. The perpetrator blames her through some imagined provocation. It is unlikely that the violence will be deterred by the minor sanctions of criminal justice action unless it occurs in the early stages and in certain types of battering relationships. Societal pressures frequently force the woman into "making the best of it."

Phase III: A change in the severity or frequency of the abuse may trigger a transition into this stage. *Defensive violence* is one tactic that may be used to ward off attacks. The woman may attempt to leave the emotional and economic bond that had developed. Threats or psychological torture make early attempts difficult and often they return. About one-half of those who leave are successful in this attempt toward survival.

Phase IV: Convinced by threats from constant surveillance and punishments, women believe that they cannot get away. Failed attempts to leave reinforce the perception. This stage is horror filled and may bring about depression and posttraumatic stress syndrome. Suicide may be contemplated. A severe altercation may lead to homicide as the final stage in what becomes a "kill or be killed" scenario.

Figure 4–3   Surviving violence. *(Adapted from Ferraro, 1997.)*

contradiction of being in love with a partner who both loves and hurts her. As the situation worsens, the survivor comes to the realization that the battering has become a permanent part of their relationship, and she refuses to take the blame that her batterer heaps on her.

The later stage that Tifft describes involves the methods that the family has adopted to alter life according to the abuse. Children may withdraw from school activities to get home and protect their mom. The family becomes socially isolated to accommodate the presence of the batterer. Overwhelmed by the atmosphere of violence, the mother may become less able to care for the children as all of her attention becomes focused on the abuser. Sexual violence may also occur as the batterer becomes more jealous of what he has already lost. The battering may stop temporarily due to his being arrested or the survivor's seeking refuge at a shelter. Typically they reunite, and he resumes his pattern of battering. The survivor who hangs on to her love for him will have a difficult time in severing the relationship. It may take numer-

Figure 4–4 Men who abuse their wives may also abuse their children.

ous attempts at separations and rejoinings before the survivors are permanently able to "freeze out" the batterer.

Female Victims

Suman Kakar suggests that victims have both internal and external factors that explain why they tolerate violence (Kakar, 1998). The internal traits that victims possess may be natural or due to the experiences of the battering relationship, however. Examples are timidity and low self-esteem. Feelings of helplessness can be acquired when the victims feel trapped and unable to escape. Some researchers suggest that through controlling tactics, the perpetrator "brainwashes" the victim, and a traumatic bonding occurs, according to Kakar. Overly optimistic victims may feel that they love the offender and hope that they can change the abuser's behavior. External factors that influence the victim can be summed up through economic dependence on the perpetrator. Women often remain economically dependent on the man while they care for children in the home; they may delay their education and forgo employment outside the home. Social factors make up another external influencing factor. The lack of friends and supportive adults may increase the sense of futility and increase the victim's feeling of isolation and despair.

In *Battering of Women: The Failure of Intervention and the Case for Prevention*, Larry Tifft likens battered women to the "peoples of invaded nations ... perceived by the general culture as the cause of their own invasion, torture, and anguish" (p. 5). After 15 years of empirical research focused on the characteristics of women who have been battered, few risk markers have been identified (Tifft, 1993). When low self-esteem, codependency, or lack of assertiveness is suggested, says Tifft, it blames the victims and draws attention away from the real problem. Rather than viewing women who are battered as in need of therapy, advocacy, justice, and support are the needed responses. According to a recent study, cultural differences account for high rates of women violence within Asian communities (Yoshioka et al., 2000). An astounding 25 to 38 percent of the entire sample reported knowing a woman who met at least one criterion of abuse. It is imperative that we acknowledge the scope and seriousness of this problem. Strong patriarchal beliefs coupled with the shame associated with female battering lead most victims to keep silent on their abuse.

Effects of Rape.   Marital rape accounts for approximately 25 percent of all rapes (Bergen, 1999). Between one-third and one-half of battered women are raped by their partners at least once, suggesting that this is just another form of domestic violence. The physical effects of domestic partner rape may include injuries to the vaginal and anal areas, lacerations, soreness, bruising, torn muscles, fatigue, and vomiting. Other physical symptoms may include broken bones, black eyes, bloody noses, and knife wounds that occur during the sexual violence. Approximately one-half of the survivors report having been kicked or burned during sex (Bergen, 1999). Miscarriages, stillbirths, bladder infections, infertility, and the potential contraction of sexually transmitted diseases including HIV are specific gynecological consequences of marital rape.

Survivors of rape often experience changes in their overall health. Sleep disorders such as insomnia or eating disorders often occur following rape or sexual assault. Some women experience nightmares and flashbacks. Others encounter body aches, headaches, and fatigue. Posttraumatic stress disorder (PTSD) is the most common disorder seen in

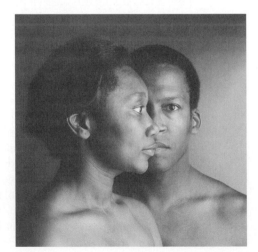

Figure 4–5   Marital rape is more likely to occur in relationships characterized by other forms of violence, earning the label "battering rape."

victims of rape or sexual assault. Rape victims sometimes experience anxiety, depression, self-injury, and/or suicide attempts, as well as other emotional disorders. They sometimes try to cope with their feelings by indulging in alcohol or drugs.

Women with Disabilities.   Approximately 54 million Americans report some level of disability (Sigmon & Edmunds, 2002). National studies of victimization to the population of women with disabilities are lacking, but generalizations have been made possible due to smaller research projects (Sigmon & Edmunds, 2002). Research confirms that women with disabilities are at least twice as likely to be victimized by all forms of domestic violence as the general population of women; some reports estimate that the victimization is as high as 85 percent of the population of women with disabilities (Fiduccia & Wolfe, 1999). The vast majority of abuse toward women with disabilities is perpetrated by males. These women experience a high probability of victimization, repeat victimizations, and of more severe abuse that occurs over longer periods of time as compared to the general population of women (Milberger, LeRoy, Martin, & Israel, 2002). Compared to women without disabilities, these victims frequently experience greater dependence on their abusers for personal care.

Of all women, those with developmental disabilities have among the highest rates of physical, sexual, and emotional violence by spouses, ex-spouses, boyfriends, and family members (Emanuel, 2000). Developmental disability includes mental retardation, autism, cerebral palsy, and severe learning disabilities. For women with physical disabilities, the level of victimization by a husband or live-in partner is similar to women without physical disabilities, but the duration of abuse is longer (Milberger, et al., 2002). Estimates on the prevalence of domestic abuse for women with disabilities range from a low of 50 percent to a high of 83 percent depending on the study (Milberger et al., 2002). Predisposing personality characteristics include high levels of dependency on others, lack of assertiveness, overcompliance, and low self-esteem (Carlson, 1997). The absence of family support systems may further isolate the victims.

Violence Against Same-Sex Partners

Since the numbers of lesbian households have only recently been documented within the United States, their numbers are expected to reflect those that are openly gay. For the second time in its history, the 2000 United States Census permitted same-sex couples living together to identify as unmarried partners. There are approximately 300,000 same-sex female couples of the nearly 1.2 million gay and lesbian adults recorded in this census (Bradford, et al., 2002). Almost one in five lesbian households reported having children under the age of 18 living in the home. Violence in heterosexual, gay, transsexual, and lesbian relationships occurs at approximately the same rate as heterosexuals, 2 in 5 (NCAVP, 2003).

Issues related to sexual orientation and gender identity are specifically stated on the Web site of the Gay Men's Domestic Violence Project (2002):

Services—Lesbians and gay men, bisexual and transgender (LGBT) people who have been abused have fewer services available to them.

Isolation—The isolation that accompanies domestic violence can be compounded by being LGBT in a homophobic society. Silence about domestic violence within the LGBT community further isolates the victim, giving more power to the batterer.

Heterosexist manipulation—A batterer may threaten to "out" a person's sexual orientation or gender identity to friends, family, coworkers, or a landlord. In addition to this, existing services may require an individual to "come out" against his or her will.

Community myths—Many LGBT individuals do not want to challenge the myth of community nonviolence.

Protectionism about "queer love"—The discrimination LGBT people face can lead to our overprotection of same-gender relationships and an unwillingness to recognize abuse when it happens. Some idolize "queer love" as a deconstruction of many of the power differences in heterosexual relationships and defend same-gender relationships against a homophobic society bent on invalidating them. This defensiveness can build community denial about abusive relationships.

Fear of further oppression—As an oppressed and defamed group, the LGBT community is often hesitant to address issues that many fear will further "stain" the community. "Don't we have enough to deal with?" is a common phrase from people unwilling to discuss domestic violence in the LGBT community.

Gender-based denial—The battered women's movement often avoids the fact that women do batter, and men are victims. This denial is also present among many police, hospital workers, and people in the criminal justice system.

Gender myths—People assume that two men in a fight must be equals. Similarly, GBT men often reject the idea that they can be victims.

Context of historical oppression—LGBT people often approach shelters, social service agencies, domestic violence service providers, police, and the courts with great caution. LGBT victims may fear revictimization through homophobia, disbelief, rejection, and degradation from institutions that have a history of exclusion, hostility, and violence toward LGBT people.

Shelter—No transitional, medium-term, or long-term shelters exist for battered GBT men.

Myths about S&M—Misconception that LGBT victims of domestic violence are only experiencing an S&M sexual relationship.

Limited community space—Even in larger cities, the LGBT community can feel surprisingly small, privacy is often difficult to maintain, and leaving may be more difficult.

Children—Risk of losing children to third parties is greater for LGBT couples when domestic violence is involved.

Lesbian Partnership Violence.   The battered woman's movement has been slow to recognize domestic violence perpetrated within female relationships; few significant studies have documented its prevalence. From these rare and outdated studies comes the suggestion that violence among lesbian partners may be occurring at a rate of 50 percent within the population (NCAVP, 2003). A contrary finding is that women living with a female intimate partner experience less partner violence than heterosexual women (Tjaden & Thoennes, 2000). Antidotal evidence suggests inappropriate social and criminal responses to same-sex domestic violence (Leventhal & Lundy, 1999; Ristock, 2002).

Societal notions on the role of women have contributed to the reluctance of lesbian victims to identify the abuse (Coleman, 1996). Lesbians fear reporting domestic violence battering due to the double victimization that is likely to occur. Women are expected to be nonviolent in this culture that attributes battering primarily to males. Accusations of violence by a female toward another female may be met with disbelief.

Gay Male Partnership Violence.   Domestic violence is the third leading health problem facing gay men today, second to substance abuse and AIDS. Additional problems for these victims are the silence about same-sex battering and the risk of a homophobic response. These factors contribute to the tendency for gay and bisexual men not to report domestic violence. Gay men and bisexual men are likely to deny or minimize the violence that is perpetrated against them.

Documented rates of battering victimization in gay male relationships range from 12 to 36 percent, which is less than reported lesbian domestic violence and comparable to family violence among heterosexual women (Greenwood et al., 2002). In their recent study approximately two of five gay men (39 percent) reported experiencing partner violence during the previous 5 years.

Victims of violence are created by batterers, suggest Island and Letellier (Island & Letellier, 1991). They state that it is all too easy to lump together victims and offenders in the same psychological package. Why male victims stay is a much more difficult question to answer. Each gay victim has his own set of reasons for staying with

Figure 4–6 Regardless of sexual orientation, victims' experiences are similar when mistreated through family violence.

his batterer. The cycle of violence theory and learned helplessness theory offer theoretical explanations. Fear, they contend, is the most powerful reason.

Male Victims

Sexual and physical crimes committed against men and boys are believed to be underreported. Male victimization is slowly coming to the surface. In 1999, one in every ten rape victims were male (Rennison, 2000). Approximately 15 percent of domestic violence victims are male whose batterers are their female partners; in 2001 the total was estimated to be 103,220 victimizations (Rennison, 2003). Since the male identity includes expectations of problem solving and self-protection, battered men often do not perceive their victimization as abuse. In *The Sexually Abused Male*, Jim Struve applies the dynamics of patriarchy and the learned helplessness theory to the sexual victimization of boys (Struve, 1990). *Sexual entitlement*, the belief that sex is the privilege of dominant adult males, blurs the boundaries between adult and child in this patriarchal view. The legal, economic, and social dependency on parents leaves no feasible alternative for children when their safety is threatened, and they learn to accommodate. Cultural dictates on sexual secrecy and misinformation on sex serve to perpetuate the shroud of secrecy that envelops this form of male abuse. Struve suggests nine socialization factors that make it more difficult for male survivors to achieve recovery.

1. *Treatment.* Men are not as likely as women to seek treatment. This is a reluctance to see oneself as a victim—a female-associated persona.

2. *Minimization.* Males are reluctant to make a disclosure about sexual abuse for fear that it will not be seen as a victimization experience. If the victim is a self-identified homosexual, the abuse may be seen as the result of sexual choice.

3. *Shame.* The male victim typically focuses on why he failed to protect himself. Male survivors frequently report internalized anger, according to Struve, as well as their having failed at their manly responsibility of inflicting serious physical harm on the offender.

4. *Masculine identity.* The male survivor may overcompensate for the anxiety surrounding his inability to protect himself by using macho behaviors to project a strong male image. For the heterosexual male, fears that he will be "branded" as homosexual will plague him.

5. *Male intimacy.* Intense anxiety or anger is produced in settings with other males that might create intimacy. The victim typically will avoid relationships with other males, to avoid appearing weak or needy.

6. *Sexual identity.* A male that has been sexually assaulted may assume that his failure to protect himself equates with passivity, wrongly considered a female trait. Since the majority of perpetrators are also male, the self-perception of arousal or physical pleasure from a same-sex assault can lead to the false assumption of homosexuality.

7. *Power and control dynamics.* Low self-esteem is related to having been victimized sexually. It may lead to an exaggerated effort to control others.

8. *Externalization.* Victimizing others sexually is one way that victims externalize their feelings. Isolation surrounding his own victimization and patriarchal values place the victim at risk for offending against others.

9. *Compulsive behaviors.* Some male survivors mask their emotional anxiety and pain through compulsive behaviors. These may include alcohol and substance abusing, or rigid repetitive behaving patterns.

Male victims of physical battering must overcome the social barriers that do not recognize their abuse as legitimate. Philip Cook suggests that physical injury should not be the measure of an abusive relationship (Cook, 1997). He maintains that abused men do exist and in greater numbers than people realize. Battered men frequently stay in marital discord for reasons similar to those of women. Cook maintains that it is false to assume that economic resources offer greater escape possibilities for men; they are held responsible for financially supporting a former spouse and children regardless of abuse. Fear of losing contact with children also inhibits fathers from leaving abusive relationships: Women most often receive physical custody of children. Additionally, abused men feel powerless due to their inability to change the situation in the past.

Why Do Domestic Violence Victims Stay?

All too often the question "Why do women stay in violent relationships?" is answered with a victim-blaming attitude. The fact is, women do leave their abusers. It simply is not up to us to determine when or if she should stay. In a recent study of married female respondents reporting having experienced a violent victimization, those who reported that an intimate had victimized them were substantially more likely to also report a change in their marital status six months after an initial interview (Rennison, 2001). This special report on intimate violence found that for female victims of intimate partner violence, 30 percent of those who were married during the first interview were separated at the interview in which they reported the victimization. An additional 8 percent were divorced.

Female victims of abuse often hear that they must like or need such abuse, or they would leave. Others may be told that they are one of the many "women who love too much" or who have "low self-esteem." No one enjoys being beaten, no matter what their emotional state or self-image. A woman's reasons for staying are more complex than a statement about her strength of character. In many cases it is dangerous for a woman to leave her abuser. If the abuser has all of the economic and social status, leaving can cause additional problems for the woman. Leaving could mean living in fear and losing child custody, losing financial support, and experiencing harassment at work. Battered women experience shame, embarrassment, and isolation. Here are some of the many reasons why a victim may not leave battering immediately:

- She realistically fears that the batterer will become more violent and maybe even fatal if she attempts to leave;
- Her friends and family may not support her leaving;
- She knows the difficulties of single parenting in reduced financial circumstances;
- There is a mix of good times, love, and hope along with the manipulation, intimidation, and fear;
- She may not know about or have access to safety and support;
- Many women are socialized to believe that they are responsible for making their marriage work. Failure to maintain the marriage equals failure as a woman;
- Many women become isolated from friends and families, either by the jealous and possessive abuser, or to hide signs of the abuse from the outside world;
- The isolation contributes to a sense that there is nowhere to turn;
- Many women rationalize their abuser's behavior by blaming stress, alcohol, problems at work, unemployment, or other factors;
- Many women are taught that their identity and worth are contingent upon getting and keeping a man.

Dating Violence Victims

Years after adult victimization was recognized, scholars began to look at violence during the courtship phase. Research has indicated that approximately one out of ten high school students experience physical violence in dating relationships. For college students the figure rises to 22 percent, which is the same as violence in adult relationships (Gamache, 1998). Clearly, violence occurs in the context of both marital and dating partnerships. Yet dating someone is different than being married. The two most stressful events of marriage, money management and childrearing, don't exist in the context of courtship. Problems associated with having a place to live and going to work are not involved. It sounds as though dating would be free of any factors that are associated with violence. Why does it happen?

Scholars are beginning to associate intimacy with violence, in both adult and dating relationships. James Makepeace, for example, suggests a developmental theory based on the need for intimacy between partners as his explanation for courtship violence (Makepeace, 1997). He states that intimacy is a fundamental individual need, and its attainment is both magnified and romanticized in our culture. The frustrations to satisfy that need begin early during the courtship stage. Youngsters often begin dating when they have not yet gained the maturity to handle the frustrations of satisfactory intimacy and may react in inappropriate ways. He cites jealousy as the most frequent reason for courtship violence, and hitting as a response to jealousy is often accepted by both males and females.

Makepeace reports that the majority of respondents (54 percent) first experienced violence in courtship between ages 16 and 18. The life experiences that are significant in predicting this violence include the family background, such as absent, emotionally distant, or harsh parents; school difficulties; difficulties in employment; and having begun dating at an early age. Consistent with studies on adult interpersonal violence, the use of drugs and alcohol is a consistent risk factor in abuse. Neither can be used as an excuse for perpetration, however.

For lesbian teens, an absence of role models may lead the adolescents to engage in destructive behaviors that they falsely assume are characteristic of the sexual choice that they have made (Levy & Lobel, 1998). Confusion about what is normal behavior makes this population especially vulnerable to abuse. The isolation due to the sexual identity adds to their low self-esteem and creates an intense bond with their lover. When the victim is unable to trust others, it is difficult to seek support if a partner becomes abusive.

Date Rape.   Since the 1980s the term *date rape* has been used to describe rape of young women or adolescent girls perpetrated by casual or intimate dating partners. There is no crime called "date rape." This is a social term used to explain the context under which the crime is occurring; it brings attention to the fact that rape occurs within relationships. The legal term for date rape is simply rape. Studies on the prevalence of acquaintance rape have indicated shocking rates of occurrence. Women are five times more likely to experience rape in a dating relationship than from strangers (DeKeseredy & Schwartz, 1998).

In addition to the fear and depression that is common to rape victims, adolescent survivors suffer in ways that are unique (Gallers & Lawrence, 1998). In their review of the literature, Gallers and Lawrence explain that teenagers experience a sense of loss of personal integrity as well as trust of the world around them. Young people frequently feel invincible, and the personal violation shatters that myth, altering their reality. The self-esteem of a normally narcissistic adolescent may be damaged from an assault. Victims tend to internalize and falsely blame themselves for being with the offender in the first place. Sudden personality changes, such as a drop in school performance, withdrawal from usual school or social activities, and flagrant promiscuous behavior are among the symptoms that adolescent rape victims display. They may engage in self-destructive behavior such as drug or alcohol abuse or develop eating disorders such as bulimia or anorexia.

A concern now is the increasingly predatory nature of rape indicated by the use of date rape drugs by high school and college students. The most common is Rohypnol, often called **"roofies"** and "forget pill." According to the Drug Enforcement Administration, this illegal drug is manufactured worldwide and brought in through Mexico. Its popularity among young people is due to the drug's low cost, usually below $5 per tablet. Placed into the drink of an unsuspecting victim, the drug is tasteless and odorless. Within 15 to 30 minutes, the effects include dizziness, drowsiness, confusion, and memory impairment. Another drug, gamma-hydroxybutyrate (GHB), is also being used to incapacitate victims in order to abuse them sexually. Its side effects are similar to those of Rohypnol. Most commonly found in liquid form, it is also colorless and odorless.

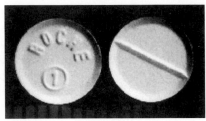

Figure 4–7   "Roofies" or Rohypnol tablets are white and are single- or cross-scored on one side with "ROCHE" and "1" or "2" encircled on the other.

People who suspect that they have been drugged and sexually violated should have their urine and blood tested within 24 hours. All clothing and physical evidence should be kept and given to the police. It is important not to change, shower, or douche, so that a hospital protocol and rape examination may be made to secure evidence of the assault.

EFFECTS OF VICTIMIZATION

Throughout this chapter, a number of different responses to personal violence have been offered. The reactions of victims may vary greatly. The severity and frequency of the abuse, the personal characteristics of the victim, and the form of abuse all contribute to the range of victim reactions. Presented here are some responses that have been identified from the psychological viewpoint. Although attributing mental health disorders to victims of domestic violence is hotly debated, these characterizations are interwoven into the literature on victimization. The disorders are not specific to any group or determined by race, ethnicity, gender, or age.

Borderline Personality Disorder

Described as a pervasive pattern of instability of mood, interpersonal relationships, and self-image, the **borderline personality disorder** affects functioning in numerous areas of life (Alderman, 2000). Examples include employment or school, social relationships, and/or personal well-being. Alderman explains that this disorder is a chronic, intense instability, and chaos characterized by fluctuating extremes. She likens the personality disorder to the video game "Sonic the Hedgehog" (pp. 105–106):

> In the game, Sonic was safe from his enemies as long as he curled up in a tight ball and kept spinning. Once he stopped and stood up, he was vulnerable to the attacks of various creatures. As long as the people with borderline personality keep spinning, creating and repairing chaotic situations within their lives, they feel safe. When their lives get too calm or too stable, vulnerability, tension and anxiety emerge, causing them to seek new chaos. Stability sends these people spinning.

Posttraumatic Stress Disorder

Posttraumatic stress disorder (PTSD) is the diagnostic category most frequently used by psychotherapists to explain the trauma associated with rape, battering, and sexual abuse. Often, it is experienced as the result of one severely traumatic event; its application to domestic violence is limited.

The Diagnostic and Statistical Manual of Mental Disorders (American Psychiatric Association, 2000) defines posttraumatic stress disorder as a type of anxiety disorder caused by trauma and prolonged stress. First applied to Vietnam veterans, it is also reported in victims of violence. The diagnostic criteria for this psychological condition are these:

1. That the person has experienced an event outside the range of usual human experience that would be distressing to almost everyone.

2. That the person re-experiences the trauma as evidenced by at least one of the following:

   a. Recurrent or intrusive recollections of the event

   b. Recurrent dreams of the event

   c. Sudden acting or feeling as if the traumatic event were recurring because some stimulus triggers an association (including a sense of reliving the experience, illusions, hallucinations, and dissociative [flashback] experiences)

   d. Intense psychological distress at exposure to events that resemble or symbolize the traumatic event

3. That the person has a numbing of responsiveness to, or reduced involvement with, the external world beginning sometime after the trauma, as shown by at least one of the following:

   a. Markedly diminished interest in one or more significant activities

Figure 4-8 Personal violence can have devastating and long-term effects on its victims.

    b. Feelings of detachment or estrangement from others

    c. Constricted affect

4. That the person shows persistent symptoms of increased arousal that were not present before the trauma:

    a. Hypervigilance

    b. Sleep disturbance

    c. Memory impairment or trouble concentrating

    d. Irritability or outbursts of anger

    e. Exaggerated startle response

    f. Intensification of symptoms (and physiological reactivity) by exposure to events that symbolize or resemble the traumatic event

5. That these symptoms last for at least one month.

Stockholm Syndrome

Characteristics common to hostage taking have been identified in nine groups examined by Graham (Graham & Rawlings, 1998). The bidirectional bonding between the captor and the hostage appears to occur between the abuser and physically and/or emotionally abused children, incest victims, battered women, and procured prostitutes, as well as cult members, concentration camp prisoners, prisoners of war, civilians in Chinese prisons, and people in hostage situations. Known as the **Stockholm syndrome**, the condition occurs as a survival strategy. Graham proposes that the following conditions precede the phenomenon:

- The victim perceives a threat to survival along with the belief that the captor is willing to carry out that threat.
- The captive perceives that some small kindness from the captor occurred within the context of terror of the situation.
- An isolation from perspectives other than those of the captor narrows the victim's perception of the events.
- The captive perceives an inability to escape.

Self-Inflicted Violence

Victims of abuse do not always resort to *self-inflicted violence* (SIV), states Alderman. Trauma is not believed to cause SIV but seems to be related to childhood victimization. She notes that the majority of people who engage in self-destructive practices have previously been victimized by physical, sexual, or emotional abuse (Alderman, 2000).

    SIV involves acts done to oneself by oneself that are physically damaging and intentional but not suicidal. Cutting, burning, and hitting oneself are examples. Pulling out hair and excessive nail biting are others. Razor blades and lit cigarettes are common tools in the practice. Equally important to the description is that these are repetitive and extremely private actions. SIV is not done to conform to cult requirements or as a fashion statement. It is a self-destructive coping mechanism and often the response to stress.

THE COST OF FAMILY VIOLENCE

In terms of personal pain and suffering, it is impossible to gauge the costs of family violence. The damaged lives and generations of troubled persons due to abuse are something that we have only recently begun to understand. A recent report estimated that 1.3 million adults received hospital emergency treatment for physical and sexual assaults in the one-year period before the survey (Tjaden & Thoennes, 1998). The figure includes personal assaults against males by strangers but not victimization against children. According to recent figures from the National Center for Injury Prevention and Control, the cost of medical and mental health care that is estimated to be directly related to intimate partner violence is $5.8 billion annually (2003).

Those who do not personally experience violence should realize that there is a cost to society as well. Researchers have attempted to assess the costs and place dollar amounts on them. The National Research Council has analyzed the data and estimated that family violence in the United States costs somewhere between $1.7 billion and $140 billion annually (Chalk & King, 1998). Included in the estimate are medical costs, foster care, and lost productivity due to victimization. Chalk and King explain that the variation among cost estimates stems from differences in the variables selected to generate the figures. One estimate included a high set of indirect costs associated with pain and suffering. The use of different prevalent rates of violence is a factor that also contributes to the wide range of cost. Regardless of the lack of an exact figure, it should be apparent that the problems of victimization are far from personal; it affects us all.

CONCLUSIONS

The key emphasis in this chapter is emphasis on understanding domestic violence from the viewpoint of the victim. This shift grew out of complaints concerning the criminological explanations that included victims but tended to assign to them a responsibility for personal violence. The *victim movement* was born during the 1960s to address the victim blaming that occurred. The two movements outlined here are the children's rights movement and the battered women's movement. Both have attempted to remedy the lack of attention to victimization and the consequences of victimization. Social and legal changes have been the focus of both. Of note is the interconnection between child abuse and women abuse. Men who batter their wives are more likely to abuse their children as well. The witnessing of domestic violence against women is now considered an abuse against the children. Childhood abuse is a problem that has both criminal and social consequences—its prevalence cannot be ignored.

Due to the struggle, we now recognize that children can be harmed physically, sexually, and through neglect. In addition, they are abused psychologically through witnessing violence. As increased attention was given to the victims of child abuse, activists sought similar recognition of the abuses perpetrated against women. One of the major theories that explained battering in intimate relationships is based on the perception that violence begets violence, known as the intergenerational transmission of violence. The research conducted relative to child abuse both supported and connected the effort to understand violence against women. Although the two movements are separate, they are so interconnected that it is impossible to study one without the other.

The health and safety concerns of women who survive battering in an intimate relationship are predicated on research that documents the possibility of severe injury. The physical injury due to abuse of both children and women is a significant social problem. Women with disabilities are particularly vulnerable to abuse from an intimate partner. This chapter specifically addressed the risks of injury during pregnancy. Homelessness has been defined as a problem related to domestic violence.

For female and male victims of domestic battering and rape, the psychological effects can be devastating. Numerous mental and emotional problems associated with victimization at the hands of an intimate point to the need for increased sensitivity to all victims of abuse. Gender has been the primary victim characteristic in the past, but this does not mean that men do not experience forms of domestic violence or that women do not commit it.

The gender lines that previously marked family violence have become obsolete with the realization that intimate abuse occurs with high levels of frequency in relationships that involve lesbian women. Gay men are also victimized in domestic partnerships. With fewer legal and social resources for homosexual victims, their struggles to overcome violence may be intensified.

A new domestic relationship has been established concerning the victims of dating violence. Recent studies point to an alarming rate of both physical and sexual abuse within the courtship context. The response to this information has been an outpouring of research into the causes and effects of premarital abuse. Most surprising is the seemingly nonchalant attitude of teens that are affected by this violence. Most distressing is the current predatory nature of drug use for the purpose of gaining control and sexually abusing young women.

QUESTIONS FOR REVIEW

1. Violence against women has reached epidemic proportions. What are some major consequences of the violence against women?

2. Can the consequences of child abuse be predicted?

3. What is the sexual abuse accommodation syndrome?

4. Explain the accomplishments of the women's movement.

5. What are the socialization factors that make it more difficult for male survivors to achieve recovery?

6. Explain the dynamics of courtship violence.

7. Explain posttraumatic stress disorder.

8. Homosexual intimate partnership violence has similarities as well as differences from heterosexual domestic violence. What does this mean?

9. Give examples of self-inflicted violence. Why does it happen?

10. Why would a victim of domestic violence stay in the relationship?

INTERNET-BASED EXERCISES

1. Search online to find out what is being done to protect women and children from domestic violence. A good place to start your search is the "Violence against Women online resources." This Web site provides law, criminal justice, advocacy, and social service professionals with up-to-date information on interventions to stop violence against women. Here you will find at least eight model programs: http://www.vaw.umn.edu/mp.asp. Compare and contrast at least two program models.

2. What can you do to prevent domestic violence? For ideas, go to the National Advisory Council on Violence Against Women Web site. They have developed the Toolkit to End Violence Against Women. Each Toolkit chapter focuses on a particular audience or environment and includes recommendations for strengthening prevention efforts and improving services and advocacy for victims. http://toolkit.ncjrs.org/

REFERENCES

Adams, David. 1992. *Historical Timeline of Institutional Responses to Battered Women, 1850–1992.* Cambridge, MA: Emerge.

Alderman, Tracy. 2000. *The Scarred Soul.* Oakland, CA: New Harbinger Publications.

American Academy of Pediatrics. 2001. "Assessment of Maltreatment of Children With Disabilities." *Pediatrics* 108(2):508–12.

American Psychiatric Association. 2000. *The Diagnostic and Statistical Manual of Mental Disorders,* 4th ed. Washington, DC: APA.

Amir, Menachem. 1971. *Patterns in Forcible Rape.* Chicago: University of Chicago Press.

Belitz, Jerald, and Anita Schacht. 1995. "Satanism as a Response to Abuse: The Dynamics and Treatment of Satanic Involvement in Male Youths." Pp. 82–95 in *Family Violence: Readings in the Social Sciences and Professions,* James Makepeace (ed.). New York: McGraw-Hill.

Bergen, Raquel K. Mar. 1999. "Marital Rape" [Web page]. Accessed Apr 2004. Available at *http://www.vaw.umn.edu/library/dv/.*

Bradford, J., K. Barrett, and J. A. Honnold. 2002. *The 2000 Census and Same-Sex Households.* New York: The National Gay and Lesbian Task Force Policy Institute, the Survey and Evaluation Research Laboratory, and The Fenway Institute.

Carlson, Bonnie E. 1997. "Mental Retardation and Domestic Violence: An Ecological Approach to Intervention." *Social Work* 42(1):79–89.

Carlson, Bonnie E. 2000. *Violence Against Women: Synthesis of Research for Service Providers.* NCJ 199578. Washington, DC: U.S. Department of Justice.

Chalk, Rosemary, and Patricia A. King (eds.). 1998. *Violence in Families: Assessing Prevention and Treatment Programs.* Washington, DC: National Academy Press.

Cohen, Elena, and Barbara Walthall. 2003. *Silent Realities: Supporting Young Children and Their Families Who Experience Violence.* Washington, DC: The National Child Welfare Resource Center for Family-Centered Practice.

Coleman, Vallerie E. 1996. "Lesbian Battering: The Relationship between Personality and the Perpetration of Violence." Pp. 77–101 in *Domestic Partner Abuse*, L. K. Hamberger and Claire Renzetti (eds.). New York: Springer Publishing Company.

Cook, Philip W. 1997. *Abused Men: The Hidden Side of Domestic Violence.* Westport, CT: Praeger Publishers.

Crime Victim Compensation Quarterly. 2003. "Compensation at Record Heights!" [Web Page]. Accessed 30 Oct 2003. Available at *www.ncvc.org/resources/statistics/costofcrime.*

Crosse, Scott B., Elyse Kaye, and Alexander C. Ratnofsky. 1993. *A Report on the Maltreatment of Children With Disabilities.* Washington, DC: Office on Child Abuse and Neglect.

DeKeseredy, Walter S., and Martin D. Schwartz. 1998. *Woman Abuse on Campus: Results from the Canadian National Survey.* Thousand Oaks, CA: Sage Publications.

DiLillo, D., G. Tremblay, and L. Peterson. 2000. "Maternal Anger." *Child Abuse and Neglect* 24(6):767–79.

Emanuel, Elllie J. 2000. "Breaking the Power of Discrimination." *Impact* 13(3):6–7.

Ferraro, Kathleen. 1997. "Battered Women: Strategies for Survival." Pp. 124–40 in *Violence between Intimate Partners: Patterns, Causes, and Effects*, Albert P. Cardarelli (ed.). Needham Heights, MA: Allyn & Bacon.

Fiduccia, Barbara W., and Leslie R. Wolfe. 1999. *Violence Against Disabled Women.* Washington, DC: Center for Women Policy Studies.

Gallers, Johanna, and Kathy Lawrence. 1998. "Overcoming Post-traumatic Stress Disorder in Adolescent Date Rape." Pp. 172–83 in *Dating Violence: Young Women in Danger*, 2nd ed., Barrie Levy (ed.). Seattle, WA: Seal Press.

Gamache, Denise. 1998. "Domination and Control: The Social Context of Dating Violence." Pp. 69–83 in *Dating Violence: Young Women in Danger*, 2nd ed., Barrie Levy (ed.). Seattle, WA: Seal Press.

Garrett, Athena, and Heather Libbey. 1997a. "Common Outcomes of Abuse and Neglect." *Theory and Research on the Outcomes and Consequences of Child Abuse and Neglect*, Vol. 2. Washington, DC: National Institute of Justice.

———. 1997b. *Theory and Research on the Outcomes and Consequences of Child Abuse and Neglect.* Child Abuse Intervention Strategic Planning Meeting, Washington, DC. Washington, DC: National Institute of Justice.

Gay Men's Domestic Violence Project. 2002. *http://www.gmdvp.org/index.html.* 2002.

Geffner, Robert, Ingelman, Robyn Spurling, and Jennifer Zellner. 2003. *Effects of Intimate Partner Violence on Children.* Binghamton, NY: Haworth Press.

Graham, Dee and Edna Rawlings. 1998. "Bonding with Abusive Dating Partners: Dynamics of Stockholm Syndrome." Pp. 119–35 in *Dating Violence: Young Women in Danger*, 2nd ed., Barrie Levy (ed.). Seattle, WA: Seal Press.

Greenfield, Lawrence, Michael Rand, Diane Craven, Patsy Klaus, Craig Perkins, Cheryl Ringel, Greg Warchol, Cathy Matson, and James Fox. 1998. *Violence by Intimates: Analysis of Crimes by Current or Former Spouses, Boyfriends, and Girlfriends.* NCJ 167237. Washington, DC: U.S. Department of Justice.

Greenwood, Gregory, Michael Relf, Bu Huang, Lance Pollack, Jesse Canchola, and Joseph Catania. 2002. "Battering Victimization Among a Probability-Based Sample of Men Who Have Sex With Men." *American Journal of Public Health* 92(12):1964–67.

Groves, Betsy M., Marilyn Augustyn, Debbie Lee, and Peter Sawires. 2002. *Identifying and Responding to Domestic Violence: Consensus Recommendations for Child and Adolescent Health.* San Francisco, CA: Family Violence Prevention Fund.

Island, David, and Patrick Letellier. 1991. *Men Who Beat the Men Who Love Them: Battered Gay Men and Domestic Violence.* Binghamton, NY: Harrington Park Press.

Jacobson, Wendy. 2000. *Safe from the Start: Taking Action on Children Exposed to Violence.* NCJ 182789. Washington, DC: U.S. Department of Justice.

Kakar, Suman. 1998. *Domestic Abuse: Public Police/Criminal Justice Approaches towards Child, Spousal and Elderly Abuse.* San Francisco: Austin & Winfield.

Kilpatrick, Dean, Benjamin E. Saunders, and Daniel W. Smith. 2003. "Youth Victimization: Prevalence and Implications." *NIJ: Research in Brief.* NIJ 194972. Washington, DC: U.S. Department of Justice.

Letellier, Patrick. 1996. "Gay and Bisexual Male Domestic Violence Victimization: Challenges to Feminist Theory." Pp. 1–22 in *Domestic Partner Abuse,* L. K. Hamberger and Claire Renzetti (eds.). New York: Springer Publishing Company.

Leventhal, Beth, and Sandra E. Lundy, editors. 1999. *Same-Sex Domestic Violence.* Thousand Oaks, CA: Sage Publications, Inc.

Levy, Barrie, and Kerry Lobel. 1998. "Lesbian Teens in Abusive Relationships." Pp. 203–8 in *Dating Violence: Young Women in Danger,* 2nd ed., Barrie Levy (ed.). Seattle, WA: Seal Press.

Makepeace, James M. 1997. "Courtship Violence as Process: A Developmental Theory." Pp. 29–47 in *Violence between Intimate Partners: Patterns, Causes, and Effects,* Albert Cardarelli (ed.). Needham Heights, MA: Allyn & Bacon.

McFarlane, Judith. 1998. "Violence during Teen Pregnancy: Health Consequences for Mother and Child." Pp. 137–41 in *Dating Violence: Young Women in Danger,* 2nd ed., Barrie Levy (ed.). Seattle, WA: Seal Press.

Meadows, Robert J. 1998. *Understanding Violence and Victimization.* Upper Saddle River, NJ: Prentice Hall.

Milberger, Sharon, Barbara LeRoy, Angela Martin, and Nathaniel Israel. 2002. *A Michigan Study on Women with Physical Disabilities.* NCJ 193769. Washington, DC: U.S. Department of Justice.

NAIC. 2003. "Children and Domestic Violence: A Bulletin for Professionals" [Web page]. Available at *http://nccanch.acf.hhs.gov/pubs/factsheets/domesticviolence.cfm.*

National Center for Injury Prevention and Control. 2003. *Costs of Intimate Partner Violence Against Women in the United States.* Atlanta, GA: Center for Disease Control and Prevention.

National Coalition Against Domestic Violence. 1998. "About the National Coalition Against Domestic Violence." *http://www.ncadv.org/.* 2002.

National Domestic Hotline. 2003. "Hotline Services." *http://www.ndvh.org/.*

National Information Clearinghouse. 2001. "Understanding the Effects of Maltreatment on Early Brain Development." Washington, DC: U.S. Department of Health and Human Services.

National Resource Center on Domestic Violence. 2002. *Children Exposed to Intimate Partner Violence.* Harrisburg, PA: National Resource Center on Domestic Violence.

NCAVP. 2003. "National Report on Lesbian, Gay, Bisexual, and Transgender Domestic Violence in 2002." New York: National Coalition of Anti-Violence Programs.

NCH. 2002. *Why Are People Homeless?* Washington, DC: National Coalition for the Homeless.

Osofsky, Joy D. 2001. *Addressing Youth Victimization.* NCJ 186667. Washington, DC: U.S. Department of Justice.

Pagelow, Mildred D. 1984. *Family Violence.* New York: Praeger Publishers.

Rennison, Callie. 2003. *Intimate Partner Violence, 1993–2001.* Bureau of Justice Statistics. NCJ 197838. Washington, DC: U.S. Department of Justice.

Rennison, Callie Marie. 2001. *Intimate Partner Violence and Age of Victim, 1993–99.* NCJ 187635. Washington, DC: U.S. Department of Justice.

Rennison, Callie M., and Sarah Welchans. 2000. *Intimate Partner Violence.* NCJ 178247. Washington, DC: U.S. Department of Justice.

Rennison, Callie Marie. 2000. *Criminal Victimization 1999: Changes 1998–99 with Trends 1993–99.* Bureau of Justice Statistics, National Crime Victimization Survey. NCJ 182734. Washington, DC: U.S. Department of Justice.

Ristock, Janic L. 2002. *No More Secrets: Violence in Lesbian Relationships.* New York: Routledge.

Rodrigues, M., H. Bauer, E. McLoughlin, and K. Grumbach. 1999. "Screening and Intervention for Intimate Partner Abuse: Practices and Attitudes of Primary Care Physicians." *Journal of the American Medical Association,* 282(5), 468–474.

Rudman, W. 2000. *Coding and Documentation of Domestic Violence.* Washington, DC: Family Violence Prevention Fund.

Sigmon, Jane, and Jane Edmunds. 2002. "Victimization of Individuals with Disabilities." Chapter 15 in *National Victim Assistance Academy: Foundations in Victimology and Victims' Rights and Services.* Washington, DC: Office for Victims of Crime.

Struve, Jim. 1990. "Dancing with Patriarchy: The Politics of Sexual Abuse." Pp. 3–45 in *The Sexually Abused Male,* Vol. I, Mic Hunter (ed.). New York: Lexington Books.

Summit, Roland. 1982. "Beyond Belief: The Reluctant Discovery of Incest." In *Women's Sexual Experience: Explorations of the Dark Continent,* Martha Kirkpatrick (ed.). New York: Plenum Press.

Tifft, Larry L. 1993. *Battering of Women: The Failure of Intervention and the Case for Prevention.* Boulder, CO: Westview Press.

Tjaden, Patricia, and Nancy Thoennes. 1998. *Prevalence, Incidence, and Consequences of the Violence Against Women: Findings from the National Violence Against Women Survey.* NCJ 172837. Washington, DC: U.S. Department of Justice.

Tjaden, Patricia, and Nancy Thoennes. 2000. *Extent, Nature, and Consequences of Intimate Partner Violence: Findings from the National Violence Against Women Survey.* NCJ 181867. Washington, DC: U.S. Department of Justice.

Von Hentig, Hans. 1948. *The Criminal and His Victim: Studies in the Socio-Biology of Crime.* New Haven, CT: Yale University Press.

Walker, Lenore E. 1995. "Battered Women and Learned Helplessness." Pp. 243–51 in *Family Violence: Readings in the Social Sciences and Professions,* James Makepeace (ed.). New York: McGraw-Hill.

Whitfield, Charles, Robert Anda, Shanta Dube, and Vincent Felitti. 2003. "Violent Childhood Experiences and the Risk of Intimate Partner Violence in Adults: Assessment in a Large Health Maintenance Organization." *Journal of Interpersonal Violence* 18(2):166–85.

Widom, Cathy S. 2000. "Childhood Victimization: Early Adversity, Later Psychopathology." *National Institute of Justice Journal* NCJ 180077. Washington, DC: National Institute of Justice.

Widom, Cathy S., and Michael G. Maxfield. 2001. *An Update on the "Cycle of Violence."* NCJ 184894. Washington, DC: National Institute of Justice.

Wolfgang, Marvin. 1975. *Patterns in Criminal Homicide.* Montclair, NJ: Patterson Smith.

Yoshioka, Marianne R., Quynh Dang, Nanda Shewmangal, Carmen Chan, and Cheng Imm Tan. 2000. *Asian Family Violence Report: A Study of the Cambodian, Chinese, Korean, South Asian, and Vietnamese Communities in Massachusetts.* Boston, MA: Asian Task Force Against Domestic Violence, Inc.

Part Three

Crime Identification

Generally, the level of brutality in an abuse situation determines the severity of the domestic crime that has been committed. Some crimes stand out and deserve particular attention due to their unique characteristics or brutality. The classification of an act as a domestic violence crime may be based on the nature of the offense or the vulnerability of the victim population. Are women and children particularly vulnerable as abuse victims? Is the problem of child abuse or woman battering overstated? Do elders need additional legal protections? At what point should police intervene in protecting elders against their wishes?

Throughout Chapter 5, "Dynamics of Partner Violence," we look at the role of substance abuse and the characteristics of abusers to better understand the occurrences of partner violence. Is there more than one type of abuser? Does it make a difference whether the relationship is between heterosexual or homosexual adult partners? What are the common characteristics of abusive men? Female offenders, though small in numbers, are included in this chapter. Date rape is also examined. We present many common characteristics of marital sexual offenders and delve into the research that often guides policy decision making. Interventions aimed at stopping battering are explained. New information on programs for persons who batter elders is included in this third edition.

In Chapter 6, "Recognizing Child Abuse," we delve into the forms of domestic violence perpetrated against children and the indicators of this abuse category. Emotional and psychological abuses are the most frequently reported types of child maltreatment and are often indicators of physical and/or sexual abuse crimes. Can the location of abrasions, bruises, lacerations, and welts aid in the difficult determination of child abuse versus child accidents? What are the symptoms of sexual abuse? When should a parent be charged with parental kidnapping? Who are the people mandated by law to report cases of abuse and neglect of children? These are some of the questions answered.

"The Identification of Elder Abuse," Chapter 7, addresses the unique problems associated with old age. What choices does an elder have when he or she is in ill health and dependent on a family member for care? At what point does gift giving turn into financial exploitation? Who makes this determination? Are adult children responsible for providing care for an infirm parent? Why don't we hear more about the sexual abuse of elders? Who is mandated to report elder abuse and neglect to the authorities? New in the third edition is a discussion of the styles of violence from the perspective of the offender.

CHAPTER 5

DYNAMICS OF PARTNER VIOLENCE

SIMPLY SCENARIO

Police Officers Who Batter

Jill has recently moved in together with the police officer she had been dating. Due to his shift work and demanding overtime schedule, he bought her a cell phone so that they could keep in touch during the day. One day she had gone shopping and forgot to turn the phone on. When he came home Al was furious, accusing her of cheating on him. He was yelling and throwing things around the house. Jill was very angry and yelled back at him, demanding that he leave her house. Al responded by pushing her down, then he started to kick her repeatedly. When Al left Jill went to the hospital and received treatment for broken ribs. She was frightened—after all he is a police officer!

Question: What is the policy recommended by the International Association of Chiefs of Police?

KEY TERMS

Attachment theory
Exploder offender
Family systems model
Marital rape
Mutual battering

Patriarchal theory
Power and control wheel
Self-defending victims
Tyrannical offender
Unified court system

INTRODUCTION

> The difference between domestic violence and most other fields is that the theoretical debate affects the practice of the professionals that deal with the problems. (Healey & Smith, 1998)

The closer we look at domestic abusers, the more significant their differences appear. As we recognize numerous forms of family violence, no single theory seems to fit all the categories. Yet batterer programs and criminal justice practices have been based on these models! The intervention may not be appropriate—it may even make things worse. If we are to make an impact on the problem, it becomes important to understand the offenders and the available strategies, in addition to those theories that drive them. In the first part of the chapter we focus on the perpetrators of domestic battering. In the second half we examine domestic rape and sexual assault offenders.

The dispute between the **family systems model** and the feminist position is one example. It is often a heated and uncompromising debate. The **patriarchal theory** assumes that the major cause of domestic violence is the social order, where men are the offenders and women are the victims. It stresses the empowerment of women and the criminal prosecution of assaultive men. Men's power over and control of women is believed to occur through psychological and emotional abuse as well as physical assault and rape. Aggressive law enforcement action, including mandatory arrest policies, has become a typical response. Therapy involving couples is strongly discouraged in this model because it encourages the victim to discuss openly issues that may later be used by the batterer. The terms *educational* and *psychoeducational* are associated with interventions based on this perspective.

On the other hand, the family systems theory assumes that the major cause of family assaults is inadequate interpersonal skills and a dysfunctional relationship. The anger and frustration that results is believed to lead to violence. Batterer intervention emphasizes building communications skills and may involve the use of couples counseling with the aim of family preservation (Healey & Smith, 1998). Power inequality is only one of the problems that is addressed through joint counseling. According to this perspective, both partners may contribute to the escalation of conflict, and either partner may resort to violence. No one is considered the perpetrator or the victim, even if only one person is physically violent. Intervention that is termed couples therapy is usually associated with the family systems approach.

The focus on standardizing batterer programs developed during the mid-1980s as a response to interventions that were deemed by political activists as distancing the problem from its intended focus on the oppression of women and of concerns that rehabilitation might overshadow the safety issues for victims (Austin & Dankwort, 1998). By 1997 forty-five states had developed, or were in the process of developing, standards for batterer intervention programs (Austin & Dankwort, 1998). Currently 90 percent of these batterer intervention programs are based on the power and control feminist model (Austin & Dankwort, 1998). Arguing that standardizing domestic violence intervention infringes on their right to practice according to their professional training, some professionals in the mental health community strongly criticize proscribing practice in the absence of empirical evidence to support particular interventions (Austin & Dankwort, 1998).

Family systems interventions are therefore less common than the other models and have limited application for criminal justice professionals who are looking for alternatives. Individually based models represent the third major theoretical intervention approach. This category includes the psychological theories that attribute domestic violence to personality disorders, the batterer's social environment during childhood, biological disposition, or attachment disorders. The term *group process* is usually associated with the psychotherapeutic interventions that target individual problems and/or build cognitive skills to help the batterer control violent behaviors (Healey et al., 1998). When treatment for domestic violence is suggested from the psychotherapeutic viewpoint, cognitive and behavior modification are often mentioned. Can these positions reconcile the major theoretical assumptions that appear to be mutually exclusive? A review of the literature suggests that the answer to this question becomes vitally important to the criminal justice community.

CHARACTERISTICS OF DOMESTIC VIOLENCE ABUSERS

The theories on the causes of family violence still do not tell us very much about the individual batterer. What type of person commits violence in a domestic relationship? What behaviors indicate an abusive partner?

The majority of heterosexual domestic violence victims are females who were physically assaulted by a male intimate partner, according to the National Violence Against Women Survey (Tjaden & Thoennes, 1998). An intimate partner is defined as a current or former spouse, opposite-sex cohabiting partner, same-sex cohabiting partner, date, or boyfriend or girlfriend. Estimates on heterosexual domestic violence suggest 85% of the perpetrators are male and 15% are female.

The National Violence Against Women Survey confirmed that male intimate partners were the most frequent perpetrators of adult rape and physical assault against women (Tjaden & Thoennes, 1998). Seventy-six percent of the women who were raped and/or physically assaulted since the age of 18 reported being assaulted by a current or former husband, cohabiting partner, or date, compared to 17.9 percent of the men. Relatives other than the spouse accounted for assaults toward 8.6 percent of women and 6.8 percent of men. In a recent study of a sample of men who have intimate same-sex relationships, the incidence of violence was found to be quite high, approximately 2 out of 5 persons reported battering by a partner during the past five years (Greenwood et al., 2002). Preliminary studies show that 22 to 46 percent of all lesbians have been in a physically violent same-sex relationship (Renzetti & Miley,

1996) and the rate of perpetration may be as high as 50 percent within the population (NCAVP, 2003).

Descriptions of the Batterer

The following descriptors have developed from studies on the battering male. Although illustrating the characteristics of an abusive male, they are listed here because they have been applied to the identification of perpetrators in homosexual and lesbian relationships, elder and child battering, and female offenders.

Controlling Behaviors.   A tendency for the abuser to dominate the victim has been noted in the various forms of domestic violence (Ramsey-Klawsnik, 1997). Sometimes the control is due to jealously; the perpetrator often seeks control over the victim's time, dress, and behavior. Controlling behaviors show contempt and a general lack of respect for the partner.

Excessive name-calling and putdowns are techniques used to attack the confidence of the victim and assure future dominance. Calling a partner a "bitch" or similar derogatory terms devalues the person. An abuser may refer to the other as a "pig," "lousy housekeeper," "bad mother," or "lousy father." The use of derogatory language

Figure 5–1   Perpetrators of domestic violence use a variety of techniques to control the victim.

in addressing one's partner may start as the intimates develop a familiarity with each other. Such a pattern is not legally prohibited. It signifies emotional abuse, however, which often accompanies physical battering.

Fear and Intimidation.   Fear and intimidation is achieved through violence or the perception of impending violence. Victims of repetitive abuse recall a particular "look" from the offender that serves as a warning signal of an explosion that is about to occur. A raised fist or hand in a threatening gesture serves the same purpose.

Discharging or displaying a firearm in or around the house or at pets is a severe form of intimidation. It is the ultimate display of power. Even the presentation of a weapon raises the level of acceptable violence that is difficult to decrease. Any direct or indirect threat that involves a gun or other weapon should not be taken lightly, due to the desperation that it signifies.

Killing or Mutilating a Pet.   There is a renewed interest in the link between domestic violence and animal abuse. If a batterer assaults or mutilates pets, he is more likely to kill a partner (Meuer, Seymour, & Wallace, 2002). Violence against pets is considered to be a predictor of adult violence in children. Adults who perpetrate domestic violence often abuse the victims' pet(s). One of the first empirical analyses of the prevalence of animal maltreatment in a small sample of battered women in shelter found that 71 percent of the women who reported current or past pet ownership reported that their partner had threatened and/or actually hurt or killed one or more of their pets (Ascione, 1998). Fifty-seven percent of the reports involved actual rather than threatened harm to pets. The killing of a pet is meant to convey the message, "you could be next." For the many victims of domestic violence there is no such thing as an idle threat.

A recent commentary entitled *Domestic Violence and Animal Abuse: The Deadly Connection* reported on a study of 111 battered women who sought shelter; almost half reported that their current or former male partners had threatened or abused their animals (Cohen & Kweller, 2000). Cited was an example where a man, whose wife went to a shelter, sent a picture of him using gardening shears to chop off the ears of his wife's dog. After receiving the photo the wife told the shelter counselor she had to go home to save the lives of her dog and other animals. Abusers harm animals to

---

Been There . . . Done That!

Penny recounted coming home in the near dark one evening to find the severed head of her horse in the walkway. She recoiled in horror, asking herself, "Why would he do such a horrible thing?" Many years later, Walter still shoots at trees around the perimeter of her country home that he has been restricted from entering through a permanent court order.

punish their wives for leaving and for real or imagined injustices. Common types of cruelty include torture, shooting, stabbing, drowning, burning, and bone breaking.

Manipulation.   Abusers have been characterized as the masters of manipulation. After an abusive attack, it is not unusual for the offender to beg for forgiveness. Gifts and flowers may accompany the statements that they will never "do it" again. Another destructive behavior is the unrealistic demand for proof of love or loyalty characteristic in abusive dating relationships. Coercion into sexual relations as a condition of a continued relationship can be extremely dangerous for the victim during a dating relationship.

Excessive Rule Making.   When a partner makes rules that the other must follow, it signifies an unequal relationship based on dominance. One way to recognize this pattern is to notice when a penalty or punishment is attached to the failure to fulfill expectations. A healthy request does not begin with the phrase "you had better . . ." and it is not followed with the statement, "or else . . .". Taking back a gift or present because "you are not a good girl" indicates an anticipation of rule following by the abuser. It implies that some form of punishment will result for unfulfilled expectations.

Isolation.   The role of geographical isolation is explained by Neil Websdale in *Rural Woman Battering and the Justice System.* Women who live in secluded areas with no public transportation report not having had any friends for years (Websdale, 1998). Websdale suggests that the choice to reside in isolated areas of the country may stem from their batterers' calculated decision. Control tactics include removing the phone receiver (when the batterer goes to work), disabling or destroying motor vehicles to limit the victim's mobility, closely monitoring the odometer reader on motor vehicles, and locking the thermostat in the winter (as a form of torture).

B e e n   T h e r e . . . D o n e   T h a t !

Penny knew that her husband did not like her to have friends over to the house. He made it quite clear. But she was a self-employed woman who was confident about herself and of the friends that meant so much to her. During the early years of their marriage she continued to invite them. Over time she drifted away from them—it became too difficult, she stated. She thought she was going mad and couldn't face them with the confusion that she felt. Things that she did, she couldn't remember doing or didn't ever know. For example, the plates were kept in the cupboard to the right of the sink. Then they were on the left side. They always were, said her spouse. The clothes she wore were in her bedroom closet, or were they kept in the hall closet? Dog food was always in the cellar—why was it in the garage? Years later, she realized that she was not going crazy at all—it was her husband who had tried to convince her otherwise. He frequently moved things and insisted that she was "losing it." He loved her; she had believed it.

Demands for constant attention to the exclusion of friends and family are one form of isolating the victim. Although it may be attractive in the beginning of a relationship, it becomes a form of isolation when the abuser insists on being the only focus of the victim's life. Extreme forms include demands that the victim not work, or denial of transportation to leave the home. These accomplish economic and physical isolation that cuts the victim off from resources or protection from abuse.

The Role of Drugs and Alcohol in Domestic Violence

In October 1997, the National Institute of Justice released findings from a research study conducted in 1995 in Memphis, Tennessee, on the extent of drug and alcohol use/abuse in domestic violence incidents. The report, entitled *Drugs, Alcohol, and Domestic Violence in Memphis*, revealed important data (Brookoff, 1997):

- Almost all assailants had used drugs or alcohol during the day of the assault.
- Two-thirds had used a dangerous combination of cocaine and alcohol.
- The vast majority of those assaulted were repeat victims of the current assailants.
- Two-thirds of the assailants were on probation or parole at the time of the assault.
- A majority of battering incidents involved the assailant's use or display of a weapon.
- A number of victims suffered injuries severe enough to require immediate medical attention.
- Based on these findings, researchers recommended that future responses to domestic violence should include (1) testing assailants at the time of arrest for alcohol or other drug intoxication; (2) detoxifying arrested drug- or

Figure 5–2 Do not refer to strangulation as choking; this is strangulation.

alcohol-dependent assailants prior to release from jail; (3) assessing children who directly witness domestic violence to determine if psychological treatment is needed; and (4) allowing domestic assault victims to swear out arrest warrants at the scene.

One-half of all state inmates and a third of convicted jail inmates serving time for a violent crime against an intimate reported that they had been drinking for six or more hours prior to the offense (Bureau of Justice Statistics, 1998). Researchers estimate that one-fourth to one-half of men who commit acts of domestic violence also have substance-abuse problems.

There is substantial evidence of a link between alcohol use and domestic violence. Between 1980 and 1988, the results of 23 studies on batterers indicated that 24 to 86 percent had prior histories of drug and/or alcohol abuse (Burnley et al., 1996). Some experts suggest that perpetrators drink alcohol in order to become violent (Gelles, 1974). Aggression has also been linked with psychoactive drugs such as barbiturates, amphetamines, opiates, phencyclidine, cocaine, and alcohol–cocaine combinations (Fagan, 1990). The need to achieve personal power and control through woman abuse may be similar to the origins for substance abuse (Gondolf, 1995).

Larry Bennett shatters the myth that substance abuse begets domestic violence (Bennett, 1997). He conducted a study in 1995 that shows that while there is a 50 to 70 percent overlap between batterers and substance abusers, other studies indicate that 75 percent of batterers are not drinking when they batter, and 80 percent of heavy drinkers don't batter at all. Bennett acknowledges that the two forms of abuse appear to be linked because both may be related to feelings of powerlessness, but he suggests that power is a critical factor in whether someone batters. Drinking tends to increase men's sense of personal power, which can lead to a higher "need" for dominance. Substance abuse is most likely first used as a vehicle, than as an excuse for being controlling and violent.

In 1999 the Safety and Sobriety: Best Practices in Domestic Violence and Substance Abuse task force agreed on the following principles relative to domestic violence and substance abuse (Bennett, 1999):

- Substance abuse problems and domestic violence overlap and they often co-occur. However, substance abuse and domestic violence are different problems, and they require different interventions.
- There are multiple causes for both substance abuse and for domestic violence. There is little evidence that one problem causes the other.
- Active substance abuse by the perpetrator of domestic violence or active substance abuse by the victim of domestic violence threatens the safety of the victim.
- Domestic violence impairs the opportunity for addiction recovery and threatens sobriety.

Figure 5-3 Substance abuse frequently is associated with domestic battering.

Regardless of setting, workers in all fields will be more effective if they consider the perspectives of safety, sobriety, and justice for the people with whom they work.

Substance Abuse and Elders.   Heavy alcohol use is reported by 13 percent of men and 2 percent of women aged 60 to 94 (Knauer, 2003). As the body ages, the normal effects of alcohol are compounded along with the possibility of drug interactions and falls for the elder. Alcohol abuse by either the victim or the perpetrator increases the risk of domestic elder abuse (Knauer, 2003). Heavy drinking by an elder may also be a sign of ongoing or severe victimization (Osgood & Manetta, 2002).

In a recent study of domestic violence comparisons by age cohorts, elder women were victimized at a lower rate compared to young and middle-aged women (Rennison & Rand, 2003). These women aged 55 and older reported that their perpetrator was under the influence of alcohol or drugs in nearly half of the instances. Over 60 percent of the perpetrators against the older women were their current spouse; reports were made to the police in only half of the violent occurrences.

Abusive Men

Remember that the majority of domestic violence perpetrators are men, according to government studies that use arrest as a criterion. The average abuser brought to court for restraining orders or to police attention for a domestic disturbance call is 32 years

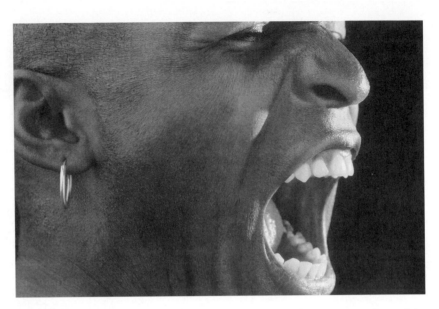

Figure 5–4 The vast majority of domestic violence is perpetrated by men.

old, with two-thirds being in their mid-twenties (Burnley et al., 1996). They often have low self-esteem and are overly dependent on the victim. Most are extremely jealous and possessive. Almost always the abuser blames others for his actions and denies or minimizes the effects of his violence on his victims. Abusers often present a very different posture in public than they do in the privacy of their own homes. Although they may be charming on the outside, they can terrorize their partner behind closed doors!

Personality risk factors in male batterers include

- Aggressive and hostile personality
- Antisocial personality
- Depression
- Emotional dependency
- Insecurity
- Low impulse control
- Low empathy
- Narcissism
- Poor communication and social skills

Next we look at some specific red-flag identification characteristics in these men.

1. *Men who abuse alcohol and other drugs.* As noted previously, substance abuse often coexists with domestic battering.

2. *Men who have explosive tempers.* Daniel Sonkin and Michael Durphy state that abusive men often confuse anger and violence (Sonkin & Durphy, 1997). Violence is just one expression of anger; abusive men insist that it is a behavior that can be controlled.

Experts caution against a one-size-fits-all description of the male batterer, however. In a review of the different types of men who abuse their spouses, colleagues Holtzworth-Monroe and Stuart categorize three types of violent men (Holtzworth-Monroe & Stuart, 1994):

1. *Family-only offenders.* The perpetrators in this category may have a history of exposure to aggression in their family of origin. Relative to nonviolent men, they are poor communicators and lack social skills. They rank as less deviant than the other two categories of men in areas of impulsivity, substance abuse, and criminal behavior. They would rarely require personality disorder treatment, according to Holtzworth-Monroe and Stuart.

2. *Dysphoric or borderline offenders.* These men are believed to have had a history of child abuse and parental rejection. Delinquent behavior has been an early indicator of problems for these men. They are marked by negative attitudes toward women and positive attitudes toward violence, coupled with low remorse. Additionally, this group has a high dependency on their partners and poor social and communication skills.

3. *Generally violent or antisocial offenders.* The batterer in this category is the most aggressive. He is profoundly deficient in communicating and social skills. Believed to have been abused as a child, he comes from a violent family of origin. This abuser has developed antisocial behavior and views violence as an appropriate response to any provocation due to his socialization. Treatment for personality disorder is suggested for this type of offender.

Police Officers Who Batter. Of particular concern to professionals is the abuser who is legitimately carrying a firearm for work, business, or pleasure. Acts of domestic violence by a police officer against a partner are estimated to be at least as common as acts committed by the general population. Recent limited research indicates the possibility of higher incident rates of domestic violence among law enforcement professionals, according to the International Association of Chiefs of Police (IACP, 1999). The IACP takes the position that the problem exists at some serious level and deserves careful attention regardless of estimated occurrences.

Research also indicates that documentation of such incidents by departments varies dramatically, with some incidents reported in great detail, others handled through informal actions, and still others undocumented in any way. Departmental positions on police officer domestic violence also significantly differ: Some departments have clear "zero tolerance" positions, other departments have less-defined positions, and still others have no articulated position at all. In cooperation with the Violence Against Women Office, IACP worked to develop a comprehensive policy response for reports of police battering. The IACP 2003 policy on *Domestic Violence by Police Officers* establishes the policy and procedures for handling domestic violence committed by police officers. It recognizes that federal law prohibits police officers convicted of qualifying misdemeanor domestic violence crimes from possessing firearms and states that officers found guilty of a domestic violence crime through criminal proceedings shall be terminated (IACP, 2003).

Perpetrators in Gay Male Relationships.   Domestic violence is considered one of the most severe health problems facing gay men today. Gay perpetrators exhibit negative behavioral traits that are similar to those of heterosexual offenders, such as a narcissistic personality and the externalization of blame (Potoc/ niak et al., 2003). Coercion, jealousy, criticism, isolating of the victim, lying, and humiliation are noted as typical controlling behaviors (Merrill, 1998).

In *Men Who Beat the Men Who Love Them*, authors David Island and Patrick Letellier describe the following characteristics of violent gay males:

1. Gay batterers are those who are unclear on the concept of masculinity. For gay men the concept of masculinity is confused because being gay itself is considered unmasculine in our culture. Negative stereotypes about how men should behave are adopted by these males in their attempt to control others so that they are not controlled. Island and Letellier reject the overgeneralization of gender-role stereotyping and patriarchal rhetoric, however. They insist that the majority of men in the United States cannot be identified as aggressive, sexist patriarchs.

2. They choose to abuse their lovers. Most men do not batter; those gay men who engage in family violence do so by choice. The authors call it the "cowards' choice."

3. Their violence is criminal. Committing an act against a gay lover is no less a crime than in any other domestic relationship. It cannot be explained away as a "lovers' quarrel" or minimized because of the sexual orientation.

4. The conduct is a learned dysfunctional behavior. Since battering is a learned condition, it is treatable. Gay abusers should be classified by the psychological community as dysfunctional and afforded opportunities for treatment.

Male Perpetrators of Dating Violence.   Men who have a family history of observing or experiencing abuse are more likely to inflict abuse, violence, and sexual aggression during the courtship years. As the consumption of alcohol by either the victim or perpetrator increases, the rate of serious injuries associated with dating violence also increases. Studies have found the following to be associated with sexual assault perpetration: the male having sexually aggressive peers; heavy alcohol or drug use; the man's acceptance of dating violence; the male's assumption of key roles in dating such as initiating the date, being the driver, and paying dating expenses; miscommunication about sex; previous sexual intimacy with the victim; interpersonal violence; traditional sex roles; adversarial attitudes about relationships; and rape myths.

Abusive Women

Some evidence suggests that women perpetrate minor violence in domestic relationships at an equal rate to men (Straus et al., 1980). This fact is highly disputed; however, the rate of female offenders convicted of felonies has grown at more than two times the rate of increase in male defendants. Almost three out of four violent victimizations committed by female offenders are simple assaults compared to half of the violence committed by male offenders (Greenfeld, & Snell, 2000). Based on self-reports of victims of violence, women account for approximately 14 percent of violent offenders, an annual average of about 2.1 million violent female offenders (Greenfeld & Snell, 2000).

Lesbian battering is believed to be occurring as often as heterosexual domestic violence (Renzetti & Miley, 1996). Young women are suspected to be the instigators of violence in the majority of dating relationships, according to numerous studies (Sugarman & Hotaling, 1998). Physical abuse against children is as likely to be committed by mothers as by fathers (U.S. Department of Health and Human Services, 1996). Domestic battery in elderly couples may be perpetrated more often by the woman (Wolf, 1996). On the surface it appears as though women are as capable as men of being violent and acting out the tendency.

Critics argue that there is no such thing as a battered husband syndrome. Government studies indicate that approximately 15 percent of perpetrators against men are women. In the majority of these cases, the female is responding to long-term wife battering (Hattendorf & Tollerund, 1997). In every report that documents women as offenders, a disclaimer is attached: Most are believed to be **self-defending victims**. What does this mean? Self-defending victims are women who use physical aggression to prevent further injury; they are not batterers but victims. They are believed to be women who act in self-defense against the men that are abusing them. If there is a typology that can describe a woman prone to violence, it has not been forthcoming. There is no argument among professionals that women receive severe injuries from male battering and that this type of battering is in no way comparable with women's battering of men.

Lesbian Domestic Offenders.   The feminist model of power and control is often used to describe the context of battering within a lesbian relationship. In discussing lesbian teen abuse, authors Levy and Lobel state that the same elements of hierarchy, power, ownership, entitlement, and control exist in lesbian as in nonlesbian relationships (Levy & Lobel, 1998). An added isolation for these young women exists due to their sexual orientation and resulting homophobia. Like most teens, they have difficulty trusting adults; additionally, they have few supportive peer relationships.

Been There . . . Done That!

Marilyn was a middle-aged professional woman in a ten-year relationship. The reality that her lesbian partner was leaving did not sink in until Betty came home to pack her belongings, bringing her new companion for support. Marilyn burst into the room waving a gun. Stating that she could not stand it any longer, she threatened to kill herself and maybe take someone with her. Fortunately, the two women were able to get out of the house and call the police. After hours of negotiation, the STOP team was able to remove Marilyn to safety without anyone being hurt.

Young lesbians are at risk of being trapped in abusive relationships with no role models and no resources. While many similarities exist between lesbian offenders and heterosexual perpetrators, a number of significant differences do exist. Dynamics of the abuse may also include HIV-related abuse, heterosexism, and homo/biphobia. Gender-based theory that is typically used to explain male domestic violence offending dynamics may also be applicable to understanding lesbian offenders. Lesbian victimization in this perspective is a patriarchal social construct rather than a biological fact (Ristock, 2002). Domestic violence is seen clearly as a pattern of behaviors designed to control another and that women as well as men are capable of physical, sexual, emotional, verbal, and economic abuse and other controlling behaviors (Peterman & Dixon, 2003).

The forms of violence include physical, sexual, and emotional abuse. The editors of *Violence in Gay and Lesbian Domestic Partnerships* suggest that lesbian battering is

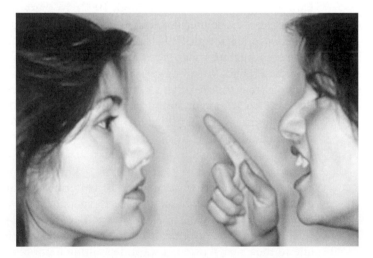

Figure 5–5   Are women becoming more violent?

often dismissed by myths of mutual battering and notions that women can't really harm each other. This dismissal puts the victims of domestic violence at risk for future harm and emboldens the perpetrators (Renzetti & Miley, 1996).

Female Offenders and Dating Violence.   David Sugarman and Gerald Hotaling refer to dating or courtship physical violence as a problem of pandemic proportions (Sugarman & Hotaling, 1998). Major studies on the gender of the offender suggest that women have higher levels than men of both inflicting and sustaining physical dating violence.

In contrast, Walter DeKeseredy and Martin Schwartz are openly annoyed at the contention that "women do it too" when it comes to discussions on intimate violence (DeKeseredy & Schwartz, 1998). They point out that there is a scarcity of solid empirical information about the men who claim to be battered by women. In their analysis of dating violence, they delved into the question of why women use violence during courtship. A common motive for violence was self-defense, they found; a majority of women did not initiate an attack. Moreover, women using defensive violence experienced higher rates of severe victimization, including physical and sexual assault after they had used defensive violence.

Two recent studies of university students also reported high incidence of female offending in dating relationships. Straus and Ramirez stated that women self-reported physical assaults against their partner at a rate of 32 percent versus 29 percent males revealing (Straus & Ramirez, 1999). The higher incidence of female offending appeared to be linked to a history of prior criminal offending. Rates of physical offending for both males and females were similar in a similar study of undergraduate and graduate students (Hanard, 2001). Hanard suggests that this research differs from other social studies, indicating that females were victimized more frequently because there was no consideration regarding the impact of such violence.

No research has documented the characteristics of females that physically assault their courtship partners. The consequences for personal violence differ significantly between the sexes, however. Typically, women are injured more frequently and severely when they are victimized by violence.

Mutual Battering: Challenging Criminal Justice

The idea of mutual battering in domestic violence is one of great controversy and presents enormous challenges to the criminal justice community. In the heterosexual community, it implies that both men and women initiate physical and emotional violence to resolve conflicts in the relationship. We typically think of domestic abuse as gender specific: a male batterer and a female victim. In mutual battering, both parties are believed to be equally involved in initiating the violence, although not necessarily at the same time. Mutual battering as an explanation for domestic abuse blurs this picture of who is the victim and who is the perpetrator. The victim and offender roles may not exist in this relationship or may change as one or the other becomes the aggressor.

The challenge for the criminal justice community is in assigning blame. One party must be responsible and held accountable in the criminal justice paradigm. Some police officers respond by arresting both the male and female in the domestic violence dispute to avoid having to sort it out. This practice of mutual arrest is strongly discouraged by the courts. Not only does it confuse the court as to how to proceed, but it often results in neither party's being prosecuted. Victims are not being protected and batterers are empowered. In addition, this tactic serves to punish the victims of domestic violence because they are being put before the court as if they were the abusers.

Dismissing domestic abuse as **"mutual battering"** causes concern to those confronting problems of violence within homosexual and lesbian communities. Abuse among same-sex couples can be confusing to law enforcement officers; traditionally, they have looked at gender and physical size when determining who is at fault in a domestic dispute. A clearer picture of who is in need can be made when one person is obviously dominant in a relationship due to stature or gender. When the relationship involves two persons of the same gender, the determination becomes more difficult. Critics argue that police officers dismiss claims of same-sex battering as "mutual" rather than taking the time to access the situation adequately. The failure to assign any blame by viewing the situation as mutual is detrimental to the victim.

Experts are beginning to acknowledge the dilemma and offer direction on how to proceed. In a domestic dispute, determine the primary physical aggressor! Healy and colleagues explain this criterion (Healey et al., 1998):

Figure 5–6   The primary aggressor determination is not based on gender, nor is the physically larger partner always the primary aggressor.

1. Do not assume that the physically larger partner is always the primary aggressor. Care must be taken to question the couple and any witnesses closely before making an arrest.

2. Be aware that bruises may take hours to appear, whereas signs of defensive violence, such as scratching or biting, are immediate. Question the partners separately and determine how the visible marks were made, and why. Did the victim bite an arm that was holding him or her down, for example?

3. Determine if there has been a history of abuse. Batterers tend to recommit. It is more likely that the perpetrator of violence in the past has perpetrated again. Ask if there has been a recent escalation in the violence, and why.

4. Victims may feel free to express their anger about the violence to police. Anger or the expression of anger should not be mistaken for primary aggressive behavior.

5. Do not allow yourself to be provoked into arresting both partners. An angry victim's conduct is not a justification for arresting. Failure to "shut up" is not criminal behavior or indicative of who the batterer is.

6. Determine who the initial aggressor was. When signs of injury are exhibited by both parties, consider the possibility of self-defense and examine the relative level of injury or force involved.

Elder Battering

Compared to other forms of family violence, elder abuse research is in its infancy. In part due to the demographics of aging in the United States, increased attention has been focused on elder issues. In 1990, the over-65 age group accounted for just 4 percent of the population. Between 1989 and 2030, the 65-year-old and over population is expected to more than double; the 85-year-old and over group is expected to triple. An increased demand for domestic violence protective services has already been noted for this second age group. Indications are that resources will continue to be in demand as the elder population explodes.

The information on perpetration for elder violence is conflicting. In some studies, spouses were found more likely than adult children to abuse elders physically; adult children were more likely than spouses to abuse elders financially (Brandl & Cook-Daniels, 2002). The largest category of perpetrators (47.3 percent) of the substantiated incidents of elder abuse are the adult children of the victims (Administration on Aging [AOA], 1998). Spouses represented the second largest group of perpetrators, comprising 19.3 percent in the AOA study. Some studies found more females perpetrate abuse than males; others found males the primary offenders. Clearly more information is needed on the perpetration of elder violence.

The National Center on Elder Abuse estimates that for every incident of elder abuse or neglect that is reported, approximately five go unreported (Administration on Aging, 1998). The popular myth that abuse in later life is caused by stressed caregivers has been found untrue, one of the few areas where the researchers agree (Brandl & Cook-Daniels, 2002). Elder violence has similar characteristics to battering in younger relationships. Professionals who believe that abusers are stressed caregivers are likely to unwittingly collude with the batterer by accepting their excuses (Brandl, 2000).

Similar to the violence in heterosexual relationships, changes occur over time within gay male relationships. The extent of violence within elder homosexual relationships is less frequent than their younger counterparts, but this incidence appears to be on the rise (Peterman & Dixon, 2003). Men younger than 40 are approximately 6 times as likely to report multiple forms of partner violence as men aged 60 or older (Greenwood et al., 2002).

Elder Abuse Offender Characteristics.   Holly Ramsey-Klawsnik has proposed a new typology of five elder abuse offenders along with their characteristics (2000):

1. *Overwhelmed offenders:* These are well-intentioned and capable individuals who are unable to meet the demands of caring for the elder. Victims may feel guilty for "causing" the abuse and the offender often feels shame and remorse.
2. *Impaired offenders:* These are well-intentioned care providers that have physical or mental impairments where they do not realize the inappropriateness of their actions. Improper use of restraints and medications is common in this category of abuser.
3. *Narcissistic offenders:* These are not involved with the elder out of good intentions. They treat the elder like an object and lack empathy or support. Financial abuse is not uncommon for this offender.
4. *Domineering or bullying offenders:* These are prone to outbursts of rage. Demanding and explosive, they misuse relationships to justify exerting coercive control over others.
5. *Sadistic offenders:* These enjoy harming, humiliating, terrifying, and overpowering others. They are extremely harmful to an elder. They are prone to inflict severe, chronic, multifaceted abuse, including human bite marks, burns, sexual and physical assaults, assaults to genitals, and restraining the elder.

HIGH-RISK VIOLENCE

Most researchers agree that domestic battering is a pattern of behavior that follows somewhat predictable stages. As noted earlier in this chapter, the frequency of the abuse differs depending on the relationship. In severe cases, the battering incidents may be as frequent as 60 times a year, while the average abuse cycle occurs only about 5 times a year (Straus, 1993). The length of time in each stage also can vary from hours to weeks. Education groups for men who batter frequently use the **power and control wheel** developed by the Duluth model to illustrate the elements of a battering relationship. The tactics used by the batterer are similar to those used to sustain many other forms of group domination (Pence & Paymar, 1993). According to the authors of *Education Groups for Men Who Batter*, even though the men may feel out of control when battering, the actions are intentional. At the core of the cycle is the element of power and control—all actions are for the purpose of dominating and controlling the spouse. Each cog in the wheel represents a form of behavior that in total makes up the abusive conduct. This represents the feminist idea of the battering relationship.

Murray Straus questions the appropriateness of applying criminal justice sanctions to all family disputes. Acknowledging that the police and courts are not equipped to understand the unique circumstances of each family that can lead to violence, he argues that they also cannot be expected to determine what the best interest of either the victim, the offender, or the family might be. Additionally, numerous reports have indicated that in approximately half of the cases, women are the first to commit a physical assault. If men are arrested "only" for slapping their wives a few times, shouldn't women receive equal treatment? "If even half of the domestic assaults came to the attention of the police, the courts would have to deal with literally millions of such incidents and would be overwhelmed" (Straus, 1993).

Risk Factors

It is necessary to distinguish between high-risk violence and the more usual marital violence, according to Straus. The high-risk offenders assault their partners on an average of 60 times per year, whereas the partners of battered women in the general population engaged in an average of 5 assaults a year. Straus suggests the following checklist to help identify high-risk cases (1993):

Been There . . . Done That!

The relationship was over—moving out was the next step. Debbie explained that she had returned home one day to an ominous setting that convinced her that moving day had come! He had "set up" the house to appear as though he had committed suicide, she stated. The gun drawer was left open, with an empty holster and an open box of ammunition. The house alarm was not set. All indications were that he was somewhere in the house, possibly dead or dying, maybe lying in wait for her. She made an excruciating search through every closet, behind every door, and throughout the cellar before she realized he was not there at all. Then another fear set in: He would be back, and he had a loaded weapon on him! What would happen then?

Figure 5–7 Power and control wheel: Duluth model. *(From* Education Groups for Men Who Batter *[1993, copyrighted], Ellen Pence and Michael Paymar, Springer Publishing Company, Inc., New York 10012. Adpated by permission.)*

Criterion A

- Suspect initiated three or more instances of violence in the preceding year

Criterion B

- Threatened partner with a weapon in hand or verbally threatened to kill the partner

- Medical treatment needed by the victim (regardless of whether it was obtained)
- Physical abuse of a child
- Physical abuse when a child
- Severe violence between parents
- Drunk more than five times in the past year
- Drug abuse in the past year
- Extreme dominance or attempts to achieve such dominance
- Thinks there are some situations when it is okay for a man to hit his wife
- Physically forced sex on the partner
- Extensive or repeated destruction of property
- Threats or actual killing or injuring of a pet
- History of psychological problems
- Assault of a nonfamily person or other violent crime
- Extreme jealousy and surveillance or restriction of partner
- Police involved in domestic assault incident in the preceding 12 months

Straus maintains that after identifying those most at risk for severe or repeated battering, programs to treat male batterers would be appropriate. The intervention is consistent with the feminist model. Since almost 90 percent of couples fall in the low-risk category, however, these might be more suited to the family theory approach of couples counseling, he suggests.

The idea that dangerousness might be predicted and appropriate interventions be made is an appealing one. In jurisdictions that do not mandate arrest as a police response, Straus's idea holds the greatest potential. Its usefulness is toward predictions of future occurrences. Since the information is most important to the victims, it should be shared with them. Victims can assess their own potential for severe attacks if they know the signs to look for. For that reason, therapists and domestic violence shelters frequently use a variation of the Straus list on predicting the dangerousness of the offender. Keep in mind that it is not necessary to satisfy all the elements for a prediction of dangerousness to be made.

According to the guidelines established by EMERGE, the first program in the United States to treat male batterers, concrete and direct questions must be asked of the batterer to determine dangerousness (Figure 5–8). Examples of the questions include, "And what happens when you lose your temper?" and "What about grabbing or shaking?" "Have you hit her?" "When you hit her, was it a slap or a punch?"

Styles of Violence

From the perspective of offenders themselves, two violent styles used by men against women have been identified. Both groups of men used violence as a method of response to intolerable emotions of anxiety or anger and were unable to state the

Duluth Curriculum: based on feminist theory; issues of power and control as primary targets.

Program structure: 2 or 3 sessions on each of eight themes: nonviolence; non-threatening behavior; respect; support and trust; honesty and accountability; sexual respect; partnership; negotiation and fairness.

EMERGE: blend of feminist educational approach with more in-depth and intensive group work.

Program structure: 48-week program divided into two stages: 8 weeks of orientation and 40 weeks of group work. About one-third of the batterers require additional time in the program.

Orientation topics include: defining domestic violence; negative vs. positive "self talk"; effects of violence on women; psychological, sexual and economic abuse; abusive vs. respectful communication; effects of partner abuse on children.

Groups meet weekly for 2 hours. Sessions typically include:
1. A short check-in to recount any conflicts during the week; a long check-in for new members to detail the last abusive episode and focus on batterer responsibility
2. Longer discussions concerning issues raised during check-in that focuses on alternatives to violence
3. Development of individualized goals based on current and past abuse

The Amend Model: blend of feminist educational approach with more in-depth and intensive group work.

Program structure: Variable—from 36 weeks to 5 years for the most difficult cases. AMEND takes a "multimodal" approach centered on group therapy, but it may also include some individual counseling or couples work.

Approach: AMEND's philosophy has seven tenets:
1. Belief in the feminist "power and control" theory of battering is central.
2. Intervention with batterers cannot be value-neutral—violence is a crime.
3. Counseling aims to teach behavior change to stop violence and abuse and addresses the psychological features of the batterer's problem.
4. Violence and abuse are choices, and the victims are not responsible for the violence.
5. Ending violence is a long-term process, from 1 to 5 years.
6. Ending violence is complex and requires "multimodal" intervention.
7. Treatment of batterers requires special skills and training.

Figure 5–8   The three major intervention programs are EMERGE, the Duluth curriculum, and the AMEND model. *(Adapted from Healy et al., 1998.)*

violence in terms of its impact on their partners. The characteristics of tyrannical offending versus exploder offending are described by authors James, Seddon, and Brown (2002) as follows:

The Tyrannical Offender

- Uses aggression, intimidation, verbal abuse, and physical assault to control and dominate his partner
- Knows what he is doing and intends to fright, intimidate, and punish his partner
- Sees his violence as justified or understandable response to frustration and anger
- Tends to minimize his violence by admitting to having committed verbal abuse
- Describes their partners as being submissive and careful around them

The Exploder Offender

- Experiences the violence as being out of control, sudden, and explosive, typically in response to partner criticisms, challenge, or pursuit (like being in his face)
- Uses the violence to get distance from his partner and to silence her
- Usually acknowledges that he has used violence, but blames his partners for provoking him

A different perspective on the typologies of batterers is offered by Gondolf (1992) as reported by Peterman and Dixon (2003). The typical batterer is one that has no personality disorder or diagnosable mental illness. Usually there is no criminal record associated with this person and he is not violent to people outside of the family. The sociopathic batterers may have a diagnosable personality disorder, a problem with substance abuse, and are more likely to severely injure their victims. Threats to kill or do more violence are associated with this type, along with a tendency to make sexual demands after committing the violence. These batterers are not apologetic and some-times use religious beliefs to justify the violence. The most dangerous group of offend-ers is the antisocial batterer. These individuals have diagnosable mental illnesses or personality disorders, substance abuse problems, and criminal records. They are more likely to have a criminal record.

DOMESTIC RAPE AND SEXUAL ASSAULT

Relatively little has changed in the characterization of rapists over the last decade. What is new is the application of this knowledge to our understanding of rape within a domestic relationship. As with every other family violence crime, a relationship between the victim and the perpetrator is not a factor in the determination of rape. It becomes an element only when the considered criminal charge is incest. Follow the criminal elements defined in your jurisdiction to determine if this crime has been committed. Consent is a legal consideration in cases that involve adults only. Consent is not an issue when rape is committed against a child.

Sexual offenders are best described initially through their diversity. Although sexual offenders are usually male, the offender sometimes is reported to be a female. They may be juveniles or elders and every age in between. Perpetrators are found in every race and ethnic background; they may be gay or straight, religious and nonreligious; professionals or criminals already found guilty for some other crime. A relatively unknown category is the sexual abuse of the elderly. The largest category of suspected offenders against elders is thought to consist of sons who were sexually abusing their elderly mothers (Ramsey-Klawsnik, 1991).

Marital Rape and Male Offenders

Sexual offenders who perpetrate in domestic relationships can readily be compared to stranger rapists. No personality or physical characteristics make them stand out from others. They are not identified through their social status, occupation, race, or ethnic group. Rapists may be power- or anger motivated (Bradway, 1990). Those who commit the crime of rape do so with purpose. It may be to confirm their own manhood or to express their manhood to the victims, as in the power rapist category. Anger rapists are considered extremely dangerous because they may obtain pleasure from inflicting pain and seek to degrade the female victims.

Authors David Finkelhor and Kersti Yllo graphically point out in *License to Rape: Sexual Abuse of Wives* that rape is not a trivial family quarrel over sex, with the man getting his way. It is a brutally forced act, designed to humiliate and harm the woman. In their study on the topic, one-fourth of the wives spoke of forced anal intercourse; a fifth stated that they were forced to perform oral sex; almost one-fourth of the women were raped in the presence of others, usually their children; and the majority reported brutal vaginal intercourse. These authors illustrated three types of **marital rape** (Finkelhor & Yllo, 1985):

1. *Battering rape.* Battered women are believed to be at high risk for marital rape. The type of man who beats his wife is also more likely to rape her.

2. *Force-only rape.* In relationships that have little or no other violence, force-only rape is linked with the power to control the frequency of sexual relations within the marriage. The assaults are typically after the woman has refused sex and is characterized by physical brutality of slapping, hitting, and holding the woman down despite her pleas for him to stop. The goal of the rapist is sexual conquest, by any force necessary.

3. *Obsessive rape.* This form of rape is characterized by the bizarre, strange, and perverse sexual interests and fantasies of the husband, often inflicting pain on the woman. An example provided by victims included being tied up and having objects inserted, as well as being burned, bitten, or beaten during the act.

Taking pictures of the wife is a common part of the abuse, according to Finkelhor and Yllo.

Had any of these forms of violence been perpetrated by a stranger, there is little doubt that the offender would be prosecuted if caught.

Female Sex Offenders

It is difficult to determine the exact prevalence of sexual abuse perpetrated by women since there are few studies that look strictly at that offender population. In her review of the literature on child sexual abuse, Kim Menard found a range of 1 percent to 32.5 percent of perpetrators who were women (Menard, 1997). She suggests that the disparity in female perpetration rates that exist among studies may be due to the criterion when defining abuse (rape versus sexual conduct) as well as the source of the data (convicted offenders versus self-reports). In part this may be due to the absence of terminology in government studies that include female-perpetrated sex crimes. As late as 1994, the Uniform Crime Reporting System still defined rape for female victims only.

The most comprehensive estimates on the prevalence of female sexual abuse have been compiled by David Finkelhor and Diana Russell, cited by Mic Hunter (Mathews et al., 1990). They found that 24 percent of sexually abused males and 13 percent of sexually abused females were victimized by females either acting alone or with an accomplice. In approximately 2 percent of the cases of male sexual victimization and 54 percent of the cases of female victimization by females, the female offender was acting in the company of others.

What we do know about female sexual offenders has largely been derived from small samples of adjudicated adults (Atkinson, 1996). In a review of the literature on the population, Atkinson identifies three typologies:

1. *Teacher or lover sex offender.* This offender initiates the sexual abuse of an adolescent from a position of power obtained through either age or status,

---

B e e n   T h e r e . . . D o n e   T h a t !

One by one, the prosecutors laughed at my request to bring forward a rape case that involved a female perpetrator in her thirties and a 15-year-old boy. Comments like, "I should have been so lucky," and "Are you kidding? That is every boy's dream," to "We would never win a case like that in court!" were among the responses. Never mind that the crime of statutory rape was committed or that the youngster suffered great emotional and psychological harm from the relationship. Forget that she threatened to kill the child that she bore from him if he cut off the relationship! I suggest that we need to know more about these infrequent but occurring instances of sexual abuse by women.

including that of mother, aunt, or guardian. The offender would probably be a person who had suffered severe emotional and verbal abuse as a child, but not necessarily sexual abuse. The offender views her victim as an equal, thus denying the seriousness of the offense. A minority of this population has been found to be developmentally delayed.

2. *Male-coerced sex offender.* Male-coerced offenders, who induce or are forced into sexual abuse by a male, are the most frequent type reported in adult clinical research. They are typically passive and nonassertive, which may have resulted from childhood sexual and physical abuse. A frequent offender in this category is the daughter of a male aggressor.

3. *Predisposed sex offender.* Without male accomplices, the offender in this group usually perpetrates against her own children. Seventy-five percent of these offenders are believed to have been victims of incest.

Ruth Mathews and colleagues suggest another category in addition to the above (Mathews et al., 1990):

4. *Experimenter or exploiter.* This is a juvenile female offender who tends to be 16 years old or younger and generally chooses a young male child (6 years old or younger). Typically, this is a one-time event that is characterized by detachment, no intimacy, and low emotionality. The offender is very anxious and naive about sexual relationships and fearful of advances from peers.

Faller (1987) reports on a clinical sample of 40 women who were judged by staff to have sexually abused at least 63 children. These women represented 14 percent of the total of 289 perpetrators of sexual abuse. Many of the women had significant difficulties in psychological and social functioning. About half had mental problems, both retardation and psychotic illness. More than half had chemical dependency problems, and close to three-fourths had maltreated their victims in other ways in addition to the sexual abuse. The women fell into five case types (four were sexually abusive in more than one context). Faller concludes that the circumstances that lead women to abuse children sexually can be differentiated from those causing men to abuse sexually.

1. *Polyincestuous abuse.* Twenty-nine (72.5 percent) of the women fit into this category. In such cases, there are at least two perpetrators and generally two or more victims. Usually, a male rather than the female offender instigated the abuse. The woman went along with the male and played a secondary role.

2. *Single-parent abuse.* Six (15 percent) of the women who sexually abused were single parents. These mothers did not have ongoing relationships with men and the oldest child seemed to serve as a surrogate partner for the mother, often having adult role responsibilities.

3. *Psychotic abusers.* Only three (7.5 percent) of the women were classified as psychotic at the time of the sexual abuse. Therefore, this study does not sup-

port the clinical assumption that most female perpetrators are highly disturbed and often psychotic at the time of the sexual abuse.

4. *Adolescent perpetrators.* Three (7.5 percent) were adolescent girls who had difficulty with peer relationships and lacked alternative sexual outlets.

5. *Noncustodial abusers.* There was only one woman who was the noncustodial mother of her victims and sexually abused them during visitation. Faller believes that in such cases the noncustodial parent is apt to be devastated at the loss of her spouse and the children become the source of emotional gratification.

Male Date Rape Offenders

Unlike the picture presented for physical dating violence, sexual aggression is almost exclusively male perpetrated, according to Py Bateman (Bateman, 1998). She states that although reports of date rape are rare, it is significant to note that many adolescents don't recognize the pressures that lead to unwanted sex as rape. Experts agree that the crime is grossly underreported. A number of studies indicate that both men and women often share the belief that women are responsible for both stimulating and satisfying men's sexual urges, a factor that might contribute to a victim's unwillingness to view the event as criminal. Cultural pressures on young men lead them to insist on sexual relations, using whatever psychological or physical force is necessary.

Nearly 3 percent of college women (1 in 36) are victims of rape or attempted rape in an academic year, according to a study entitled *Sexual Victimization of College*

Figure 5–9   Reports indicate that dating violence is reaching epidemic proportions. What can you do to reduce these incidents?

Women (Fisher et al., 2000). It finds that violence against women, sexual assault, and stalking on college campuses is prevalent, yet less than 5 percent of sexual assaults or attempted sexual assault on college campuses are reported to the police. Most of the sexually assaulted women knew the person who victimized them. For completed and attempted rapes, nearly 90 percent of the victims knew the offender, who was usually a classmate, friend, ex-boyfriend, or acquaintance.

BATTERER INTERVENTIONS

In a recent report to the National Institute of Justice, Kerry Healey and Christine Smith point out another compelling reason for the reconciliation of theory with practice. They contend that the requirement that batterers attend intervention programs as a condition of probation, or as part of a pretrial or diversion, is fast becoming a part of the response to domestic violence in many jurisdictions (Healey et al., 1998). Although that may be the practice, they suggest that judges and probation officers often lack basic information about program goals and methods. Since deterring future violence is the objective of criminal justice, it may be the reward for astute attention to the program goals and careful selection.

Major Theoretical Models That Influence Batterer Intervention

The trend toward specialized batterer treatment programs came with the recognition that the batterer's socioeconomic status, racial or ethnic identity, country of origin, and sexual orientation can affect intervention, according to Healey and Smith. In response to concerns regarding diversity, culturally competent interventions were developed to draw on the strength of the offender's family or community social systems (Healey & Smith, 1998). Programs for men of African descent, recent Asian immigrants, and Latinos who speak Spanish are examples of culturally based intervention programs. Recognizing ethnic and racial differences in curriculum planning is central to the specialized approach. African American groups enable men to focus on what they did instead of social injustice or racism; Asian programs counter the social acceptability of private violence; and the concept of machismo is challenged in strategies used with Latino groups.

Attachment theory provides the basis for the opposite approach seen in the Compassion Workshop, based in Silver Spring, Maryland (Healey & Smith, 1998). Several types of offenders, including male and female heterosexual batterers, gay and lesbian perpetrators, victims, and child abusers, work together to develop trust, intimacy, and commitment. The positive development of emotions is meant to overcome the anger rooted in powerlessness and worthlessness, which is believed to trigger offender behavior. This approach is considered highly controversial.

Program Procedures for Male Perpetrators

Batterer programs typically consist of five stages: intake and assessment, orientation, victim orientation, program, and ending the program.

Intake and Assessment.   The intake interview may take place at the court-house after the perpetrator has been seen by a probation officer. In some jurisdictions, a representative from the program attends the civil court hearings. After the judge has issued an order, the staff member will meet with the perpetrator and explain the program. In other jurisdictions it is the responsibility of the batterer to initiate the contact and arrange for the assessment interview. During the intake process, the interviewer seeks information on the pattern and severity of the abuse toward current and past partners, children, and others. Not all batterers are accepted at this stage. Much depends on whether the offender has substance abuse or mental illness problems that might make him or her more suitable to a different program that can address those needs. Many programs will not admit a person who denies being violent or appears likely to disrupt the group.

Orientation.   During the orientation session, the new clients meet and are told the rules and goals of the program. One purpose of the orientation is to establish rapport between the participants and the counselors. Since a majority of clients are court ordered to attend the session, it is an effort to reduce their defensiveness. It is important to find out as much as possible about the abuse that was perpetrated so that effective intervention can occur. Counselors meet one-on-one in addition to the group meeting in order to assess how the program can best benefit each person.

Victim Orientation.   Many programs offer an opportunity for the person who was battered to meet with the staff. Some states require that partners be notified at various points of intervention. The purpose of meeting with the victims is threefold. First, it allows a counselor the opportunity to explain the program goals and philosophy. Second, it is an opportunity to get the victim's assessment of the abuse in the relationship. Third, safety issues and protection options can be discussed so that the battered person is aware of the resources available if services are needed. Shelter locations and orders for protection are among the topics that may be discussed.

Program.   Anger management skills training in a group setting are common components of batterers' programs. Education on power and control issues and the development of critical-thinking skills are emphasized to help batterers understand and change their behavior. Some programs offer in-depth counseling that is designed to force the batterer to accept responsibility for his or her actions. Others focus on the relationship between the batterer and the victim to promote respect and positive behavior.

The group sessions may involve role-playing based on personal experiences to teach appropriate ways to deal with family situations that batterers find frustrating.

They may discuss situations that have caused men or women to batter and apply alternatives to violence. Videos and stories about abuse from the victim's perspective are designed to sensitize the perpetrators about the effects of abuse on their partners.

Ending the Program.   A client may be terminated prior to completion of the program for a number of reasons. Among them are revocation of probation, alcohol and drug abuse, disrupting the sessions, failure to take responsibility for abusive acts, and not attending group sessions regularly. Successful completion of the program may involve an exit project, such as a letter on how the client was affected by the process. Some programs offer follow-ups at specified time periods after a client has been discharged from the program.

Program Procedures for Women Who Batter

Researchers are in disagreement on the existence of females as batterers. Clinicians, on the other hand, have had to face increasing numbers of women in need of treatment. Numbers of women arrested for domestic violence have grown in recent years, despite the decline in the rates of intimate violence (Clifford, 1999). Typically the response to these offenders is a feminized version of male intervention. The strategies are inconsistent and in many parts of the United States nonexistent.

The Domestic Abuse Project (DAP) put together the first published manual specifically intended to address the problems and behaviors of female offenders (DAP, 1998). Their approach is inclusive on the growing needs in the field for facilitators connected to the gay, lesbian, bisexual, and transgender communities. Providing guidelines for the treatment of women that batter, the program philosophy is grounded in the belief that violent behavior is learned and that it is a chosen behavior. Their Women Who Abuse program is a four-step process consisting of a thorough intake assignment with referral options for the survivors, assessment follow-up sessions, a psychoeducational therapy group, and individualized therapy.

Intake Assessment.   A major focus in this stage is the assessment on offender readiness to change her abusive behavior. A thorough screening is included to assure that the referred woman is not a self-defending victim.

Individual Sessions.   In preparation for group sessions, this stage is used to build rapport with the client and assist the women in the difficult process of acknowledging their abusive behavior and developing a self-control plan.

Education Component.   During a 20-week period, approximately 16 educational topics are covered. Examples include sessions on shame versus responsibility; communication skills; anger management; costs and payoffs of being violent; and the effects of violence on children.

Individualized Treatment. This final section of the program focuses on the development of the self-control plan. Central are the cues of escalation prior to violence and plans for avoiding violence. Stress management and prevention are the desired outcomes.

CAN PROGRAM INTERVENTIONS STOP BATTERING?

Referral to batterer treatment programs is fast becoming the usual procedure for the courts. How well do these programs work at lowering recidivism? According to Healy and Smith, the majority of studies that have attempted to evaluate batterer treatment programs have netted inconclusive results. Methodological problems such as sample size and unreliable sources of follow-up have caused uncertainty. A few evaluations have found modest but statistically significant reductions in recidivism among men participating in batterer interventions. A 40 percent recidivism rate was found after 5 years in a study of the graduates of Duluth's domestic abuse intervention project (Pence & Paymar, 1993). At issue are the criteria for evaluating a batterers' program. Although it would be the goal of every project to end domestic violence, practitioners wonder if that is a realistic expectation.

Promoting the safety of the victims is an important consideration, for example. When the Duluth program measured victims' perception of increased safety due to their partners' participating, they were pleased with the results. The majority of women stated that they felt safer during the program. Further, the victims reported increased safety when the community was actively involved in the coordination of services to both protect the woman and provide alternatives to the perpetrator. It takes a community effort to affect domestic violence. Those options included mandating jail when the men reoffended.

These findings point to the success of a coordinated community approach to combat domestic violence that involves the courts, the police, the community, and the batterers' programs. Other studies concluded that educational programs were successful at transmitting information but not deterring violent behavior. If deterrence is not a

---

Been There . . . Done That!

The marital relationship of Frank and Martha was described by witnesses as mutually combative. Frank was a police officer. His wife called the station to report that during an argument, he had held a gun to the head of their child. Officers who responded confiscated all of his weapons and arrested him for assault and battery with a dangerous weapon. He was suspended without pay and denied access to any guns pending a full investigation.

likely outcome of an intervention, suggests Healy, then punishment, education, behavioral monitoring, or social change must be explicitly advanced (Healey et al., 1998).

Unified Court System Partnered with Probation

Policy makers and clinicians, however, question the extent to which abusers are held accountable for their actions. The effectiveness of batterers' intervention programs (BIPs) is uncertain at best and often relied upon as a "quick fix" for batterers, they contend. In support of this position, authors Heckert and Gondolf found only half of the batterers in their study perceived that they would be jailed as a likely outcome from program dropout or reassault (Heckert & Gondolf, 2000). When programs contained a court review process for program compliance, the batterers were more likely to perceive jail as likely. However, neither perceived certainty of sanctions (jailing likely) nor perceived severity of sanctions predicted dropout and reassault.

One response to these concerns has been the development of specialized domestic violence courts. The first domestic violence court opened in Brooklyn, New York, in 1966. Designed to increase victims' safety and hold defendants accountable, judges, along with extensive partnerships with criminal justice and social service agencies, staff it. The Department of Probation dedicated several officers from the "intensive supervision program" to work on these domestic violence cases. For the past several years, the probation violation rates at the Court have been nearly half the violation rate typical of this probation population (Office for the Prevention of Domestic Violence, 2000). The successes of the program have led to it being replicated and adapted to other courts.

CONCLUSIONS

The characteristic descriptions of domestic violence batterers based on gender give an idea of the type of person who commits these crimes. Controlling tactics and methods of intimidation are part of the domestic violence cycle. Aside from their social and personality deficiencies, we found that the majority of offenders are males who perpetrate against females. The typology typically used to describe heterosexual offenders differs when homosexual relationships are included in the discussion. Criminal justice professionals need to be sensitized to all forms of family violence, regardless of preexisting notions about gender and perpetration. Age is no longer a factor when we put juvenile offenders into the mix. Actions that constitute domestic violence must be considered as such despite age, gender, or sexual orientation. A crime is a crime.

Presenting information about female perpetrators is not meant to minimize the severity of abuse toward female victims. The offenses are usually minor and far less frequent than those committed by men. Ignoring acts because the offender is a female is unfair to the victim, whoever he or she may be.

A promising direction for law enforcement is in the concept of the primary physical aggressor determination. If you missed that part, go back to the section on mutual battering (p. 149). It can be difficult for professionals to distinguish between acts of primary and mutual battering; this is one method that tries to define what the officer should be looking for. Of course, it is still a difficult process, and the primary aggressor may also change within a relationship. Focus on the facts at hand and don't rush to make a judgment. To understand better the dynamics of battering, three models through the stages of abuse are offered: cognitive, feminist, and integrated.

The next part of the chapter focused on marital rape and sexual assault. Offender characteristics and typology give insight to the behaviors of the marital rapist. As in battering, the vast majority of sexual offenders are men, although some women are known to offend. Rape within the dating relationship is a newly discovered problem that needs to be addressed.

Batterer programs and typical procedures are explained. The lengths of time in the programs vary, but the structure is similar in the major models that were presented. This is not meant to imply that all batterer programs are the same. Many grassroots efforts have emerged that do not easily fit into the major model descriptions. They include specialized or culturally competent interventions and models based on the attachment theory. It was noted that efforts to evaluate the effectiveness of batterer intervention programs have brought mixed results. It appears that a greater emphasis needs to be placed on identifying the goals that are desired from intervention programs. Are we trying to stop it totally? Is victim protection the major purpose? Does recidivism matter? These are all questions that need to be explored.

Intensive supervised probation in conjunction with specialized domestic violence courts has seen surprising results in lowering domestic violence recidivism. The New York model is one worth further study.

Q UESTIONS FOR R EVIEW

1. Compare heterosexual domestic violence and homosexual domestic violence. How are they similar? What are the differences?

2. According to the National Violence Against Women Survey, who are the majority of domestic violence victims?

3. What behaviors or actions would a batterer exhibit?

4. Describe the average male batterer and his personality.

5. What results did Island and Letellier find in their study about men who batter men?

6. Given your status as a college student, what is your reaction to the incidence of females offending in physical dating violence?

7. What is the significance of alcohol and drug abuse in violent relationships?

8. Explain why it might be difficult to determine the primary abuser in a case where there is mutual battering.

9. Define marital rape and describe the three types according to Finkelhor and Yllo.

10. Compare the reports of successes in batterer treatment programs versus the unified court model.

INTERNET-BASED EXERCISES

1. The fastest population of rape victims is students. What are the chances that you will be victimized? Find out more about the problems by going to The National Center for Victim Assistance at http://www.ncvc.org/infolink/main.htm. Once you know the odds, calculate the figures at your college to determine how many women may be victimized.

2. What are the similarities and differences in domestic violence for lesbian, gay, bisexual, transgender, and queer/questioning (LGBTQ) communities compared to heterosexual couples? Two good sites to begin your research are http://www.gmdvp.org/ and http://www.cuav.org/. Write a report comparing the reported rates of domestic violence and suspected nonreported rates. What factors might deter nonheterosexual victims from reporting to the police?

REFERENCES

Administration on Aging. 1998. The National Elder Abuse Incidence Study; Final Report. Washington, DC: U.S. Department of Health and Human Services.

Ascione, Frank. 1998. "Battered Women's Reports of Their Partners' and Their Children's Cruelty to Animals." *Journal of Emotional Abuse*, 1(1):119–133.

Atkinson, J. L. 1996. "Female Sex Offenders: A Literature Review." *Forum* 8(2):39–42.

Austin, Juliet, and Juergen Dankwort. 1998. *A Review of Standards for Batterer Intervention Programs*. Washington, DC: National Resource Center on Domestic Violence.

Bateman, Py. 1998. "The Context of Date Rape." Pp. 95–99 in *Dating Violence: Young Women in Danger*, 2nd ed., Barrie Levy (ed.). Seattle, WA: Seal Press.

Bennett, Larry W. 1997. "Substance Abuse and Woman Abuse by Male Partners." Violence Against Women Online Resources. *http://www.vaw.umn.edu/Vawnet/substanc.htm*. 2002.

Bennett, Larry W. 1999. Safety and Sobriety: Best Practices in Domestic Violence and Substance Abuse. Task Force Report. Bureau of Domestic Violence Prevention & Intervention of the Illinois Department of Human Services. *http://tigger.uic.edu/~lwbenn/taskforce/introduct.html*. 2002.

Bradway, William C. 1990. "Stages of a Sexual Assault." *Law and Order*, September, 119–24.

Brandl, Bonnie. 2000. "Power and Control: Understanding Domestic Abuse in Later Life." *Generations* 24(2): 39–45.

Brandl, Bonnie, and Loree Cook-Daniels. 2002. "Domestic Abuse in Later Life." Available at *http://www.vaw.umn.edu/documents/vawnet/arlaterlife/arlaterlife.pdf*

Brookoff, D. 1997. *Drugs, Alcohol, and Domestic Violence in Memphis.* National Institute of Justice, Research Preview. Washington, DC: U.S. Department of Justice.

Bureau of Justice Statistics. 1998. *Violence by Intimates, Analysis of Data on Crimes by Current or Former Spouses, Boyfriends, and Girlfriends.* Washington, DC: U.S. Department of Justice, p. 28.

Burnley, Jane et al. (eds.). 1996. *National Victim Assistance Academy Textbook.* Washington, DC: Office for Victims of Crime.

Clifford, James O. 1999. "Spouse Abuse Crackdown, Surprisingly, Nets Many Women." Associated Press. November 24, 1999. *http://www.vix.com/menmag/batapwmn.htm.* 2002.

Cohen, Murry J., and Caroline Kweller. 2000. "Domestic Violence and Animal Abuse: The Deadly Connection." Physicans Committee for Responsible Medicine. *http://www.pcrm.org/issues/Commentary/commentary0010.html.* 2002.

DeKeseredy, Walter S., and Martin D. Schwartz. 1998. *Woman Abuse on Campus: Results from the Canadian National Survey.* Thousand Oaks, CA: Sage Publications.

Domestic Abuse Project. 1998. *Women Who Abuse in Intimate Relations.* Nancie Hamlet (ed.). Minneapolis, MN: DAP.

Fagan, J. 1990. "Intoxication and Aggression." Pp. 241–320 in *Drugs and Crime,* M. Tonry and J. Q. Wilson (eds.). Chicago: University of Chicago Press.

Faller, K. C. 1987. "Women Who Sexually Abuse Children." *Violence and Victims* 2(4):263–76.

Famularo, R., R. Kinscherff, and T. Fenton. 1992. "Parental Substance Abuse and the Nature of Child Maltreatment." *Child Abuse and Neglect: The International Journal* 16(4):475–83.

Feld, S. L., and M. A. Straus. 1990. "Escalation and Resistance from Wife Assault in Marriage." Pp. 489–505 in *Physical Violence in American Families: Risk Factors and Adaptations to Violence in 8,145 Families,* M. A. Straus and R. J. Gelles (eds.). New Brunswick, NJ: Transaction Publishers.

Finkelhor, David. 1984. *Child Sexual Abuse: New Theory and Research.* New York: Free Press.

Finkelhor, David, and Kersti Yllo. 1985. *License to Rape: Sexual Abuse of Wives.* New York: Holt, Rinehart and Winston.

Fisher, Bonnie S., Francis T. Cullen, and Michael Turner. 2000. *Sexual Victimization of College Women.* NCJ 182369. Washington, DC: National Institute of Justice.

Gelles, Richard. 1974. *The Violent Home: A Study of Physical Aggression between Husbands and Wives.* Beverly Hills, CA: Sage Publications.

Gondolf, E. W. 1995. "Alcohol Abuse, Wife Assault, and Power Needs." *Social Service Review* 69:275–83.

Greenfeld, L., and T. Snell, BJS Statisticians. 2000. *Women Offenders.* Bureau of Justice Statistics: Special Report. NCJ 175688. Washington, DC: U.S. Department of Justice.

Greenwood, Gregory, Michael Relf, Bu Huang, Lance Pollack, Jesse Canchola, and Joseph Catania. 2002. "Battering Victimization Among a Probability-Based Sample of Men Who Have Sex With Men." *American Journal of Public Health* 92(12):1964–67.

Hanard, Melanie S. 2001. "Abused Women or Abused Men? An Examination of the Context and Outcomes of Dating Violence." *Violence and Victims* 16(3):269–85.

Hattendorf, Joanne, and Toni R. Tollerund. 1997. "Domestic Violence: Counseling Strategies That Minimize the Impact of Secondary Victimization." *Perspectives in Psychiatric Care* 33(1):10–14.

Healey, Kerry, Christine Smith, and Chris O'Sullivan. 1998. *Batterer Intervention: Program Approaches and Criminal Justice Strategies.* NCJ 168638. Washington, DC: U.S. Department of Justice.

Healey, Kerry M., and Christine Smith. 1998. *Batterer Programs: What Criminal Justice Agencies Need to Know*. NCJ 171683. Washington, DC: U.S. Department of Justice.

Heckert, Alex, and Edward W. Gondolf. 2000. "Effect of Perceptions of Sanctions on Batterer Program Outcomes." *Journal of Research in Crime and Delinquency* 37(4):369–91.

Holtzworth-Monroe, A., and G. L. Stuart. 1994. "Typologies of Male Batterers: Three Subtypes and the Differences Among Them." *Psychological Bulletin* 116(3):476–97.

International Association of Chiefs of Police. 1999. *Police Officer Domestic Violence Concepts and Issues Paper*. Washington, DC: U.S. Department of Justice.

International Association of Chiefs of Police. 2003. *Domestic Violence by Police Officers*. Alexandria, VA: IACP.

Island, David, and Patrick Letellier. 1991. *Men Who Beat the Men Who Love Them: Battered Gay Men and Domestic Violence*. Binghamton, NY: Harrington Park Press.

James, Kerrie, Beth Seddon, and Jac Brown. 2002. " 'Using It' or 'Losing It': Men's Constructions of Their Violence Towards Female Partners." *Australian Domestic & Family Violence Clearinghouse* 1:1–20.

Knauer, C. 2003. "Geriatric Alcohol Abuse: A National Epidemic." *Geriatric Nursing* 24(3):152–54.

Levy, Barrie, and Kerry Lobel. 1998. "Lesbian Teens in Abusive Relationships." Pp. 203–208 in *Dating Violence: Young Women in Danger*, 2nd ed., Barrie Levy (ed.). Seattle, WA: Seal Press.

Mathews, Ruth, Jane Mathews, and Kate Speltz. 1990. "Female Sexual Offenders." Pp. 275–93 in *The Sexually Abused Male: Prevalence, Impact, and Treatment*, Mic Hunter (ed.). New York: Lexington Books, citing Finkelhor, David, and Diane Russell. 1984. "Women as Perpetrators: Review of the Evidence." Pp. 171–87 in Child Sexual Abuse: New Theory and Research, David Finkelhor (ed.). New York: Free Press.

Menard, Kim. 1997. *Female Sexual Offenders: A Review of the Literature with Research and Policy Implications*. Academy of Criminal Justice Sciences Annual Conference, Albuquerque, NM, March. Unpublished.

Merrill, G. S. 1998. "Understanding Domestic Violence Among Gay and Bisexual Men." Pp. 129–41 in *Issues in Intimate Violence*, R. K. Bergen, (ed.). Thousand Oaks, CA: Sage.

Meuer, Tess, Anne Seymour, and Harvey Wallace. 2002. *Domestic Violence*. National Victims Assistance Academy Textbook. Washington, DC: Office for Victims of Crime.

NCAVP. 2003. *National Report on Lesbian, Gay, Bisexual, and Transgender Domestic Violence in 2002*. New York: National Coalition of Anti-Violence Programs.

Office for the Prevention of Domestic Violence. 2000. Bulletin 12(2). Mendands, NY: New York State Office for the Prevention of Domestic Violence.

Osgood, N., and A. Manetta. 2002. "Physical and Sexual Abuse, Battering, and Substance Abuse: Three Clinical Cases of Older Women." *Journal of Gerontological Social Work* 38(3):99–113.

Pence, Ellen, and Michael Paymar. 1993. *Education Groups for Men Who Batter*. New York: Springer Publishing Company.

Peterman, L. M., & Dixon, C. G. 2003. "Domestic Violence Between Same-Sex Partners: Implications for Counseling." *Journal of Counseling & Development*, 81(3), 40–47.

Potocziak, Michael, Jon E. Mourot, Margaret Crosbie-Burnet, and Danial Potoczniak. 2003. "Legal and Psychological Perspectives on Same-Sex Domestic Violence: A Multisystemic Approach." *Journal of Family Psychology* 17(2):252–59.

Ramsey-Klawsnik, Holly. 1991. "Elder Sexual Abuse: Preliminary Findings." *Journal of Elder Abuse and Neglect* 3(3):73–89.

————. 1997. *Sessions I and II; III and IV, Workshop Handouts.* Canton, MA: Massachusetts Executive Office of Elder Affairs.

Ramsey-Klawsnik, H. 2000. "Elder-Abuse Offenders: A Typology." *Journal of the American Society on Aging*, XXIV(11), 17–22.

Rennison, C., and M. Rand. 2003. "Nonlethal Intimate Partner Violence—A Comparison of Three Age Cohorts." *Violence Against Women* 9(12):1417–28.

Renzetti, Claire M., and Charles H. Miley (eds.). 1996. *Violence in Gay and Lesbian Domestic Partnerships.* Binghamton, NY: Harrington Park Press.

Ristock, Janic L. 2002. *No More Secrets: Violence in Lesbian Relationships.* New York: Routledge.

Sonkin, Daniel J., and Michael Durphy. 1997. *Learning to Live without Violence: A Handbook for Men*, 5th ed. Volcano, CA: Volcano Press.

Straus, Murray A. 1993. "Identifying Offenders in Criminal Justice Research on Domestic Assault." *American Behavioral Scientist* 36(5):587–99.

Straus, Murray A., Richard J. Gelles, and Suzanne K. Steinmetz. 1980. *Behind Closed Doors: Violence in the American Family.* Garden City, NY: Anchor Press/Doubleday.

Straus, Murray A., and Luis Ramirez. 1999. *Criminal History and Assault of Dating Partners: The Role of Gender, Age of Onset, and Type of Crime.* NCJ 186240. Washington, DC: U.S. Department of Health and Human Services.

Sugarman, David B., and Gerald T. Hotaling. 1998. "Dating Violence: A Review of Contextual and Risk Factors." Pp. 100–18 in *Dating Violence: Young Women in Danger*, 2nd ed., Barrie Levy (ed.). Seattle, WA: Seal Press.

Tjaden, Patricia, and Nancy Thoennes. 1998. *Prevalence, Incidence, and Consequences of the Violence Against Women: Findings from the National Violence Against Women Survey.* NCJ 172837. Washington, DC: U.S. Department of Justice.

U.S. Department of Health and Human Services. 1996. *Study of the National Incidence and Prevalence of Child Abuse and Neglect.* FS-13. Washington, DC: DHHS.

Websdale, Neil. 1998. *Rural Woman Battering and the Justice System: An Ethnography.* Thousand Oaks, CA: Sage Publications.

Wolf, Rosalie S. 1996. "Understanding Elder Abuse and Neglect." *Aging* (367):4–17.

CHAPTER 6

RECOGNIZING CHILD ABUSE

Mandated Reporting

As a new teacher in the Springfield elementary school, Maryanne had her hands full. There were forty children in her classroom. The first year was frustrating! The lack of books and supplies gave her the impression that the administration did not care about the children, many of whom were not English speaking. Maryanne overheard some girls laughing at Susan and the dirty clothes she was wearing. Taunting Susan, the girls said it was no wonder she was filthy because her mom was always high and her dad was in jail. Maryanne began to watch Susan closely. She noticed that some days Susan appeared to have difficulty walking.

Question: Does this constitute a reportable condition of child abuse?

KEY TERMS

Active maltreatment
Battered child syndrome
Brittle bone disease
Failure to thrive
Immersion burn
Incest

Mandated reporting
Osteogenesis imperfecta
Parental kidnapping
Passive maltreatment
Shaken baby syndrome

INTRODUCTION

> I mentioned to one of our lawmakers that while a parent's death caused by his child is called murder and taken very seriously, a child's death caused by his parent usually results in lesser charges. He said, half in jest, "They [parents] are adults like me, and children don't vote; furthermore, they [children] are not very vocal before my committee!" (Foreword by C. Henry Kempe; Helfer & Kempe, 1988).

Until the late 1970s and early 1980s, the criminal justice professions rarely intervened in crimes against children. Allegations of child abuse were investigated only in the most serious cases or when a death obviously due to abuse had occurred. Even then, a female matron would probably be assigned to investigate—a strong message to police officers that child abuse was a "family problem" and not important enough for real police attention. With limited exceptions, the problem was referred to a social service agency for family intervention. This attitude reflected a greater social problem: the devaluation of children and the lack of societal protections under the guise of parental rights. Every state now has legislation to prohibit crimes against children. The legal transgression depends on the statute language of each state.

In addition to the identification and recognition of child abuse, the impact of violence is of consequence to the investigator. Insight into the reactions of the victim may provide an accurate portrayal of the situation that is harmful to the child. The investigator has a unique opportunity to document the full extent of injury, both physical and psychological, if those signs and symptoms present themselves. Keeping in mind that the role of investigators from different agencies may conflict at times, the child protection worker must determine if a child is in need of protection and/or services. The mandate may or may not include family preservation. Law enforcement officers first have the duty to protect, which is emergency intervention only. The job of law enforcement is to determine if a crime has been committed and, if so, by whom.

Back Then . . .

C. Henry Kempe and colleagues were largely responsible for the shift in public attitude, in the increased awareness, and ultimately in the legal responses to child abuse. They raised consciousness through their first presentation about the battered child syndrome in 1961. **Battered child syndrome** refers to the repeated mistreatment or beating of a child that results in physical and psychological injuries. Their contributions to our understanding the complexities of child victimization continue through *The Battered Child* (Helfer & Kempe, 1988).

Civil Versus Criminal Action

Should the perpetrator be arrested and prosecuted criminally? The district attorney makes the final decision based on the following factors:

- Age of the child
- Seriousness of the offense
- Reluctance to testify
- Evidence
- Probability of successful prosecution

Recent research indicates that violence toward an intimate partner causes a variety of psychological problems for the children and places them at greater risk for delinquency and adult criminality. Known as indirect abuse, this form might constitute criminal neglect. Those who reside in violent homes are also at greater risk of becoming victims of direct abuse. Ongoing research efforts continue to identify the impact of violence on children in a variety of settings. In this chapter we identify and define the direct forms of child abuse and discuss the indirect effects of witnessing abuse.

CATEGORIES OF ACTIVE MALTREATMENT

Active Maltreatment

An injury or a pattern of injuries that is nonaccidental characterizes this direct child abuse of **active maltreatment**. It is damage to a child for which there is no explanation that is reasonable or fitting to the injuries that the child has sustained. The most frequent category of violence that comes to the attention of investigators is the active abuse, sometimes referred to as maltreatment. Such abuse may take these forms:

- Emotional abuse and psychological maltreatment
- Physical injury abuse
- Sexual abuse

Passive Maltreatment

Passive maltreatment is the action or inaction of a legally recognized caretaker who fails to fulfill his or her responsibility to a dependent child identifies the second category of direct violence. These neglectful categories of abuse are becoming more familiar to criminal justice and social service agencies as they struggle to enforce an increasing number of child protection statutes:

- Neglect, which may be physical or emotional
- Educational neglect

Been There . . . Done That!

Having been part of the 1980s transition in policing for Massachusetts, I am still frustrated by the lack of understanding and the failure of some police departments to use traditional investigative techniques during child abuse investigations. When queried, officers with years of experience will admit to never having executed a search warrant to obtain evidence in child abuse allegations. Although this is not the case in all jurisdictions, rigor and consistency are lacking. Some agencies have created detective divisions to investigate and follow through with the prosecution of crimes against children, but all criminal justice professionals need to be educated to recognize the signs and symptoms of child abuse. I believe the larger problem comes from not understanding the crimes, what might constitute evidence, and how the evidence should be gathered.

What kind of information and evidence might be gathered? Everything and anything that gives credibility to the statement or medical condition of a child! The first step toward the goal of evidence gathering lies in the recognition of abuse, which is the basis of this chapter. Assessing the injury or harm is done through detection (visual and medical diagnosis) along with the medical and family history of the events leading up to the injury.

- Inadequate care in such areas as food, clothing, and shelter
- Lack of supervision
- Lack of medical care
- Nonsupport of minor child
- Parental kidnapping

Back Then . . .

A classic case of child abuse is that of Mary Ellen Wilson. In 1874, the 8-year-old child came to the attention of the judicial system due to repeated beatings with a rawhide whip and scissors, as well as severe neglect. Concerned neighbors reported the case to numerous authorities, even the New York City Police Department, which said that there was no proof of a crime! Legend says that the Society for the Prevention of Cruelty to Animals ultimately intervened on Mary Ellen's behalf and persuaded the courts to accept the case because she was a member of the animal kingdom. This account is less than truthful, according to Sallie Watkins, who reports that Mr. Bergh made it clear to the court that he was not acting in an official capacity as president of the Society of Prevention of Cruelty to Animals, but as a humane citizen (Watkins, 1995).

CATEGORIES OF SECONDARY MALTREATMENT

There are two categories of secondary abuse: witnessing domestic violence and witnessing the homicide of a parent. Secondary abuse can be described as the consequence of residing in a violent home. Violence toward an intimate partner causes a variety of psychological problems for the children and places them at greater risk for delinquency and adult criminality. As you read in Chapter 4, child witnessing of domestic violence is being linked with a variety of problems, from aggression and hostility to depression and cognitive impairment. Although we cannot predict which children will become victims of abuse, those that reside in violent homes are at greater risk. How many children witness violence in the home? We can only speculate based on those we know who live with a mother who is being battered. Approximately 43 percent, or 4 out of 10, of abused women live with children under the age of 12 (Rennison & Welchans, 2000).

THE VICTIMS OF CHILD ABUSE

The estimated numbers of child abuse victims are staggering. In 1999, child protective services agencies received reports on about 2.97 million allegedly maltreated children (U.S. Department of Health and Human Services [DHHS], 2001). Of these allegations, 28 percent of the 1999 reports were substantiated. Eighty-seven percent of the victims were maltreated by one or both parents; 44.7 percent of the substantiated cases involved a mother acting alone (U.S. Department of Health and Human Services, 2001). Children under age 6 accounted for 86 percent of fatalities caused by child abuse and neglect, with children less than a year old accounting for 43 percent (U.S. Department of Health and Human Services, 2001). The number of children substantiated as abused or neglected has dropped from 13.4 per 1,000 children in 1990 to 12.3 per 1,000 children in 2002 (McDonald, 2004).

Age

The victims can be found throughout society with no regard to age or gender. This does not mean that all children are victimized, but that boys and girls of all ages are represented as victims. A child is defined as a person under the age of 18, except in those states that specify a younger age. Young children are reported as the victims of neglect most often. Children age three and younger had the highest rates of victimization (16 per 1,000 children), with girls being slightly more likely to be victims than boys (McDonald, 2004). Categorizing by age difference has become less important for the investigator, with findings that all age groups are at risk for some form of maltreatment. Children between the ages of 4 and 7 are victimized at the rate of 13.7 per 1,000 children; from 8 years old to 11 years old the rate drops to 11.9 per 1,000 (McDonald, 2004).

TABLE 6–1

Child Maltreatment, 2002

Perpetrators of Child Abuse	Percentage
Parent	81
Other relative	66
Other	47
Unknown or missing	33
Unmarried partner of parent	29
Child daycare provider	7
Foster parent	5
Residential facility staff	2
Legal guardian	2

Source: McDonald, 2004. National Clearinghouse on Child Abuse and Neglect Information.

Gender

Boys and girls are victimized almost equally. In 2002, over 48 percent of child victims were boys and 52 percent were girls (McDonald, 2004). Boys are at higher risk of serious physical injury and for emotional neglect than are girls (Kilpatrick et al., 2003). Official statistics reflect that girls are sexually abused more often than boys. The U.S. Department of Health and Human Services reports that boys were sexual abuse victims in 23 percent of substantiated cases versus girls in 77 percent (U.S. Department of Health and Human Services, 1998). Keep in mind that the statistics on abuse are based

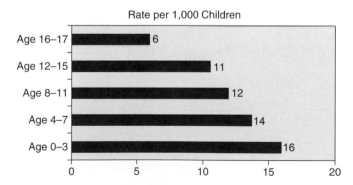

Figure 6–1   Victimization by age group: The victims of domestic violence can be found in every age group. Those under age 3 are considered the most vulnerable to child abuse. *(Data from McDonald, 2004.)*

on cases that are reported to social service agencies; the true incidence of sexual abuse to boys is believed to be equal to the victimization of girls (Hunter, 1990).

Race

According to the U.S. Department of Health and Human Services, victimization rates varied by race and ethnicity. African American children had the highest rate of victimization (25.2 per 1,000), followed by Hispanics (12.6 per 1,000), whites (10.6 per 1,000), and Asian/Pacific Islanders (4.4 per 1,000) (U.S. Department of Health and Human Services, 2001).

In contrast, the Third National Incidence Study did not find any significant differences in the rates of abuse according to the race of the child. Although this runs counter to the representation of minorities in the child protection agencies, the authors suggest that this may be due to differential attention during the process (U.S. Department of Health and Human Services, 1996).

Perpetrators of Child Abuse

The report entitled *Child Maltreatment: 2002* (McDonald, 2004) sheds light on our understanding of adults that offend against children in family violence. In part it states the following:

- Over 80 percent of perpetrators are parents. Other relatives accounted for 7 percent, and unmarried partners of parents accounted for 3 percent of perpe-

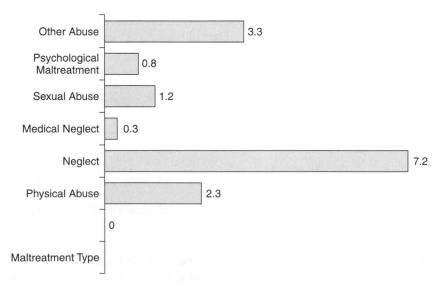

Figure 6–2 Child maltreatment by type and frequency. Note that neglect is the most frequent form of child abuse. *(Data from McDonald, 2004.)*

trators. The remaining perpetrators include persons with other (camp counselor, school employee, etc.) or unknown relationships to the child victims.

- Female perpetrators, who were mostly mothers, were typically younger than male perpetrators, who were mostly fathers.
- Women also comprised a larger percentage of all perpetrators than men, 58 percent compared to 42 percent.
- Of all parents who were perpetrators, less than 3 percent were associated with sexual abuse. Of all perpetrators of sexual abuse, nearly 29 percent were other relatives, and nearly one-quarter were in nonrelative or non-child-caring roles.

THE MAJOR FORMS OF ABUSE

It is not unusual for a victim to present more than one form of abuse at the same time. A child who is battered will frequently have been subjected to emotional or psychological maltreatment and/or neglect. A legitimate criticism about the frequency of child abuse is that some states report more than one type of maltreatment as separate cases of abuse, which makes it difficult to determine exactly how many children are abused. These criticisms have brought attention to state reporting methods and point to the need for clear and standardized procedures.

Emotional Abuse and Psychological Maltreatment

Emotional abuse involves a pattern of behavior that impairs a child's emotional development and sense of well-being. Approximately 5 percent of substantiated child abuse cases involve emotional abuse or psychological maltreatment (U.S.

Been There . . . Done That!

A student once said that she could tell if a child was abused by just looking at him or her. Having interviewed over 1,000 children who were victims and countless others who were not, I assure you that you cannot tell simply by outward appearances! Disheveled or unkempt appearances are not necessarily signs of abuse. Not all children respond to abuse by becoming surly or openly angry; some children react to abuse by adapting—they learn how to please others and appear overly willing to do so.

When indicators are present, they should serve as the catalyst for investigation, not as confirmation in the determination of abuse. Trained investigators, along with a team of professionals, should be consulted for abuse to be substantiated. The information presented in this book provides guidelines to conduct thorough investigations, and since social and medical research is providing new information constantly, do not expect this book to include every indicator or symptom.

Department of Health and Human Services, 1997). In the mildest form, emotional abuse occurs when a caretaker belittles or ridicules a child frequently. It also includes the absence of supporting language such as praise or expressions of love and concern.

Most often, emotional abuse is considered reprehensible behavior that may indicate the need for social service or therapeutic intervention but is not criminal. However, emotional maltreatment often accompanies other forms of abuse to children and should serve as a red flag to investigators that other types of abuse may be occurring. A full investigation of abuse should document emotional and psychological maltreatment in addition to other forms to show the atmosphere of abuse under which the child resides, even if it is not criminal conduct. In its most extreme form, emotional abuse is considered criminal activity. When a caretaker uses extremely restrictive methods to bind a child or places a child in close confinement such as a closet or trunk for an extended period of time, the victim suffers emotional abuse.

Indicators of Physical Abuse

Criminal prosecution of physical abuse is more common than the prosecution of emotional maltreatment, but it is less frequent than prosecution for sexual abuse (Smith, 1995). The recognition of abuse and collection of substantiating evidence becomes extremely important in these cases. The line between accident and intentional harm can be blurry, making the determination difficult. The multiagency or interdisciplinary team approach is helpful in gathering information from various sources to portray an accurate picture of the abuse.

Been There . . . Done That!

Susan came into my office with a big smile on her face! A charming 4-year-old, she was sparkling clean—the kind of child whose face shines. Her hair was tied in a ponytail topped with a pink ribbon, which matched her dress. Within moments of meeting, she spun around in circles to show off her frilly outfit! In an apparent effort to please me, she smiled broadly and chatted incessantly.

Yet I already knew that there was a dark side to the life of this little girl. Months earlier, she told her mother that daddy had touched her and that he had hurt her where she pees. Frustrated in her lack of ability to protect the child, her mother fled with her and had been living in hiding ever since. A medical exam had found trauma to the vagina that "might indicate" sexual abuse. During our videotaped interview, Susan told me that daddy had put his pee "down there" and white stuff had come out of it. It hurt her, and she did not want to see daddy again.

Regardless of the nature or role of the initial investigating agency, any reports and other documentation generated may become the focus of the court if prosecution proceeds. Whenever possible, obtain a written report from a medical professional on his or her opinion of the cause of injury. Medical records of the victim may be summoned if necessary. Gathering information on the nature, type, and location of injury is the first step toward a determination of physical abuse. This history should be collected before the victim is interviewed, then compared with the explanations. An allegation of abuse is not confirmation that a child has been victimized. Approximately two-thirds of the cases reported to child protective agencies were not substantiated after an investigation (Wang & Daro, 1998).

Since bruises and cuts are often legitimate accidental injuries (Figure 6–3), the age and mobility of the child is considered along with the explanation given for the injury. The greatest asset that an investigator can possess is the ability to remain objective and nonjudgmental when a child has suspicious injuries. Children can become injured during play; bruises, burns, and even broken bones do occur that are not due to parental abuse. Gather information on the location and type of injury, and speak with the caretaker about the incidents that preceded the injury.

Location of Abrasions, Bruises, Lacerations, and Welts.   Infants who are not mobile are not capable of inflicting severe injury to their bodies. In the absence of a medical condition such as **brittle bone disease**, such an explanation is not plausible. Infants who are thrown or dropped, hit or slapped, burned, or poisoned may have visible signs of injury. Any location of injury that the child is incapable of

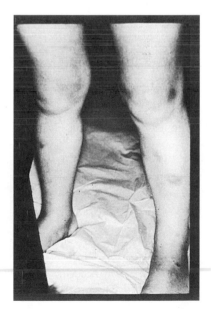

Figure 6–3   Normal bruising encountered on the legs of an active child. *(Photo used with the permission of the American Academy of Pediatrics.* Visual Diagnosis of Child Physical Abuse; *Bk&Acces edition; AAP [January 1995].)*

Been There . . . Done That!

During an investigation of the suspected sexual abuse of a 4-year-old boy, the child drew a crude picture of an erect penis. His father was thought to have been the perpetrator. Insufficient evidence of the crime prevented my bringing criminal charges against anyone. Regardless of my suspicions that the child had been raped, probable cause to make an arrest did not exist in this case. Here is just one example of sexual abuse to a male child that would not be included in the statistics.

Whenever I made an arrest for sexual abuse crimes, an attempt was made to determine whether the men had themselves been victimized. Many told me "off the record" about their own childhood victimization. Almost all the male perpetrators who had been sexually abused as children knew that their offenders had never been prosecuted.

self-inflicting is cause for concern. Keep in mind that children often scratch their faces if their fingernails are not kept cut; many hospitals, for example, put mittens on newborns for this reason. Note the bruise on the infant in Figure 6–4; the outline of fingers is readily identifiable on the cheek.

When an injury is caused through discipline or for the purpose of inflicting injury, it is an example of nonaccidental injury. If a child is punched, kicked, thrown, or shaken and sustains injury, no matter how slight, the abusers could be held legally responsible regardless of a preexisting medical condition.

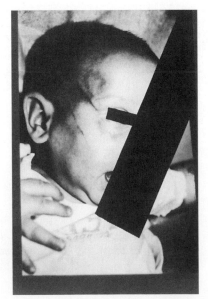

Figure 6–4 This child was slapped with a human hand. *(Photo used with the permission of the American Academy of Pediatrics.* Visual Diagnosis of Child Physical Abuse; *Bk&Acces edition; AAP [January 1995].)*

Been There . . . Done That!

The interdisciplinary or multiagency team is an example of recent attempts to provide coordination among child protection workers, the police, the medical community, and the prosecutor's office. It is helpful to include a forensic mental health specialist or child psychologist on the team if possible. They share information and discuss options for the child. In 1984, I was a member of one of the first interdisciplinary teams to investigate child abuse in Massachusetts at the Northwestern District Attorney's office under Michael Ryan. It worked like this: Once a week, the team would meet for one to two hours. The department of social services investigator would bring the week's list of child abuse allegations of serious physical or sexual abuse. The team, including a doctor, prosecutor, mental health worker, victim witness assistant, and me as the police representative, would discuss the cases.

We determined who would conduct the interview of the child in order to minimize the number of interviews. The interviewer could be any team member or a forensic interviewer. Then we discussed the cases already in the process of investigation.

In cases that the prosecutor thought were likely to go to trial, I would conduct the interview because I also videotaped the first interview with the victims. The videotape would be shared with the necessary agencies, or they could watch through a two-way mirror as the interview was being conducted. The police would always interrogate the perpetrator, with a full report made to the social service agency to complete their mandate to talk with the abuser.

When present (it was difficult to have a doctor or representative present at all meetings), the physician or representative would advise on the necessity of a physical exam. He or she would explain the findings if an exam had already been done. The victim witness advocates and mental health professional would express their concerns about any mental health problems and address the victim's perceived ability to withstand the rigors of a criminal trial. We discussed the reliability of the victim and the consistency of any reports regarding the abuse. This coordinated response resulted in many child abuse cases never coming to trial, for any number of reasons that the team might bring up, including the needs of the victim. Successful prosecution of these difficult cases increased with the team approach.

Since my own experiences, multidisciplinary teams have sprung up across the nation. Experts suggest the team approach as the best method of investigation for child abuse cases (Sgroi, 1984; Smith, 1995). I agree.

Age Dating of Bruises.   Multiple bruises, abrasions, or other wounds in varying stages of healing may indicate repetitive physical assault, particularly if they are in the same location on the child. Documenting the color of the bruises will assist in determining if repetitive abuse has occurred. It may also be helpful to see if the age of the bruise matches the explanation for the presenting injury, since a timeline of the

---

Been There . . . Done That!

Interviewing parents or the caretaker of a child should always be done with respect. The feelings or personal opinion of the investigator should never enter into the conversation, no matter how severe the injuries may be. There is a distinct difference between an interview and an interrogation of the suspect. The interview is a gathering of information and should not be confrontational. Keep it nonjudgmental and thorough to assure compliance of the interviewee; there is always time later for an interrogation if a suspect is identified.

Once an accusation is made, or the parents feel they are being accused, they will hesitate to answer the many questions that you have. The majority of parents whose children have injuries did not intend to harm the child. Some may believe that they have the right to punish in any form they choose, or have gone too far in the form of punishment they gave. It is the role of the court to make these parents accountable, not that of the investigator.

Additionally, leave the door of communication open, taking care not to accuse someone falsely of abuse. The consequences of false allegations by authorities cannot be underestimated: Humiliation, shame, loss of job, and in some cases loss of the custody of their children can result.

Figure 6–5 Accidental injury locations, front and back. Bruises on the walking child are usually accidental if they appear on the forehead, elbows, and stomach, and the outside of the thighs, knees, and ankles.

Figure 6–6 Nonaccidental injury locations, front and back. Bruises or fractures to a child that are suspicious for an intentional injury are located on the ears and cheeks, neck, shoulders and upper arms, genitals, and inner thighs. Bruising on locations other than bony prominences is questionable. Defense posturing can cause injuries to the outside of the lower arm. Suspicious bruising locations include the buttocks, lower back, earlobes, mouth, and neck.

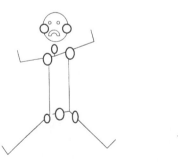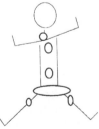

injury is possible. The age of a bruise is generally determined by its color, although the location can change the color somewhat.

- Bright red bruises are indicative of an injury 0 to 2 days old.
- Bluish or purple bruises are 2 to 5 days old.
- Green indicates a bruise 5 to 7 days old.
- Yellow bruises are 7 to 10 days old.
- Brown bruises are 10 to 14 days old.
- No evidence of bruising occurs after 2 to 4 weeks.

Many factors influence expected bruising patterns and colors. Some people merely bruise more easily than others; bruises are harder to see on people with very dark skin, and the colors usually seen when the bruise fades may not be apparent. How hard the person is hit and the location of the injury may alter the expected bruise colors or patterns. Persons with medical conditions, particularly leukemia, may have what appear to be severe bruises when no beating occurred.

Patterns of Bruising Abrasions, Bruises, Lacerations, and Welts.   Common household items are frequently used as weapons against children in abusive situations. Examples include hairbrushes, flyswatters, hangers, belts, and baseball bats. The most common dangerous weapon remains the hand. Look for the patterns on the locations that have been identified as suspicious. Even if the child is unable to articulate, bruise patterns on the child may help to identify and retrieve the weapon as evidence.

More About It: Osteogenesis Imperfecta

The technical term for **brittle bone disease** is **osteogenesis imperfecta** (OI). Bones that break easily characterize the condition. There are four forms of OI, with bone fragility ranging from mild to very severe, depending on the type. A minor accident may result in a fracture; some fractures may occur while an infant with the condition is being diapered, lifted, or dressed.

Child abuse is also characterized by broken bones. Consult a physician in cases of multiple fractures in multiple stages of healing, rib or spiral fractures, and when there is no adequate explanation for the trauma. In most cases, radiographic, clinical, and historical features are present and obvious, allowing easy detection (Ablin, 1998). A skin biopsy for collagen analysis in difficult cases may help to identify mild forms of OI. Since child abuse and OI have been reported together, the presence of OI does not exclude the possibility of child abuse.

Infants are not capable of "falling" down, but once they begin to walk, they begin to fall. Young children who are active are more capable of hurting themselves physically.

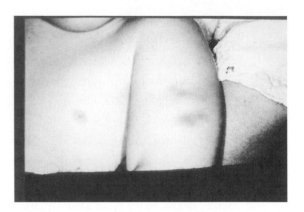

Figure 6–7   Grab mark. *(Photo used with the permission of the American Academy of Pediatrics. Visual Diagnosis of Child Physical Abuse; Bk&Acces edition; AAP [January 1995].)*

Small oval patterns or imprints suggest an inflicted injury due to being grabbed, pinched, squeezed, or slapped. Figure 6–7 shows a grab mark on the upper arm: Notice the two bruises caused by fingers; there may be a thumb mark on the other side of the arm of the child. These oval marks, which are characteristic of fingertips, may be found on the trunk of a child who has been shaken, and around the throat if strangulation was attempted.

Another indication of attempted strangulation is a wrapping mark around the throat indicating that a rope, cord, or wire might have been used. Tethering or tying up of the child may also cause a bruise around the mouth, neck, wrists, or ankles. Wraparound or tethering or binding injuries on the neck, ankle, or wrist suggest that a child is being tied with a rope or cord.

As stated earlier, punishment gone too far is at the root of most abuse. Refer to Figure 6–8 for a clear example of punishment that is considered abusive. Not all physical abuse cases are this extreme. When minor injury is present, the investigation becomes difficult. The final resolution for the child should not be the result of a gut reaction, however. Consider the physical evidence as an outside indication of abuse; look to see if behavioral symptoms and signs are present. Look for other forms of abuse, such as emotional or psychological abuse, sexual abuse, or neglect. If you do not find signs of these, the case may have to be closed. Objects used to hit a child may leave a distinguishable pattern of bruise identifiable, for example, as that of a hairbrush, cord, or coat hanger. The doubled-over cord or coat hanger will leave a loop mark, as shown in Figure 6–9. A human bite also leaves a distinguishable pattern of injury that can be distinguished from animal bites by the configuration of the teeth, as in Figure 6–10. Tearing or shearing injuries are more likely to be caused by an animal (Jenny & Day, 1994).

Injuries to the Head.   Infants rarely suffer head injuries that are accidental. A child riding a bicycle, roller skating, dirt biking, or four-wheeling might suffer accidental head injuries. Car accidents may also be responsible for the harm to a child.

Child protective services, known as the Department of Social Services in Massachusetts, called to notify me of a young child at the local hospital who was suspected to have been shaken. The child was presumed to have serious brain damage and was not expected to live through the night. The child's infant brother, who had brittle bone disease, had died on the previous day. The initial determination was that the infant had died of complications due to the osteogenesis imperfecta.

An interview with the mother provided information that she and her boyfriend shared a one-bedroom apartment with the two children. In the middle of the night, the crying of the sick child, who in turn woke the other child, awakened the boyfriend. The desperate mother had carried both children into the kitchen to appease her boyfriend. She said that she stumbled over a toy in the doorway and had dropped the toddler. A search warrant executed at the apartment found there were no toys in the apartment. A dent on the side of the stove was noted in the doorway where the mother claimed to have stumbled. Her story of how the child "rolled" to the opposite side of the room was indicative of his having been thrown against the stove before coming to rest a few feet away in the opposite direction. In addition to the brain damage, he presented with retinal hemorrhage, suggestive of shaken baby syndrome. This child became ill the next day, throwing up, and he had stopped breathing before he was rushed to the hospital. Although the toddler lived, his doctor predicted that the brain damage would prevent him from developing past his age of two.

The infant was presumed to have died immediately from the incident. It was never clear whether he was also thrown or had been mishandled, causing his brittle bones to break.

Toddlers just learning to walk present a different picture; they frequently have "goose eggs" on their foreheads because of falling. Examples of intentional injury include

- Hemorrhaging beneath the scalp or when hair is missing due to being pulled
- Retinal hemorrhage, the hallmark of **shaken baby syndrome** and only rarely associated with some other kind of injury
- Injury from multiple slapping or hitting on the head, causing neck injury, with the child unable to turn his or her head
- Whiplash (without an auto accident history)
- Any bruising to the ear, a cause for suspicion that the child has been hit on the side of the head
- A "cauliflower ear," similar to a boxing injury, caused when the ear is hit numerous times

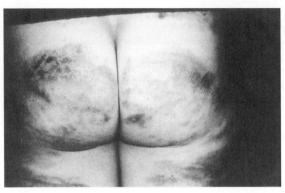

Figure 6–8 This child was beaten on the buttocks with a plastic pipe. Notice the outline of the pipe that was used. *(Photo used with the permission of the American Academy of Pediatrics.* Visual Diagnosis of Child Physical Abuse; *Bk&Acces edition; AAP [January 1995].)*

- A black or swollen eye, which can be accidental or the result of abuse (the history of the accident is important)

Shaken Baby Syndrome.   Shaken baby syndrome (SBS) is the medical term used to describe the violent shaking of a child and the injuries that can occur. Shaken baby is relatively new classification of death or injury to infants, and the number of child victims is uncertain. Some professionals believe that 10 to 12 percent of all deaths due to abuse and neglect are attributable to the syndrome (Seymour et al., 2002). Children from birth to age two are at the highest risk of suffering harm from shaking because their neck muscles are underdeveloped and their brain tissue is fragile.

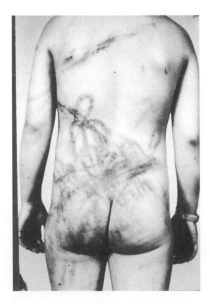

Figure 6–9 Looped cord mark. *(Photo used with the permission of the American Academy of Pediatrics.* Visual Diagnosis of Child Physical Abuse; *Bk&Acces edition; AAP [January 1995).]*

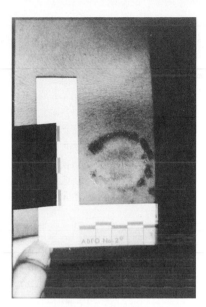

Figure 6–10 Human bite mark. *(Photo used with the permission of the American Academy of Pediatrics. Visual Diagnosis of Child Physical Abuse; Bk&Acces edition; AAP [January 1995].)*

Repeated vigorous shaking causes the brain to slam against the skull from side to side. It can cause brain damage, blindness, paralysis, seizures, and death. Most SBS victims present with retinal hemorrhages that look like broken blood vessels and small pooling of blood on the white of the eye. Between 1,000 and 3,000 children are diagnosed with shaken baby syndrome every year; about 100 to 120 of them die (Seymour et al., 2002). Violent shaking of infants is a common cause for abusive brain injury.

According to Seymour and colleagues (2002), the perpetrators of shaken baby syndrome are about 80 percent male: 37 percent are the biological fathers and 20.5 are percent boyfriends to the mother of the child. The biological mother is the perpetrator in approximately 12.6 of the instances; female babysitters account for 17.3 percent of the shaking abuse.

Burns.   Punishment in the form of burns may involve forcing a child under hot water, inflicting cigarette or lighter burns, or pushing/holding a child on a heating or electrical unit. In extremely rare cases, children have been placed in ovens and in a microwave, which caused death. When a child has a burn that is described as accidental, the injury is probably located on the front of the child's body. This can happen if a child pulled over a pot on the stove or a container of hot liquid. A young child might also touch or step on a heating unit, injuring the bottom of a foot or hand.

Immersion in hot water causes symmetrical patterns that are distinct from accidental burns and are the most common burns caused by child abuse (Jenny & Day, 1994). A person who steps into a hot bath or bumps into a pot of boiling liquid that spills on him or her will move away and jump in pain—the burns caused by this are not

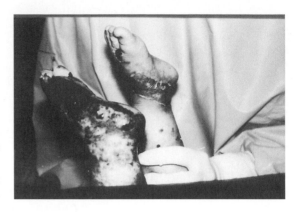

Figure 6–11   Immersion burn. *(Photo used with the permission of the American Academy of Pediatrics. Visual Diagnosis of Child Physical Abuse; Bk&Acces edition; AAP [January 1995].)*

even across the body; splash marks result. An **immersion burn** occurs when a child is held or forced into the hot water. What results is a distinct shape or series of burns:

- An oval burn usually includes buttocks and genitals; it is caused when a child is submerged and held in hot water. The burn may not be totally symmetrical; some areas of the body can be protected from the burn, due to the position of the arms and legs of the child.

- A glove or stocking burn results when a hand or foot is held in hot water. An example of a stocking burn is seen in Figure 6–11. Notice the splash marks on the less severely burned leg, which indicates that the child managed to free that leg partially while being held.

- A donut-shaped burn surrounding the buttocks indicates being forced to sit on a hot object, which could be an electric heater, stove, or other electrical unit.

Forms of Sexual Abuse

Girls are more likely to be sexually abused, with 12- to 15-year-olds in the most danger (2.8 per 1,000), according to recent government reports (U.S. Department of Health and Human Services, 2001). It is commonly accepted that sexual crimes are under-reported; self-reports typically report higher levels. Debates on the prevalence of sexual abuse against both boys and girls rage on. All agree, however, that sexual abuse of a child is contemptible. When family members perpetrate the abuse, it usually involves multiple episodes over a period of time from one week to years. However, there is no "typical" victim. Sexual abuse has been known to be committed against all ages of children, even infants. Over 50 percent of male victims experienced anal penetration (Hammerschlag, 1996). A sexual assault on a child is any forced, exploitive, or coercive sexual contact or experience with a child. Statutes typically address the issue of force, and they vary widely. Due to the usual age difference in sexual victimization and the lack of sexual maturity in a young person, force can be as minimal as instructing a child in a sexual activity.

Most often, there are no physical signs of the sexual misuse of children. Types of sexual assault include the following:

- *Molestation:* Involves indecent touching of the child or forcing the child to touch the perpetrator on the genitals or breasts.
- *Rape:* The insertion of any object into any orifice for sexual gratification. Penile penetration usually comes to mind, but rape also includes digital penetration into the child's vagina or anus (use of fingers), or oral penetration of breasts, penis, or vagina (use of the mouth). In fact, any object can be used to effect a rape; common weapons include bottles, sticks, and curling irons. Any object used to penetrate a child is a weapon of rape. Rarely, there may be a visible indication that force was used in the attempt of a rape. Notice the bruise around the neck of the rape victim in Figure 6–12.
- *Voyeurism:* Includes looking at the victim in various stages of undress. The victims may or may not be aware that the perpetrator is watching them.
- *Exhibitionism:* When a person exhibits his or her genitalia to a child.
- *Pornography:* For the crime to be pornography, the victim does not have to be aware that the perpetrator is filming or videotaping.
- *Forced prostitution:* A child is always considered to be forced when he or she is engaging in prostitution at the instruction of an adult.

Incest.   When a blood relative perpetrates sexual abuse, it is known as **incest**. If the sexual relationship is between a parent and child, the power position of the parent identifies the perpetrator. Parental/child incest is the type that is most commonly reported, but sibling incest may be the most frequent form (Sgroi, 1984). Including stepparents or foster parents is common in nonlegal definitions of incest, particularly in clinical settings. When sexual interactions take place between children who have the same parents, they are incestual. The relationship may be consensual in the absence of

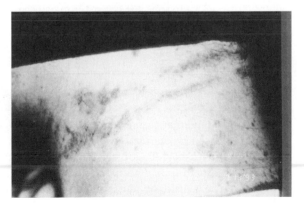

Figure 6–12 Bruise due to strangulation attempt. *(Photo used with the permission of the American Academy of Pediatrics.* Visual Diagnosis of Child Physical Abuse; *Bk&Acces edition; AAP [January 1995].)*

threats or harm in order to gain compliance when both individuals are legally capable of giving consent.

Symptoms of Sexual Abuse

Sexually Transmitted Diseases in Children. Gonorrhea, syphilis, AIDS, herpes, venereal warts, and pubic lice are examples of sexually transmitted diseases (STDs). The presence of an STD in a child over the age of one month is suggestive of sexual abuse, but exceptions do exist (Hammerschlag, 1996).

Physical Indicators

1. Enlarged vaginal or anal opening
2. Bleeding or discharge from the vagina, penis, or anus
3. Scratching or rubbing the genitals
4. Walking with the buttocks and legs apart (as if the child has to have a bowel movement)
5. Current physical injury accompanied by signs of multiple prior injuries

Behavioral Indicators

1. Complaining that his or her genitals hurt or were touched
2. Acting out sexually with other children
3. Inappropriate sexual knowledge for his or her home environment and age
4. Child fearful or unwilling to explain the cause of any injury
5. Regression

Caretaker Indicators

1. Delay or failure to seek medical treatment for a child in circumstances that would warrant medical attention
2. History not consistent with the child's developmental level or ability to harm himself or herself
3. Historical details change or are different from the caretaker's original version

---

More About It: Maltreatment

Keep in mind that as individuals, we have our own perspective on how children should be raised, based on our upbringing and family history. Be careful not to impose your standards on another family! Additionally, families living in poverty will appear different due to a lack of resources and should not be accused of abuse simply because they don't live the way you do! Abuse is maltreatment, not a result of the living standards or values of other families.

Neglect

Child neglect is the form of violence that is most commonly found in cases of abuse. More than 60 percent of the estimated 896,000 children were neglected by their parents or other caregivers in 2002 (McDonald, 2004). Neglect is often present when other forms of abuse are reported. In some states, that would constitute a separate report; in others, it would not be substantiated if it were the "minor" form that the child presents. The accuracy of our statistics is questionable due to obscure definitions and differential reporting methods. Still, the problem of assuring adequate care for children is a huge one that requires education. When neglect is noted, it should be documented in a comprehensive report of the child's situation.

Neglect is difficult to define because there is no consensus. Inadequate parenting can include a number of different acts or omissions that might be considered neglectful. The concept of neglect is predicated on a parental duty to provide the basic needs for one's children. These needs include food and adequate shelter. A parent is expected to seek medical attention and provide educational opportunities for the child. Providing supervision and nurturing is also expected. The failure to provide these necessities within socially acceptable standards may be considered neglectful.

Along with the idea of parental duty, the concept of children's rights has been established. Children have been afforded legal protections to assure that the parent is providing the necessities of life and promoting well-being. As early as 1838, the U.S. Supreme Court ruled in *Ex Parte Crouse* that the right of the parent is not inalienable. The extent to which children must be protected and the expanse of child rights has always been controversial in social and legal forums.

Educational Neglect.   At the most basic level, the education of a child includes providing behavioral limits that are age appropriate. All states have mandatory formal educational requirements that a child must attend school until age 16. Educational neglect includes failure to enroll a child of mandatory school age in school, the allowing of chronic truancy, and the failure to attend to a special educational need.

Inadequate Care Such as Food, Clothing, and Shelter.   Children are unable to seek out nutrition that is necessary for body growth and development. A healthy baby should double his or her birth weight by four to six months and triple it by about one year (Rosenberg, 1996). Food should be of the quality and amount that is appropriate for the age of the child. Inadequate nutrition or a disease may cause a condition in children called the **failure to thrive**, where sufficient weight for normal growth is not attained. Acute starvation is the result of lack of nutrition on a short-term basis. If a child has been dehydrated (by a failure to provide fluids), the child may present with severe vomiting or diarrhea. If failure to thrive, dehydration, or starvation is suspected, the child requires immediate medical attention, as illness or death can result. According to a report from the National Clearinghouse on Child Abuse and Neglect (2001), research has determined that malnutrition during the first few years after birth can result in stunted brain growth and slower passage of electrical signals in the brain. Cognitive, social, and behavioral deficits are associated with these effects on the brain. Malnutrition can result in anxiety, depression, social problems, and attention disorders when it is due to iron deficiency.

Clothing should be sufficient to protect the child from the elements, minimally clean, and in decent repair. Infants must have diapers that are cleaned and changed frequently to avoid severe diaper rashes. Shelter must provide protection from extreme weather and allow a safe place for sleep.

Lack of Supervision.   Supervision is necessary to prevent harm or to intervene when harm is occurring. Leaving a young child unattended or locking the child in a room are examples of failure to provide supervision if the age and maturity of the child are insufficient to respond to problems that might occur. Young children have been known to play with matches and lighters while locked in a room, which has led to a fire and ultimate death. Parents must be sure that when children are left alone—such as latchkey kids—they are reasonably able to care for themselves in case harm arises.

Failure to Seek Medical Care.   The parent has the duty to seek medical care for a child when necessary. Withholding of medically necessary treatment has been defined by the Child Abuse Prevention and Treatment Act of 1996 as the failure to respond to an infant's life-threatening conditions by denial of treatment that would probably be effective in ameliorating all life-threatening conditions. A religious exemption from medical neglect is permitted in some states if the withholding of medical care is based on religious grounds. Each state determines if it will recognize this federal standard expressed by the U.S. Department of Health and Human Services.

Nonsupport.   The court determines child support when a family divorces or separates. It is like an allowance for the child that is administered by the parent who has

---

Been There . . . Done That!

Although I was not a narcotics investigator, there were times when that unit would ask for assistance in executing warrants. I remember such a case where we "hit" an apartment with a search warrant for drugs. As I came through the door, I couldn't help but notice a child of about six years old sitting at the breakfast table. He would put his fingers into the bowl and pull out a cockroach, then take a spoon full of cereal. He repeated this until he had finished eating, literally "flicking" the cockroaches across the room each time. As I searched his bedroom, the contents of each dresser drawer would appear to "move" in unison when opened to the light. When I lifted his mattress to look at that space between the mattress and box spring, thousands of cockroaches scurried to the same beat. Was this child neglect? I spoke with a social worker who reminded me that the apartment was one of approximately 150 in the block and that cockroaches are a hazard of the poverty in that neighborhood.

legal physical custody. It allows the custodial parent to provide adequate care for the child who lives with him or her at a level roughly equivalent to the family's status had the separation not occurred. Both biological parents have the responsibility to care for their offspring; this method attempts to share the financial assets of the parents for the benefit of the child. Failure to provide for a child financially directly affects the quality of life for the child and may cause illness or neglect. Recent campaigns to decrease nonsupport have attained a high level of media coverage. Most people are familiar with the terms *deadbeat dad* and *deadbeat mom*. These refer to parents who attempt to avoid their financial responsibility through nonsupport of a minor child.

Parental Kidnapping

Parental abduction of children has become a serious concern in the United States, where approximately one-third of all children live in single-parent households. The term is used when a parent abducts a child in violation of custody or visitation rights or prior to the filing of custody decree. Approximately 203,900 family-abducted children were kidnapped in 1999 (Hammer et al., 2002). Abductors may flee to avoid further abuse to themselves or children, or the abuser may abduct in an attempt to intimidate a battered parent who is attempting to leave the relationship. In either situation the legal remedies remain the same.

While society may be sympathetic to situations where a parent flees to avoid abuse, there is no legal exemption per se from prosecution for **parental kidnapping**. Some states, however, provide an affirmative defense for victims who are fleeing domestic violence situations (Johnston et al., 2001). A "defense" is not an exemption; any case where parental kidnapping is alleged would be evaluated on its merits; the defense is not always successful (Johnston et al., 2001). Abused women are strongly encouraged to seek legal advice and pursue all available legal remedies for child protection and custody before taking the decisive step of kidnapping.

The majority of perpetrators are the parent of the child, yet other family members kidnap a small percentage of these victims. Family abductions can be viewed as two separate categories, according to severity. In the first are situations in which a family member took a child in violation of a custody agreement or decree, or in violation of a custody order failed to return a child at the end of the legal or agreed-upon visit. The second type involves an attempt to conceal the taking or whereabouts of the child or to prevent contact with the child; it may involve taking the child out of state. The vast majority of these child-kidnapping cases involving family occur within the context of divorce. Males and females are equally liable to kidnap their offspring; however, most cases are quickly resolved.

Due to the seriousness of the problem and the consequences for the child, all 50 states and the District of Columbia have enacted criminal parental kidnapping statutes. When confronted with an allegation of child kidnapping by a parent who names the other, a check begins with a determination as to who has physical legal custody. The reporter should be able to supply documentation from a family court or from a divorce proceeding on the custody and specifics for child visitation if the parents have appeared before the court. A frequent resolution in the absence of child abuse allegation is the awarding of shared legal custody to the parents upon separation and divorce.

ADOLESCENT OFFENDING AS A CONSEQUENCE OF VICTIMIZATION

First it must be stated that child abuse does not end with the onset of adolescence. Until recently, the frequency of adolescent physical and sexual victimization went unnoticed. Adolescents are thought to be capable of protecting themselves; the numbers indicate that this misconception could cause inappropriate responses to allegations of abuse by teenagers. In 2002, almost 17 percent of child abuse victims were between the ages of 12 and 17 (McDonald, 2004).

High school students with histories of maltreatment experience significant adjustment and emotional problems as compared to students without maltreatment experiences (Wolfe, 2001). For female students, risk of clinically significant anger and depression problems was found to be seven times greater among those with a history of maltreatment. Risk anxiety and posttraumatic stress problems for the girls were over nine times greater than for students without maltreatment experiences (Wolfe et al., 2001).

The effects of sexual assault, physical assault, physically abusive punishment, and witnessing an act of violence have severe consequences during adolescence. Kilpatrick and colleagues (2003) found higher rates of posttraumatic stress disorder (PTSD), alcohol abuse, marijuana abuse, hard drug abuse, and delinquent behavior for both boys and girls that had been victimized. Boys that had been sexually assaulted were three times more likely to have committed a major crime than female victims, according to the study. Kilpatrick and associates found a strong link between physical assault or abusive punishment and delinquency.

Severe dating violence among and against high school students has been documented in many communities. Nearly 12 percent of adolescents self-reported severe dating violence in one South Carolina study (Coker et al., 2000). Of these students, 7.7 percent self-reported as a perpetrator and 7.6 percent reported severe victimization. The adolescent female victims experienced suicide ideation or attempts; male perpetration was strongly associated with suicide attempts. The need to address relationship violence among adolescents is strongly indicated; education regarding positive relationship building is warranted.

Risk of Adolescent Sexual Reoffending

Frequently, sexual offenders report that they began offending in their adolescent years. An early target may be a younger sibling. The child may abuse because he or she has learned that this is acceptable or may act out of rage due to his or her own experiences of being abused.

Juvenile sex offending may include bestiality, sometimes combined with other violent behavior toward animals (Lane, 1997). Frank Ascione recently reported on "Animal Abuse and Youth Violence" (Ascione, 2001). He finds a connection between child abuse and neglect, domestic violence, and animal abuse. Animal abuse is more likely to occur in homes where children are abused or neglected and in homes where spouse battering occurs. Based on the available literature, Ascione documents that sexually abused children are more likely to be cruel to animals and to engage in bestiality as adolescents as compared to those without a history of maltreatment.

Risk of Juvenile Battering Behavior

For male high school students the risk of using physical abuse against their partners was over three times greater among those with a history of maltreatment compared to students without a history of abuse (Wolfe et al., 2001). Child maltreatment is firmly interwoven with juvenile dating violence.

Against Parent(s) or Caretakers.   Langer (1997) found that a significant proportion of cases involved domestic violence perpetrated by a juvenile against parents or siblings. The data suggest that the percentage has increased and is likely to continue. Reasons for the increase in reported cases may include better training that enables police to identify domestic violence, a broader definition of domestic violence that includes family members other than parents, and greater awareness of what is unacceptable behavior within a family. In this limited data set, the primary victim of juvenile violence in the family is the mother.

Data from calls to a 24-hour hotline for the Violence Intervention Program (VIP) in New Orleans, Louisiana, support the findings. Of the 300 calls received in 1999, more than half were from parents concerned about violent behavior by their 13- to 17-year-old children (Osofsky & Fenichel, 1999). Courts nationwide have developed innovations to address child maltreatment and the problem of abuse perpetrated by children that results in calls to police by a parent.

Against Siblings.   Violence between siblings is underreported and underdocumented. Most instances of this type of family violence are attributed to sibling rivalry, but its effects can be serious. Adults and children commit similar types of abuse: physical, sexual, and emotional abuse. The acts involve punching, hitting, kicking, biting, and rape. Critics have argued that most aggression between siblings is not serious and should not be considered abuse; proponents suggest otherwise.

Sibling abuse goes beyond child play and contains strong elements of violence. It is not an isolated act but a cycle of behavior that looks very much like spouse abuse. The child who is violent is often male and larger than his siblings. According to Vernon Wiehe, it looks like the stronger beating up the weak (Wiehe, 1997). The size of the child is deceiving, however, as the abuse is a way to compensate for a lack of power or perceived loss of power. The child may feel jealous toward siblings who appear to please the parents through better academic achievement, looks, or personality. Given the opportunity to express feelings of inadequacy, the child may direct them at the siblings.

Researchers suggest that abused children learn to be abusive through modeling and instrumental learning, according to the social learning theory. This may explain why juveniles who are abused, physically or sexually, sometimes perpetrate against others. However, critics using the cycle of violence theory as an intervention point out that only 20 to 30 percent of child abuse and neglect victims become involved in abusive and criminal behavior as adults (Garrett & Libbey, 1997).

MANDATED REPORTING

Mandated reporting is the legislative requirement that certain professionals must report cases of suspected child abuse or neglect for investigation to a designated authority within a specified period of time. All 50 states and the District of Columbia have legislation that mandates reporting of child abuse and neglect. These mandates differ slightly from state to state as to what agency must receive and investigate the report and the time to accomplish the investigation. The primary objective for agencies that investigate child abuse is to determine whether the child is in need of care and protection. The investigator must next assess the level of risk to the child in his or her present living arrangements. Protection options include the removal of the suspected offender from the home if he or she lives with the child. A parent or legal guardian of the victim should be encouraged to file for a no-contact restraining order to protect the child during the investigation from further violence and threats, whether or not the suspect resides with the child.

To prevent the child from feeling punished for having divulged abuse, removal of the child from his or her home to a safe living environment is an option that should be exercised only if a nonoffending parent or guardian is unwilling or unable to protect the child from the suspect. Additional social services are provided according to the resources of the area in which the abuse is alleged to have occurred. An investigation to determine if a crime has been committed is conducted by law enforcement officials and may be done jointly with a social service agency or independently. Although the initial concern of any investigation involving a child is the safety of the child, law enforcement and social services have different mandates for investigative procedures.

False reporting of child abuse has been a concern of practitioners and parents since enactment of legislation requiring reporting. The Pennsylvania Department of Public Welfare acknowledged that knowingly false and malicious reporting is considered to be a serious problem that is on the increase. After careful and lengthy consideration, recommendations were made to adopt a protocol for the screening of anonymous referrals of suspected abuse (Cosner et al., 1997).

Who Must Report?

Any person who has a duty to care for or protect a child may be considered a mandated reporter, governed by the requirements of each particular state. Typical mandated reporters include physicians, childcare givers, police officers, and teachers. It is difficult to determine the exact number of children who are reported and substantiated for child abuse because of the wide variation among states' data collection procedures. Compliance for reporting of child abuse is also difficult to determine, and we can only speculate on the cases that are not investigated due to a lack of reporting.

CONCLUSIONS

The recognition of child abuse and neglect is an important step in the determination of domestic violence involving children. Victims may have experienced numerous kinds of injury and harm that can sometimes be confused with nonabusive injury. Forms of direct abuse include active and physical maltreatment; the general categories include physical, sexual, and emotional maltreatment. Secondary abuse is the consequence of witnessing violence in the home.

No profile can be drawn to describe the victims of abuse. All ages, gender, and races are represented. Although confusion may exist on the exact numbers of those maltreated, certainly we can conclude that it is high—unacceptably high for our society. Medical history and injury inspections are part of the process in determining abuse. Age dating of bruises and pattern identification are tools to assess the condition of the child and provide the necessary protection options. Multidisciplinary teams are helpful for providing insights into the injury and harm and for decisions on intervention. Ultimately, it is the responsibility of the parents or legal guardians to provide for the care and protection of their children physically, mentally, and financially. Intervention must take place only when the needs of the child are not being met to a minimum standard of care or when abusive conditions exist.

For accurate determinations regarding allegations of child abuse or neglect, sexual or physical, proper preserving and gathering of evidence is essential. In this chapter numerous methods of distinguishing between abuse and nonaccidental injury have been documented. Further, the identification of bruises and injury patterns has been presented.

We frequently dismiss or ignore concerns about juvenile violence. New events have forced us to look again at the consequences of abuse and neglect and its effects on adolescents. It is important not to underestimate the devastating effects that family violence has on all children, adolescents included. Juvenile crime is a concern that must be addressed through prevention strategies.

QUESTIONS FOR REVIEW

1. What made the public shift attitudes toward child abuse?

2. Describe direct abuse. What is the difference between active and passive maltreatment?

3. What is secondary abuse?

4. What are the major forms of child abuse?

5. What is brittle bone disease?

6. How can one determine the age of a bruise?

7. Are victims that flee to avoid abuse exempted when they have kidnapped their child?

8. What are the elements of sexual abuse?

9. List and define the types of sexual abuse.

10. Who is obligated by law to report abuse?

INTERNET-BASED EXERCISES

1. Conduct online research on sudden infant death syndrome (SIDS). Explain the "Back to Sleep" Campaign. What is the relation of SIDS to child abuse? Start your search at the American Academy of Pediatrics: http://www.aap.org/.

2. Describe the signs and symptoms of shaken baby syndrome. What are some challenges prosecutors face in the prosecution of these cases? Explain. Go to http://www.shakenbaby.com/default.htm.

REFERENCES

Ablin, Deborah S. 1998. "Osteogenesis Imperfecta: A Review." *Canadian Association Radiological Journal* 49:110–23.

Ascione, Frank. 2001. "Animal Abuse and Youth Violence." *Juvenile Justice Bulletin*. NCJ 188677. Washington, DC: U.S. Department of Justice.

Children as Victims. 2000. 1999 National Report Series. Office of Juvenile Justice Delinquency Programs. NCJ 180753. Washington, DC: U.S. Department of Justice.

Coker, Ann L., Robert McKeown, Maureen Sanderson, Keith Davis, Robert F. Valois, and E. Scott Huebner. 2000. "Severe Dating Violence and Quality of Life Among South Carolina High School Students." *Urology* 19(4):220–27.

Cosner, R. E., N. A. Weiner, V. Huang, R. Rendon, U. Bischoff, and I. M. Schwartz. 1997. *Knowingly False and Malicious Reporting of Child Abuse and Neglect in Pennsylvania: Critical Questions, Findings, and Recommendations.* NCJ 171798. Washington, DC: U.S. Department of Justice.

Garrett, Athena, and Heather Libbey. 1997. *Theory and Research on the Outcomes and Consequences of Child Abuse and Neglect.* Child Abuse Intervention Strategic Planning Meeting. Washington, DC. Washington, DC: National Institute of Justice.

Hammer, Heather, David Finkelhor, and Andrea Sedlak. 2002. *Runaway/Thrownaway Children: National Estimates and Characteristics.* NISMART-2. NCJ 196469. Washington, DC: Office of Juvenile Justice and Delinquency.

Hammerschlag, Margaret R. 1996. *Sexually Transmitted Diseases and Child Sexual Abuse.* NCJ 160940. Washington, DC: U.S. Department of Justice.

Helfer, Ray E., and Ruth S. Kempe (eds.). 1988. *The Battered Child,* 4th ed. Chicago: University of Chicago Press.

Hunter, Mic. 1990. *Abused Boys: The Neglected Victims of Sexual Abuse.* Lexington, MA: Lexington Books.

Jenny, Carole, and Thomas Day. 1994. *The Visual Diagnosis of Child Physical Abuse.* Denver, CO: American Academy of Pediatrics.

Johnston, Janet R., Inger Sagatun-Edwards, Martha-Elin Blomquist, and Linda K. Girdner. 2001. *Early Identification of Risk Factors for Parental Abduction.* Juvenile Justice Bulletin, Office of Juvenile Justice and Delinquency Prevention. NCJ 185026. Washington, DC: U.S. Department of Justice.

Kilpatrick, Dean, Benjamin E. Saunders, and Daniel W. Smith. 2003. *Youth Victimization: Prevalence and Implications.* NIJ: Research in Brief. NIJ 194972. Washington, DC: U.S. Department of Justice.

Lane, S. 1997. "Assessment of Sexually Abusive Youth." In *Juvenile Sexual Offending: Causes, Consequences, and Correction.* Ryan, G. and S. Lane (eds.), pp. 219–263. San Francisco: Jossey-Bass.

Langer, L. 1997. *Final Report of the Juvenile Domestic Violence Project.* Miami, FL: 11th District Court.

McDonald, Walter. 2004. *Child Maltreatment 2002.* Washington, DC: Department of Health and Human Services.

NAIC. 2003. "Children and Domestic Violence: A Bulletin for Professionals" [Web Page]. Available at *http://nccanch.acf.hhs.gov/pubs/factsheets/domesticviolence.cfm*.

National Clearinghouse on Child Abuse and Neglect. 2001. *Understanding the Effects of Maltreatment on Early Brain Development.* Washington, DC: U.S. Department of Health and Human Services.

Osofsky, J. D. 2000. *Final Report: Violence Intervention Program, Mental Health Initiative with Police.* New Orleans, LA: Louisiana State University Health Sciences Center.

Osofsky, J. D., and E. Fenichel. 1999. *Infants and Violence: Building Community Strengths.* Washington, DC: Zero to Three/National Center for Infants, Toddlers, and Families.

PBS Online. 1998. "Innocence Lost: The Plea." *http://www3.pbs.org/wgbh/pages/frontline/shows/innocence/etc/chronology.html*. 1998.

Rennison, Callie M., and Sarah Welchans. 2000. *Intimate Partner Violence.* NCJ 178247. Washington, DC: U.S. Department of Justice.

Rosenberg, Donna. 1996. *Child Neglect and Munchausen Syndrome by Proxy.* NCJ 162841. Washington, DC: U.S. Department of Justice.

Seymour, A., M. Murray, J. Sigmon, M. Hook, C. Edmunds, M. Gaboury, and G. Coleman (eds.). 2002. *National Victim Assistance Academy Textbook.* Washington, DC: Office for Victims of Crime.

Sgroi, Suzanne M. 1984. *Handbook of Clinical Intervention in Child Sexual Abuse.* Lexington, MA: Lexington Books.

Smith, Barbara. 1995. *Prosecuting Child Physical Cases: Lessons Learned from the San Diego Experience.* NCJ 152978. Washington, DC: U.S. Department of Justice.

U.S. Department of Health and Human Services. 1997. *Child Maltreatment 1995: Reports from the States to the National Child Abuse and Neglect Data System.* 2–7. Washington, DC: National Center on Child Abuse and Neglect.

———. 1998. *Child Maltreatment 1996: Reports from the States to the National Child Abuse and Neglect Data System.* Washington, DC: DHHS.

————. 2001. *Child Maltreatment 1999: Reports from the States to the National Child Abuse and Neglect Data System.* Washington, DC: U.S. Government Printing Office.

Wang, Ching-Tung, and Deborah Daro. 1998. *Current Trends in Child Abuse Reporting and Fatalities: The Results of the 1997 Annual Fifty-State Survey.* Working Paper 808. Chicago: National Committee to Prevent Child Abuse.

Watkins, Sallie A. 1995. "The Mary Ellen Myth: Correcting Child Welfare History." Pp. 46–53 in *Family Violence: Readings in the Social Sciences and Professions*, James Makepeace (ed.). New York: McGraw-Hill.

Wiehe, Vernon R. 1997. *Sibling Abuse: Hidden Physical, Emotional, and Sexual Trauma*, 2nd ed. Thousand Oaks, CA: Sage Publications.

Wolfe, D. A., K. Scott, C. Wekerle, and A. Pittman. 2001. "Child Maltreatment: Risk of Adjustment Problems and Dating Violence in Adolescence." *Journal of the American Academy of Child and Adolescent Psychiatry* 40:282–98.

Wolfe, David. 2001. "Preventing Abuse in Adolescent Dating Relationships." *Research Bulletin* 1(3). Ontario, Canada: Centre for Research on Violence Against Women and Children.

CASE

Ex Parte Crouse, 4 Wharton 9, PA 11 (1838).

CHAPTER 7

THE IDENTIFICATION OF ELDER ABUSE

SIMPLY SCENARIO

Concern for the Elderly

Mary is a 71-year-old widow who is living alone in her own home. Joanne, a granddaughter who lived in another state, came to visit after not seeing Mary for over a year. Joanne noticed that there was no food in the house and that Mary looked frail and did not recognize her.

Question: What form(s) of abuse does this describe?

KEY TERMS

Abandonment
Active maltreatment
Adult protective service
Alzheimer's disease
Dementia
Domestic abuse
Financial exploitation
Institutional abuse

Misuse of restraints
Ombudsman
Passive maltreatment
S.E.A.M.
Self-neglect
Triad
Undue influence

INTRODUCTION

> I'm growing fonder of my staff; I'm growing dimmer in the eyes;
> I'm growing fainter in my laugh; I'm growing careless of my dress;
> I'm growing frugal of my gold; I'm growing wise; I'm growing—yes—
> I'm growing old. (J. G. Saxe, "I'm Growing Old")

People age 65 or older are the least likely to become victims of violent crime in the United States. The elderly, persons age 65 or older, experienced less violence and fewer property crimes than younger persons between 1992 and 1997 (Rennison, 2001). Retirement can be a peaceful age, a time to sit back and reminisce on the accomplishments of a more active period. Increased leisure time becomes available for activities that were not possible in younger years. Elders as a group are doing well in a number of ways. While the number of children living in poverty has risen, elders on the whole are more financially secure than ever before. In 1959, one-third of elderly were poor; today, the poverty rate for elders is less than the national average (DiLeonardi, 1995). About 3.4 million elderly persons (10.2 percent) were below the poverty level in 2000. This poverty rate was not statistically different from the historic low reached in 1999 (Administration on Aging, 2001). Another 2.2 million or 6.7 percent of the elderly were classified as "near-poor" (income between the poverty level and 125 percent of this level).

For some, however, growing old can become a time of increased fear and victimization. The most probable source of violence is adult children, spouses or partners,

Figure 7–1   Elders are the least likely to be victimized by violent crime but have the highest rate of fear of victimization. *(Photo courtesy of the Administration on Aging.)*

friends, and other caregivers (Executive Office of Elder Affairs, 1998). Yet this area of domestic abuse is unlike any other; a "Just the facts, ma'am" approach will not work. Policing elder violence for the upcoming generation will involve intellect and patience on the part of police officers. Strength and aloofness must be replaced with confidence and compassion when responding to this population. Some consider this a departure from traditional police work; it is. Now the job of law enforcement means incorporation of appropriate responses to reports from older Americans so that it becomes the tradition of good police work in the future.

Compared to the other forms of domestic violence, elder abuse response is in its infancy. Some credit the report entitled *Battered Parents* (American Psychiatric Association, 1979) with bringing the idea of elder abuse to contemporary study. Much later, the work of researchers Finkelhor and Pillemer first looked at its prevalence and characteristics (Finkelhor & Pillemer, 1988).

The criminal justice community has been slow in responding to the needs of the elderly. Prosecutions of elder abuse have been rare in the past. Significant changes have been seen in the last decade along with new criminal justice system responses. Increasingly, elder abuse is being recognized as more than just an act against the individual victim, but also against the entire community (Heisler, 2000). Challenging the traditional response that elder victims did not want help from the criminal justice system, alternative approaches that include aggressive prosecution are evolving. Multidisciplinary teams are forming nationwide as the best approach to elder abuse prevention (Nerenberg, 2003). Although the make-up of multidisciplinary teams varies from state to state, they share common prevention goals. For the victims, the enhanced autonomy and improved access to service options are evident. Professionals share information as well as the needs and approaches of the protective services, the criminal justice system, victim witness assistance programs, and aging services. Additionally the approach acts as a support system for the various professionals who are concerned with elder abuses, providing an environment for sharing frustrations and the uncertainty that these cases might bring. For the communities, the team approach acts to identify gaps in services and ultimately provide an improved system response. Since the various agencies have conflicting goals and perspectives on how cases of abuse should be handled, the team approach offers a forum for balancing their different goals and aids in case resolution in the best interest of the elder.

Community policing for the elderly is another attempt to remedy this problem and to combat the excessive fear that plagues many elderly citizens. The American Association of Retired Persons (AARP), the International Association of Chiefs of Police (IACP), and the National Sheriffs' Association (NSA) signed an agreement in 1988 to work together to reduce crime against the elderly and to improve law enforcement services to older citizens (Office of the NY State Attorney, 2003). Referred to as **triad**, community-based programs that involve law enforcement, concerned citizens, and advisory boards are being formed across the United States to improve education and police response to this population of citizens.

Back Then . . .

Early references to elder abuse in Britain coined such phrases as granny battering, granny bashing, and granny abuse according to the authors of Elder Abuse in Perspective (Biggs et al., 1995). These terms conjure up images of the little old white-haired lady, someone frail and considered incompetent. Now the stereotypical elder is anything but typical, and current research cautions against identifying elders as one age group of 65 and beyond (Doerner & Lab, 1998). Approximately 34 million elders span four decades as senior citizens (Administration on Aging, 1998b). Their health and functional abilities have greatly improved with innovations in medical technology. Increased income, educational attainment, and access to support services for some elders accompany improved standards of care.

Early retirement programs have brought people aged 50 to 55 into the category of senior citizens. Qualifying membership into the American Association of Retired Persons (AARP) is age 50. The spouse of an AARP member is admitted at any age. Since the category of senior citizen has expanded along with the life expectancy, social investigation may necessitate more specifically defined categories of elders. Although states have the flexibility to define elders in law, they do not differentiate between categories such as early old age or advanced old age. The ability or lack of ability to protect oneself is of little consequence when applying legal protections to the elderly. It does, however, make prosecutions more difficult. Social intervention can and often does differentiate between those who are able and those who require additional consideration. The term *granny bashing* is no longer applicable to describe elder victimization, if it ever was.

Civil Versus Criminal Action

Should the perpetrator be charged criminally? The determination on civil versus criminal action for elder abuse is extremely complex. Prosecution is rarely presumed, as with other adult domestic crimes. Neither is the decision made with purely protective concerns, as with child domestic cases. The elder victim is assumed to have an interest in protecting family relationships due to some dependence on the perpetrator. Often, the relationship is of value to an increasingly isolated elder, and threats of **abandonment** or commitment to an institution make the elder reluctant to follow through with criminal court proceedings. Institutional settings often prefer to handle their own "problems" and historically do not pursue criminal avenues for redress. An institutionalized resident is already limited in ability and may be severely disabled, further complicating determinations in an abusive situation.

Examples of civil actions include assault and battery for physical abuse; false imprisonment when excessive restraints have been used; negligence for mismanagement of funds; and/or restraining orders against perpetrators of abuse. Although this approach could serve to free assets or provide compensation to the victim, he or she must be competent and able to pay the costs of litigation.

More About It: Triad

Since its inception in 1988, 32 states have formally committed to work together to increase use of the triad approach, according to the National Sheriffs' Association (NSA). In several other states, the office of the attorney general is involved in promoting triad. The national model now includes state and local efforts that survey the needs and concerns of older citizens, expand crime prevention programming, and provide reassurance programs to local seniors. It is called triad because it consists of a partnership with seniors, law enforcement, and the community to provide much needed services. Increasing public awareness and decreasing victimization against older people are the guiding principles. A senior advisory counsel called SALT is established for each chapter to integrate the triad activities and tailor them to fit a community's particular needs.

Providing law enforcement services for elders means accepting that this group of citizens is not incompetent. Understanding the unique character and needs of the people in every age category allows dignity and life choices. These are adults with constitutional protections. Sometimes an elder will make decisions in a manner that is perceived as inappropriate. Could it be that their concerns and considerations are simply different? When age or illness overcomes an elder's ability, interventions become more complex and crucial. Although technically not "domestic," institutional abuse is included because of the caretaker status that nursing homes take on in behalf of the elder.

Back Then . . .

The apparent lack of criminal justice response to this category of maltreatment is evidenced in this historical example of elder abuse. Referring to the preference for health care facilities to deal internally with problems, one author cites *Long v. Brookside Manor*, 1994 (McDaniel, 1997):

> This negligent hiring action suit was brought against a nursing home, based on the assault of a resident by a nursing home employee. Facts indicate that an employee, upon observing that the nursing home resident had accidentally soiled herself, became enraged and grabbed the elder by the hair, jerking her out of the chair and then began beating her about the head, kicking her and punching her. Judgment for plaintiff was reversed and claims dismissed because the court of appeals found that the plaintiff had failed to show that the nursing home's failure to do a background check on the employee was the proximate cause of her injuries.

Based on the information above, should this case have proceeded with criminal charges of assault and battery? Should the law be applied equally to residents in institutional facilities? What do you think?

Criminal actions include assault and battery for physical abuse, burglary or extortion for financial abuse, as well as specific elderly crimes with enhanced penalties. Some states have a caretaker statute that makes it a specific crime to omit care to a dependent or vulnerable person. The advantage to criminal prosecution is the possibility of court-mandated counseling or removal from the victim's presence. Prosecution may serve as a deterrent to future abuse. However, the elder may refuse to press charges due to a fear of retaliation, or may change his or her mind and drop all charges. It is not uncommon for an older adult to be ashamed or embarrassed to admit that his or her family member is abusive.

Prosecution attorneys make the final decision on criminal complaints and must consider the status of each person as well as the severity of the abuse. In some cases adult protection services seek custody of the elder who is unable physically or mentally to make determinations for his or her best interests. Although criminal statutes do not differentiate by age category and ability to self-protect, the choice between civil intervention and criminal prosecution may involve that differentiation.

Categories of Abuse

There are two general categories of elder abuse: domestic and institutional. The use of these terms may be a bit confusing; remember that they all refer to family or domestic violence. We specify the place of elder maltreatment because this population can reside both at home and in institutional settings. The relationship of the perpetrator to the victim along with the loose definition of *residence* will allow elder abuse to come under the umbrella of domestic violence, regardless of the setting. The location of the victimization is important to distinguish in order to understand the differences in abuse and likeliness of perpetrator. Bear in mind that these categories are terms used to specify the setting in which the maltreatment occurs.

Domestic elder abuse refers to the victim who lives in his or her own home or in the home of a caregiver. Abuse of an elder who lives in a nursing home, foster home, or group home is termed *institutional*. The forms of abuse remain the same regardless of the environment. For example, physical abuse may occur in a **domestic abuse** situation or institutional setting. The category of abuse does influence the appropriateness of the responding agency. **Ombudsman**, health care services, or adult protective services would probably respond to allegations of **institutional abuse** and neglect, since the majority of complaints would not be criminal. Police would be more involved in the investigation of physical or sexual violence in domestic settings (alone or in conjunction with social service organizations) but may also become involved in severe institutional abuses. It is necessary that all agencies that are charged with response contact each other and work together to resolve conflicts and protect the elder victims.

In any category of abuse, the **maltreatment** may be either **active** or **passive**. This refers to the difference between intentional abuse of the elderly and benign neglect, which could be unintentional. Intervention may be necessary for the protection of the elder in either case, and a determination would have to be made as to

The elder-at-risk program is a short-term, program-focused, goal-oriented crisis intervention. Offered to self-neglecting and/or self-abusing elders aged 60 years and older, it is strictly voluntary. Usually, its clients have demonstrated reluctance to accept interventions by more traditional efforts. The programs provide nontraditional services for those elders seriously in need.

whether the action or inaction of the caregiver was criminal behavior. Social services are provided to elders on a consent basis. If elders refuse services, they may be enrolled in an elder-at-risk program and offered whatever services are appropriate. Law enforcement has a responsibility to uphold the law.

Active Abuse and Neglect

The forms of active abuse and neglect should sound familiar to you by now, because they exist in other categories of domestic violence. **Financial exploitation** and **misuse of restraints** are examples of specific offenses in this category. **Self-neglect**, a noncriminal activity, might result in civil intervention on the victim's behalf. Feeling stress and acting out against the elder is not an acceptable excuse for causing harm to an older person.

- Financial exploitation
- Misuse of restraints
- Neglect and abandonment
- Physical abuse

Figure 7–2   Financial exploitation and misuse of restraints are examples of specific offenses committed against the elderly. *(Photo courtesy of the Administration on Aging.)*

- Psychological abuse and emotional abuse
- Sexual abuse

- Self-neglect

Passive Maltreatment

Caring for an infirmed or impaired person that results in unintentional injury or neglect is a passive category, necessitating social intervention. Caregiver stress is not the most common cause of elder abuse as many had previously assumed, but it may be a factor in some cases. Caregiver emotional and psychological problems or drug or alcohol addictions are all indications that the caregiver may not be capable of providing adaquate care to elder. Signs that the older person may be suffering from benign neglect include some of the following:

- Sunken eyes or loss of weight
- Extreme thirst
- Bed sores

THE VICTIMS OF ELDER ABUSE

Authors found a victimization rate of 32 elders per 1,000 in the first major study of elder maltreatment (Finkelhor & Pillemer, 1988). Suggesting that a unique classification of elder abuse be recognized, they encouraged professionals to define this category and begin work on profiling the victims involved. Over 1 million older Americans were estimated to have been victimized in 1988 alone.

In part due to the demographics of aging in the United States, increased attention has been focused on elder issues. In 1900, the over-65 age group accounted for just 4 percent of the population. Between 1989 and 2030, the 65-year-old and over

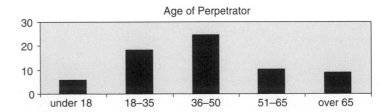

Figure 7–3   Elder abuse perpetrators by age. The adult children of the elderly are the most frequent source of abuse and neglect toward an older person. This chart illustrates that the perpetrators are also most likely to be between the ages of 18 and 50. (*Source: Adapted from Teaster, 2003.*)

population is expected to more than double; the 85-year-old and over group is expected to triple. The U.S. Bureau of the Census predicts that by 2030 the population over age 65 will be more than 70 million people, and older people will make up more than 20 percent of the population (up from 12.3 in 1990) (Smith, 2003). An increased demand for domestic violence protective services has already been noted for this second age group. A survey of state social service departments by NCEA noted a 50 percent increase in elder abuse between 1980 and 1990 (National Aging Resource Center on Elder Abuse, 1992). A steady increase in reported elder abuse cases was noted each year between 1990 and 1994 (Kohl et al., 1995). Indications are that resources will continue to be in demand as the elder population grows.

Estimates on the rate of abuse to elders showed an increase by 150 percent between 1976 and 1986, when 293,000 cases were reported of suspected abuse. In 1996 it was estimated that there were between 820,000 and 1,860,000 abused elders in the country (Tatara, 1996). In 1997, estimates showed over 2.1 million older persons were abused, neglected, or exploited (Administration on Aging, 1998a).

Both social service agencies and the criminal justice community are affected by these changes. All states and the District of Columbia have passed legislation to protect this population because of the impairments associated with old age. Every state has also passed legislation that mandates police to intervene in domestic violence. Police already respond to domestic elder abuse because law requires it.

Age

A baby born in 1900 was expected to live an average of 47.3 years. In the United States, this figure rose to an average of 75 years in 1987! Males average 72 years of life, and the average woman lives to 79 years old (Administration on Aging, 1998b). This trend in life expectancy changes the face of Americans from visions of the young to the wrinkles of the old. If there were such a thing as a "typical" victim, she would be 80 years old, frail, and dependent on others for her care (Young et al., 2000). Excluding self-neglect adults, substantiated reports show that persons aged 80 and old suffer the greatest share of abuse (46.5 percent) (Teaster, 2003).

Illness and disability associated with old age complicate the investigations of elderly maltreatment. Excluding those who do not live in institutions, approximately 12 million elderly are limited by chronic conditions (Administration on Aging, 1997b). Of these, 3 million are unable to perform by themselves activities such as bathing, shopping, dressing, or eating.

Gender

In 2002, 26.6 million men and 33.0 million women were aged 55 and over, meaning a sex ratio of 81 men per 100 women nationally (Smith, 2003). As they get older the distribution of women and men changes. For example, 41 percent of women and 47 percent of men were aged 55 to 64 in 2000; at age 85 this drops to only 7 percent of women versus 4 percent of men (Smith, 2003). During their elder years, men and

Figure 7–4 Age and infirmities make elder abuse investigations difficult.

Figure 7–5 The importance of financial exploitation against an elder cannot be understated. With the majority of the nations' wealth controlled by persons aged 50 and older, this population represents a target to those who may feel privileged to the funds due to their relationship or caretaking roles. This abuse can devastate the victim, and it may be accompanied by physical abuse, neglect, and even homicide.

women are equally likely to become victims of physical abuse, the current rate is 3 victimizations per 1,000 persons over age 50 (Rennison & Welchans, 2000).

Age or gender of the perpetrator does not excuse abusive behavior defined as criminal, nor does it exclude law enforcement action. In addition to the general criminal codes that address domestic violence, legislation provides protections that are specific to the elderly. Some of these laws are criminal, and some are civil. Financial exploitation in a domestic setting is criminal, for example. Self-neglect is usually a civil matter. National standards for protection have been established through the Older Americans Act. Each state interprets the mandates and makes the laws for its jurisdiction. It is important to research the civil as well as criminal statutes to know the exact duties and responsibilities.

Almost all of the sexual assault victims are women (Brandl & Cook-Daniels, 2002). We know that younger male victims have been slow in coming forward with complaints of sexual assault, and therefore we cannot assume that elder males are not also at risk of sexual abuse. In the Ramsey-Klawsnik study, all the victims were limited in their ability to protect themselves (Ramsey-Klawsnik, 1991). The majority of elder victims were aged 70 to 80 years old. In 61 percent of the reports, the victim had been raped at least once; vaginal rape was the most common form. Surprisingly, a third party witnessed the sexual victimization of these women in approximately one-third of the cases. In institutional settings, the typical victim of abuse is thought to be a female and in poor health (Pillemer, 1988). The Bureau of Justice Statistics estimates that persons age 65 or older comprise 1 percent of the victims of sexual assault or rape in the United States (Perkins, 1997). The literature tells us that any elder woman is susceptible to being sexually abused; frailty and infirmity are not the defining victim characteristics.

Race

By the year 2020 the elderly minority populations will have increased substantially, from 14 percent in 1985 to approximately 21 percent. Minority populations are believed to be increasing at a faster rate than the white population. Because cultural and ethnic factors are thought to influence whether or not families turn to law enforcement or social service agencies for help, it is difficult to assess the risk of elder abuse in this rising portion of our population (Brandl & Cook-Daniels, 2002). Between 1993 and 1999 no significant difference was found by race in the pattern of intimate partner violence of those aged 50 and over (Rennison, 2001).

Cultural Differences

Cultural differences among minority elderly may have an impact on the reporting of abuse. Since the minority population is expected to comprise 33 percent of the over-65 population by the year 2050, these differences are important (Nerenberg, 1993). If a translator is necessary to conduct interviews with the victim, care must be taken to

Been There . . . Done That!

No one tells the rookie officer what to expect during routine patrol. You have to experience it yourself. Let me tell you of my first experience with Gertrude.

One night while on highway patrol, I noticed a car swerving from lane to lane. Pulling the vehicle over, I expected to find a drunk driver. To my surprise, a petite gray-haired lady opened the door and stepped out as I approached. She took a swing at me, knocking my hat into the travel lane, where the oncoming truck driver delighted in running it over. Admittedly, it took me a moment to reconcile that some little old lady had just hit me, for no reason! I hadn't even said anything yet!

She took off, running up an embankment to the right of the highway. On hands and knees I reached her, holding her first by the ankle so she couldn't go any further. While I was trying to talk to her, she bit me, punched me, and kicked me. I remember yelling, "What is the matter with you? You should be home knitting!" It is really difficult to put someone under arrest when you are afraid of hurting him or her. Ask any police officer; it is a dangerous situation. You are the one most likely to get hurt in the process.

The next day in court, my fellow officers kidded me on my "big" arrest of that poor little old lady for assault and battery on a police officer. I felt so humiliated until the judge yelled at my victim: He was tired of her picking fights with the cops, he said. Then and only then, my fellow officers told me that Gertrude had been beating up her husband for over 50 years. Since he had died, she resorted to fighting with any police officer she could get to approach her.

Figure 7–6 African Americans comprise the largest group of minority elderly in the United States. *(Photo courtesy of the Administration on Aging.)*

assure that exact words are translated and statements are not paraphrased. An adult child of the elder should not be used as a translator as this may violate cultural norms. Shame and embarrassment are frequent reasons why elders across cultural boundaries are reluctant to report domestic violence. Significant differences on what constitutes domestic violence are noted in various cultures (Brandl & Cook-Daniels, 2002). Brief profiles offer the following to consider when responding to reports of elder abuse:

1. Older African Americans form the largest group of minority elderly in the United States. Often residing in central city areas, the average African Americans have lower income and health status than elderly Caucasians (Nerenberg, 1993). This population is more likely than other elders to have dependent children or grandchildren living with them. According to a recent study, African Americans are four times more likely than Caucasians to be affected by **Alzheimer's disease** (Mayeux, 1998). These characteristics may increase the vulnerability to abuse.

2. Hispanics/Latin Americans represent the fastest-growing segment of the elder population. They are twice as likely as compared to other elders to live in poverty and may have a limited command of the English language (Nerenberg, 1993). Their lack of resources teamed with insufficient communication skills makes intervention difficult. Their risk for Alzheimer's is now thought to be twice as likely as for whites (Mayeux, 1998). Bilingual investigators are important resources for these cases.

3. Older Asian Americans represent still another set of challenges. Their suicide rate is three times higher than the national average for seniors (Nerenberg, 1993). Language barriers inhibit intervention.

4. Native Americans reside in each of the 50 states and the District of Columbia, according to the 1990 census (Administration on Aging, 1997a). They are likely to be rural dwellers. Although they make up less than 1 percent of the total population, the number of elder Native Americans increased 35 percent more than the total non-Indian older population in the United States.

Vulnerability and Undue Influence

Older people and their families worry about crime. Though older people are less likely to be victims of crime than teenagers and young adults, the number of crimes against older people is hard to ignore. Each year hundreds of thousands of older persons are abused, neglected, and exploited by family members and others. Many victims are people who are older, frail, and vulnerable and cannot help themselves. Some may depend on others to meet their most basic needs. People 80 and older, and women of all ages, are at greater risk. Older adults who are dependent on others for basic care are particularly vulnerable.

Three out of four elder abuse and neglect victims suffer from physical frailty. About one-half (47.9 percent) of substantiated incidents of abuse and neglect involve elderly persons who are not physically able to care for themselves (National Center on Elder Abuse, 1998). When these conditions cause concern that there might be a problem, it is time to get the older person some help. Confronting the abuser is not likely to be helpful. Some of the reasons why people may not seek help for the elder are

- Uncertainty about who to talk to
- Uncertainty about what can be done
- Fear of not being believed
- Fear of getting involved

As people age it is normal to experience some decline in certain mental functions, particularly memory. Pronounced decline may signal illness or disease, which may be treatable. Poor nutrition, depression, and medication interactions may be a

---

Been There . . . Done That!

Phyllis lived alone, widowed for many years. She had only one child and no one else to turn to for help. What could she do? she wondered. She loved her son, but she didn't have much money and was afraid that he was going to take it all. Her son was taking money out of her purse after she had cashed her Social Security check. He had a drug problem, she confided, and she was afraid to confront him about the missing money.

She did not know exactly how much money had been taken, or when the stealing had begun. She had never seen her son go into the purse; it must have happened while she slept. No, Phyllis did not want to press criminal charges against her son. Phyllis wanted me to make her son stop taking her money—that's all. Hardly the job for a supercop, I thought. This was not really what I expected to be doing in the major crime bureau! It was easy, though; a little time spent with Phyllis to assess the problem made the choices clear.

First, I spoke to Phyllis about a security alarm for her house—it might make her feel more comfortable knowing that she had the ability to decide who would enter her home while she slept. We discussed having her checks sent by direct deposit to her bank so that she would not have large amounts of cash in the home. Finally, I told her about adult protective services, the social service agency that could help her to make those things happen. They could check up on her and provide a place to call if she had further problems. A small thing, right? Phyllis sent a letter of thanks to the district attorney, which didn't hurt me a bit. It has occurred to me that I had the opportunity to make a difference, a small one to be sure, but it might have made her life a little better. All it cost was my time, and I was already being paid for that! Although the lack of evidence made prosecution impossible, we found an acceptable alternative.

factor that contributes to the elder's vulnerability to undue influence. **Undue influence** occurs when people use their role with the elder to exploit the trust, dependency, and fear of others. This deceptive use of power is used to gain control over the decision making of the vulnerable adult. Vulnerability to undue influence is not related to the person's intelligence, but cognitive impairment may make the manipulation easier to accomplish.

During a domestic crime, an older person is more likely to be seriously hurt and may die from the abuse. The **adult protective service** (APS) is the agency to contact when elder neglect or abuse is suspected. A local police department can be contacted to obtain the information if needed. The professionals who investigate the situation are trained to deal with the elder in a sensitive and caring manner. The resolution will depend on what is in the best interests of the older person. It may mean that other agencies will be involved to assist with the care, meals might be delivered, and medical needs may be met. Contacting APA is not an accusation or indictment against someone; rather it is a positive move toward protecting a vulnerable adult. Getting involved may be exactly what is needed! Neglect and abuse are conditions of social concern, not private family problems. Reducing the isolation of the elder, introducing better nutrition, and monitoring medications are all ways to help elders to feel less vulnerable and more able to help themselves.

CATEGORIES OF ELDER ABUSE

The environment under which elder abuse occurs provides some insight into the condition of elders as well as their ability to protect themselves. Knowledge of that environment is extremely important to assure that everything that can be done for the elder is put into motion. In each setting, the rights of the victim must be fully protected. Adult protective services are available in every state and the District of Columbia to assist in the protection of elder abuse victims, alone or in conjunction with law enforcement.

Domestic Abuse

Law enforcement is encouraged to use a multidisciplinary approach to elder abuse and neglect investigation. Overlapping responsibilities of multiple state agencies, including long-term ombudsmen, adult protective services, department of social services, and law enforcement, make this category of abuse particularly amenable to agency cooperation. As mentioned earlier, the call for services from all agencies is expected to increase dramatically in future years. A 1992 survey by the Police Executive Research Forum (PERF) identified elder abuse training as the most necessary, according to 81 percent of police chiefs (Nerenberg, 1993).

Due to the dependence that an elder may have on an abusive caretaker, PERF recommends a modified police response to this category of domestic violence. Arrest and removal of the perpetrator may sometimes cause more harm than good. Research suggests that mandatory arrest may sometimes lead to further violence. The situation must be evaluated, and flexibility must be part of the standard operating procedure. Knowing the resources in your area beforehand will make assisting the domestic violence victim much more efficient. Is there emergency care that can be arranged in the event that the abuser/caretaker must be removed from the home? Where is the emergency care provider, and has a protocol been set up with that agency for quick response?

Institutional Abuse

Elders enter nursing and adult foster homes when they become limited in the ability to care for themselves in some way. An elder may have become ill or injured and need this form of temporary assistance until he or she is able to care for himself or herself. It is false to assume that going into a nursing home is permanent. Approximately 30 percent of elders return to their own homes or to assisted living situations after a recuperative stay in a nursing home.

It is also false to assume that all residents of nursing homes are demented. Symptoms of maltreatment can be confused with conditions that are nonabusive. When an elder's abilities appear to deteriorate quickly in the institutional setting, it should be standard procedure to seek a medical cause. A simple cold would not seriously affect a 25-year-old, yet to a 90-year-old who weighs only 85 pounds, a cold could involve a number of unexpected side effects, such as increased confusion, restlessness, or rapid weight loss. A medical checkup should be a standard part of the investigation into elder abuse since it may help to confirm or negate abuse allegations.

Aggression, agitation, and depression may be symptoms of a form of dementia such as Alzheimer's disease. These symptoms may be mistaken for abuse if organic causes have not been ruled out. At the same time, **dementia** is a factor that also puts the resident at higher risk for abuse. Present in 50 to 75 percent of patients who reside in nursing and foster homes, dementia is the leading risk factor for maltreatment (Weinberg & Wei, 1995). So although illness or disease may explain away the behavioral indicators of abuse, it does not mean that abuse is not occurring. Diminished capacity does not mean that abuse cannot occur: It can and does. However, only 4 percent of elders resided in nursing or foster homes in 1997; therefore, the risk of abuse in institutional settings is considered relatively small (Doerner & Lab, 1998).

Both state and federal statutes regulate and monitor nursing homes in the United States. The responsibility for protection, however, rests principally with the states. Obtaining a clear picture of maltreatment to the elderly is difficult in part due to the diverse agencies and definitions that are involved. In some states, as many as seven different agencies may investigate complaints of institutional abuse. Primarily, the state long-term care ombudsman's office and adult protective service agencies handle these allegations; however, law enforcement or state health department officials might be charged with the task. In light of former President Clinton's announcement

---

More About It: Dementia

The term *dementia* comes from Latin for "madness" or "senseless." We use the word to describe the deterioration of intellectual faculties, such as memory, concentration, and judgment. Many conditions can cause dementia. It may be related to depression, drug interaction, thyroid imbalances, and other problems. Emotional disturbance and personality changes are indicative of this brain disorder or disease. Some diseases that can cause dementia include Parkinson's, Creutzfeldt–Jakob, Huntington's, and multi-infarct or vascular disease, caused by multiple strokes (Alzheimer's Association, 1998).

Alois Alzheimer (1864–1915), a German neurologist, first diagnosed Alzheimer's disease in 1906. This is the most common form of dementia. Nearly half of women over the age of 85 suffer from this disease, which involves memory loss and decline in cognitive abilities. The Alzheimer's Association reports that 4 million Americans have Alzheimer's disease now and that experts expect that 14 million will be affected by the middle of the next century if a cure is not found.

---

in July 1998 of a new initiative to improve the quality of nursing homes, the future involvement of law enforcement is likely to increase. Included in this announcement is "the need to prosecute egregious violations of care practices through civil and criminal investigation and prosecution" (National Senior Citizens Law Center, 1998).

Compounding the problems associated with obtaining reliable statistics, states report instances of institutional abuse differently. Although the majority of states do provide statistics for institutional abuse separately from those for domestic abuse, some do not collect data on this category at all (Tatara, 1990). Although we don't know the exact prevalence of maltreatment in this setting, reports received by authorities have been increasing steadily in the past few years.

What we do know is that nursing home residents can be vulnerable due to low staff ratios, poor working conditions and wages, and inadequate supervision, to name a few of the problems. In any case of suspected abuse, it is critical that documentation begin at the onset of an investigation. Once the facility records abuse, it may become admissible in a criminal court and therefore should be stored properly and with limited access allowed to the professional staff of the facility.

Current controversies surrounding institutional abuse and neglect involve the character of nursing and foster home care. In a society that is ambivalent about institutional residential settings, there is little consensus on the nursing or adult foster home. Some authors suggest that the institution itself is oppressive, due to the invasion of personal privacy and forced dependency, a setting that by its very nature abuses residents (Biggs et al., 1995). Others argue this perspective while citing the need for increased awareness that institutional abuse is a category of family violence, deserving attention and concern. This view can be summarized with this statement: "The first step towards resolving mistreatment is to uncover it" (Biggs et al., 1995).

More About It: Ombudsman

Federal legislation has provided the standards for elder care through the Older Americans Act of 1965. An amendment in 1987 provided for the creation of a long-term care ombudsman's office to act as the agency for nursing home certification and licensure. The amendments of 1987 and 1992 included services to prevent abuse of older people. Bringing together the long-term care ombudsman program with programs for the prevention of abuse, neglect, and exploitation and state elder rights and legal assistance development programs, the act calls for a coordination and linkage within each state. It establishes a requirement that each state agency on aging provide a person who will investigate and resolve complaints made by or on behalf of older persons who are residents of long-term care facilities. This person, the ombudsman, is responsible for investigating complaints and providing or arranging appropriate resolutions for complaints. He or she might become a reporter of abuse that is discovered and provide information to criminal justice or health department agencies. An ombudsman may be a paid staff member or a trained volunteer. In addition to being an impartial fact finder, the ombudsman is an advocate for improving the quality of life for nursing home residents.

Investigations require knowledge of state and federal regulations concerning nursing and foster homes. Most often, an ombudsman investigates in these settings initially. Joint interviews with adult protective services and law enforcement personnel can be valuable, since determinations must be made on the victim's mental status.

THE MAJOR FORMS OF ABUSE

In part, the problems of elder abuse are confusing because of the lack of definitional consensus within the professions that investigate, research, and document cases concerning elders. Hudson (1991) does not include self-neglect as a category of abuse. Additionally, his classification considers sexual abuse as a subgroup of physical abuse (Hudson, 1991). Another author includes "violation of individual or constitutional rights" as an abusive category (Boudreau, 1993). Vague categories that are difficult to understand assure the continuing controversy on the meaning of elder abuse. For the purposes of this book, seven forms of abuse, in two categories, domestic and institutional, have been identified.

Just as with other victims of abuse, it is not unusual for an elder to have more than one injury or different forms of abuse and/or neglect. Physical abuse may be the tool to accomplish financial exploitation, and vice versa. Determining the cause of injury begins with ruling out the obvious and looking toward possible explanations that are nonabusive. If an elder is mentally incompetent, his or her patterns of behavior should be observed to assure that the person is not self-neglecting.

When abusive conditions seem likely, the ability of some elders to protect themselves against abuse must be assessed. Elders are often dependent on others for their care, which is a factor contributing to their vulnerability. What is the source of the maltreatment? Is the elder able to take adequate steps in preventing further abuses? Cognitive, physical, mental, and sensory impairments may make elders susceptible to many forms of abuse, including financial exploitation (Brandl & Cook-Daniels, 2002)

Financial Exploitation

Financial exploitation is also known as fiduciary abuse, financial abuse, economic abuse, and financial mistreatment. It covers a broad range of conduct that is difficult to define and to prove. The determination is often subjective, and rarely is it possible to prove criminal knowledge of incompetence and intent (Commonwealth of Massachusetts, 1995). Although prosecution of the perpetrator has been rare (Wilber & Reynolds, 1996), it is possible in some cases. A civil lawsuit, for the purpose of recovering misappropriated property, is also an option for the victim. As the phenomenon of exploitation becomes better understood, its indicators will increasingly be recognized and successful intervention more commonplace. This form of violence to the elderly could be called the invisible tragedy; without the external signs of abuse, it has often been unrecognized and its effects minimized.

Since people over the age of 50 control 70 percent of the nation's wealth (Nerenberg, 1996), the motivation for this form of abuse is clear. The impact of financial exploitation is not as obvious. Losing financial resources can be especially worrisome to a person who is of an age when he or she cannot replenish them. Anguish about the lack of adequate resources and confusion over financial arrangements can be devastating. Loss of property rights to one's home may mean institutional commitment or

---

More About It: Adult Protective Services

Most states have an adult protective services (APS) program. The purpose is to provide services and receive reports of adults who are abused, neglected, exploited, or otherwise mistreated by their families or caretakers (American Association of Retired Persons, 1987). Social services are offered to consenting older adults and personnel may intervene following court authority on behalf of incompetent persons without consent. There is no national consistency, however. APS may be part of a social services department or contracted to a private, nonprofit agency; eligibility may be based on age (50, 60, or 65), incapacity, or vulnerability. It is believed that APS originated in 1958 (Mixson, 1996). At that time, the National Council on Aging created an ad hoc committee to investigate the need for national protective services for the elderly. Implementation of elder protective services nationwide was slow since federal funds were not appropriated until 1991.

dependence when the elder would have otherwise been able to care for himself or herself. Financial abuse does not always occur in isolation and may be accompanied by physical abuse, neglect, homicide, and other crimes. Approximately 12 percent of cases investigated by protective services involve financial exploitation (Fox et al., 1995).

The National Center on Elder Abuse warns that the following may be indicators of financial abuse (Nerenberg, 1996). By no means is this an exhaustive list.

- Uncharacteristic bank activity is noted for an elder.
- Suspicious activity appears on the person's credit card accounts.

Since the banking industry has a stake in protecting its clients, educational efforts should be aimed at bank personnel in addition to protective service agencies and law enforcement. This model, which includes the banking business in efforts to combat financial exploitation, is outlined in *The Bank Reporting Project* (Fox et al., 1995). The design includes a sample protocol for reporting and responding to financial exploitation by bank personnel in addition to consumer education. A similar program with the Milwaukee Police Department and area banks reduced confidence crime against elders in that city by 80 percent, according to the Fox report.

- Bank activity is noted that is inconsistent with the abilities of an elder.
- There are changes in property titles, will, or other documents of the elder.

Tellers are trained to be observant of client behaviors, such as the behavior of elders when withdrawing large cash amounts or those accompanied by others who appear domineering. Elders who appear confused or coerced into banking activity would prompt the senior bank officers or security to speak privately with the client about the transaction.

- An elder does not understand recently completed financial transactions or seems unaware of the transactions.
- An older person is uncared for.
- An elder seems to be isolated by others.
- An elder has untreated medical or mental health problems.
- A power of attorney is executed by a confused older person.
- Forged and/or suspicious signatures appear on an elder's documents.

The National Association of Adult Protective Services Administrators (NAAPSA) conducted a survey in 2001 to determine the extent of financial exploitation of vulnerable adults (NAAPSA, 2003). They found that 29 states have a mandatory reporting statute that includes financial exploitation against elders. Eleven of those states included financial institutions among those mandated to report and almost half made financial institutions reporting voluntary. Over 76 percent of those victimized by financial exploitation were aged 51 and older. More than half of the victims are female and aged 66 or older.

Police officers found themselves inundated with investigations involving complex misappropriation of property through powers of attorney, quitclaim deeds, wills, and living trusts. In response to these crimes, fiduciary abuse specialist teams, or multidisciplinary FASTs, have been developed to meet the investigative need. Typical professionals included on these teams are law enforcement and mental health professional, consultants with expertise in financial matters, bank personnel, realtors, real estate attorneys, insurance brokers, and Medicaid fraud investigators (Nerenberg, 2003). A rapid response FAST team exists to respond to imminent danger and in cases of emergency in some jurisdictions. Examples of financial abuse that has been evidenced in recent years according to Nerenberg (2003) are

- Home equity loan scams
- Misuse of "protective" legal instruments such as powers of attorney and trusts
- Confidence crimes
- Identity theft
- Investment scams
- Telemarketing fraud
- "Sweetheart" scams
- Homicide for profit

Misuse of Restraints

Although misuse of restraints is usually associated with institutional settings, it may also be identified in an abusive home. It involves the chemical or physical control of an elder beyond physician's order or outside accepted medical practice. The U.S. Department of Health Services concluded in a 1990 report that 24 percent of nursing homes improperly administered drugs against the written orders from attending physicians.

Restraints (cloth bindings on chairs or beds) may be used in nursing homes only under two conditions:

1. When a person is confused and unable to comprehend or remember that by moving about, he or she may harm himself or herself or someone else.
2. When a person is unable to maintain his or her position because of a severe physical handicap such as paralysis.

Restraints are used only for a resident's safety; they are never to be used without a physician's order and even then only for the span of time absolutely necessary. A restraint used for the convenience of the caretaker is never acceptable. Used in anger or for punishment, a restraint constitutes abuse. Caretakers at home may not be familiar with state laws on abuse and need to be educated about its limited acceptable use. Educating the caretaker on alternative methods may be helpful. If the restraints are used as a punishment or for the purpose of inflicting pain, particularly if the practice is an ongoing or repetitive action, prosecution may be a feasible option. The misuse of restraints can cause physical injuries such as rope burns. Look for rope burns on the extremities, neck, or torso that result from being tied up or restrained for long periods of time. While some patients themselves may not think that the use of restraints is improper, their use does not allow the person to be able to flee in the case of fire or other emergency.

Neglect and Abandonment

The frequency of neglectful behavior, and its duration, intensity, severity, and consequences, all are taken into account when making a determination as to elder abuse and neglect (Wolf, 1996). It is not a simple decision that can be made haphazardly. Controversy exists between the child abuse model and spousal abuse model, both of which have been applied to address the needs of the elder victim. The child abuse model uses language similar to child abuse protective statutes and takes a stronger view of victims as unable to protect themselves. Conversely, the spousal model assumes elders to be victimized yet legally independent adults. Some researchers claim that the family violence paradigm is not suitable for these cases because cases of neglect are forms of inadequate care, not violence. Concerned about the civil rights of elders, professionals disagree on this area of government interference (Biggs et al., 1995). Since many adult protective services have modeled legislation after child abuse statutes, this raises questions on freedom of choice. Some suggest that the government-defined level of care denies elders basic constitutional rights.

Abandonment. If a special relationship exists between a caretaker and the elder, the caretaker can be held legally responsible for a failure to act on that duty of care in some states. California is one state among six that has adopted criminal abandonment legislation, making it a felony to cause or permit a dependent elder to suffer harm. In 1995, the California Supreme Court put that law to test. They tried family members for "abandonment" after the death of 67-year-old Robert Heitzman, Sr. His "body was found in his bedroom on a mattress covered with feces and rotted through with urine" (National Committee for the Prevention of Elder Abuse, 1995). Two sons who lived with the elder were found guilty of 368(a) of the California Penal Code. Upon appeal, the California Supreme Court held that the statute was not unconstitutional or vague—yet a duty to care for an elder, through a special relationship, must be present for legal liability to attach. A daughter who did not live full-time with her father was found not guilty. In 1998 cases of abandonment were relatively small; they comprised 3.6 percent of the total substantiated cases against the elderly (Administration on Aging, 1998a).

Figure 7–7   If a person discontinues taking care of an elder, and harm results to that dependent elder, the caretaker may be held criminally liable. California is an example of a state that has adopted such criminal abandonment legislation.

Active Neglect.   A deliberate attempt by a caregiver to inflict injury or emotional stress on an older person characterizes active neglect. This is an intentional condition that is inflicted on the elder by an act or an omission: for example, failure to provide needed medication for the elder because of the high cost of the prescription. Half of substantiated abuse reports involve neglect (Administration on Aging, 1998).

Passive Neglect.   The passive form of neglect occurs when a caregiver is unable to provide the necessary care for an elder. Passive neglect may be caused by caretakers who are too young or inexperienced to take care of an older person who has special needs. Sometimes the person responsible for elder care is handicapped by a mental or physical disability and is unable to handle the difficult chores of caring for an elder. Passive neglect is defined by AARP as the unintentional failure to fulfill a caretaking obligation. There is no willful desire to inflict physical or emotional distress on the older person.

Symptoms for both types of neglect include the following:

1. *Withdrawal or denial of health services.*   Overmedication may be purposeful to keep an elder "quiet" or might be due to ignorance and carelessness on the part of the caretaker. Either way, it can be extremely dangerous to the person, and intervention is necessary. This could be a life-threatening situation for the elder. Deliberate overmedication is a form of an improper use of restraint. In some instances, a lack or perceived lack of financial resources could cause the withdrawal or denial of health services. Medical attention for

the elder should be sought to determine the condition and provide necessary medications. Untreated injuries and illnesses may alert the responder to neglect or abuse. Although it is not life threatening to be denied eyeglasses, dentures, or hearing aids, this would constitute a lower standard of life for the senior and is neglectful.

2. *Denial of adequate food.* The elder may become malnourished or dehydrated as a result. If the elder is living alone, the investigator should look into the refrigerator and cupboards to confirm suspicions that food is not being supplied or made available to the elder.

3. *Lack of proper hygiene.* If the older person smells of old urine or is caked with feces, he or she is not being cleaned properly. Other signs of neglect include matted, unclean, or uncut hair, bodily crevices caked with dirt, or overgrown finger/toe nails. The presence of a serious rash, bedsores, urine burns, or impetigo is also suggestive of neglect.

The neglected elder's environment may also provide clues that abuse is occurring (Ramsey-Klawsnik, 1997). Evidence demonstrating neglect includes

- An excessively cluttered or dirty home
- Lack of heat, running water, electricity, or air conditioning in extremely hot climates
- Infestation by cockroaches or rodents

Self-Neglect and Abuse

When an older person threatens his or her own health or safety, it is called self-neglect or self-abuse, depending on the actions of the elder. Self-neglect is the most common form of elder mistreatment and must be differentiated from maltreatment caused by another person. Nationally, about 42 percent of elder abuse cases involve self-neglect (Teaster, 2003). Self-neglect and self-abuse are included as a separate form of violence because it is extremely rare that they would be considered a criminal offense. This type of abuse may accompany other forms of abuse for which there are criminal consequences. The differences are important, and an investigation of neglect must include the consideration that abuse may be in part or wholly self-inflicted.

The National Association of Adult Protective Services Administrators formed a committee to study and report on the characteristics of adults identified as self-neglectful in addition to providing a definition for this form of abuse (NAAPSA, 1991). As a result, NAAPSA adopted the following definition:

Self-neglect: the result of an adult's inability, due to physical and/or mental impairments or diminished capacity, to perform essential self-care tasks, including providing essential food, clothing, shelter, and medical care; obtaining goods and services

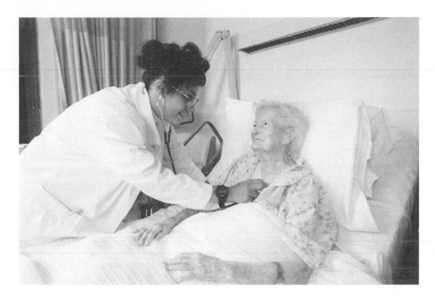

Figure 7–8   This elder needs medical care and attention, regardless of who the abuser is. Since self-neglect is the most common form of elder mistreatment, you can expect that over half of abuse allegations involve this form of maltreatment.

necessary to maintain physical health, mental health, emotional well-being, and general safety, and/or managing financial affairs.

Generally noninstitutionalized, self-neglectors frequently have a mental and/or physical impairment. Service needs for this population can be substantial. Recognition of this form of abuse by law enforcement is crucial to make the appropriate referrals to social service agencies that can provide appropriate intervention. Self-abuse is not a criminal violation, and necessary emergency intervention should come from a social service or adult protective service agency.

Physical Abuse

The symptoms of elder physical abuse are similar to the other categories of domestic violence. Approximately one-quarter of all substantiated reports of abuse involve physical abuse (Administration on Aging, 1998). Human bite marks, bruises, bleeding, and burns are all indicative of maltreatment. Gag marks, or the indication that the elder has been tied or taped, should make investigators highly suspicious of elder abuse. Slapping an elder is an example of physical abuse. Injuries that are not consistent with the explanation given for their cause are a red flag that should cause an investigator to look deeper into the situation. Does the elder have a history of similar injuries or hospitalizations? Do people in the household give varying accounts of how the elder was injured?

However, injuries due to falls or accidents may not be caused by abusive conditions. Observing the behavior of the elder may help to clarify the situation if abuse is suspected. Presence of fear, agitation, contradictory statements, or refusal to talk openly should alert officers of a potential abuse situation. It is not confirmation of abuse but should focus further investigation.

Spouse Abuse.   Adult children are the most frequent abusers of elderly. The second most frequent physical abuser is the elder spouse. Although the incidence of spouse abuse in older couples is significantly less than that of younger couples, many of the risk factors present in abusive couple relationships are the same (Harris, 1996). There are several patterns of domestic violence among the elderly, and the following situations have been observed (Nerenberg, 2000):

- "Spouse abuse grown old" in which the victims have been abused for most of their adult lives.
- "Late onset" cases in which the abuse begins late in life by partners who had not previously been abusive. This type of abuse seems to be associated with age-related conditions or stresses including retirement, dependency, changing patterns in relationships, or sexual dysfunction.
- Cases involving women who enter into abusive relationships late in life. In these cases, the abusers are frequently the victim's second or third spouse or intimate partner, and in many instances, financial gain through financial abuse also accompanies the physical abuse.

Figure 7–9 We now know that the second most frequent physical abuser of the elderly is his or her own spouse. It is equally likely that the perpetrator is the husband or wife.

- Situations in which elderly women who had been battered earlier in their lives by their husbands (or who, in some cases, previously abused their children) are battered by their sons or daughters.

There is a lack of consensus among service providers as to whether or not battering by adult offspring falls under the rubric of domestic violence.

Psychological and Emotional Abuse

Psychological and emotional abuse is the willful infliction of mental or emotional anguish by threat, humiliation, intimidation, or other abusive conduct. Psychological and emotional abuses are the most difficult forms to identify. Isolation, name-calling, or being treated like a child by a caretaker are recognizable conditions. Usually, there is a lack of evidence to support these claims. If an elder is suffering from another type of abuse, it is not unusual for psychological and/or emotional abuse to be present also. Documenting signs of psychological and/or emotional abuse in conjunction with other more visible forms of abuse will provide an accurate statement of the general living conditions that are indicators of abuse as well as strengthen the case against the suspect. This is the second largest category of domestic violence against an elder. In 1998 more than one-third of substantiated cases were for psychological and emotional abuse (Administration on Aging, 1998).

Additionally, investigation may find the elder to be in need of services. A referral to the local elder protection agency is warranted when the complainant seems confused or unable to distinguish between reality and fantasy. It is appropriate to contact a caregiver or protection agency when a person is displaying inappropriate behaviors.

Sexual Abuse Indicators

Research on sexual abuse against elders is emerging slowly. We know that it is happening because the professionals in the field are identifying cases. Sexual maltreatment may be "covert" or "overt," as described in one major study from Massachusetts (Ramsey-Klawsnik, 1991). The author describes covert sexual abuse as a sexualized relationship. It involves sexual interest, jokes, comments, and harassment of the victim or discussion of sexual activity in front of the victim. Overt sexual abuse is any type of unwanted or forced sexual conduct with an elder. Overt sexual abuse can be any form of sexual activity, including but not limited to kissing and fondling, oral–genital contact, penetration of the vagina or anus, voyeurism, and exhibitionism. Reported in 1998, .03 percent of all substantiated cases involved sexual abuse to the elder (Administration on Aging, 1998).

It may be surprising to know that many sexual assaults against the elderly are witnessed by a third party (Burgess et al., 2000; Teaster et al., 2000). In one study, 7 percent of the older battered women had been forced to have sexual intercourse with their husbands (Mouton, 2003). Victims of sexual abuse are not spared due to infirmity.

More About It: Attempted Suicide

There is at least one situation where self-neglect or abuse may be a criminal offense: Some states outlaw suicide. The law of Massachusetts, for example, allows for a person to be brought before the court on a complaint of "attempted suicide." This is common law crime, but rarely is it enforced.

An officer in western Massachusetts has used it, however. The case involved a man who after repeated unsuccessful suicide attempts refused medical assistance or evaluation. Brought before the court on criminal attempted suicide, he was ordered to have a psychiatric evaluation and a temporary commitment to a local hospital. This method was used to obtain emergency help for the victim.

This issue raises some important considerations for criminal justice on the acceptable extent of government interference. The suicide rate for the elderly is higher than for any other age group. Is it the role of law enforcement to prevent or intervene in such attempts? Jack Kevorkian has brought the issue to the forefront in the United States through his multiple assisted suicides for terminally ill patients.

Burgess, Dowdell, and Prentky (2000) found that 80 percent of the women in their study were bedridden or could only get around in a wheelchair; over half had dementia. The sexual assault victims in another study lived in a nursing home and many could not walk without assistance (Teaster et al., 2000).

Sexual assault victims share the same or similar symptoms regardless of their age or gender. The following signs are suspicious for sexual abuse, although their presence doesn't verify that abuse to the elder is occurring and may be indicative of other problems.

Sexually Transmitted Diseases.   Presence of a sexually transmitted disease (STD) if the elder is not engaged in consensual sexual activity and does not have a prior record of STD is cause for concern when present with other indicators, such as fear, apprehension, or neglect. Some STDs are related to poor hygiene and would not indicate abuse, so caution is recommended. Examples of STDs that could be caused by poor hygiene or sexual abuse include *Trichomonas vaginalis* (vaginitis) and bacterial vaginosis (Hammerschlag, 1996). Herpes and herpes simplex may be self-infected in the genital area if the person was infected with mouth sores previously. Severe and untreated infections may be indicative of neglect rather than abuse.

Physical Indicators
1. Injury such as bruising, bleeding, or pain to the genitals, rectum, mouth, and breasts should be investigated thoroughly. Urinary incontinence would complicate the diagnosis for abuse if the elder is not cleaned and cared for properly. Redness of the genital area could be caused by poor hygiene.

2. When bruising or pain is evidenced with injury to the face, neck, cheek, abdomen, thighs, or buttocks, the patterns of bruising might be suggestive of grab marks or the use of restraints.

3. Evidence of torn, stained, or bloody underwear is highly indicative that sexual abuse is occurring.

Behavioral Indicators

1. Intense fear, anxiety, or mistrust of one person, along with other indicators of sexual maltreatment, is a sign of sexual abuse.

2. The victim of sexual abuse may offer a "coded" disclosure to someone that she or he trusts. Ramsey-Klawsnik suggests that the elder may give hints about the sexual abuse, described as "testing of the waters" (Ramsey-Klawsnik, 1993). This may include statements about a dislike for a particular caregiver or a reluctance to be bathed by that person.

3. Depression without other explanation or cause may indicate sexual abuse.

4. Self-destructive behavior or suicide attempts without a history of mental illness or underlying medical causes may indicate sexual abuse.

Consequences of Elder Abuse

The severe emotional distress experienced by older persons as a result of mistreatment has been well documented. It is important to note that elders have the highest rate of suicide of any age category; reporting an individual as being in need of services may save his or her life. If a person is considered a risk to himself or herself or others, regardless of age, either law enforcement or social service agencies may seek assistance from the civil or family court. Even abuse that is not defined by state law as elder crimes may be addressed by using other provisions of the mental health, social service, or penal code (Nerenberg, 1993).

Rates of depression are higher in abused elders as compared to nonabused persons. Social supports have had a positive effect on the level of psychological distress in victims, indicating that victims benefit more from the social supports they receive (Wolfe, 2000). According to the National Victims Assistance Academy (2000), elderly victims of sexual assault are confronted with the psychic trauma of victimization as well as possible physical injuries that can pose significant health threats due to the victim's age and physical well-being. To many older victims, rape is the worst form of lost dignity. Shame may be exacerbated by misplaced feelings of self-blame and guilt. There may be profound shame in discussing the crime or participating in a medical exam with law enforcement and medical personnel. There may be feelings of embarrassment that family members and/or neighbors will find out or that the media may somehow access and release the information to the community.

Perpetrators of Elder Abuse

Compared to the other forms of family violence, there is relatively little information about domestic abuses toward the elderly. The extent of spouse abuse is believed to be lower than other forms of violence in the family (Pillemer & Finkelhor, 1998). Adult children are often in the caretaking role, and they are represented as the most frequent abusers of the elderly (Tatara, 1996).

Along with the possible approaches to these situations, Ramsey-Klawsnik describes three general categories under which elders are abused (Ramsey-Klawsnik, 1997).

1. *The stress-precipitated abuser.* This form of abuse to an elder is intentional, yet it is caused by stress and abuse is not necessarily the intended result. It is used to describe the situation where abuse is related to stress, low resources, or impairments. Caring for an elder can be an extremely difficult situation for a family member who is already overburdened with his or her own family responsibilities. This abuser might benefit from and be willing to accept services.

2. *The greedy abuser.* The second category is related to greed and lack of concern for the elder. This abuser intentionally denies care and services; may cause physical or sexual harm; or takes money and possessions directly from the elder. The purpose is to control and acquire whatever financial resources the elder may possess. The abuser should be removed from the caretaking role. Criminal intervention may be necessary, particularly in cases of financial exploitation.

3. *The intentional harm perpetrator.* The third category is the most dangerous abuser, having the intention to harm through power and control over the victim. Protection for these elders may be through empowerment. Prosecution for severe harm caused the elder should be considered.

Both males and females are likely to commit abuse against the elderly. Interestingly, neglect is the only type of maltreatment that is committed with approximately equal frequency by females and males. For the remainder of the maltreatment types, males clearly are more likely to commit abuse and neglect. The Administration on Aging (1998) gives some insight into the gender of these perpetrators:

- Neglect was the most frequently committed offence. The Administration reports that slightly more than half of the perpetrators are female.
- Emotional/psychological abuse was the second most frequent type of maltreatment. Data show that just over one-half of the perpetrators were male (60.1 percent) while the remainder were female (39.9 percent).
- Financial/material exploitation was the next most frequent type of abuse perpetrated. Perpetrators of this type of abuse were approximately 60 percent male, while the remaining were females.

- Almost two-thirds of the perpetrators of physical abuse were males (62.6 percent) while the remaining one-third (37.5 percent) were females.
- Abandonment was predominately perpetrated by males (83.4 percent) while the remainder were female.

The largest category of perpetrators (47.3 percent) of the substantiated incidents of elder abuse was the adult children of the victims (Administration on Aging, 1998). Spouses represented the second largest group of perpetrators comprising 19.3 percent. In addition, other relatives were the third most frequent category of perpetrators (8.8 percent), with grandchildren following closely behind (8.6 percent).

Elder Abuser Treatment Program. Domestic violence against an elder family member has unique issues when compared to abuses against younger persons. Court referrals to batterer treatment programs are the most frequent criminal sanction for batterers generally. Now program development has expanded to include services for holding elder perpetrators accountable. **S.E.A.M.**, or Stop Elder Abuse and Mistreatment, is one example of a psychoeducational program for abusers of the elderly (Mason, 2003). It is a 12-week educational and rehabilitative program that teaches abusers to recognize unacceptable behaviors and teach alternative acceptable behaviors. It is not mental health, psychiatric, or substance abuse counseling but a court-referred abuser program. Using the curriculum created by LIFESPAN, it has been attended by physical abusers, financial exploiters, sexual abusers, and verbal abusers. Both genders and age range from 19 to 76 have taken part in this program. LIFESPAN is a non-profit agency located in Rochester, New York.

Been There . . . Done That!

A report came into the barracks of theft from an elder. When responding to the call, I found the man extremely agitated as he described his wallet being stolen. His fear of being victimized was real, but the account of how it happened didn't sound plausible. After careful consider of his narration and interviewing of the suspect, I doubted that the wallet had been taken. We slowly retraced his steps throughout the day. Actually walking the property where he had been, I found the wallet lying on the ground in the barn. He was embarrassed to find that it had been dropped, not stolen.

Complaints from seniors should never simply be dismissed. If possible, they should be resolved. The elders' fear of victimization is high even though the actual incidence may be low. Failure to be sensitive to elderly fears will leave the person in emotional turmoil, if not psychological pain. Although frivolous complaints may occur from time to time, we have no way of determining if the abuse is occurring without an investigation. A case solved is a case solved, regardless of the complaint!

DUTIES AND RESPONSIBILITIES

Since elder abuse and neglect is a new area of intervention for the criminal justice community, it is important to consider the duties and responsibilities that are in place to direct law enforcement. Police officer liability is a factor that must be taken into account. If your state has a mandated or preferred arrest policy for domestic abuse that does not specifically exclude elders, it must be enforced. If the state has a more liberal policy involving discretionary action, police can consider the entire situation before taking any action. Depending on the severity of the abuse and the likelihood of repeated assaults, an arrest, further investigation, or referrals are all options to consider.

In neglectful situations, it may be more difficult to determine an appropriate course of action. Any investigation is first concerned with the safety of the victim. Can the person protect himself or herself against further abuse or neglect? Referrals, arrest, or continued investigation are all options. The first guiding principle should be the determination of probable cause. If probable cause to believe a crime has been committed does exist, officers must consider already existing domestic violence law in their state. Does your jurisdiction mandate arrest in an abuse situation?

MANDATED REPORTING

Forty-five states and the District of Columbia have mandatory reporting laws under which physicians, nurses, social workers, and others designated by the state are legally required to report suspected elder abuse (Teaster, 2003). The remaining states have voluntary reporting laws. A mandated reporter is required to report when he or she saw abuse or when there is a reasonable belief that it is occurring. It is difficult to identify abuse in some instances, since many elderly are reluctant to tell and since many physical and mental difficulties that older adults suffer from have results that can easily be mistaken for some forms of abuse. Since it is extremely hard to determine if elder abuse is actually occurring, the trend in most states is to grant immunity from legal sanctions for reporting abuse when in fact it is not occurring, if that report was based on a good faith belief that it was.

States that have mandated reporters seem to create a duty to report for almost all professionals with whom the elderly come into contact. Following is a list that identifies the percentage of state laws that include the professionals cited as mandated reporters (Tatara, 1995): social workers, 75 percent; physicians, 70 percent; nurses, 69 percent; police, 52 percent; and dentists, 50 percent. If a mandated reporter believes that abuse is possible but fails to report it, legal repercussions could be taken against the reporter. For failing to report abuse, for example, a reporter can be found to have committed a misdemeanor (Stiegel, 1995). Most states do not, however, take such aggressive action against this omission. In fact, only one prosecution occurred in the United States between 1994 and 1997 under these mandated reporting laws (Moskowitz, 1998).

Figure 7–10 A mandated reporter has a duty to report the suspicion of elder abuse, even when he or she believes that the elder will not cooperate with an investigation. Reluctance to cooperate may be due to an unwillingness to give information about a family member, particularly when the elder depends on the person for care or attention.

CONCLUSIONS

As a society, we are faced with many challenges in the upcoming years. Our elder population is exploding, and the call for services is increasing as well. In an area where law enforcement has been involved only sporadically, the need for continued self-education and involvement is imperative. Community triad programs demonstrate the commitment of this generation of law enforcement personnel toward protecting the next. Fiduciary investigation units such as LAPD's FAST provide an example of one police department's response to the unique problems that elders face. Most officers can expect to be faced with these elder issues throughout their careers and should remember that they, too, will one day be elderly.

Physical and sexual abuse of the elderly shares many identifying physical characteristics with other forms of family violence. The signs and symptoms are nearly the same; injury is still the obvious indicator. The possible extent of injury for the elderly can be higher than for other populations, however, due to infirmity and old age. The emotional and psychological harm of abuse, which is impossible to measure, may be taken to the grave.

Change in abilities and dependencies make elders susceptible to abuse in ways that don't apply to other age groups. Due to the vulnerability of elders, legislation has been enacted that will guide enforcement action for the future. Financial exploitation, the invisible abuse, should be a growing area of specialization for law enforcement in the future. Compassion and empathy will go a long way toward preserving the dignity of seniors in the United States.

QUESTIONS FOR REVIEW

1. Name criminal actions against the elderly.

2. What are the two types of elder domestic abuse, and what agencies handle each?

3. Name the forms of active elder abuse.

4. Define *passive maltreatment*.

5. Describe the demographics of the "typical" elderly victim of abuse.

6. What is dementia, and how is it related to abuse?

7. What is an ombudsman?

8. What is financial exploitation?

9. Explain the category of self-neglect and abuse. What is the seriousness of this type of abuse?

10. Name some of the symptoms that indicate physical abuse of an elder.

INTERNET-BASED EXERCISES

1. Every state is required to have an ombudsman program—can you find the one in your home state? Go to http://www.ltcombudsman.org/static_pages/ombudsmen.cfm.

2. What does it mean for a group of people to grow old together? What can one generation tell us about the future of our aging society? Go to the following site and gather information on the aging population. How will this affect you and your future? http://www.generationsjournal.org/

REFERENCES

Administration on Aging. 1997a. *Native American Elder Population, 1990.* Washington, DC: U.S. Administration on Aging.
———. 1997b. *Older and Younger People with Disabilities: Improving Chronic Care Throughout the Life Span.* AOA Fact Sheet. Washington, DC: U.S. Department of Health and Human Services.

————. 1998a. *The National Elder Abuse Incidence Study; Final Report*. Washington, DC: U.S. Department of Health and Human Services.

————. 1998b. *Older Women: A Diverse and Growing Population*. AOA Fact Sheet. Washington, DC: U.S. Department of Health and Human Services.

————. 2001. *A Profile on Older Americans: 2001*. Washington, DC: U.S. Administration on Aging.

Alzheimer's Association. 1998. "Alzheimer's Disease: A Major Health Issue for Women." *http://www.alz.org/news/right.htm*. August 1988.

American Association of Retired Persons. 1987. *Decision-Making, Incapacity, and the Elderly*. Washington, DC: Legal Counsel for the Elderly.

American Association of Retired Persons Foundation. 1998. *Elder Abuse: Training Module*. Washington, DC: National Legal Assistance and Elder Rights Project.

American Psychiatric Association. 1979. "Battered Parents—A New Syndrome." *American Journal of Psychiatry* 136(10):1288–91.

Biggs, Simon, Chris Phillipson, and Paul Kingston. 1995. *Elder Abuse in Perspective*. Bristol, PA: Open University Press.

Boudreau, F. A. 1993. "Elder Abuse." Pp. 142–58 in *Family Violence: Prevention and Treatment*, R. L. Hampton, T. P. Gullotta, G. R. Adams, E. H. Potter, and R. P. Weissberg (eds.). Newbury Park, CA: Sage Publications.

Burgess, A., E. Dowdell, and R. Prentky. 2000. "Sexual Abuse of Nursing Home Residents." *Journal of Psychosocial Nursing*, 38(6), 10–18.

Brandl, Bonnie, and Loree Cook-Daniels. 2002. "Domestic Abuse in Later Life." Available at *http:www.vaw.umn.edu/documents/vawnet/arlaterlife.pdf*

Commonwealth of Massachusetts. 1995. *Investigation of Financial Exploitation: Skill-Building for Protective Services Caseworkers*. Boston: The Commonwealth.

DiLeonardi, Joan W. 1995. "Families in Poverty and Chronic Neglect of Children." Pp. 145–51 in *Family Violence: Readings in the Social Sciences and Professions*, James Makepeace (ed.). New York: McGraw-Hill.

Doerner, William, and Steven Lab. 1998. *Victimology*, 2nd ed. Cincinnati, OH: Anderson Publishing Company.

Executive Office of Elder Affairs. 1998. *Elder Protective Services 1997 Program Report*. Boston: Commonwealth of Massachusetts.

Finkelhor, David, and Karl Pillemer. 1988. "Elder Abuse: Its Relationship to Other Forms of Domestic Violence." Pp. 244–54 in *Family Abuse and Its Consequences: New Directions in Research*, Gerald Hotaling, David Finkelhor, John Kirkpatrick, and Murray Straus (eds.). Newbury Park, CA: Sage Publications.

Fox, Craig R., Gillian Price, John S. Scheft, and Bonita Irving. 1995. *The Bank Reporting Project: An Edge against Elder Financial Exploitation*. Boston: Commonwealth of Massachusetts, Executive Office of Elder Affairs.

Hammerschlag, Margaret R. 1996. *Sexually Transmitted Diseases and Child Sexual Abuse*. NCJ 160940. Washington, DC: U.S. Department of Justice.

Harris, S. 1996. "For Better or Worse: Spouse Abuse Grown Old." *Journal of Elder Abuse and Neglect* 8(1)1–32.

Heisler, Candace. 2000. "Elder Abuse and the Criminal Justice System: New Awareness, New Responses." *Generations* XXIV(II):52–64.

Hudson, M. F. 1991. "Elder Mistreatment: A Taxonomy with Definitions by Delphi." *Elder Abuse and Neglect* 3(2):1–20.

Kohl, Rhiana, Diana Brensilber, and William Holmes. 1995. *Elderly Protection Project*. Washington, DC: U.S. Department of Justice.

Mason, Art. 2003. "S.E.A.M., Stop Elder Abuse and Mistreatment: A Psycho-Educational Program for Abusers of the Elderly." *Domestic Violence Report* 8(6):87–88.

Mayeux, Richard. 1998. "The APOE-E4 Allele and the Risk of Alzheimer Disease among African Americans, Whites and Hispanics." *Journal of the American Medical Association* 280(19): 1661–63.

McDaniel, Christine L. 1997. "Elder Abuse in the Institutional Setting." May. *http://www.ink.org/public/keln/bibs/medaniel2.html*. August 1998.

Mixson, Paula M. 1996. "How Adult Protective Services Evolved, and Obstacles to Ethical Casework." *Aging* 367:14–17.

Moskowitz, Seymour. 1998. "Private Enforcement of Criminal Mandatory Reporting Laws." *Journal of Elder Abuse and Neglect* 9(3):1–22.

Mouton, Charles P. 2003. "Intimate Partner Violence and Health Status Among Older Women." *Violence Against Women* 9(12):1465–78.

NAAPSA. 2003. *State Adult Protective Services Program Responses to Financial Exploitation of Vulnerable Adults.* Washington, DC: The National Center on Elder Abuse.

National Aging Resource Center on Elder Abuse. 1992. *Elder Abuse: Questions and Answers.* Washington, DC: NARCEA.

National Association of Adult Protective Service Administrators (NAAPSA). 1991. A National Study of Self-Neglecting Adult Protective Services Clients. Wheaton, IL: NAAPSA. *http://www.naapsa.org*

National Center on Elder Abuse. 1994. *Findings from a National Study of Domestic Elder Abuse Reports.* Washington, DC: NCEA.

———. 1996. *Highlights of a National Study of Domestic Elder Abuse Reports.* Washington, DC: NCEA.

———. 1998. *The National Elder Abuse Incidence Study.* Washington, DC: The Administration for Children and Families.

National Committee for the Prevention of Elder Abuse. 1995. "California Supreme Court Rules on Family and Neglect." *Nexus* 1(2):6.

National Senior Citizens Law Center. 1998. "Betrayal: the Quality of Care in California Nursing Homes." July 27. *http://www.nsclc.org/testate.html*. 2002.

National Victims Assistance Academy, 2000. *Office for Victims of Crime.* Anne Seymour, Morna Murray (eds.). NCJ 184052. Washington, DC: U.S. Department of Justice.

Nerenberg, Lisa. 1993. *Improving the Police Response to Domestic Elder Abuse.* Washington, DC: Police Executive Research Forum.

———. 1996. *Financial Abuse of the Elderly.* San Francisco: San Francisco Consortium for Elder Abuse Prevention.

———. 2000. "Older Battered Women: Integrating Aging and Domestic Violence Services." In National Victim Assistance Academy, 2000. *Office for Victims of Crime.* Anne Seymour, Morna Murray (eds.). NCJ 184052. Washington, DC: U.S. Department of Justice.

———. 2003. *Elder Abuse Prevention Teams: A New Generation.* Washington, DC: National Center on Elder Abuse.

Office of the NY State Attorney. 2003. "What is a Triad?" [Web page]. Accessed 2004. Available at *http://www.oag.state.ny.us/seniors/triad.html*

Office for Victims of Crime (OVC). 1997. *VOCA Victim Assistance Final Program Guidelines.* Washington, DC: Office for Victims of Crime.

Perkins, C. 1997. *Age Patterns of Victims of Serious Violent Crime: Special Report.* Washington, DC: U.S. Department of Justice, Bureau of Justice Statistics.

Pillemer, Karl, and David Finkelhor. 1998. "The Prevalence of Elder Abuse: A Random Sample Survey." *Gerontologist* 28(1):51.

Pillemer, Karl A. 1988. "Maltreatment of Patients in Nursing Homes: Overview and Research Agenda." *Health and Social Behavior* 29:227–33.

Ramsey-Klawsnik, Holly. 1991. "Elder Sexual Abuse: Preliminary Findings." *Journal of Elder Abuse and Neglect* 3(3):73–89.

———. 1993. "Interviewing Elders for Suspected Sexual Abuse: Guidelines and Techniques." *Journal of Elder Abuse and Neglect* 5(1):5–17.

———. 1997. *Sessions I and II; III and IV, Workshop Handouts.* Canton, MA: Massachusetts Executive Office of Elder Affairs.

Rennison, Callie. 2001. *Criminal Victimization 2000, Changes 1993–2000.* Bureau of Justice Statistics. NCJ 187007. Washington, DC: U.S. Department of Justice.

Rennison, Callie. 2003. *Intimate Partner Violence, 1993–2001.* Bureau of Justice Statistics. NCJ 197838. Washington, DC: U.S. Department of Justice.

Rennison, Callie M., and Sarah Welchans. 2000. *Intimate Partner Violence.* NCJ 178247. Washington, DC: U.S. Department of Justice.

Smith, Denise. 2003. *The Older Population in the United States: 2002.* Census Bureau Current Population Reports. P20-546. Washington, DC: Census Bureau.

Stiegel, Lori. 1995. *Recommended Guidelines for State Courts Handling Cases Involving Elder Abuse.* Washington, DC: American Bar Association.

Tatara, Toshio. 1990. *Elder Abuse in the United States: An Issue Paper.* Washington, DC: National Aging Resource Center on Elder Abuse.

———. 1995. *An Analysis of State Laws Addressing Elder Abuse, Neglect, and Exploitation.* Washington, DC: National Center on Elder Abuse.

———. 1996. *Elder Abuse in Domestic Settings.* Washington, DC: National Center on Elder Abuse.

Teaster, Pamela. 2003. *A Response to the Abuse of Vulnerable Adults: The 2000 Survey of State Protective Services.* Washington, DC: National Center on Elder Abuse.

Teaster, Pamela B., Karen A. Roberto, Joy O. Duke, and Myeonghwan Kim. 2000. "Sexual Abuse of Older Adults: Preliminary Findings of Cases in Virginia." *Journal of Elder Abuse & Neglect* 12(3/4):1–16.

Tennessee Department of Social Services. 1991. *A National Study of Self-Neglecting Adult Protective Clients.* NAAPSA #1. Nashville, TN: National Association of Adult Protective Services Administrators.

Weinberg, Andrew D., and Jeanne Y. Wei. 1995. *The Early Recognition of Elder Abuse.* Bayside, NY: American Medical Publishing Company.

Wilber, Kathleen H., and Sandra L. Reynolds. 1996. "Introducing a Framework for Defining Financial Abuse of the Elderly." *Journal of Elder Abuse and Neglect* 8(2):61–80.

Wolf, Rosalie S. 1996. "Understanding Elder Abuse and Neglect." *Aging* 367:4–17.

Wolfe, Rosalie. S. 2000. "Emotional Distress and Elder Abuse: Special Research Review Section." National Center on Elder Abuse Newsletter. December 1999/2000. *http://www.elderabusecenter.org/research/emotional.html.* 2002.

Young, Melinda G., Donna Benton, Cheryl Phillips, and Matthew Wayne. 2000. "Recognizing the Signs of Elder Abuse." *Patient Care* 34(20):56–64.

CASE

Long v. Brookside Manor, 885 S.W. 2d 70 (1994).

Part Four

Legal and Enforcement Responses

The criminal justice system is the focus of Part Four. What laws have been enacted to protect victims of abuse and to make the perpetrators responsible for their actions? How did the criminalization of domestic violence emerge in recent times? Why did law enforcement, rather than social service, become the primary tools to eradicate domestic abuses in our society? What should police officers do in cases of criminal domestic violence?

Chapter 8, "Legal Responses," includes an examination of federal and state legislative action that has poured forth in response to the problems of domestic abuses. A new section on domestic violence courts is included in the third edition. Every state has criminalized partner violence, child abuse, and elder abuse, yet little consistency exists among the states. In this chapter we look at the criminal statutes that define and prohibit crimes against intimate and family members. Discussions are included here relative to the civil protections for victims in domestic violence and the remedies that may be available after victimization occurs. Antistalking legislation and gun control emerge as recent components to both federal and state efforts in combating domestic violence. For the first time in history, domestic violence has become a federal concern. Information concerning the full faith and credit provision of the Violence against Women Act of 1994 has been newly expanded for this edition.

In Chapter 9, "The Role of the Police," the pivotal responsibility that police officers have in cases involving domestic violence is acknowledged. Here the nature of policing is examined along with the trends toward a problem oriented approach that is consistent with the needs of the victims of family violence. This chapter sets forth the three law enforcement goals that specifically address domestic violence yet are relevant to the overall organizational goals of policing. Common myths about domestic abusers and victims are discussed as well as the realities that police must acknowledge when responding to these crimes. Note the new section, "The Role of Police in Cases Involving Persons with Disabilities." It includes a discussion on obtaining truthful information for the determination of criminal responsibility in domestic situations involving an allegation of abuse.

The ambivalence toward the role of police in response to domestic violence is presented in Chapter 10, entitled "Law Enforcement Response." New for the third edition is a section, "Primary and Dominant Aggressor Determination." How do the police get involved in these cases? In this chapter, mandated arrest policies are examined in addition to alternative resources for police to consider. Civil protection codes and mental health codes appear to complicate the law enforcement response at first glance, but ultimately they are tools for officers to use toward resolving conflict. The determination of probable cause is critical to any police action that may involve an arrest; therefore, the officer must collect evidence and interrogate suspects. Also discussed are the constitutional constraints that law enforcement must work within in order to gather information and evidence.

"Associated Major Crimes: Stalking and Homicide" is the title for Chapter 11. In-depth examinations of the crimes of stalking and domestic homicide are the focus of this chapter. Stalking has been termed the crime of the 1990s. Although stalking behaviors are not new, they are newly prohibited. Are domestic violence victims more vulnerable to being stalked? How can someone protect himself or herself against becoming a victim of stalking? Have you ever heard of the false victimization syndrome? You may be surprised to learn that the rate of homicide committed by intimates is declining. In this chapter you will also study the prevalence of murder in the family and consider the different forms that it takes. What about the murder scene exception to the requirement for a search warrant in cases of suspected homicide? Does it exist? New to this chapter are a section on death review teams and expanded information on stalking. These questions and more will be addressed in Part Four.

CHAPTER 8

LEGAL RESPONSES

SIMPLY SCENARIO

Full Faith and Credit

Brian obtained a protection order against his same-sex abuser. The provisions of the court order require that Tom must refrain from abusing, threatening, or attempting to harm Brian in any way. Further, Tom is ordered not to contact Brian or come near his residence. Brian decided to move to another state in order to start a new life without fear. He learns that Tom is looking for him and he wonders what to do. In the state where he now lives, same-sex partners are not eligible to obtain protection orders.

Question: Is Brian's protection order enforceable in his new home state?

KEY TERMS

Civil law
Concurrent jurisdiction
Driver Privacy Protection Act
Full faith and credit
General jurisdiction
Jurisdiction
Marital rape
National Center for Missing and
   Exploited Children

National Incidence Study
National Instant Criminal Background
   Check System
Parental kidnapping
Petition
Pro se

INTRODUCTION

> The people reign in the American political world as the Deity does in the universe. They are the cause and the aim of all things; everything comes from them, everything is absorbed in them. (Alexis de Tocqueville; Knopf, 1994)

In his classic description of equality in the American political system, Alexis de Tocqueville (1805–1859) expressed the spirit of our nation that has resurfaced. Claims that the U.S. criminal justice system has been way out of balance are being addressed. Small grassroots movements that began nearly four decades ago to right injustices for victims of crime have gained significant ground. Although insignificant when weighed against the rights of the government and that of the accused, enormous changes have occurred.

Historians will someday look back on the twentieth century and judge the society in which we live today. A progression will be evidenced during which tremendous gains toward equality and protection for crime victims will be noted. The domestic social problems that are identified throughout this book and the responses to them have been well documented. Legislative responses have come forward in both the criminal and civil arenas. Never before in the history of men and women have so many statutes been enacted toward the goal of equal protection.

Strong victims rights' laws make a difference, but a question remains as to whether victims' needs are being met. It is not enough to enact statutes unless they are given full force by the criminal justice community, which is positioned to give them meaning through enforcement. Since education has often been recognized as the most effective method of bringing about social change, that initial step is being taken now. Knowledge is power—in this case, it is the power for the present generation to be successful in implementing the vast amounts of legislative amendments that seek to protect victims' rights.

In this chapter we present a brief overview of the legal codes, which have come about so fast that it is difficult to keep up with them. For persons involved in protection of the public, we provide a starting point to use when examining particular state statutes.

COURT JURISDICTION

Before we can consider laws governing domestic violence and personal relations, it is necessary to understand the complexity of the U.S. court system and the positioning of domestic violence legislation. With the recent criminalization of domestic violence, the lines between criminal and civil actions are blurring. Protection and relief from domestic violence are both criminal and civil in nature. Domestic law is now located within both federal and state court jurisdictions.

A network of courts across the United States makes up the judicial system. The scope and power of authority for each court is called its **jurisdiction**. The constitutional or statutory parameters within which judicial power may be exercised limit the court to a geographical area and to specific subject matter. One group of courts in the system maintains federal jurisdiction: It tries crimes and hears controversies that have occurred anywhere in the nation that a federal law is alleged to have been violated. The U.S. Supreme Court interprets the U.S. Constitution. The federal court system is made up of the U.S. Supreme Court, the U.S. Courts of Appeals, and the U.S. District Courts.

Within each state are one or more federal judicial districts, within each of which is a U.S. District Court. There is also a U.S. District Court in the District of Columbia. These are the trial courts with **general jurisdiction** over cases involving federal law violations, crimes committed on federal property, and disputes between citizens of different states. General jurisdiction refers to the court's authority to hear any case put

United States Supreme Court

This is the highest court in the nation. It has the power to choose the cases that it wishes to hear, through the writ of certiorari. Cases are presented through appeals from lower federal courts and from state supreme courts on the interpretation of federal law or of the Constitution itself. The opinions of the Courts provide precedent or guidelines for the states to follow. The decisions of the Court become case law. The states cannot take away any citizen rights afforded by the U.S. Constitution as interpreted by the U.S. Supreme Court.

↑

United States Court of Appeals

These federal courts have jurisdiction over decisions of U.S. District Courts. The country is broken down into areas referred to as *circuits*. They hear appeal from the lower courts.

↑

United States District Courts

Only when federal laws are alleged to have been violated will the case come before a U.S. District Court. These courts have original jurisdiction in all matters of federal criminal law. Domestic violence offenses committed after crossing a state line, for example, may be prosecuted here.

Figure 8–1   Federal court system.

before it that does not belong exclusively to another court. The authority to consider a case in the first instance, and to try it and pass judgment on the law and facts, begins in these courts of original jurisdiction.

District Court is also the name given to many lower courts of the states and in the Commonwealth of Puerto Rico. These general jurisdiction courts are sometimes called superior or circuit courts. State courts of general jurisdiction have the authority to try all cases, both civil and criminal. When a court is given limited original jurisdiction, it may, for example, hear only misdemeanor cases. Lower courts may then bind over felony cases to the higher court. Large urban areas commonly have divisions that specialize in different kinds of cases, such as juvenile or family matters.

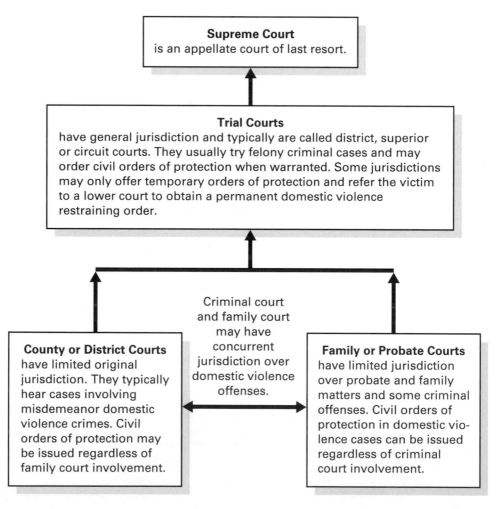

Figure 8–2   This represents the typical state court process. Note that not all state court systems are the same.

Codes governing domestic relations belong in a body of law that is called **civil law**. Contrasted with criminal law, these codes are concerned with civil or private rights and remedies. Family and probate courts typically have jurisdiction over divorce, custody, and guardianships. In some states these courts have a limited jurisdiction in civil and criminal domestic violence cases. Those with appellate jurisdiction review the judgments of these lower courts. Laws prohibiting domestic violence are within the subject matter of original jurisdiction courts. For example, a district or lower court has original jurisdiction to hear the facts and pass judgment on violations of criminal law.

Federal Versus State Jurisdiction

Until recently, domestic violence was not within the federal jurisdiction. One early attempt to provide federal sanctions to those who battered was a bill introduced in the U.S. Congress in 1906. This attempt to impose federal whipping of wife beaters was defeated. In January 1978, the U.S. Commission on Civil Rights sponsored a consultation to look at the issues of public policy concerning battered women. Many people presented evidence on the problem of domestic violence and the inadequate police response to its victims.

The first two federal efforts to assist victims of domestic violence failed in 1978 and 1979. They would have provided federal grants to states to be used for spouse abuse shelters. Legislative responsibility as well as police domestic abuse response were identified as areas of concern. Since family relations were under the exclusive jurisdiction of state courts, there was no protection against domestic violence committed on federal property. Crimes against the person would have been prosecuted, even in the absence of domestic violence law; however, no civil protection was available for families in the military and on tribal lands.

Domestic violence continued to be under the exclusive jurisdiction of the states until 1984. It was not until the passage of the Family Violence Prevention and Services Act and the Victims of Crime Act that Congress approved federal legislation to aid victims of domestic violence. The 1984 acts provided federal funding to help states provide shelters for domestic violence victims, education, research, and crime victim compensation.

The Violence Against Women Act (VAWA) of 1990 introduced for the first time in history legislation that called for the federal prosecution of a person who has traveled across state lines and intentionally injures or sexually abuses his or her spouse or intimate partner. Originally defeated, the bill was reintroduced in subsequent years until some provisions were incorporated into the Violent Crime Control and Law Enforcement Act of 1994, referred to as Title IV of VAWA.

The states continue to legislate and control criminal and civil actions relative to domestic violence for the majority of cases. Federal legislation is not meant to take away the jurisdiction of the states in these matters. Instead, it is a body of law that represents a joint effort between the federal and state governments to close the loopholes and provide more comprehensive protection for victims of family violence. Travel

State Court Jurisdiction   **Federal Court Jurisdiction**

Domestic violence offenses have traditionally been state crimes. State statutes and civil codes protect citizens within their jurisdiction.

New federal offenses make it unlawful to cross a state line to commit domestic violence crimes or to violate a protection order. Federal statutes prohibit domestic violence crimes on federal property.

The full faith and credit provision of VAWA requires that foreign orders of protection be recognized and enforced in every state as if they had originated in the jurisdiction of the offense. Some states have responded with their own statutes to implement the requirement; others rely on the federal mandate.

Federal Statutes may be used when

1. An interstate crime makes it difficult for local law enforcement to gather evidence.

2. Penalties for domestic violence, because of old statutes or early parole, don't fit the crime.

3. Release of the defendant on bond is an issue.

4. The offense occurs on federal property, such as tribal lands or military installations.

5. A civil rights violation that is gender motivated is alleged.

Figure 8–3   Federal versus state court jurisdiction in cases involving domestic violence.

between states is a common occurrence. The likelihood of escaping responsibility for domestic crime due to differing jurisdictions is now diminished due to the possibility of federal prosecution.

Civil Versus Criminal Court in the State System

The allegation of a criminal law violation can be tried in a court of general jurisdiction at the state level. Provisions for civil protection orders when a domestic relationship exists are found in the state codes. An overlap between the criminal and civil law is inherent in domestic violence cases. Traditionally, family courts of limited jurisdiction handled relationship issues. For this reason, a person can obtain a civil order of protection in a family or probate court in addition to filing a petition for protection in the lower criminal courts. Moreover, some criminal offenses have been added to the juris-diction of family court through state statutes. This is called **concurrent jurisdiction**. It occurs when different courts are each authorized to deal with the same subject mat-ter within a similar geographical area.

No clear guidelines on whether an offense belongs in family or criminal court can be given due to the numerous variations from state to state. Significant points that lead to the decision of whether a case belongs in the family or in a criminal court include the following:

- Type of offense
- Relationship of the victim to the offender
- Age of the perpetrator

The victim makes the choice to file in civil court; the prosecutor makes the choice in criminal court. Making that choice in domestic violence cases does not exclude the possibility of dealing with both criminal and civil courts at the same time. For example, a person may file criminal charges in a trial court and obtain a civil restraining order in the family court.

Criminal Law.   Since 1984, all states, the District of Columbia, the Common-wealth of Puerto Rico, and the Virgin Islands have enacted some form of legislation specific to domestic violence. The first domestic abuse statutes applied only to adult married spouses of abusers, and only to women as victims. Today, the majority of statutes include domestic partners regardless of gender, age, or marital status. Case law has clarified disputes of gender, age, or marital status where the statutes have failed to do so adequately.

A crime can be a positive or negative act in violation of law. Many crimes have originated from common law, while most have been created by statute. In many states, criminal violations have been codified. Each law describes the act that is forbidden, called the elements of the crime. Unless all legal elements of the crime are met, there is no crime.

Police action is not limited by the relationship of the victim to the offender. Law enforcement response occurs when any criminal violation comes to the attention of the police, regardless of any family relationship. For example, a drug addict may break into the home of his or her parents and steal money. The crimes charged would be breaking and entering and larceny (or the appropriate statute in that state). The ele-ments of the crime must still be satisfied and police powers of arrest for the crime remain the same. The penalty for committing the forbidden act, contained within the statute, does not change.

There is no such thing as a crime entitled domestic violence. The term refers to one or more illegal acts that are coupled with a domestic relationship and recognized though legislation. It can be confusing when specific crimes are identified as domestic through violence protection acts. This legislative classification does not exclude other

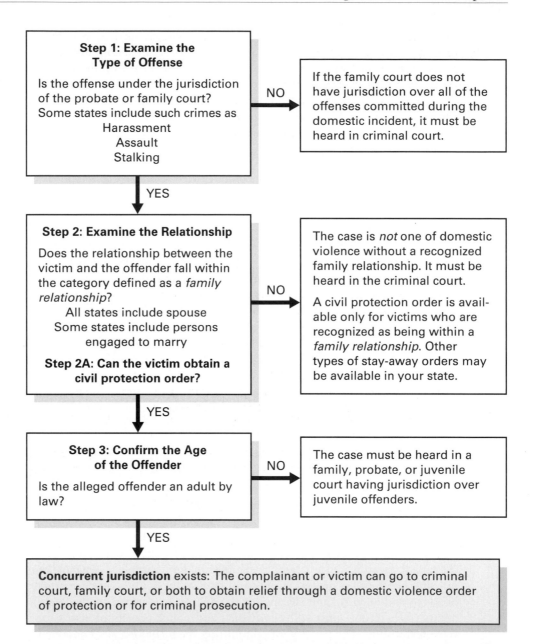

Figure 8-4 Resolving concurrent jurisdiction. *(Adapted from the Capital District Women's Bar Association Legal Project, 1998.)*

crimes from being domestic; instead, it identifies those crimes that bring additional responsibilities and specific commands to law enforcement for those crimes when they occur within the relationship.

Domestic violence arrest laws authorize warrantless arrests when particular conditions are met and encourage or mandate police officers to arrest for certain crimes. Domestic violence arrest laws can be classified as mandatory, discretionary, or hybrid (Lehrman, 1997). The mandatory arrest statutes require that police officers make a warrantless arrest of an abuser when called to the scene of a complaint of domestic violence. The discretionary arrest statutes allow the police officer to make the decision on whether or not to arrest. A hybrid statute mandates an arrest in some circumstances and grants discretion to police officers under some other situations.

Civil Protection Orders.   The most significant legislative change for protection against domestic violence is the civil protection order. Until recent times the use of protective orders has been restricted to protect crime victims and witnesses from harassment by defendants. Women who were unwilling to divorce at the same time as applying for protection were denied the legal process of the civil restraining order until the legal reforms of the 1970s (Fagan, 1996). Civil protection orders are now available to adults in every state and in the District of Columbia (Hart, 1992). These orders are generally referred to as restraining orders since their intent is to restrain the

---

More About It: Police Procedures and Abuse Prevention Law

Each state specifies the responsibilities of police within its abuse prevention law. Excerpts from the Massachusetts General Laws ch. 209A, §6, Abuse Prevention Law, show some of the specific procedures that are required when a Massachusetts police officer responds to a domestic abuse scene.

4:1 The Officer's Responsibilities. Whenever any officer has reason to believe that a family or household member has been abused, or is in danger of being abused, such officer shall use all reasonable means to prevent further abuse. The officer shall take but not be limited to the following action:

a. Remain on the scene where the abuse occurred or was (or is) in danger of occurring as long as the officer has reason to believe that at least one of the parties involved would be in immediate physical danger without the presence of an officer for a reasonable period to prevent abuse.

b. Give abuse victims immediate and adequate notice of their rights by handing them and reading a form detailing their rights. Where said person's native language is not English, the statement shall be provided in said person's native language whenever possible.

perpetrator from further abusive behavior and to grant relief. To qualify for this type of order, an abuse must have occurred that places the victim in fear of imminent, serious physical harm. Violation of a civil protection order carries some penalty. The penalty for a violation is a criminal offense, usually a misdemeanor.

For an order to be valid, a magistrate, a clerk, or a judge authorized to issue such orders must sign it. It contains the name of the person who is under the order as well as the name of the complainant or victim. An attempt to serve the order on the offender must be made. In some cases, the offender cannot be located. Failure to accept service of the order does not invalidate its provisions. In some jurisdictions, provisions exist to obtain an emergency judicial order when the court is not in session. Referred to as the emergency judicial response system in Massachusetts, it places a judge on call to be reached by telephone when one is not available through the court. The judge can issue a temporary protection order over the phone and instruct the police officer to take protective measures. The victim must then go to the court on the next business day to obtain the order in writing.

Obtaining the order may prove challenging and burdensome to the women in stress. It requires an excessive amount of paperwork, upward to six pages, in addition to testifying in front of a judge on the necessity of the order. If the victim is even aware of her right to obtain a protection order, misconceptions on how to obtain one without legal counsel persist. Economic and cultural barriers may be factors. In one study, 40 percent of women who had applied for a temporary restraining order failed to appear in court for a permanent order (Harrell & Smith, 1998). The most frequent reason for not returning, given by 64 percent of respondents, was that the offender had stopped bothering her. Continued abuse, however, was reported for the year following receipt of restraining order in approximately 60 percent of cases. A few states impose a mandatory minimum term of confinement; Hawaii, Illinois, and Iowa provide these examples, imposing between 24 hours and 7 consecutive days in jail (OVC, 2002). Restraining order violations might also provide the basis for bail forfeiture, bail, probation revocation, or imposition of supervision. Use of the courts to enforce violations of protection orders is rare, despite its criminalization. Less than one-quarter of calls to the police for restraining order violations actually result in the offenders' arrest, according to Harrell and Smith (1998).

As with any court order, the civil protection order restricts or instructs only one person to conform to the provisions within it. This is frequently misunderstood. For example, an order that directs Barney to stay away from Betty means that Barney alone is responsible for maintaining the distance between himself and the subject. If Betty calls Barney and invites him over to dinner, she is not in violation, because the order is not directed to her. But if Barney accepts, and comes to dinner when he is under order to stay away, he is in violation of a court order and alone must face the consequences. The invitation does not render the protective order void. In many states, Barney is subject to arrest for his actions—but not Betty! Violation of some of the provisions contained in a civil protection order may be a criminal offense. The order remains valid until it expires or the judge changes it no matter what Betty does! Each state has passed legislation describing the portions that are enforced though criminal action and the criminal penalties.

Domestic Violence Courts

As domestic violence awareness has increased, courts across the country have responded with specialized response calendars and procedures. The term *domestic violence courts* refers to those courts that assign judicial officers to hear a special domestic violence calendar, regardless of whether they hear those cases exclusively. Such courts have developed along with the realization that noninjury cases of domestic violence cases are often upstaged by "more serious crimes" irregardless of the potential for escalation into high-injury or homicide (Fritzler & Simon, 2000). While specialized courts have emerged slowly over the past several years, the reluctance for judicial participation in part is due to the concern that its position of neutrality would be compromised by joint procedures favoring one side of the community over another (Keilitz, 2000). The development of other court specializations such as drug courts and balanced justice initiatives has contributed to the overcoming of such barriers. One local study found that arrests for domestic abuse increased 74 percent in a two year period along with a 200 percent increase in domestic violence related homicides (Fritzler & Simon, 2000). Domestic violence courts have emerged for the following reasons:

1. There has been a large increase in the numbers of domestic violence cases.
2. There is an increasing awareness that specialized services and responses are needed.
3. When left in traditional courts, those with low injury or non-injury cases tend to be upstaged by more serious crimes, regardless of the potential violence attached by these offenses

Studies suggest the potential for intervention to contribute to the empowerment and victim satisfaction with the legal system. This therapeutic approach to jurisprudence seems to have contributed to the "one stop shopping" concept for domestic violence victims, a coordination of services approach (Fritzler & Simon, 2000). Some significant benefits of domestic violence courts cited by advocates (Keilitz, 2000) include

- Advocacy services
- Enhanced coordination of cases
- Greater understanding by judges of the dynamics
- Improved batterer compliance with orders

FEDERAL LEGISLATION

As indicated earlier, Title IV of the Violence Against Women Act of 1994 was incorporated into the Federal Crime Bill of 1994. Through this legislation the government committed substantial federal funds to support state and local prosecutions of domestic violence. It encourages states to adopt mandatory arrest policies for abusive partners and for the aggressive enforcement of domestic violence law. VAWA provides federal penalties for sex crimes as well as mandatory restitution and assistance to the victim of sexual offenses. Interstate domestic violence was also criminalized. It is now a federal offense to cross state lines for the purpose of engaging in conduct in violation of a domestic violence restraining or protection order.

The VAWA of 2000 (P.L. 106–386), enacted on October 28, 2000, improved legal tools and programs addressing domestic violence, sexual assault, and stalking. VAWA 2000 reauthorized critical grant programs created by the original VAWA and subsequent legislation, established new programs, and strengthened federal laws. It removed the requirement that the victim suffer bodily injury as a result of the action from the definition of domestic violence and stalking. One important change made in VAWA 2000 is the inclusion of dating violence in several VAWA programs; STOP grants, Grants to Encourage Arrests, Rural Domestic Violence and Child Abuse Enforcement Grants, and Grants to Combat Violent Crimes Against Women on Campus. While all VAWA grants and programs were not amended to include dating violence, its inclusion in parts of the bill is a significant victory for advocates, victim service providers, and victims. Dating violence is defined as violence committed by a person who is or has been in a social relationship of a romantic or intimate nature with the victim. The existence of such a relationship is determined by the following factors: (1) length of the relationship; (2) type of relationship; and (3) frequency of interaction between the persons involved.

To assist states in drafting their own domestic violence legislation, the National Council of Juvenile and Family Court Judges developed a Model Code on Domestic and Family Violence (McHardy, 1994). The model includes a range of crimes that should be considered domestic, from arson to trespass; suggests an enhanced penalty for second or subsequent crimes of family violence; and provides an expansive list of duties for law enforcement officers to aid victims of domestic abuse. Addressing a common concern for police officers who face opposing complaints in domestic violence calls, the model suggests that officers determine the primary physical aggressor in these cases. Stressing that police are not obligated to arrest both parties believed to have committed family violence, the council suggests that the officer consider these points in identifying primary physical aggressors:

- Prior complaints of domestic or family violence
- The relative severity of the injuries inflicted on each person
- The likelihood of future injury to each person
- Whether one of the persons acted in self-defense

Antistalking Legislation

The Interstate Stalking and Punishment Act of 1996 prohibits people from traveling across a state line with the intent to cause injury or to harass another person or placing such a person in reasonable fear of death or bodily injury. According to the National Institute of Justice, strangers are the perpetrators in 23 percent of female stalking incidents (Tjaden & Thoennes, 1998). Current or former husbands are the perpetrators 38 percent of the time; current or former cohabiting partners are the perpetrators 10 percent of the time; and current or former boyfriends are the perpetrators 14 percent of the time.

The legislation was developed as a result of a directive from the U.S. Departments of Commerce, Justice, and State; the judiciary; and related agencies under the Appropriations Act for fiscal year 1993. The act congressionally mandated the creation of a model antistalking code to assist states in developing their own antistalking laws (Bureau of Justice Assistance, 1996). Key elements in the model code that emerged included (National Institute of Justice, 1996)

- Conduct occurring against an individual or his or her family members
- Multiple incidents
- Conduct that involved following or threatening behavior, or both

The VAWA 2000 amended the interstate domestic violence and stalking offenses to clarify the elements of these offenses and to improve effective prosecution of these crimes. It further expanded the interstate stalking law to include interstate cyberstalking (over the Internet) and stalking that occurs by mail or by telephone.

Domestic Violence Across State Lines

Interstate domestic violence and interstate violation of protection orders are two new federal offenses under VAWA. This code section applies if a batterer travels across state lines to reach the victim and also if the victim was induced to travel across state lines to come to the batterer. The law is gender neutral; it applies to both male and female victims and their intimate partners. In 1995, the first successful federal prosecution for interstate domestic violence took place in the Southern District of West Virginia (Lehrman, 1997). Christopher Bailey battered his wife into a coma in their West Virginia home and then drove through Ohio and Kentucky for several days, abusing her throughout. Despite a bleeding head wound, he confined her in the trunk of the car. Several days later he brought her to a hospital in Kentucky. Because of the delay in treatment, Sonya Bailey is now in a permanent vegetative state. Bailey was convicted of kidnapping and interstate domestic violence and is now serving a life sentence. On May 2, 1997, the Fourth Circuit affirmed Bailey's conviction in *United States v. Bailey*, 112 F.3d 758 (4th Cir. 1997).

Full Faith and Credit. **Full faith and credit** is mandated by VAWA. This means that a state must enforce a sister state's protection order, even where the enforcing state would not issue such an order itself. States have implemented this provision by including the language of full faith and credit in their own statutes and codes on domestic violence prevention. New provisions under VAWA 2000 prohibits states and tribes from requiring notification (to the perpetrator) of the registration of an out-of-state or tribal protection order, unless the victim requests the notification. Further, the victim cannot be required to register and/or file the order in the new state as a prerequisite for enforcing out-of-state or tribal orders of protection. Huge improvements have been made since that time, but recent progress has slowed down to a standstill.

Paving the way for the nationwide reciprocal enforcement of protection orders, the National Stalker and Domestic Violence Reduction Act, 28 U.S.C. §534 (1997), authorizes civil restraining and abuse protection orders to be entered in all National Crime Information Center databases. Since the authorization in 1997 only 19 states have begun to enter their data, less than 5 percent of the estimated 2 million eligible orders (OVC, 2002). Without participation in the database the effective nationwide enforcement of existing orders remains doubtful. Without enforcement of the protection order it represents a false sense of security to the victim. Indications are that enforcement practices across the nation are inconsistent; less than one-quarter of the states have either established a streamlined method of verifying protection orders or operate a state-wide registry (OVC, 2002).

Domestic Violence on Federal Enclaves

An important void was filled by the VAWA of 1994 with respect to military installations. Since jurisdiction of federal court did not previously reach into domestic relations, the victims who resided within federal enclaves were not ensured legal recourse for domestic violence protection (Malinowski, 1990). When the victim was a child,

---

More About It: Full Faith and Credit

Police have a duty to enforce domestic violence restraining orders that were issued from another state under the Violence Against Women Act (VAWA), passed by Congress as part of the Federal Crime Bill of 1994. The act contains the provision for interstate enforcement of protection orders (Title II of VAWA), which is referred to as full faith and credit. It establishes that states must recognize and enforce protection orders issued in foreign states or tribal courts. Expressly forbidden in providing full faith and credit in instances where cross or counter petitions have been filed. The provision is otherwise vague, however, and states are left to set up procedures to implement the requirement effectively (Klein, 1995). Any victim with a valid order continues to receive protection until the expiration of that order, regardless of which state she or he has entered and regardless of the issuing state. VAWA does not require that a victim register the foreign protection order in the enforcing state to validate it. Whenever a state fails to provide for full faith and credit, the federal VAWA standards apply. Given this, many states have adopted their own procedures for complying with the VAWA requirement. Check with your state to find the procedures for interstate enforcement. If none exists, the federal statute applies.

there was no clause in military or federal law authorizing the removal of the child. Abusers were subjected only to military authority, which was without domestic violence law. Previously, a conflict of interest existed, in that military officials represented military personnel but not the spouses who were being abused. Without domestic violence jurisdiction, federal installations had not adequately addressed victim needs.

The Department of Defense (DOD) recognizes that domestic violence is a serious problem within the military (Beals, 2003). Unique problems such as deployments, reunification, and constant relocations of military families are acknowledged as contributing factors for this population. In 2001, over 18,000 incidents of spouse abuse were reported. The abuser was most often an active duty military member (62 percent); the victim was frequently female (66 percent) and male in approximately one-third of the reports (Beals, 2003).

Indian reservations represent another area where federal protection failed to include domestic intervention and legal recourse for citizens. The Indian Child Welfare Act of 1978 was an early attempt to meet the needs of Native American children. Through this act, Congress declared its commitment to the establishment of foster or adoptive homes that would reflect the unique values of Native American culture and promote the security of Indian tribal families. Exclusive jurisdiction was recognized for Indian trial courts in proceedings that involved Indian child custody. The Act also provided for full faith and credit in every state to the judicial proceedings, records, and public acts of Indian courts. Emergency removal of a child from Indian land was retained by state authority to prevent imminent physical damage or harm to the child.

Although information on the prevalence of partner violence among the Native American population is scarce, it is believed to be higher than in non–Native American families. One study conducted on a Navajo reservation found out of 341 women who reported for health care, 107 participants reported at least 1 episode of domestic violence. Fifty-six (16.4 percent) reported violence within the previous 12 months. Age under 40 years and living in a household receiving governmental financial assistance were independently associated with the 1-year prevalence of adult domestic violence, according to the authors (Fairchild et al., 1998).

Overall, American Indian women identified significantly higher rates of intimate partner violence than women of other racial backgrounds in the National Violence Against Women Survey (Tjaden & Thoennes, 2000). The Survey indicated that 37.5 percent were victimized by their intimate partners (Tjaden & Thoennes, 2000). Recent reports indicate, however, that this population is no more likely to have higher levels of domestic violence.

Gun Control

Proclaimed as one of the most significant advances to end domestic violence, the Domestic Violence Offender Gun Ban was passed as part of the Omnibus Consolidated Appropriations Act of 1997 (Smeal, 1997). Hotly debated, opponents referred to the ban as excessive. Arguments focused on the failure of the bill to exclude police and military personnel from its provisions.

This federal legislation amended the Gun Control Act of 1968 (GCA). It makes it illegal for any person convicted of a misdemeanor or felony crime of domestic violence to ship, transport, possess, or receive firearms or ammunition. Selling or disposing of a firearm or ammunition to any person knowing or having reasonable cause to believe that the recipient has been convicted of a misdemeanor is also unlawful.

A misdemeanor crime of domestic violence is defined in the act as an offense that (1) is a misdemeanor under federal or state law; and (2) has, as an element, the use or attempted use of physical force, or the threatened use of a deadly weapon, committed by a current or former spouse, parent, or guardian of the victim; by a person with whom the victim shares a child in common; by a person who is cohabiting with or has cohabited with the victim as a spouse, parent, or guardian; or by a person similarly situated to a spouse, parent, or guardian of the victim. The law became effective on September 30, 1996. Application of this legislation is retroactive. It prohibits people convicted of domestic violence offenses from purchasing a weapon or ammunition even if the offense occurred before the legislation became effective, regardless of whether a weapon was used during a domestic assault.

The system for assuring proper gun ownership is partially achieved through the **National Instant Criminal Background Check System** (NICS). NICS is a national database that contains records on individuals who are disqualified from possessing a firearm under state or federal law. These records include an individual's name, sex, race, other personal descriptive data, date of birth, state of residence, and sometimes a unique identifying number. This information is maintained so that gun dealers may determine if the sale of a firearm to a prospective purchaser would violate federal or state law. The purpose of the NICS check is to insure timely transfer of firearms to law-abiding citizens while denying those transfers to persons who are prohibited under the Brady Act from receiving firearms.

Specific concerns about the extent of domestic violence among police officer families prompted the legislative change that did not exempt them from the gun ban. The instance of domestic violence among families in the general population is estimated at 10 percent, contrasted with an estimated 40 percent of police officer families (Feminist Majority Foundation, 2004). The GCA was purposefully amended to prohibit all law enforcement officers and government employees convicted of domestic violence offenses—misdemeanor or felony—from carrying, owning, or possession for any purpose. This provision, known as the Lautenberg Amendment to Public Law 104–208, has caused considerable controversy among law enforcement officers. Police officers without the ability to carry a weapon in the performance of their duties might lose their jobs. Apart from the federal initiative, numerous state and local police departments have instituted policies that conform to the Lautenberg gun ban. Recent state law also reflects the trend in nonexemption for police officers who batter a child or spouse. A clear trend has emerged that will include, not excuse, police officers who commit family violence crimes.

Possession of Firearm While Subject to Order of Protection. 18 U.S.C. §922(g)(8).   As the result of the Lautenberg Gun Bill, it is now illegal for a person to possess a firearm while subject to a court order restraining such person

Figure 8–5 Police officers are not exempt from the Lautenberg Gun Ban. A domestic violence conviction will result in the loss of the right to carry a firearm. For those interested in becoming police officers, it means the loss of a career.

from harassing, stalking, or threatening an intimate partner or the child of an intimate partner. The protection order must have been issued following an evidentiary hearing as to which the defendant had notice and an opportunity to appear. The protection order must also include a specific finding that the defendant represents a credible threat to the physical safety of the victim or must include an explicit prohibition against the use of force that would reasonably be expected to cause injury.

Possession of Firearm After Conviction of Misdemeanor Crime of Domestic Violence. 18 U.S.C. §922(g)(9). As of September 30, 1996, it is illegal to possess a firearm after conviction of a misdemeanor crime of domestic violence. This prohibition applies to persons convicted of such misdemeanors at any time, even if the conviction occurred prior to the new law's effective date. The official use exemption does not apply to Sections 922(d)(9) and 922(g)(9). This means that law enforcement officers or military personnel who have been convicted of a qualifying domestic violence misdemeanor will not be able to possess or receive firearms for any purpose, including the performance of official duties.

Privacy for Domestic Violence Victims

A concerted effort is being made at the federal level to offer protection to victims of domestic violence who fear that public information will be made available to an abuser or stalker. The **Driver Privacy Protection Act**, which became effective on September 13, 1997, is one example. Under this act, personal information can be disclosed only to

---

In the News: National Instant Criminal Background Check

As of December 1998, the Federal Bureau of Investigation (FBI) began the new National Instant Criminal Background Check System (NICS). Within 14 days, the system had processed 372,565 background checks on people who sought to purchase firearms. There were 3,348 gun sales denied to those attempting to purchase weapons in violation of federal law during that period. Domestic violence offenders have lost the right to purchase weapons and ammunition, along with fugitives, the mentally ill, those dishonorably discharged from the military, illegal aliens, drug users, and those under domestic violence restraining orders.

The Instant Criminal Background Check System eliminates the need for the waiting or "cooling off" period that had been required under the Brady Bill. Sarah Brady, wife of James Brady for whom the gun control law is named, expressed concern over the removal of that safeguard. On the other hand, the National Rifle Association (NRA) has filed a federal suit against the new FBI background check system. The NRA claims that the system is a violation of a federal law prohibiting the establishment of a national registry of gun buyers. *(Source: Family Violence Prevention Fund, 1999).*

---

certain categories of requestors. Personal information is defined as including a person's name, address, and driver license number. Redisclosure of personal information from Registry of Motor Vehicle records to an authorized person will remain on record and retained for five years.

Another measure to protect victims of abuse from being located is the recent policy change announced by the Social Security Administration (NCADV, 2004). Because employers, banks, credit card companies, health care providers, and many other organizations have used the numbers routinely, it has been almost impossible for a domestic violence victim to change identity. For those who flee from an abuser, the difficulty in obtaining a new Social Security number was another insurmountable problem. The new rules require a victim to provide proof of current abuse simply by presenting a protection order or statements by law enforcement officers or other knowledgeable persons. Previously the Social Security Administration (SSA) required the individual to establish that the abuser had either misused the individual's Social Security number or could be expected to misuse it to locate the individual. Only in cases of extremely severe abuse or endangerment of the person's life did social SSA assume misuse. Now SSA will presume Social Security number misuse is possible in all abuse cases.

Child Abuse Initiatives

Our national concern regarding the welfare and well-being of abused and neglected children initiated several federal and state laws that provide safeguards for young victims. The first major effort came from the Child Abuse Prevention and Treatment Act of 1974, which required states to assign an agency to receive and investigate reports of alleged child abuse and neglect. Social service departments are those most frequently designated to receive the reports. Some state laws have since expanded their reporting system with a reciprocal reporting to a designated criminal justice agency.

The act also created the **National Center for Missing and Exploited Children** (NCMEC). Pursuant to 42 U.S.C. §5771, and 5780, this nonprofit organization was established in 1984. It provides technical information on missing and exploited children, offers training programs to law enforcement and social service professionals, distributes photographs and descriptions of missing children nationwide, and coordinates child protection efforts with the private sector. NCMEC also maintains a 24-hour toll-free telephone line open for those who have information on missing and exploited children.

Reporting Laws. While the government has mandated child abuse reporting within the states since 1974, it was not until the Victims of Child Abuse Act of 1990 that similar provisions were created for federal reporting laws. This act requires professionals to report on child abuse and neglect for cases arising under federal jurisdiction. Child abuse and neglect that involves any Native American as perpetrator or victim that occurs on Indian reservations must be reported to the FBI under the Indian Child Protection and Family Violence Prevention Act of 1996.

Child Abuse Information. Numerous sources have recently been created on issues concerning child protection. One of the earliest and most significant was the First **National Incidence Study** (NIS) in 1974. The NIS was congressionally mandated under Public Law 93–247 and represents the periodic efforts of the National Center on Child Abuse and Neglect to gather information and analyze the incidence of child abuse and neglect in the United States. It was repeated in 1984 and again in 1996. There are immense advantages to having a comparable source of data such as NIS. The most obvious is that it enables researchers to identify problem areas that require additional support and to contrast present figures with previous years. For example, the Third National Incidence Study (Sedlak & Broadhurst, 1996) reported that more children are now being abused and neglected than in 1986 and that their injuries are more serious. The report identified neglect as the most frequent maltreatment activity, which needs greater attention from social service response agencies.

Parental Kidnapping. The Census Bureau estimates that over half of marriages that have occurred since 1970 end in divorce and that over half of divorces involve couples with children under the age of 18. These statistics give rise among other things to concerns relative to **parental kidnapping** in cases where domestic violence is alleged. The U.S. Congress passed the Missing Children's Assistance Act in 1984 as Title IV of the Juvenile Justice and Delinquency Prevention Act. Through this initiative, Congress mandated a national response to the problem of missing and exploited children to be coordinated by the Office of Juvenile Justice and Delinquency Prevention (OJJDP) along with the National Center for Missing and Exploited

Children. A major source of information on parental kidnapping comes under the direction of OJJDP from the National Center for Prosecution of Child Abuse, a non-profit agency.

The National Incidence Studies of Missing, Abducted, Runaway, and Thrown-away Children (NISMART-2) was recently published (Hammer, Finkelhor, & Sedlak, 2002). These studies were undertaken in response to the Missing Children's Assistance Act (Public Law 98–473), which requires that the OJJDP conduct periodic studies to determine the number of U.S. children reported missing and the number of children recovered during a given year. Family abduction is a type of crime and child welfare problem for which only limited statistical information has been available. Among the key findings from this Bulletin are the following:

- An estimated 203,900 children were victims of a family abduction in 1999.
- Forty-four percent of family-abducted children were younger than age 6.
- Fifty-three percent of family-abducted children were abducted by their biological father, and 25 percent were abducted by their biological mother.
- Forty-six percent of family-abducted children were gone less than 1 week, and 21 percent were gone 1 month or more.

All states and the District of Columbia have statutes that prohibit parental kidnapping. In addition, the International Parental Kidnapping Crime Act of 1995 makes it a federal offense for a parent to abduct a child from the United States to another country. It also criminalizes keeping a child who is in the United States away from a person with parental rights to custody. Provisions of the act allow that if a battered woman with custody is fleeing abuse from her current partner, she can invoke the defense that return of the child was not possible. She must, however, notify her children's father within 24 hours that the children are safe.

STATE INTERVENTION

Codes in most states address the need for crisis intervention, counseling, and advocacy services for battered women and children (Hart, 1992). This means that funding is made available for such services to victims as emergency shelters, information and referrals, counseling, and legal advocacy. Due to the high demands for services and the lack of adequate funding, those available are usually strained. Legal assistance for victims of domestic violence comes through the victim assistance programs described next.

Victim Assistance

Victim assistance programs are located in law enforcement and prosecutors' offices. Staffed with a mixture of full-time, part-time, and volunteer workers, these state-run programs receive funding from various sources, including the federal government.

The services that are offered vary widely, as well as the training that staff members receive. Advocates provide information about legal rights and the criminal justice process. Assistance in applying for state victim compensation aid and referrals to social service agencies are also key services. An advocate is an individual with experience and training related to domestic violence and/or crime victim's advocacy. She or he may be required to attend court hearings in support of victims; assist in filing of forms for domestic violence criminal and civil restraining orders; and respond to hospital or law enforcement referrals to provide advocacy.

In 2002, over 70,000 women and men served as volunteers in the National Court Appointed Special Advocate Program (CASA, 2004). The trained community volunteers are appointed by judges to advocate for the best interests of abused children in 45 state organizations and over 930 local programs.

Antistalking Laws

In response to the murder of actress Rebecca Schaeffer, California became the first state to pass an antistalking law, in 1990 (California Penal Code 646.9). In a short period of time, all 50 states, the District of Columbia, Puerto Rico, and the Virgin Islands have followed suit, and there is also the federal legislation that was discussed earlier in the chapter. Nine states—Alaska, Connecticut, Florida, Iowa, Louisiana, Michigan, Minnesota, New Mexico, and Vermont—permit enhanced penalties in stalking cases involving victims who are minors.

Arrest Without a Warrant.   According to the NIJ (1998) report, 24 state statutes consider stalking a felony crime. The power to arrest without a warrant for a felony is based on probable cause, and no warrant is required. In 13 other states, stalking may be either a felony or a misdemeanor, depending on the seriousness of the action and the use of a weapon or injury. For the ten states that classify stalking as a misdemeanor, police are specifically authorized to arrest without a warrant, regardless of any domestic violence involvement. If stalking is perpetrated against an intimate or other legally recognized domestic partner, no warrant is necessary if sufficient probable cause exists. Police are authorized in 49 states to arrest, without a warrant, a person suspected of committing misdemeanor domestic violence, including stalking.

Cyberstalking.   State antistalking statutes vary widely (National Institute of Justice, 1998). Four states—Alaska, Michigan, Oklahoma, and Wyoming—specifically prohibit stalking through electronic means such as e-mail. These statutes have yet to be tested, however. They present enormous difficulty for law enforcement in identifying perpetrators, determining the jurisdiction of the crime, and satisfying necessary elements of the crime of stalking. They may be unenforceable or fall to a constitutional challenge on vagueness. Still, they represent the states' attempt to include all possible modes of victim harassment. Cyberstalking provisions may be most helpful when considered in harassment cases or in addition to other acts that together satisfy the elements of state stalking statutes.

Stalking Protection Orders. A problem identified in the NIJ report is the unavailability of stalking protection orders in most states. Civil orders of protection are available specifically for victims of stalking in only 23 states. The remaining states offer an order only as an element of a protection order issued against domestic violence or abuse.

Civil Orders of Protection

As you know, protection against domestic violence is found in various forms, including criminal law (with legal sanctions), civil orders (some provisions may include criminal/legal sanctions), and health state codes. Abuse protection acts authorize domestic violence policy. Each state has defined which relationships will be considered as domestic, set forth the forms of behavior prohibited as domestic violence and denoted which criminal laws are considered as violations of abuse protection, and stipulate avenues of redress for victims of abuse.

Additional provisions may include financial resources for domestic violence, such as shelters or training. Codes mandate specific duties and responsibilities of law enforcement. They are far from being uniform, however. Since the first protection from abuse act was passed in Pennsylvania in 1977, each state has developed considerably different acts in both form and content. The acts continue to change constantly to meet the demands of recent domestic violence legislation. Some states specifically authorize protection orders for children, although most allow this protection only for adults.

The full enforcement of civil protection orders, regardless of the original jurisdiction, has been mandated under the federal VAWA, referred to as full faith and credit. Many states have conformed with the VAWA and legislated their own statutes that include interstate enforcement. The wording found in Massachusetts General Laws ch. 209A, §3.3G is representative:

> A protective order issued in another jurisdiction shall be given full faith and credit in the Commonwealth. Therefore, officers shall make a warrantless arrest of any person the officer witnesses or has probable cause to believe has violated an emergency, temporary or permanent vacate, refrain from abuse, stay away, or no-contact order or judgment issued by another jurisdiction.
>
> In assessing probable cause, an officer may presume the validity of the protection order issued by another jurisdiction when the officer has been provided with: (A) a copy of the order, by any source; and (B) a statement by the victim that such order remains in effect.
>
> Victims who move from an issuing jurisdiction should be aware that their order has force in another county or state. They should be prepared to carry the actual order with them at all times if they fear continuing abuse.

Victim Criteria. To obtain a civil protection order, the victim must meet the following criteria:

1. The victim and abuser must be related family or household members as defined by the specific state code. In all states, this includes people who were

or had been legally married. Although marriage is generally a factor, relationships may include same-sex or living partners. The defined domestic relationships might be so broad as to include persons who had substantial dating relationships in the past. Intensity of the relationship rather than the length is significant. Know your state code!

2. Abusive or threatening behavior that is prohibited by criminal statutes or domestic violence protection acts must have been perpetrated against the victim who is filing for the protection or against a child that the adult is responsible for protecting. Generally, any act that is illegal, such as an assault where the relationship is domestic, is prohibited. Specific examples of prohibited behavior include attempting or causing physical harm, forced sexual relations, stalking, or threatening the victim.

3. The victim must make a written application for the order. The forms are available at the court and sometimes at police departments or shelters for battered women. Called a **petition**, it must include the name and address of the person seeking the protection (called the plaintiff); the name and address of the accused (the defendant); and the specific behavior that occurred, along with the date(s) of violence for which the petitioner seeks relief. Provisions exist to protect the victims of abuse through confidentiality of their residence, school, employment, and child care information.

4. The petition must be filed before a state or federal court with jurisdiction over the subject matter where the abuse occurred or where the victim is likely to be at risk. In most states, the victim appears before a probate or family court judge. A few, however, specify concurrent jurisdiction with the district court. Most of the states provide 24-hour access to the courts for the purpose of obtaining a protection order. Sometimes police officers may file the petition for the victim over the telephone when the court is not in session; the judge then issues a verbal order of protection. Sometimes called the emergency judicial system, it is activated when an officer telephones an on-call judge during evening and weekend hours.

Elements of a Petition.   Many states allow the victim to proceed *pro se* when requesting a civil order of protection against domestic violence. This means that the victim can go into court without the assistance of a lawyer and represent her- or himself. The victim of abuse must go to a court where he or she lives or where the abuse occurred to fill out the form requesting a civil protection order. The example form in Figure 8–7 is from Massachusetts. It shows typical questions that are asked on a request for protection, including, but not limited to, these:

- The name, address, phone number, and description of the victim
- The name, address (if known), and description of the defendant (perpetrator of the offense/s)

Figure 8–6   In order to obtain a civil protection order, the victim must go to court and file a petition with the judge.

- The age of the victim, or name of the adult who is filing for the victim if she or he is a minor
- Any knowledge of weapons that the defendant may possess
- Any knowledge of prior or pending court action involving the victim and defendant
- The forms of relief requested

The majority of states provide temporary custody of minor children under the prevention of abuse order. These states will also include questions regarding any minor children that the parties may have in common. It is not unusual for a court to require a sworn affidavit about the circumstances of the abuse in addition to completing the required form. When victims need help to fill out the forms, it is usually available from a clerk of court or a victim witness advocate. Some jurisdictions provide assistance from battered women shelters or police departments.

Forms of Available Relief.   The provisions contained in a protection order are referred to as relief. Violation of a civil protection order may be a misdemeanor offense, a felony offense, or contempt of court. All protection orders authorize some

<table>
<tr><td colspan="2">COMPLAINT FOR PROTECTION FROM ABUSE
(G.L. c.209A) Page 1 of 2</td><td>COURT USE ONLY – DOCKET NO.</td><td colspan="2">TRIAL COURT OF MASSACHUSETTS</td></tr>
</table>

A ☐ BOSTON MUNICIPAL COURT ☐ DISTRICT COURT ☐ PROBATE & FAMILY COURT ☐ SUPERIOR COURT _____ DIVISION

B Name of Plaintiff (person seeking protection) | Name of Defendant (person accused of abuse)

C Plaintiff's Address. DO NOT complete if the Plaintiff is asking the Court to keep it confidential. *See K. 4. below.*

Daytime Phone No. ( )

If the Plaintiff left a former residence to avoid abuse, write that address here:

G Def. Date of Birth | Defendant's Alias, if any

Defendant's Address | Day Phone ( )

Sex: ☐ M ☐ F

Social Security # | Place of Birth

Defendant's Mother's Maiden Name (first & last)

Defendant's Father's Name (first & last)

D I ☐ am over the age of eighteen.
I ☐ am under the age of eighteen, and_____
my_____(relationship to Plaintiff) has filed this complaint for me.
The Defendant ☐ is ☐ is not under the age of eighteen.

E To my knowledge, the Defendant possesses the following guns, ammunition, firearms identification card, and/or license to carry;

F Are there any prior or pending court actions in any state or country involving the Plaintiff and the Defendant for divorce, annulment, separate support, legal separation or abuse prevention? ☐ No ☐ Yes
If Yes, give Court, type of case, date, and (if available) docket no.

H The Defendant and Plaintiff:
☐ are currently married to each other
☐ were formerly married to each other
☐ are not married but we are related to each other by blood or marriage; specifically, the Defendant is my _____
☐ are the parents of one or more children
☐ are not related but live in the same household
☐ were formerly members of the same household
☐ are or were in a dating or engagement relationship.

I Does the Plaintiff have any children? ☐ No ☐ Yes If yes, the Plaintiff shall complete the appropriate parts of Page 2.

J On or about (dates)_____ I suffered abuse when the Defendant:
☐ attempted to cause me physical harm ☐ placed me in fear of imminent serious physical harm
☐ caused me physical harm ☐ caused me to engage in sexual relations by force, threat of force or duress

K THEREFORE, I ASK THE COURT TO ORDER:

1. the Defendant to stop abusing me by harming, threatening or attempting to harm me physically, or placing me in fear of imminent serious physical harm, or by using force, threat or duress to make me engage in sexual relations unwillingly.
☐ 2. the Defendant not to contact me, unless authorized to do so by the Court.
☐ 3. the Defendant to leave and remain away from my residence which is located at:
_____
If this is an apartment building or other multiple family dwelling, check here ☐
☐ 4. that my address be impounded to prevent its disclosure to the Defendant, the Defendant's attorney, or the public. *Attach Request for Address Impoundment form to this Complaint.*
☐ 5. the Defendant to leave and remain away from my workplace which is located at:
_____
☐ 6. the Defendant to pay me $_____ in compensation for the following losses suffered as a direct result of the abuse:
_____

You may not obtain an Order from the Boston Municipal Court or a District or Superior Court covering the following item 7 if there is a prior or pending Order for support from the Probate and Family Court.
☐ 7. the Defendant, who has a legal obligation to do so, to pay temporary support for me.
☐ 8. the relief requested on page two of this Complaint pertaining to my minor child or children.
☐ 9. the following:_____
_____

☐ 10. the relief I have requested, except for temporary support for me and/or my child(ren) and for compensation for losses suffered, without advance notice to the Defendant because there is a substantial likelihood of immediate danger of abuse. I understand that if the Court issues such a temporary Order, the Court will schedule a hearing within 10 court business days to determine whether such a temporary Order should be continued, and I must appear in Court on that day if I wish the Order to be continued.

DATE | PLAINTIFF'S SIGNATURE
X | Please complete affidavit on reverse of this page

This is a request for a civil order to protect the Plaintiff from future abuse. The actions of the Defendant may also constitute a crime subject to criminal penalties. For information about filing a criminal complaint, you can talk with the District Attorney's Office for the location where the alleged abuse occurred.

FA 1 (9/95)

COURT COPY

Figure 8-7 Sample civil protection request form.

ISSUES PERTAINING TO CHILDREN

A. **RELATED PROCEEDINGS.** Is there any proceeding that the Plaintiff knows of or has participated in which is pending or has been concluded in any Court in the Commonwealth or any other state or country involving the care or custody of the child or children of the parties? ☐ YES   ☐ NO

If Yes, the Plaintiff shall complete and file with this Complaint an Affidavit Disclosing Care or Custody Proceedings as required by Trial Court Uniform Rule IV, and provide copies of documents required by the Rule. This Affidavit and related information are available from the office of the Clerk-Magistrate or Register of Probate of the Court.

B. **RELATED PROCEEDINGS.** Are there any prior or pending court actions in any state or country involving the Plaintiff and the Defendant for paternity: ☐ YES   ☐ NO

C. **CUSTODY.**
The Plaintiff may not obtain an Order from the Boston Municipal Court or a District or Superior Court for custody if there is a prior or pending Order for custody from the Probate and Family Court or Juvenile Court.
☐ I request custody of the following minor child or children of the parties:

NAME	DATE OF BIRTH	NAME	DATE OF BIRTH

D. **CONTACT WITH CHILDREN.** I ask the Court to order the Defendant not to contact the following child or children unless authorized to do so by the Court:

NAME	NAME

The specific reasons for this request are: _____

_____

_____

If the Plaintiff alleges that the Defendant has abused the above-named child or children, a separate Complaint may be filed on behalf of each child.

E. **VISITATION.** If the Plaintiff is filing this Complaint in the Probate and Family Court, the Plaintiff may request a Visitation Order. Such Orders are not available in other Courts. Regarding visitation, I ask the Court to
☐ permit visitation.
☐ order no visitation between the Defendant and our minor child or children.
☐ permit visitation only at the following visitation center:_____
_____to be paid for by _____ (name) .
☐ permit only visitation supervised by _____ (name)
at the following times:_____
_____to be paid for by _____ (name) .
☐ order visitation only if a third party, _____ (name) , picks up and
drops off our minor child or children.

F. **TEMPORARY SUPPORT.**
The Plaintiff may not obtain an Order from the Boston Municipal Court or a District or Superior Court for temporary support if there is a prior or pending Order for support from the Probate and Family Court or Juvenile Court.

☐ I ask the Court to order the Defendant, who has a legal obligation to do so, to pay temporary support for any children in my custody.

DATE	PLAINTIFF'S SIGNATURE X

FA 1A (9/95)   **COURT COPY**

Figure 8–7 (cont'd)

form of relief for the victim of domestic violence. Commonly, they restrain the defendant from committing future acts of violence, grant exclusive possession of the victim's residence to the victim and/or evict the perpetrator, award temporary custody of common children, and provide child and spousal support along with stay-away or no-contact orders. Two or more court hearings may be required for the order of protection. Typically one court hearing is needed for the temporary order to issue and another for the permanent order. Some jurisdictions mandate the defendant to forfeit property such as weapons, keys to a joint residence, checkbooks, and automobiles. Common forms of relief include, but are not limited to, these examples:

1. *Restraining orders.* All states except Arkansas and Wisconsin have the restraining order provision as a general form of relief. As of 1996, Wisconsin requires the perpetrator of domestic violence to stay away from the residence of the victim for a 72-hour period following an arrest (National Council of Juvenile and Family Court Judges, 1997).

2. *Exclusive use of a residence or eviction of a perpetrator from the victim's household.* All states have some form of this provision. Some states provide for the defendant to continue to make payments for the home or apartment that defendant and victim once shared even though the perpetrator has been evicted under a prevention order.

3. *Custody or visitation.* Most states acknowledge the risk to children due to domestic violence. Those that address custody or visitation in the restraining order will specify the parent who will be granted custody. Protection orders are not meant to supersede probate and family court orders for custody and are usually temporary, pending a separate hearing to consider the best interests of the child. Arizona, Indiana, Nebraska, Oklahoma, Virginia, and Wisconsin do not address visitation or custody in the protection order. In such cases, a custody hearing may still take place apart from the protection order, through a family or probate court.

4. *Payment of child or spousal support.* Many states now authorize the payment of child or spousal support to be determined in the protection order.

Each state provides different lengths of time that the order is valid after a court order is issued, ranging from three months to over two years. Additionally, only the person who is named as the defendant on a protection order can be held liable for its violation. Every provision must be adhered to for the defendant to be in compliance with the order. If one part of the order is violated, the order itself is being violated. It is not necessary that abuse recur for a violation to take place.

Limitations of Protection Orders.   Professionals warn that obtaining a protection or stay-away order has its limitations and should not replace taking safety precautions. Although orders do provide immediate relief for the victims of domestic violence, they may only be a temporary measure. Citing frequent revictimization

TABLE 8-1

State Analysis of Civil Protection Orders

	Relationships								Remedies								Violation Penalty			Length of Order		
	Spouse or Former Spouse	Pregnant or Child in Common	Stepparent or Stepchildren	Parents and Children	Living Together	Related by Consanguinity	Dating, Engagement Relationship	Other	Restraining Order	Vacate Joint Residence	Custody	Child/Spousal Support	No Contact	Counseling	Attorney Fees or Cost	Other	Misdemeanor	Felony	Contempt	Six Months or Less	One Year	Two Years or More
Alabama	x			x	x	x			x	x	x	x				x	x	x		x		x	x
Alaska	x			x	x		x	x	x	x	x	x	x	x	x		x	x	x		x		
Arizona	x	x		x	x	x			x	x			x				x	x		x	x		
Arkansas	x			x	x	x			x	x	x	x				x	x		x		x		
California	x	x		x	x	x	x		x	x	x	x	x	x	x	x	x					x
Colorado	x			x	x	x	x	x	x	x	x			x			x	x	x				x
Connecticut	x	x		x	x	x			x	x	x			x			x	x	x	x	x		
Delaware	x	x		x	x^a				x	x	x	x	x	x			x	x	x		x		
D.C.	x	x		x	x	x	x	x	x	x	x			x	x		x	x	x		x		
Florida	x	x		x	x	x			x	x	x	x		x	x		x	x			x		
Georgia	x	x	x	x	x				x	x	x	x	x	x	x		x	x		x	x		
Hawaii	x			x	x	x			x	x	x			x	x		x	x					x
Idaho	x	x		x	x				x	x	x			x	x	x	x	x			x		
Illinois	x	x		x	x	x	x		x	x	x	x	x	x	x	x	x	x		x			x
Indiana									x	x	x			x	x		x	x			x		
Iowa	x				x	x			x	x	x	x	x			x			x		x		
Kansas					x				x	x	x	x	x	x	x	x	x	x		x		x	
Kentucky	x	x	x	x		x			x	x	x	x	x	x			x	x		x		x	
Louisiana	x		x	x					x	x	x	x	x	x	x		x	x		x	x		
Maine	x	x			x	x			x	x	x	x	x	x	x	x	x	x		x		x	
Maryland	x	x	x	x	x	x			x	x	x	x	x	x			x	x		x	x		
Massachusetts	x	x			x	x	x	x		x	x	x	x	x	x		x	x		x		x	
Michigan			x	x	x		x			x	x						x	x		x	x		
Minnesota	x	x		x	x	x		x	x	x	x	x	x	x	x		x	x		x		x	
Mississippi	x			x	x	x			x	x	x	x				x	x			x		x	
Missouri	x	x			x	x			x	x	x	x	x	x	x	x	x	x			x		

	Relationships								Remedies								Violation Penalty			Length of Order		
	Spouse or Former Spouse	Pregnant or Child in Common	Stepparent or Stepchildren	Parents and Children	Living Together	Related by Consanguinity	Dating, Engagement Relationship	Other	Restraining Order	Vacate Joint Residence	Custody	Child/Spousal Support	No Contact	Counseling	Attorney Fees or Cost	Other	Misdemeanor	Felony	Contempt	Six Months or Less	One Year	Two Years or More
Montana	x		x				x	x	x	x	x			x		x	x				x	
Nebraska	x	x	x	x	x				x	x	x		x				x				x	
Nevada	x	x	x						x	x	x	x	x			x	x	x			x	
New Hampshire	x		x	x	x	x			x	x	x	x	x	x	x	x	x	x	x		x	x
New Jersey	x	x		x		x			x	x	x	x	x	x			x		x			Not stated
New Mexico	x	x	x	x		x	x	x	x	x	x	x	x				x	x		x	x	
New York	x	x	x		x				x	x	x	x	x	x	x	x	x				x	
N. Carolina	x	x		x^a					x	x	x	x			x	x	x				x	
N. Dakota	x	x	x	x	x	x	x	x	x	x	x	x	x	x	x	x	x	x			x	Not stated
Ohio	x	x	x	x	x			x	x	x	x	x	x	x	x	x	x	x				x
Oklahoma	x	x	x	x	x			x	x	x	x	x		x	x	x		x				Continuous
Oregon	x	x	x	x	x			x	x	x	x	x	x	x	x	x					x	
Pennsylvania	x	x	x	x	x			x	x	x	x	x	x	x	x	x					x	
Rhode Island	x	x	x	x	x	x		x	x	x	x	x		x	x						x	
S. Carolina	x	x		x	x^a	x		x	x	x	x	x	x	x	x	x	x	x			x	x
S. Dakota	x	x		x	x			x	x	x	x	x	x	x		x	x					x
Tennessee	x	x		x	x			x	x	x	x	x	x	x		x	x				x	
Texas	x	x	x	x	x			x	x	x	x	x	x			x	x	x	x		x	
Utah	x	x		x	x				x	x	x	x	x		x	x	x					Continuous
Vermont		Family			x				x	x	x	x	x			x	x	x		x		FixedPeriod
Virginia	x	x		x			x		x	x		x	x	x	x	x	x				x	
Washington	x	x	x	x	x	x			x	x	x		x	x	x	x	x	x	x	x	x	
W. Virginia	x	x	x	x	x	x		x	x	x	x	x	x	x			x			x	x	
Wisconsin	x	x	x		x				x	x			x		x				x			x
Wyoming	x	x		x	x				x	x	x	x	x	x		x	x				x	

^aOpposite sex only.

Sources: Data from Hart (1992) and Lehrman (1997).

within two years of the restraining order, some experts suggest that they offer a false sense of security (Klein, 1998). Most abusers in this study had a prior history of criminal offenses; most had histories of crimes of violence with men as well as women (Klein, 1998).

A frequent concern in the criminal justice community is that of victims who obtain a temporary restraining order and do not return to make the order permanent. One study specifically addressed this problem, citing why 40 percent of victims failed to return for permanent protection orders (Harrell & Smith, 1998). The authors concluded that the majority of women who sought protection orders had serious complaints of abuse, yet chose not to return for the permanent order. Their reasons included these explanations:

- Their abusers had stopped bothering them.
- Their abusers exerted pressure on them to drop their complaints.
- They feared retaliation if they persisted in their complaints.
- They had encountered problems in getting temporary orders served on the abusers, a prerequisite to the hearing for a permanent order.

Marital Rape Laws

Rape of a woman has always been illegal, but until recently a marital privilege existed that prohibited men from being prosecuted if the crime was committed against a spouse. Rape is a crime that to which women and female children are the most frequent victims. The marital-rape exemption, which rendered a husband immune from prosecution for rape against his spouse, existed in most of the United States until the late 1970s. The exclusionary language has since been removed therefore criminalizing rape of a spouse in all 50 states and the District of Columbia (National Center for Victims of Crime, 2003). Trivializing the crime continues in less obvious ways when compared to the crime committed against a stranger. Some states mandate a shortened reporting period or provide a lesser punishment to the offender; others statutorily require the use of force versus the lack of consent (NCVC, 2003). In the wake of studies that indicated a high percentage of physically abused women who were also raped by their husbands, legislative reforms have occurred concerning this crime. The crime of rape is no longer specific to women: Legislation now includes the use of gender-neutral language that also recognizes male victims of rape.

For domestic violence victims, the battle to achieve legal protections against rape by their husbands has been a difficult one. Some of the first changes occurred in 1981 in the Massachusetts and New Jersey Supreme Courts, which acknowledged rape within a marriage relationship. As of July 1993, **marital rape** became a crime in all 50 states, the District of Columbia, and on federal lands (Bergen, 1999).

Force is usually an element considered in the prosecution of rape by a spouse, and some exceptions to prosecution still exist. A man cannot be prosecuted in some states if his wife is temporarily or permanently physically or mentally unable to consent legally.

Child Abuse Protection

In every state, police officers are permitted to take temporary emergency custody of a child in need of protection. Approximately half of the states authorize social service professionals and physicians to take custody when they have reason to believe that a child is in imminent danger. Emergency removal is a temporary measure, typically not to exceed 48 hours. A judicial review is then necessary to review the action and continue the separation if warranted.

Most state statutes also authorize emergency medical treatment of a child if the care is critically needed. When a parent refuses to allow medical care on behalf of a child whose life is in danger, a judicial review may be necessary once the child's condition is stabilized. Some states provide a religious exemption for parents who refuse medical assistance for their children. An example is the following, from Wyoming (Stat. Ann. §14-3-2029A): "Religious exemption: Treatment given in good faith by spiritual means alone, through prayer, by a duly accredited practitioner in accordance with the tenets and practices of a recognized church or religious denomination, is not child neglect for that reason alone." The religious exemption usually applies to failure to seek medical care in situations that are not life threatening. When a child dies because parents failed to seek traditional medical care due to their religious beliefs, the parents are frequently charged with involuntary manslaughter. Juries, of course, may show sympathy and not convict.

Child Victims and Criminal Law.   State criminal codes and statutes treat children differently from adults. Crimes committed against children are specifically stated offenses, such as neglect and rape without force. The majority of states have extended the statute of limitations for child sexual abuse and other crimes against children. The statute of limitation refers to the time that is allowed by law in which a case may be prosecuted after the illegal act occurs. Murder is the only crime that all state statutes agree has no time limit. Limitations vary widely from state to state and among crimes. A few states have no time limitation for the prosecution of most sexual offenses against children.

Under the Child Abuse Prevention and Treatment Act, as amended in 1990, children are allowed to submit victim impact statements "commensurate with their age and cognitive development." Hand-drawn pictures and letters from child victims may be allowed in some states. Special courtroom procedures are allowed in many states. The provisions are sensitive to the needs of children in the court process and do not require special statutes in order to be implemented (U.S. Department of Health and Human Services, 1998c). Examples of criminal justice provisions provided by the department that are specific to child victims and witnesses include

1. Allowing the judge to close the courtroom during a child victim's testimony. The purpose of these statutes is to reduce a child's fear of testifying and to protect the child from the embarrassment of talking about his or her victimization. News reporters and others not directly associated with the case would be excluded from the courtroom.

2. Allowing leading questions to be asked of child witnesses. Trial courts have the inherent authority to allow leading questions of witnesses on direct examination. Challenges to the practice of leading witnesses can occur during trial. A few state statutes grant specific entitlement for the prosecution to ask leading questions when the victim is a child.

3. Allowing the use of anatomical dolls in child abuse trials. A few states have specified that courts may allow use of anatomically correct dolls to aid a child's testimony.

A wide range of provisions has been adopted to make the child's participation in the criminal justice system less traumatic. Videotaped interviews or statements from child victims are allowed in 16 states; 27 states admit videotaped deposition in lieu of courtroom testimony (U.S. Department of Health and Human Services, 1998a). Thirty states have statutes that allow the use of closed-circuit television testimony of children under specific circumstances (U.S. Department of Health and Human Services, 1998b).

Domestic Violence and Child Custody.   The majority of states consider domestic violence as a factor when determining custody of children. The District of Columbia and at least 34 states have now enacted statutes that require the court to consider domestic violence in determining who will be awarded custody of minor children (Hart, 1992). This directly opposes the past preference for joint custody of minor children that has prevailed across the nation. Research has found that children who live under a joint custody order in high-conflict families are more likely to be emotionally troubled and behaviorally disturbed than those in sole custody (Hofford et al., 1995). Reflecting the growing movement to advocate for children's rights over parental rights, the trend is moving in the direction of denying custody and visitation to spouse and child batterers.

When allegations of abuse surface during custody hearings, the court may order an investigation. Child witnesses and expert testimony, considerations of the fitness of a parent who abuses his spouse, as well as the impact of family violence on the battered spouse's capacity to parent add to the complexity of these hearings. In many states the court will appoint a guardian *ad litem* (GAL) or an attorney to speak for the child. The GAL may be an attorney, a layperson, or a trained volunteer. The role of the GAL is different from that of the court-appointed attorney. The GAL represents the best interests of the child and speaks on his or her behalf. A court-appointed attorney, on the other hand, will advocate for the child's wishes.

Parental Kidnapping. Allegations of child and spouse abuse are common in parental kidnapping. The American Prosecutors Research Institute reported the need for a case-by-case evaluation and well-trained staffs to detect false allegations. The circumstances under which the abuse was divulged play a key role in how prosecutors and police treat the allegations. In 1999, approximately 9 percent of the children reported missing, or 117,200 children, were victims of kidnapping by a family member (Sedlak, Finkelhor, Hammer, & Schultz, 2002). Also called family abduction, Sedlak and colleagues (2002, pg. 4) define the act as occuring "when, in violation of a custody order, a decree, or other legitimate custodial rights, a member of the child's family, or someone acting on behalf of a family member, takes or fails to return a child, and the child is concealed or transported out of State with the intent to prevent contact or deprive the caretaker of custodial rights indefinitely or permanently."

Some states consider domestic violence a defense against abandonment and concealment of a child, recognizing that a battered parent may flee with the child. While society may be sympathetic to situations where a parent flees to avoid abuse, there is no per se legal exemption from prosecution for parental kidnapping. Some states, however, provide an affirmative defense for victims who are fleeing domestic violence situations (Johnston et al., 2001). A "defense" is not an exemption. Any case where parental kidnapping is alleged would be evaluated on its merits, the defense is not always successful (Johnston et al., 2001). States that allow this defense typically require proof that the parent had no alternative other than to kidnap the child.

Elder Abuse Legislation

Society has moved forward in legally protecting elders. All states agree that this population is in need of protection, since some elders may be unable to protect themselves. Every state currently has some form of adult protection program with mandated reporting of elder abuse legislated by 45 of the states (Teaster, 2003). "Adult protective services (APS) are those services provided to older people and people with disabilities who are in danger of being mistreated or neglected, are unable to protect themselves, and have no one to assist them" (Teaster, 2003, p. vii). APS programs are all authorized to investigate abuse or neglect in domestic settings and approximately over half investigate institutional setting abuses (Teaster, 2003). Although each state believes that intervention on behalf of elders is needed, each state defines this population differently. States label persons covered under their elder abuse laws as those who are 60 years of age or older, 65 years or older, disabled adults, incapacitated adults, or dependent adults. Age is a significant factor in determining who is covered under each state's statute. However, age may not matter if the person has physical or mental problems. In some states, for example, the same law used to protect 18-year-old disabled persons from abuse would also apply to the abused elderly, 60 years of age or more. An elder might also apply for protection under more than one category or definition. Central registries have been created in 21 states that serve as a repository for abuse reports on institutional elder abuse and slightly fewer for domestic abuse (Loue, 2001).

In the News: Elder in Need of Services

A home health care nurse isolated a 94-year-old woman from her family and allegedly got her power of attorney by illegal means. After obtaining such power, the nurse continued her allegedly illegal acts by stealing nearly $1 million from the elder's bank account and investments and by selling her home for $98,000 by forging the elder's name. Complaints were made to police on many occasions by friends, family, and even neighbors for over two years. The police undertook a serious investigation only after a coincidence occurred whereby a law enforcer, who had bought the elder's house, saw that something was wrong with the entire situation. The police removed the elder woman from where she was found, in a two-bedroom apartment with a feeding tube. *(Source: Wood, 1998).*

All states and territories, with the exception of Puerto Rico, have enacted legislation to protect elders from abuse in both domestic and institutional settings (Loue, 2001). Under the Older Americans Act each state Office on Aging is required to administer a nursing home ombudsman program to assist nursing home residents with the resolution of disputes encountered in the course of daily living in a nursing home (Loue, 2001). The majority of state statutes include disabled persons and others within elder abuse laws. (Tatara, 1995).

Definition of Elder	Percent of States Using the Definition
Elderly 60+	23
Elderly 65+	11
Disabled	47
Incapacitated	32
Dependent adult	30

Legal Definition of Elder Abuse.   Seven types of elder abuse have been defined in state statutes: financial exploitation, misuse of restraints, neglect and abandonment, physical abuse, psychological abuse and emotional abuse, self-neglect, and sexual abuse. States do not consistently include all these forms of abuse in their laws; abuses are also defined differently from state to state. For those states that have more than one elder abuse law, the definitions can vary within state borders. Due to repetitive and overlapping laws, there is a total of 71 state laws covering elder abuse (Tatara, 1995). Federal definitions of elder abuse, neglect, and exploitation are found in the Older Americans Act in three basic categories:

1. Domestic elder abuse,

2. Institutional elder abuse, and

3. Self-neglect or self-abuse.

Why do states have more than one law to deal with elder abuse? Some have tried to draw a distinction between those contractually obligated to care for the elderly, such as nursing homes, versus the family caregiver. The distinction must also be made between self-neglect and the right to refuse medical care by the elderly. Federal law recognizes the right of patients to refuse medical care. This Patient Self-Determination Act (PSDA) is a statute that applies to all health care facilities that receive Medicare or Medicaid funds, explicitly acknowledging the right to refuse medical treatment (Loue, 2001). Approximately 67 percent of states have one law dealing with elder abuse in both places, while the remaining 33 percent have created two or more separate laws shaped around the place of abuse (Tatara, 1995).

Legal Remedies for Elder Victims.   Significant resources are committed to ensure the safety of the elder population. The most widely available among all the states are protective services, psychiatric/medical services evaluation, guardianships, and emergency protective services. States also provide such resources as food, clothing, shelter, and psychological assistance to their abused elders. States cannot give back to abuse victims their dignity or emotional and physical well-being. However, states issue various criminal and civil penalties against their perpetrators to punish the abuser and to try and compensate the victims. Legislation is emerging that provides statutory causes of action for battery, assault, intentional infliction of emotional distress, and false imprisonment of elders (Loue, 2001). An example is evidenced in Washington, where elderly persons who have suffered from abuse in a long-term care facility or in the care of a home-health hospice specifically have cause of action for damages for injuries, suffering, and loss of property (Loue, 2001).

Criminal Remedies.   Criminal remedies are issued by courts to punish the perpetrator of a crime and to keep society safe. Crime against elders can be prosecuted under traditional criminal statutes that prohibit assault or battery. Additionally, over half of the states criminalize through specific elder legislation. Twenty-nine state laws have deemed a violation of the elder abuse law as a misdemeanor; 32 state laws consider violations a felony (Tatara, 1995). Some states have classified elder abuse as both a felony and a misdemeanor.

Civil Remedies.   Older persons may seek civil restraining orders for protection against abuse and/or neglect. These provisions may be part of a domestic violence statute or may be elder specific, depending on the state. Potential relief mirrors the protections found in domestic violence protective orders where the abuser is ordered to stay away or refrain from abusing the elder.

Civil lawsuits are brought against perpetrators to compensate the elder victim for the suffering endured as a result of the abuse. In the case of financial exploitation, where the entire purpose of the suit is to recover the money stolen, it is unlikely that money is still around to be recovered. It is also hard to prove to the court how much money was actually stolen when the person who stole it was the caretaker of the elder's financial matters in the first place. As in most types of lawsuits, it is hard to recover damages in a civil lawsuit since the elder victim is of the age where severe physical injury may lead to death. Most perpetrators do not have financial assets worth going after. These are difficulties that, coupled with the fact that most elder victims are financially unable to pay high attorney fees, make many attorneys reluctant to take the case.

When police officers are located in those states that designate some agency other than law enforcement to receive reports of elder abuse, they need to be aware of their obligation under state law to redirect those reports to those other agencies. States vary the form that these reports of elder abuse must take. Some states require a written report, while others require an oral report of elder abuse. Since circumstances are different among alleged cases of elder abuse, the states took this into consideration when allocating the time in which the reports had to be made to the designated agencies. For instance, some elders may be in imminent danger from the abuse and have to be removed immediately from the reach of abuser. A mentally competent elder cannot be removed from an abusive home without his or her consent.

The states differ when it comes to designating an amount of time to be attached to the term immediately. Some states require a report within 48 hours; others require a report within 24 hours.

There has been a tremendous move in educating the public, especially police officers, on matters of domestic violence. To ensure the enforcement and strength of all elder abuse laws, this education must be continued and extended to all professions and courts that deal with such tragedy.

CONCLUSIONS

As a society, we have always been concerned with violent crime and sought to punish offenders. Now the horrible crimes that are committed behind closed doors are recognized as illegal behavior as well. Personal actions within a family do affect the members of that family, both inside and outside the home. In this chapter you have learned that for the first time in history, domestic violence is a federal offense. An egregious act of violence on family members is no longer tolerated in the military or on tribal lands. Those who seek to escape detection for family violence by traveling to distant states are now subject to additional penalties and federal prosecution.

You have learned about abuse prevention laws that give additional guidance to law enforcement in how they should handle the cases involving victims of abuse in a domestic situation. Civil protection orders can be an effective emergency measure to assist these victims with or without criminal prosecution. They may be obtained in either civil or criminal courts as well. While the remedies available vary from state to state, in general they provide significant relief to victims of violence.

Antistalking legislation is another new area of criminal conduct that has been defined as illegal on both the state and federal levels. You will find more information about stalking in Chapter 11.

Recent gun control legislation is both controversial and encouraging. It will take time before the dust settles on the problem of police domestic offenders; meanwhile the concern has been raised. More is needed in the identification and treatment for batterers who wear the badge. It should not be a shield that offenders can hide behind if they are intent on terrorizing their family members. They must be held accountable to the same standard as that for the general population.

Advances in technology are evidenced in the ability to conduct instant background checks on people applying to buy weapons and ammunition. This is so new that it needs to be evaluated and scrutinized closely in the future. Will it even withstand a court challenge? This remains to be seen.

Unprecedented efforts are noted in government agencies that deal with personal information. It appears that there is a concerted effort to allow privacy of information in the Registry of Motor Vehicles and the SSA for victims of abuse. Abuse reporting laws are being strengthened on both the state and federal levels as well, particularly for children and elders.

In this chapter, parental kidnapping was addressed. Both the federal and state governments have commitments to protecting children who are abducted contrary to custody and visitation orders. Skepticism is noted, however, when allegation of abuse surfaces during a custody hearing. It is in the best interest of the children to have access to both parents after a separation and divorce, provided that the environment is safe.

QUESTIONS FOR REVIEW

1. What is the body of law that contains the codes governing domestic relations? Which body of law carries protections and relief from domestic violence?

2. What does it mean when a court has general jurisdiction?

3. Which court system (state or federal) has jurisdiction over crimes of domestic violence? When did this change take place?

4. What does concurrent jurisdiction mean? What is its significance for domestic violence in the state court system?

5. What are some of the most common forms of relief found in an order of protection?

6. What happens if a person needs a protection order when the court is not in session?

7. Give examples of the professionals who are authorized to take emergency custody of a child in need of protection. Is there any limitation to what can be done for a child?

8. How are children treated differently in the criminal court system?

9. Name some of the resources and accommodations associated with elder safety and criminal prosecutions.

INTERNET-BASED EXERCISES

1. Identify the domestic violence laws in your state. To begin the search, start at the Cornell Law School: http://www.law.cornell.edu.

2. Do you know how a domestic violence victim can change his or her identity? Research and document the Driver Privacy Protection Act and the Social Security Identity. Start with the Social Security Administration online at http://www.ssa.gov/.

REFERENCES

Beals, Judith. 2003. *The Military Response to Victims of Domestic Violence: Tools for Civilian Advocates.* Washington, DC: U.S. Department of Health and Human Services.

Bergen, Raquel K. Mar 1999. "Marital Rape" [Web page]. Accessed Apr 2004. Available at *http://www.vaw.umn.edu/library/dv/.*

Bureau of Justice Assistance. 1996. *Regional Seminar Series on Developing and Implementing Anti-stalking Codes.* Washington, DC: U.S. Department of Justice.

Capital District Women's Bar Association Legal Project. 1998. *Representing Victims of Domestic Violence in Family Court.* Albany, NY: Domestic Violence Legal Connection, Albany Law School.

CASA. 2004. "Court Appointed Special Advocates" [Web page]. Accessed 2004. Available at *http://www.nationalcasa.org/index-1.htm.*

Fagan, Jeffrey. 1996. *The Criminalization of Domestic Violence: Promises and Limits.* Washington, DC: National Institute of Justice.

Fairchild, David G., Molly Wilson Fairchild, and Shirley Stoner. 1998. "Prevalence of Adult Domestic Violence Among Women Seeking Routine Care in a Native American Health Care Facility." *American Journal of Public Health* 88(10):1515–17.

Family Violence Prevention Fund. 1999. Letter to News Flash (e-mail). January 4.

Feminist Majority Foundation. 2004. "Police Family Violence Fact Sheet." *http://www.feminist.org/police/pfvfacts.html.* 2004.

Fritzler, Randal, and Leonare Simon. 2000. "Creating a Domestic Violence Court: Combat in the Trenches." *Court Review Spring:*28–39.

Hammer, Heather, David Finkelhor, and Andrea Sedlak. 2002. *Runaway/Thrownaway Children: National Estimates and Characteristics.* NISMART-2. NCJ 196469. Washington, DC: Office of Juvenile Justice and Delinquency.

Harrell, Adele, and Barbara Smith. 1998. *Effects of Restraining Orders on Domestic Violence Victims.* Legal Interventions in Family Violence: Research Findings and Policy Implications. NCJ 171666. Washington, DC: U.S. Department of Justice.

Hart, B. J. 1992. *State Codes on Domestic Violence: Analysis, Commentary and Recommendations.* 43(4). Reno, NV: National Council of Juvenile and Family Court Judges.

Hofford, Merry, Christine Bailey, Jill Davis, and Barbara Hart. 1995. "Family Violence in Child Custody Statutes: An Analysis of State Codes and Legal Practice." *Family Law Quarterly* 29(2):197–227.

Johnston, Janet R., Inger Sagatun-Edwards, Martha-Elin Blomquist, and Linda K. Girdner. 2001. *Early Identification of Risk Factors for Parental Abduction.* Juvenile Justice Bulletin, Office of Juvenile Justice and Delinquency Prevention. NCJ 185026. Washington, DC: U.S. Department of Justice.

Keilitz, Susan. 2000. *Specialization of Domestic Violence Case Management in the Courts: A National Survey.* NCJ 186192. Washington, DC: National Center for State Courts.

Klein, Andrew. 1998. "Re-abuse in a Population of Court-Restrained Male Batterers: Why Restraining Orders Don't Work." In *Legal Interventions in Family Violence: Research Findings and Policy Implications.* NCJ 171666. Washington, DC: U.S. Department of Justice.

Klein, Catherine F. 1995. "Full Faith and Credit: Interstate Enforcement of Protection Order under the Violence Against Women Act of 1994." *Family Law Quarterly* 29(2):253–70.

Knopf, Alfred. 1994. P. 58 in *Alexis de Tocqueville: Democracy in America.* New York: Random House.

Lehrman, Fredrica L. 1997. Pp. 6–25 in *Domestic Violence Practice and Procedure.* Washington, DC: West Group.

Loue, Sana. 2001. "Elder Abuse and Neglect in Medicine and Law: The Need for Reform." *The Journal of Legal Medicine* 22:159–209.

Malinowski, Michael. 1990. "Federal Enclaves and Local Law: Carving Out a Domestic Violence Exception to Exclusive Legislation Jurisdiction." *Yale Law Journal* 100(189):189–208.

McHardy, Louis, Executive Director. 1994. *Model Code on Domestic and Family Violence.* Reno, NV: National Council of Juvenile and Family Court Judges.

NCADV. 2004. "Social Security Information" [Web page]. Accessed 2004. Available at *http://www.ncadv.org/publicpolicy/ssnumber.htm.*

National Center for Victims of Crime. 2003. *Spousal Rape Laws: 20 Years Later.* Accessed August 2004. Available at *http://www.ncvc.org/policy/issues/spousal rape.*

National Council of Juvenile and Family Court Judges. 1997. *Family Violence Legislative Update,* Vol. 3. Reno, NV: NCJFCJ.

National Institute of Justice. 1996. *Domestic Violence, Stalking, and Antistalking Legislation: An Annual Report to Congress under the Violence Against Women Act.* NCJ 160943. Washington, DC: U.S. Department of Justice.

———. 1998. *Stalking and Domestic Violence: The Third Annual Report to Congress under the Violence Against Women Act.* NCJ 172204. Washington, DC: U.S. Department of Justice.

OVC. 2002. *Enforcement of Protection Orders.* NCJ 189190. Washington, DC: U.S. Department of Justice.

Sedlak, Andrea, and Diane Broadhurst. 1996. *Executive Summary of the Third National Incidence Study of Child Abuse and Neglect.* Washington, DC: U.S. Department of Health and Human Services, Administration for Children and Families; and the National Center on Child Abuse and Neglect.

Sedlak, A. J., D. Finkelhor, H. Hammer, & D. Schultz. 2002. *National Estimates of Missing Children: An Overview.* NCJ 196465. Washington, DC: US Department of Justice.

Smeal, Eleanor. 1997. *Feminist Majority Commends Domestic Violence Offender Gun Ban's First Year, Calls for Stepped Up Enforcement.* Accessed August 2004. Available at *http://www.feminist.org/news/pressstory.asp?id=4568.*

Tatara, Toshio. 1995. *An Analysis of State Laws Addressing Elder Abuse, Neglect, and Exploitation.* Washington, DC: National Center on Elder Abuse.

Teaster, Pamela. 2003. *A Response to the Abuse of Vulnerable Adults: The 2000 Survey of State Protective Services.* Washington, DC: National Center on Elder Abuse.

Tjaden, Patricia, and Nancy Thoennes. 1998. *Stalking in America: Findings from the National Violence Against Women Survey*. NCJ 172837. Washington, DC: U.S. Department of Justice.

———. 2000. *Extent, Nature, and Consequences of Intimate Partner Violence: Findings from the National Violence Against Women Survey*. NCJ 181867. Washington, DC: U.S. Department of Justice.

U.S. Department of Health and Human Services. 1998a. *Child Witnesses: Admissibility of Videotaped Depositions or Testimony*. Child Abuse and Neglect State Statutes Series IV(21).

———. 1998b. *Child Witnesses: The Use of Closed Circuit Television Testimony*. Child Abuse and Neglect State Statutes Series IV(20).

———. 1998c. *Special Procedures in Criminal Child Abuse Cases*. Child Abuse and Neglect State Statutes Series IV(28).

CASE

United States v. Bailey, 112 F.3d 758 (4th Cir. 1997).

STATUTES

California Penal Codc 646.9.

Full Faith and Credit, VAWA 18 U.S.C.A., 2265 (1994).

Massachusetts General Laws ch. 209A, §6.

Older Americans Act, 42 U.S.C. § 3001 (1994).

Patient Self-Determination Act, 42 U.S.D. § 1395cc (Suppl 1999).

Prevention and Treatment Act of 1974. 42 U.S.C. §§5771, 5780.

Wyoming Stat. Ann. §14-3-2029A.

CHAPTER 9

THE ROLE OF THE POLICE

The Role of the Police

On Tuesday night Officer Jones was working the evening shift and received a call of an ongoing fight at 50 Spring Street of his city. On his arrival he heard a female yelling and screaming obscenities. He entered the house and found the female standing over a man who was obviously drunk. "She hit me," said the drunk. The woman yelled louder, calling him names and pointing to her head, "just look at this!"

Question: What are the officer's goals in this situation? Be sure to include the myths and reality of family violence.

KEY TERMS

Credibility	Lautenberg Gun Ban
Cognitive interview	Minneapolis Domestic Violence Experiment
Community policing	Problem-oriented approach
Competency	Rapport
Family crisis model	Risk assessment
Forensic interviewing	Spouse Assault Replication Program

INTRODUCTION

> Each incident of family violence which comes to public attention, each child that is beaten or battered to death, each wife who dies at the hands of her husband after having called the police for help or tried to get aid from social agencies, results in demands that something be done to prevent such incidents from occurring. Feminists, child advocates, and others plead that something be done. The question is, what? (Straus et al., 1980)

What is the police role? Increased demands for enforcement of criminal justice statutes in family violence and the creation of legislation to address newly recognized forms have not settled the debate on the role for the peace officer. If anything, they have fueled the controversy over appropriate intervention strategies for intimate disputes. A lack of consensus has resulted in practices that vary widely from state to state. Without a clear direction on how to handle these complex problems, officers will often respond inappropriately.

THE NATURE OF POLICING

Contemporary studies aimed at understanding the macrocosm of policing have developed specific categories and styles to describe what officers do. Service style and enforcement style are examples of the labels that have been applied to modern policing efforts. These terms have been beneficial in providing easily recognizable patterns of policing. Additionally, they serve to educate students on professional demands and associated problems.

At the same time, the labeling of police action over the years may have unnecessarily restricted the expected range of police action. Perceptions of policing styles should recognize the reality that every law enforcement department includes any and every type of imaginable response style. Officers themselves have preconceived notions about the job and often anticipate unrealistic drama. The media and television add to the public perception of policing as a nonstop crime-fighting business. The reality is much different, however. Crime fighters are called upon to respond to the mundane and to the domestic. Service-oriented departments also enforce laws. Road patrols may be faced with violence in rest stops and from people in vehicles pulled over to the side of the road. Service calls are a large part of police work. Writing reports and making application for warrants is more time consuming than response and service combined. In many jurisdictions, domestic violence disputes make up the majority of calls for police assistance. Understanding the range of police action is not as simple as applying a descriptive label.

As the needs of society have changed, so has the recognized role of the police officer. Is the application of the term *multifaceted* a more realistic description of the police role or just another attempt to find a label that fits? Police are increasingly expected to do all and be all—the superhero of modern day. Visions of Robocop inspire expectations that can be unrealistic. As demands increase for police officers that can do it all, the strains on modern policing show more clearly. Demands on slim police resources make it difficult to commit necessary assets. A major problem in large cities is the volume of dispute calls and a possible lack of time to spend with them.

Specialization for crime investigation is one way in which police are dealing with the pressures of increased expectations. Enhanced education and training for officers has prepared the experts; these highly trained individuals make up special units that respond to a variety of crimes. Examples of special units include child abuse divisions, juvenile crime units, and domestic abuse units. The trend is not limited to crimes of domestic violence; similar directions are evidenced with accident reconstruction teams and multidiscipline arson investigation. Although not all departments take the approach of specialized units, some have incorporated civilian expertise to enhance the job of law enforcement. An example is the use of the forensic interviewer specialist in child abuse investigations.

Figure 9–1 Today's law enforcement officer responds to the challenge of domestic violence crime through active enforcement and arrest of perpetrator when probable cause exists to do so.

Been There . . . Done That!

The crime-fighter role is easily attributed to the Massachusetts State Police. Having responsibility for rural patrol within the department made me reassess the usefulness of my job! An urgent call came in about a loose bull, for example. Since I'd never been trained in roping a bull, it was not the easiest of calls to handle. But it was my job to respond. How about a call for a man who was running down a country road banging his head on each tree that he came upon? That man had been drinking gasoline; moreover, he had a plastic windpipe from a previous suicide attempt. Don't police get calls about cats stuck in trees and barking dogs? You bet they do. Highway patrol officers come across disabled vehicles and domestic disturbances in cars pulled off the highway. As a young officer, I dealt with some ambivalence with the belief that my job should really be crime fighting! Nonsense: The job is to do whatever is necessary, I finally concluded.

Forensic Interviewing

Of all domestic cases, child abuse investigations are the most time consuming and difficult for police officers. Interviewing alleged victims is a task that requires a thorough knowledge of children's age and developmental levels. When someone uses words that a child doesn't understand, confusion and conflicting statements result. The questions cannot be leading, encouraging the child to respond with answers conforming to what the child thinks is expected. The depth of information that would lend credibility to the child's statement is different from the needs of the social service interview. Legal guidelines constrain the manner in which the juvenile can be questioned. A new specialty, **forensic interviewing**, emerged in the field to address the concerns of the criminal justice community. The American Professional Society on the Abuse of Children (APSAC) is among the many organizations that advocate specialized training for adults who investigate child abuse allegations. The trained interviewer may be a police officer or a civilian, depending on the resources of the community.

The Problem-Oriented Approach

Identifying problem areas and targeting specific populations is another response to deal with the increased demands for police service. Described as a proactive approach to reducing crime rather than random patrol efforts (Wilson, 1997), two forms are evidenced:

1. *Programs that respond to the needs of the community.* Striving to meet the needs of the young and the old and to provide positive contact with minority groups, the programs are varied. Known as **community policing**, Lawrence Sherman identifies four significant fields in the approach (Sherman, 1997).

- The neighborhood watch uses volunteer surveillance of residential neighborhoods. Involving the residents is one way to make them aware of and enabled to do something about crime. It also serves to provide police with information on crimes occurring in the community. Maintaining that police have a duty to help citizens protect themselves against crime.

- A community-based intelligence approach justifies public meetings and informal police contact. Meeting with residents and offering an outlet for their concerns may reduce citizen isolation from law enforcement. Convincing the public that police are concerned about the problems specific to a community might ease tensions between the two.

- The public information about crime version empowers citizens to protect themselves by increased information. Here officers inform citizens about the crimes they know are occurring and what has been done about them.

- The police legitimacy approach assumes that the public confidence in police will improve when citizens are treated fairly. Enforcers are encouraged to improve cooperation from residents through informal contacts. All of these efforts to reduce crime through education and outreach strive to increase the quantity and quality of police–citizen contact.

2. *Programs that respond to specific problems.* Initiatives such as zero tolerance to gang activity and gun buy-back programs illustrate the **problem-oriented approach**. In recognition that communities have different needs, police are encouraged to identify problems, seek nontraditional solutions, and test them in the field.

However one explains what police are doing now or whatever term is used to describe law enforcement today, care must be taken that these descriptive phrases do not narrowly frame the job of policing.

Police Response Strategies

Intervention approaches vary widely. There is no consistency on how police combat the challenges of family violence. Discussions about the nature and extent of acceptable police intervention for family violence occupy theorists, researchers, academics, law enforcement, and communities alike. In part, response strategies have had difficulty in keeping up with the almost constant stream of newly recognized categories that have emerged since the 1960s. Additionally, definitions vary from discipline to discipline. Research has returned conflicting theories on criminalizing intimate abuse. In the past, police did not have the power to arrest a domestic offender for crimes committed in the abuser's home. Another part of the problem is the lack of agreement about policing personal relationships. Conflicts on policing practices are as varied as the debates about police themselves.

More About It: Promising Practices Initiative

The Promising Practices Initiative of the STOP Violence Against Women Act provided many opportunities for police departments to develop coordinated approaches and identify gaps in service for domestic violence response. This example was developed as an effort under the technical assistance project. As some of the elements for law enforcement intervention it identified:

1. Dispatcher Response

    Address victim safety

    Obtain offender history and information on the likelihood of danger

2. Initial Officer Response

    Secure the crime scene

    Address victim safety and provide assistance at the scene

    Investigate at the crime scene through interviewing the victim, witnesses, and suspect

    Make an arrest decision

    Collect evidence

3. Follow-Up Investigator Response

    Address victim safety and support needs

    Gather further information to support charges

    Identify and apprehend the suspect, if not in custody

    Deliver the case to the prosecution office

Source: "Assessing Justice System Response to Violence Against Women" (Littel et al., 1998).

The Role of Police in Child Abuse.   Child abuse received great social attention with the "discovery" of the battered child syndrome in the early 1960s (Helfer & Kempe, 1988). The use of police powers in child maltreatment cases has been surrounded with controversy since the earliest attempts at intervention. Initially police agencies were named to receive mandated child abuse reports simply because they had staff available 24 hours a day (Shepherd, 1988). Child protective agencies were also expected to respond to the abuse allegations, causing confusion about who should do what in the investigation. Despite the controversy, police administrators viewed child maltreatment as an important law enforcement concern. In a relatively short time police agencies responded through increased resources to confront the challenges.

By the 1970s, specialized police units were developed to investigate and prosecute physical and sexual abuse to children. The 1980s brought a movement toward

Figure 9–2   Police respond to problems both big and small! Here a state trooper helps a child in need. *(Photo courtesy of Mark C. Ide.)*

the development of multidisciplinary teams and interagency cooperation. Thus child protective services and law enforcement have been brought together for the investigation of child abuse allegations, and this cooperation has led to an approach that is generally accepted.

Disputing the prevalence of child abuse, claims are made that inflated social statistics have invented a crisis where none exists.

Still other accusations reflect dissatisfaction with child abuse reporting statistics that may be inaccurate and inflate a problem, however real, with solutions considered phony, with poverty being confused as neglect, and with the failure of agency protection.

Been There . . . Done That!

At the same time that domestic violence became a criminal justice concern, women and minority officers were making their way into the ranks. Fertile ground for specialization existed, especially for officers with special skills or education. The belief that women would be the best investigators for child abuse was a commonly held notion. One of my academy classmates was approached to take a position for child abuse investigation. Her response, it was rumored, went something like this: I hate those little buggers. No, thank you, if I wanted to be around kids, I would have some. Don't like them, don't want them— don't make me talk to kids! *Gender alone does not qualify someone as a child abuse expert. Being a man does not exclude one from doing a great job in this field.*

Continued concerns surround the removal of children from a parent-victim of domestic violence (Baradaran-Robison, 2003). Headlines such as "The Scandalous Secret of Family Courts" report on the conflict between parental rights and government interference (Anonymous, 2004). This online magazine reported about the danger of individuals being acquitted on criminal charges of child abuse only to have their children taken by the family court under a lower standard of evidence.

Tempering accusations of child abuse when custody is being determined is still a large problem that has not been adequately addressed by mandated responses, according to some experts (Levin & Mills, 2003). Law enforcement investigators are concerned with deliberate false complaints of child sexual assault that have been estimated to occur in 14 percent of cases involving marital relations courts (Goldstein & Tyler, 1998). In a recent article from the *FBI Law Enforcement Bulletin*, these authors called such child sexual allegations frustrations of inquiry. The title is earned due to the difficulty in distinguishing a valid allegation from one that may be false. Untruthful accusations can occur from a misguided but honest belief that a child has been abused. These investigations are more difficult to solve and it is more difficult to discover the truth. The cases are time consuming and require specialized skills to uncover the evidence that will prove or disprove allegations made during marital crisis.

Day care allegations involving satanic and ritual abuse have brought national media attention, but no physical evidence and no guilty defendants. Celebrated legal cases such as the McMartin preschool case (1983–1990) and the Little Rascals Day Care case (1990–1997) invoke disbelief. After 11 years on the FBI Behavioral Science Unit and hundreds of allegations involving satanic ritual abuse, Kenneth Lanning addressed the question: Why are victims alleging things that do not seem to be true? "Some of what the victims in these cases allege is physically impossible (victim cut up and put back together) . . . some is possible but improbable (human sacrifice, cannibalism, vampirism) . . . not only are no bodies found . . . there is no physical evidence that a murder took place . . . why?" (Lanning, 1992). Pathological distortion, traumatic memory, childhood fears and fantasy, and overzealous intervenors are among the possibilities, according to Lanning. Through all the controversy, one common element emerges—there are dangers in eliciting statements from children. The warnings have not abated.

The Role of Police in Adult Violence.   Clearly, police have the duty to respond to reports of domestic disputes. Early research has documented the relationship of family crisis to crime. In Marvin Wolfgang's 1958 study, 65 percent of 500 homicide victims were found to be relatives, close friends, paramours, or homosexual partners to the principal offender (Zahn, 1991). Only 12 percent were complete strangers. The realization that family crime could be deadly was born. The criminal justice community, under attack for being lax with perpetrators of domestic violence, began searching for a way to deal with intimate violence that was consistent with crime enforcement policy. Officers were trained to negotiate with the parties and refer them to social services agencies in this mediation process.

By the early 1980s, the effectiveness of the **family crisis model** was in question. James Q. Wilson suggested that a study be conducted using various police responses to domestic violence. At issue was whether the use of criminal penalties should replace the peacekeeping efforts. The most important research efforts addressing this question were six experiments known collectively as the National Institute of Justice's (NIJ's) **Spouse Assault Replication Program** (SARP). These experiments conducted in the field were carried out between 1981 and 1991 by six police departments and research teams. They were designed to test empirically whether arrests deterred subsequent violence better than less formal alternatives.

The **Minneapolis Domestic Violence Experiment** (MDVE) was the first experiment. The study design called for officers in the Minneapolis Police Department (MPD) to carry out one of three responses when they had probable cause to believe a misdemeanor assault had occurred between cohabitants or spouses: (1) arrest the suspect, (2) order one party out of the residence, or (3) advise the couple on how to solve their problems at the scene. The researchers reported that when the suspect was arrested, there were statistically significant reductions in reoffending in the official records of all the cases and in the cases with victim interviews.

Many departments desperate for an answer that would suggest action to the complex problem welcomed the idea that police should arrest for crimes of intimate violence. Social science researchers first reported preliminary results of the MDVE in an article that appeared in the *New York Times* in 1984. Ten days after the initial report, the same paper reported that Police Commissioner Ward had issued new orders requiring police officers to make arrests for domestic violence, citing the experiment as among the reasons for the new rules. A rush to establish mandatory and preferred arrest procedures resulted, a total departure from the mediation approach that was prevalent. Arrest of the perpetrator, when probable cause exists, emerged as the preferred response in most jurisdictions.

The replication studies were conducted in Omaha, Charlotte, Milwaukee, Metro-Dade (Miami, Florida area), Colorado Springs, and Atlanta from 1985 to 1990 to determine whether the Minneapolis study's results could be reproduced in other settings. These replication studies uncovered mixed results on the effects of mandatory arrest in cases of domestic violence. Arrest was found to escalate future violence for relationships involving unemployed and unmarried couples after an initial 30-day respite. Repeat violence was found to be decreased in cases where a summons to appear in court was mailed to the batterer who had left the scene before the police arrived. In three studies, offenders assigned to the arrest group had higher levels of repeat offending (recidivism), and in the other three studies, a statistically significant but modest reduction was found among batterers assigned to arrest. Thus, rather than providing results that were consistent with MDVE, the published results from the five replication experiments produced inconsistent findings about whether arrest deters intimate partner violence. The debate on the effects of arresting the perpetrator for domestic violence crimes still rages on. A flood of literature that questioned the efficacy of criminal justice intervention followed the replication experiments. Recently a

---

In the News: The McMartin Preschool Case

The earliest and largest child sexual abuse case in this country is the McMartin preschool case, which began with an accusation in 1983 to a deadlocked jury in 1990. Today, it is a reminder of the dangers and difficulty of using children's testimony. It is thought to have been the catalyst for extensive research into determining child credibility.

The preschool was a respected institution that cared for the children of prominent local families in Manhattan Beach, California, when the first allegation was brought forth from the mother of a 2½-year-old boy. Raymond Buckey was soon arrested and then released due to lack of evidence. The following year, police rearrested Ray along with his sister Peggy Ann, his mother Peggy, and grandmother Virginia, as well as three other teachers.

Dozens of children were interviewed and examined as the result of 200 letters sent by police to the parents of children in the day care center. In part, the children reported bizarre satanic rituals, mutilating animals, touching dead bodies, and hidden underground passageways beneath the school. Over the course of the investigation, therapists evaluated approximately 400 children, with 350 children disclosing sexual abuse (Dickinson, 1985). Two hundred and nine counts of child molestation were brought in connection with the case. In 1986, charges were dropped against five of the seven. Only Ray and his mother were tried. All of the interviews were videotaped, some of which were shown to jurors at trial.

The first trial of Ray and his mother, begun in April 1987, ended in April 1989 with acquittals on some counts and a deadlocked jury on others. Ray was tried a second time, and in 1990 another jury was deadlocked on all counts. Ray had spent five years in jail and Peggy had spent two before being released. Some jurors in the first trial stated that it was the videotaped statements from the children that had prevented them from finding the McMartins guilty, according to news reports (*Frontline*, 1998).

---

recalculation of the replication research found mathematical errors—all of the studies do in fact indicate that arresting deters batterers better than other police responses (Maxwell, Garner, & Fagan, 2003).

Domestic violence calls are believed to be the largest single category of police response. In the Washington, DC Metropolitan Police Department, for example, domestic violence calls constituted 49 percent of all the violent crime calls received in 2000 (Cassidy et al., 2001). Reports indicate that some departments resist the laws requiring them to make arrests, a complaint that is ongoing. Change is occurring slowly in others. Individual officers may not always comply with the mandates. Skepticism regarding the quality of police response is grounded in reality according to a recent study of the DC Metropolitan Police Department (Cassidy et al., 2001). The authors concluded that there was a "clear and pervasive pattern" of departures from departmental policy when responding to domestic violence. For example, in only one-

Figure 9-3 Arrest is the preferred response for domestic violence crimes.

third of the domestic violence calls did an officer take photographs or ask about prior abuse. Only 17 percent of the victims were asked about a restraining order, and 83 percent were provided no printed information with contact information or resources. At the same time, social scientists question and have reexamined the results of the MDVE.

Historically, intimate violence reporting has been extremely low. Where the relationship to a victim was an intimate, relative, or acquaintances, a mere half of violent victimizations are reported to the police (Hart, 2003). To explain this phenomenon, experts suggest that police are anything but helpful to domestic violence victims, in particular gay and lesbian reports of intimate violence (Courvant & Cook-Daniels, 2003). In most areas the police response to homosexual domestic violence is lacking or even poses danger for gay and lesbian people (NCAVP, 2003).

Recent years have seen an increase in the number of women arrested for domestic violence. For example, the percentage of women arrested for domestic violence increased in Concord, New Hampshire from 23 percent in 1993 to 35 percent in 1999. Vermont saw a similar increase from 16 percent in 1997 to 23 percent in 1999. The numbers of female arrests for domestic violence in Los Angeles have increased fourfold since 1987 (Levin & Mills, 2003). Some have attributed this to the increase in "mandatory arrest" policies, in which police are required to make an arrest if there is probable cause that a person has committed domestic violence (Goldberg, 1999).

Back Then . . .

The *family crisis model* was developed from the classical study undertaken by Morton Bard in 1968 (Bard, 1969). Realizing that family disturbances constituted a major aspect of police work, the project tested an intensive training period for officers who would respond in the family crisis car. The month-long course was followed by weekly in-service training sessions. In an attempt to reduce injury to police officers who were dispatched, a mental health strategy of intervention was employed. At the same time, the participating officers also received generalized calls—rejection of an exclusively specialized role was a major goal. Emphasis was placed on the establishment of police agency relationships with other agencies in the helping system. Bard reported that the method did reduce injuries suffered by enforcers, and the community's attitude toward the police showed a marked improvement.

Further complicating this consideration of the law enforcer's role is the realization that police officers themselves have a high rate of domestic violence. Acts of domestic violence by a police officer against a partner are estimated to be at least as common as acts committed by the general population, according to the International Association of Chiefs of Police (IACP, 1999). The IACP reports that recent limited research indicates the possibility of higher incident rates of domestic violence among law enforcement professionals. The IACP, while concerned with variations in assessed levels, takes the position that the problem exists at some serious level and deserves careful attention regardless of estimated occurrences. A zero tolerance policy has been furthered by the IACP to protect intimates from domestic violence perpetrated by police officers (Lonsway & Conis, 2003). It suggests the assailant be terminated from policing when found guilty in a court for acts of domestic violence.

The Role of Police in Elder Abuse.   Protecting the elderly is a new concept without proven methods or consistent policies. Given the increasing population of elder citizenry, the need to establish acceptable police practices is imperative. This is the only form of abuse where few disputes on police intervention exist so far. A major difference between this population and the others is a perceived incompetence that may not be valid. Some victims who are in fact capable may appear unable to make decisions to protect themselves, and officers often proceed on that false assumption. Elders retain the right to participate in the decision making when offenses against them are being investigated.

Elderly domestic violence is now accepted as a mistreatment of national concern. Of the acknowledged forms of abuse, sexual abuse is the least understood (Teaster, et al, 2000). Remembering that spousal abuse perpetrators are as likely to be female as male (Mouton, et al, 2001), enforcers should keep the protection of the victim as their primary objective. For those who regard their responsibilities to children and

More about It: The Effect of Arrest on Intimate Partner Violence

The body of research—known collectively as the Spouse Assault Replication Program— fueled rather than quieted the debate on the effectiveness of arrest in cases of domestic violence. The 1984 Minneapolis Domestic Violence Experiment (MDVE) found that when the assaulter was arrested, significant reductions in subsequent offending were reported both in victim interviews and in official police records. Replication experiments conducted in Omaha, Charlotte, Milwaukee, Miami, and Colorado Springs began in the early 1990s. These five jurisdictions used a diverse set of incidents and a variety of outcome measures; consequently they reported that the use of arrest was only occasionally associated with statistically significant reductions in subsequent repeat offending. The results of the experiments varied by measures used and by the jurisdiction studied.

A new analysis of the replication studies recently reported that a consistent set of measures of repeat offending and appropriate statistical analyses for the combination of data had been developed and the studies reanalyzed. The findings of this research provide evidence supporting the argument that arresting male batterers may, independent of other criminal justice sanctions and individual processes, reduce subsequent intimate partner violence. Specifically;

- Arrest is associated with a reduction in repeat offending in all five measures of repeat offending.

- Reductions in repeat offending are larger and statistically significant in the two measures that are derived from interviews with victims.

- Reductions in repeat offending are smaller and not statistically significant in the three measures that are derived from official police records.

- The effectiveness of arrest does not vary by jurisdiction.

- The size of the reduction in repeat offending associated with arrest is modest compared with the effect of other factors (such as the batterer's age and prior criminal record) on the likelihood of repeat offending.

- Regardless of whether or not the batterer was arrested, more than half of the suspects committed no subsequent criminal offense against their original victim during the follow-up period.

- A minority of suspects continues to commit intimate partner violence regardless of whether they were arrested, counseled, or temporarily separated from their partner. Future research needs to focus on identifying such offenders and the policies and practices that will prevent their partners from being victimized further.

Source: Christopher D. Maxwell, Joel H. Garner, and Jeffrey A. Fagan, 2001. The Effects of Arrest on Intimate Partner Violence: New Evidence from the Spouse Assault Replication Program. NCJ 188199.

Figure 9–4 The elder population deserves to be treated with respect. *(Photo courtesy of the Administration on Aging.)*

grandchildren highly, the maltreatment of the elderly should be considered along lines similar to those of other forms of domestic abuse. Older persons have been identified as particularly vulnerable to financial exploitation, and care must be taken to determine if they willingly and knowingly parted with their resources or if they were duped.

The Role of the Police in Cases Involving Persons with Disabilities.   Approximately 54 million Americans live with a wide variety of physical, cognitive, and emotional disabilities (Tyiska, 1998). The situations in which police officers are handling mentally disordered persons have increased substantially since the majority of persons with disability live in the community at large. One out of every ten police calls nationally involves someone who is mentally ill, according to Lt. Woody of the Akron Police Department (Gillespie, 2001). In addition to the increased at-large population of mentally ill are persons who are developmentally delayed, the community of disabled persons is more vulnerable to victimization. Impaired adults are at a higher risk for being physically or sexually assaulted at a rate of 4 to 10 times as high as it is for other adults. Children with disabilities are also victimized more frequently than nondisabled children. Correctional inmates can be identified as disabled through self-identification; grievance; historical records; staff or health care provider observation; and third party notification.

A three-prong test is used to define disability (Ryan, 2002):

1. A person has a physical or mental impairment that substantially limits one or more major life activities; has a record of an impairment; or is regarded as having one.

2. The limitation is permanent or has long-term impact or expected impact.

3. The person meets eligibility requirements for the receipt of services or participation in programs or activities provided by the public entity.

The American with Disabilities Act.   Given the increasing likelihood of police and correctional officer encounters with persons that are disabled, training on effective communications with persons of the disabled community has taken on greater significance. Title II of the American with Disabilities Act (ADA) provides that "no qualified individual with a disability shall, by reason of such disability, be excluded from participation in or be denied the benefits of the services, programs, or activities of a public entity, or be subjected to discrimination by any such entity." This mandate of nondiscrimination extends to all state and government services, regardless of whether the person receives federal financial assistance. According to the U.S. Department of Justice, the ADA affects everything that officers and deputies do, including arresting, booking, and holding suspects (DOJ, 2003).

Most persons with disability present no additional risk to police. However, subjects with paranoid schizophrenia pose a documented rate of violence to be several times higher than members of the general population with no disorders, unless they are treated successfully (Mohandie & Duffy, 1999). Individuals with this mental disorder may present with anxiety, anger, aloofness, and argumentativeness, along with a superior or patronizing manner. Attempts to defuse a potential violent situation take a show of respect and calm, nonthreatening approach of communicating. The officer's first concern should always be toward safety and protection of persons, both for the officer and for others. The officer must determine if there are any needs or problems that must be addressed or if a situation of mandated reporting exists.

Approach the individual in a nonthreatening but controlled manner so as not to agitate or cause distress. Speak firmly and clearly, showing concern through actions and words. "Are you OK?" and "Do you need help?" are examples of introductory statements in the field used when assessing the situation.

Ask for identifying information to determine the level of stress and cognitive awareness of the person. An individual who is not aware of his or her name or address may be indicative of impairment. Do not assume that a person failing to answer your questions can hear or understand you. Failure to respond by itself is not indicative of belligerence or of criminal behavior. An indication of alcohol use does not necessarily mean that the individual is drunk; you may be dealing with a person who has a disability that also had an alcoholic beverage! Here are some guidelines that Mohandie and Duffy (1999) suggest when confronted with potentially violent mentally ill individuals:

- Assess the real risk; does the individual pose a risk, or is it merely threatened?
- Make a noticeable attempt to understand the context of the subject's comments.
- Avoid arguing about the subject's delusions while attempting to develop reality-based issues.
- Use active listening skills such as paraphrasing, and emotion labeling.
- Allow the subject to vent frustration.
- Do not crowd or violate the subject's personal body space.
- Use suggestibility and empathy to attempt a behavioral change.

LAW ENFORCEMENT GOALS

Public awareness of the various forms of violence has risen due to research efforts coupled with media coverage of the events. Their existence was not a revelation to the law enforcement community, however. Police frequently encountered intimate violence, and discussions within that community are long standing. What has changed is the availability of information on the causes and effects of family violence as well as its estimated frequency.

The signs and symptoms of domestic violence in differing populations have been covered in previous chapters. The recognition of abuse and neglect plays a significant part in determining appropriate responses. What is criminal justice trying to accomplish? The primary goals for law enforcement in responding to domestic violence are (1) to protect the victim, (2) to determine if a crime has been committed, and, if so, (3) to provide a basis for successful prosecution for the crime(s).

Goal 1: Protect the Victim

When police are confronted with stranger violence, the victim is readily apparent. That is not the case with domestic offenses. Common myths prevail with expectations that the victim and the perpetrator can be identified easily. Myths about the reliability of the witness are usual. Here are some of these misconceptions.

Victims: Myth and Reality
- *Myth:* The victim of domestic violence is the passive one in the relationship.
- *Reality:* The couple may appear to be mutually combative at the time of intervention. They may both lash out at anyone trying to help them. To

Figure 9–5 Police officers may become frustrated at repeat calls to the same household. It is important to remember that a victim making bad choices still deserves equal protection. The police officers' duty to protect is not canceled due to a frequent or repeated need of services!

determine who is the primary aggressor, it is necessary to defuse the anger and interview both parties without prejudice. There is no proper way for a victim to act. Victims may be either passive or aggressive. Victims often appear defensive. Determining who threw the first blow and why is one way to attach responsibility.

- *Myth:* The police will find the victim more likable than the perpetrator.
- *Reality:* Often, the victims of abuse will be interviewed when they are in crisis. Frustrations, anger, fear, and shame are just some of the emotions that they might be experiencing. The mix of emotions may cause the victim to yell and scream at the person attempting to intervene. It is conceivable that the victim will be the least "likable" of the people in a domestic violence situation. An objective interview will not be based on the sympathies of the interviewer toward any party.
- *Myth:* The victim will be grateful for help.
- *Reality:* Although some victims will be very grateful, that is not always the case. Past experience with ineffective interventions may cause a victim to resent interference. Presumptive prosecution could render the victim without any control of future events after an initial intervention. For the person who is

dependent on the abuser for economic or emotional support, criminal justice barging in is not welcome, and the one intervening should not expect gratitude.

- *Myth:* The woman is always the victim.
- *Reality:* Domestic abuse victims can be of either gender and of any age. The victim is the injured party; most often that is the woman, but not always. Determining the harm can be complex and at times goes beyond a simple physical assault. Injury may be due to defense posturing. The police officer is guided by legislation that dictates the manner and extent of law enforcement action in domestic violence. Your state may not recognize same-sex domestic violence or marital rape. Policy and law must guide the officer.

Perpetrators: Myth and Reality

- *Myth:* Perpetrators of domestic violence are mean and nasty people.
- *Reality:* For the "family-only" type of abuser (Rucinski, 1998), the face that is presented to the outside world is of charm and humor. These offenders are often skilled in control and manipulation. They may control themselves and attempt to manipulate officials as well. This perpetrator is just as likely to be the more calm and sweet-tempered of the two when faced with police officers. Alternatively, a generally aggressive abuser will be more apt to remain violent during intervention (Rucinski, 1998).
- *Myth:* Abusers are lowlifes and uneducated people.
- *Reality:* The perpetrator may be the pillar of the community and have a high level of education. Such abusers will attempt to explain away their behaviors, often in front of a passive victim. Abusers know that it is in their best interest to befriend the interviewer, and they do tend to act in their best interest.
- *Myth:* "She asked for it."
- *Reality:* The perpetrator may feel justified in using physical force due to a precipitating event. This does not excuse or justify violence other than for self-defense. It is a crime to use physical violence against another, regardless of the personal relationship that exists.
- *Myth:* Only women can be raped.
- *Reality:* A forced sex act can be perpetrated against a woman, a man, or a child. The operative word is *force*—a nonconsensual sex act committed with force is rape.

Witnesses: Myth and Reality

- *Myth:* Witness information is the best evidence.
- *Reality:* Witness statements are often the most unreliable of evidence and should be supported with additional proof whenever possible. This is as important in domestic violence as with any other crime. To decide if state-

ments can be relied upon, it is imperative that the motives for offering information be explored. This is not to suggest that a witness will purposefully lie about what he or she has seen but that a witness's perception may be inaccurate or lacking. The witness should not be treated like a suspect; some people simply become nervous when confronted by police officers. Treating the witness with respect can improve his or her willingness to be helpful. Determine if there is a relationship between the witness and either party in a domestic dispute. Find out if there is any prejudice against one or the other on the part of the witness. How the witness came to have the information is another area worth exploring.

- *Myth:* Witness statements will always be voluntary.
- *Reality:* There are a number of barriers to obtaining accurate information from a witness. Reluctance to give a statement could be due to a fear of reprisal or hesitation in getting involved. A witness who is related or a friend may not want to get anyone in trouble. The witness may also be dependent emotionally or economically on one or both in the relationship, such as a child or elder.

Prevention Strategies.   Efforts aimed at preventing domestic violence can be grouped into three categories: prevention, protection, and response. Interagency coordination of services has surfaced as an ideal prevention approach. However, implementing strategies for new or better procedures may be hampered by competing agency goals. Police often need specific information on improving investigative techniques, and social agencies seek to determine trends for service direction. The need for greater involvement of police personnel has consistently been found essential in developing a community response to domestic violence.

Community efforts are more responsive to particular needs but fail to provide consistency in police services across the nation. The police officers' role in prevention has taken on a new and expanded meaning because of their involvement in domestic disputes. The way that police officers respond to domestic dispute calls has an impact on future domestic violence. In a recent report to Congress, Lawrence Sherman argued that the effects of police on crime are complex, and often surprising. "Perceptions of police legitimacy is believed to strongly affect citizen willingness to obey the law. Reanalysis of the Milwaukee Domestic Violence Experiment found that repeat domestic violence was lowest among arrestees who thought police had treated them respectfully; a powerful effect on recidivism was associated with police who simply took the time to listen to the offender's side of the story. Police themselves," Sherman maintains, "create a risk factor for crime simply by failing to treat citizens with respect!" (Sherman, 1997).

Criminal justice and other professionals are repeatedly in the position to identify high-risk households. The information needs to be passed on to the agencies that can respond with services once a genuine suspicion has been documented that a child is in need. Mandated reporting legislation requires police to report severe abuse and

Been There . . . Done That!

The years that Alice was married to William can only be described as a reign of terror. Her daughter moved out of the house at an early age to escape the frequent rape and other physical assaults that she had endured at the hands of her stepfather. I knew of the sexual assaults because of the investigation prompted by the adult Deborah. It was a frustrating experience—most of the incidents had been committed past the statute of limitations for Massachusetts. So heinous were the crimes, however, that Assistant District Attorney Anger, who was handling the case, filed new legislation to extend the period under which crimes against children could be prosecuted across the state. Little was known about the conditions under which the abuse had occurred.

Then the call from Deborah came: Would I do her a favor and come to the hospital to document her mother's injuries? The face that I photographed was so swollen, blackened, and bloody that one would swear she had barely survived a fatal car accident. It was not the first time that William had beat her bloody, and it would not be the last. Prosecution did occur, but the system was not equipped to offer any protection or advice.

Approximately ten years later, I met Alice again. She has difficulty looking at me; the detached retina in one eye is a permanent condition, due to the numerous blows to her face. Hunched over, she finds it difficult to stand erect; hard objects that were used to beat her across the back took their toll. She walks with a cane; her legs had suffered many breaks. I remembered her telling how William would beat her to the ground and twist her legs backward around the kitchen table.

Now she is working as an advocate for battered women and felt able to tell me more of what had happened. Worse than the beating was the loss of her daughter, she related. She was still bitter about her inability to protect herself or her child, and their relationship was strained. Living in an isolated area of the state, she had taken solace in caring for her animals. Her precious dogs were found dead from gunshots from time to time. Anything of joy to her was broken over the years, including her spirit. My intervention was the first of many that were necessary for her to leave the situation. She had little strength left after the ordeal. What had changed? The criminal justice response. Once restraining orders were made available, she used that option. She could report the events to the police, even though it had taken years for anyone to listen. She survived, barely.

neglect to child protection services. Too often, officers are frustrated when a report is filed and no action occurs. Feelings of disappointment and frustration are at the root of an officer's future noncompliance in reporting. To enable follow-up on the initial actions, current practices should require a duplicate copy to be filed with the police department and used to document service agency culpability.

Additionally, departments themselves often fail to validate the time that officers spend for domestic investigations, which includes making referrals or filing mandated reports. A weekly or monthly activity report frequently requires officers to list the number of traffic tickets issued and arrests that they have made during a specified period. The practice serves a number of important functions. First, it makes officers accountable in a manner consistent with police department goals. Second, it identifies for the officers the work that will be recognized as legitimate use of their time. Since referrals are legally required of police, they must be identified as justifiable efforts and included in activity documentation.

The role of the police does not stop with simply making a report, however, and follow-up is suggested. Prevention of death and severe injury to children is a concern that cannot be delegated to a social service organization and forgotten. Frequent home visits can reduce child abuse and injury to children aged zero to two, according to the Sherman report, and law enforcement officers are some of the "other professionals" involved. In some cases it would be appropriate to contact parallel community services that might offer aid to the family and reduce the risk to the child. Home health aides, visiting nurses' associations, local crisis centers, YMCA, or family members could be included when appropriate. Supervisors who charge police personnel with identifying community services, establishing relationships with these agencies, and following through using available resources will arm officers with the tools needed for prevention.

Protection Efforts.   Increased protection for victims of violence is evidenced through a number of initiatives across the country that are the combined effort of government and civilian organizations; here are just a few examples.

Batterer Counseling.   EMERGE, the first counseling program for men who batter, was founded in 1977. Similar programs have since been developed in an effort to modify the violent behavior evidenced by men and women who commit domestic violence. Gay men have joined counseling groups since the first was formed at MOVE in San Francisco in 1987.

Court Advocacy.   The courts are an intimidating place for victims of crime. The forms necessary to request a civil protection or restraining order are confusing. On top of that, many victims cannot afford to hire an attorney to help with the process. The victim/witness assistance program was developed to address these needs. Typically referred to as an advocate, the victim/witness assistant does not work for the court but for the victim. Fines collected from those who are convicted criminals pay their salaries. The men and women can be found in most courthouses across the nation. Advocates provide a variety of victim-related services that had been ignored previously. They will instruct the victim or witness on the procedure itself, telling the person when she or he is required for court appearances. Frequently accompanying victims into court, advocates also track the case and provide updates for the victim.

Due to increased demands for advocate services, some jurisdictions have difficulty in arranging for assistance in filing abuse complaints. Volunteers and paid professionals from battered women shelters may supplement the advocate services with their own staff. College internship programs can arrange for appropriate undergraduate and graduate students to provide services as well.

Protection Order Confidentiality.   When filing for a court order of protection, the victim can request that his or her name, telephone number, and address not be made part of the public record. This is standard procedure for those who fear for their safety.

Victim Services.   The first rape crisis center opened in 1971; by 1976, over 400 programs for battered women and rape victims existed. Support groups for lesbian battered women first emerged in Seattle in 1985.

Victim Shelters.   The first battered women's shelter in the United States opened in St. Paul, Minnesota in 1973. Since then, the need for emergency shelters has been proven. The establishment of shelters for battered women has been supported partly through legislative funding. For those able to use this emergency measure, it provides a temporary safe haven from abuse. Only a handful of shelters exist for battered heterosexual or homosexual men. Most recently, a shelter for abused gay men has opened in California (Anon., 1998).

Voter Registration Confidentiality.   Victims of domestic violence and of sexual assault may request that their names and addresses be kept confidential on certain public lists. A police chief must supply the victim with an affidavit saying that the person qualifies to have his or her name omitted from annual street lists and the annual register of voters. This allows victims to participate in the voting process without fearing that their vital information will be accessible to their attackers.

Weapons Confiscation and Gun Ban.   The **Lautenberg Gun Ban** was passed in 1996 as part of the Omnibus Spending Bill. It prohibits anyone convicted of a domestic violence misdemeanor crime from carrying a gun. Under its provisions, officers are obligated to seize the guns and gun permits from all persons convicted of misdemeanor domestic violence.

For High-Crime Hot Spots: Extra Police Patrols.   Drug and gang task forces are two examples where police have provided extra patrols for prevention of crime. The practice is beneficial in preventing crime, according to Sherman (1997). Providing additional police patrols to high-prone areas of domestic violence is as valid as it is for combating car theft, and domestic violence is much more prevalent.

Lawrence Sherman maintains that the more focused the police strategy, the more likely it is to prevent crime. "Merely increasing police force strength does not prevent crime. Adequate numbers of police utilized for directed patrols, proactive arrests and problem-solving at high-crime hot spots have shown substantial evidence of crime prevention" (Sherman, 1997). Conclusions drawn from the report to Congress include making on-scene arrests for domestic abusers who reside in neighborhoods where most households have an employed adult, and mailing arrest warrants to suspects who leave the domestic violence scene before police arrive (Sherman et al., 1998).

Voter Registration Confidentiality Law

SAMPLE AFFIDAVIT

In accordance with the provisions of Chapter 87 of the Acts of 1998, _____

I, _____ do solemnly swear that the party

named below is duly entitled to have certain information withheld from the public pursuant

to Massachusetts General Laws, C. 265, §24C.

_____ a resident of _____ in the
           (named party)   (city/town)

Commonwealth of Massachusetts.

Executed on _____ , _____ in the
                 (date)   (city/town)

Commonwealth of Massachusetts.

I declare under the penalty of perjury that the foregoing is true and correct.

_____ of _____
    (Signature of Colonel/designee)   (city/town)

Commonwealth of Massachusetts

Figure 9-6 Victims of domestic violence and sexual assault may ask that their addresses be kept confidential on certain public lists. This is a sample affidavit for voter registration confidentiality.

Response.   Does a person retain the right to personal protection by the government even when it involves violence perpetrated from within the family? That question has been answered with the legislative changes that put a duty to respond to domestic violence on the shoulders of law enforcement. The rights of the family no longer supersede the rights of the individual. Equal protection must be provided regardless of the victim's relationship to the perpetrator. Attitudes based on gender and age bias add another dimension to the complexity of domestic violence response. Appropriate police responses are now outlined through legislation, without regard to the age or the gender of the perpetrator.

In earlier chapters, theories that would help to explain why equal protection was not afforded were put forth. Patriarchy rooted in perceptions of male supremacy is one common reason for historical noncompliance in providing police protection. From what began as the right of the husband or father to "police" his family has developed into a police liability for failure to respond to all domestic violence. What was once understood as a property issue has developed into a personal rights concern.

Exigency provides the legal reasoning that allows officers to enter and to arrest people in their homes. Excuses for lack of intervention can no longer be tolerated. The question remains how far our society is willing to commit police involvement in areas that include personal choice decisions where harm may result.

Goal 2: Determine If a Crime Has Been Committed

Using the standard of probable cause, determine if a crime has been committed. This sounds easy to someone who has never been in the position to determine culpability in an intimate dispute or family violence accusation. The reality here is that the determination takes time—facts must be gathered in a neutral and unbiased manner. The primary objective of interviewing is to gather truthful information (Figure 9–7). With this in mind, the interviewer must determine the best method of obtaining as much detail as possible in order to evaluate the truthfulness and objectivity of the person under scrutiny, whether he or she be a victim, a perpetrator, or a witness.

Interviewing the Adult.   The best method is to separate the parties and question them individually after a brief cooling-down period. The interviews should be outside the hearing range of the other, with equal levels of respect afforded to each. For crimes by intimates, the process may be a long one. Sufficient time to assess the situation involves skillful interviewing and the desire to be thorough. There is no quick resolution of a domestic dispute. The practice of "arrest everyone" punishes rather than protects the victim and is contrary to the first goal.

The three basic phases to the interview process are preparation, establishment of the psychological content, and the actual questioning. Obtaining information from the dispatcher or from officers on the scene satisfies the preparation stage. If the interview is staged at the convenience of the officer rather than a result of crisis intervention, additional preparation would include contacting agencies that have previously

Figure 9–7 The primary objective of interviewing is to obtain truthful information. *(Photo courtesy of Mark C. Ide.)*

been involved. Record checks and witness interviews would also be considered part of the necessary preparation.

The second phase contains the extremely important element of rapport, which describes the relationship established between the interviewer and the interviewee. This relationship can be constructed or destroyed within seconds if the responder shows distaste, distrust, or condemnation of the person who is confronted. Obvious bias such as asking the woman what she did to provoke an attack, or assuming that a blood-soaked man was the abuser, are examples of what breaks down rapport and inhibits information that would benefit the officer and facilitate a resolution. Victim cooperation is consistently tied to officer attitudes. Look at the evidence and question both parties without prejudice. If a victim does not believe that he or she will get fair treatment from the officer, the person won't bother to try. If victims won't give information, you can't proceed.

The third phase is the actual questioning. In addition to questions about the incident under investigation, a **risk assessment** must be made to determine the level of danger the batterer presents. The following key points should be addressed:

1. Does the suspect believe the victim is attempting to end the relationship? This is when the majority of killings take place. The most dangerous period for the victim is when the batterer realizes that this time the victim is really going through with the breakup.

2. Does the suspect possess weapons? This question must be asked in all situations. Guns, knives, *nunchaku*, and any other weapons should be confiscated

Figure 9–8 The interviewer must obtain as much detail as possible. *(Photo courtesy of Mark C. Ide.)*

if possible, even if they have not been used against the victim. If they have been used before, the danger for the victim is much greater. Threats to use weapons, even if they were not carried out, are just as serious as when a weapon has been displayed.

3. Does the suspect abuse alcohol or drugs? The batterer who is also a substance abuser is at increased risk of committing a dangerous or lethal assault.

4. Were threats made? Threats to kill the victim and/or the children and/or to commit suicide must be taken seriously. Batterers do not commonly kill themselves without first attempting to kill at least one family member.

5. Has the suspect committed any previous sexual assaults against the victim? Previous sexual assaults are indicators that the batterer is almost twice as likely to commit a dangerous act of violence against the victim.

6. Has the suspect been following the victim? Stalking, reading the victim's mail, listening in on phone calls, or other acts of surveillance should be considered an implied threat.

7. What are the frequency and severity of the violence? The best predictor of future violence is past violence. Frequent violence (two or three times per month or more) or severe violence (requiring hospitalization) places the victim in a high-risk category.

8. Is the batterer depressed or suffering from mental health problems? Some mental health problems are linked to increased propensity to commit a lethal assault. Look for delusional fears and for severe depression.

When the allegations involve child abuse or neglect, the investigator must talk with the caretaker(s). An assessment of the match between the injuries and the explanations offered by an adult caretaker might become critical during the investigation. To maximize the information, be careful not to acknowledge the impropriety of caretaker actions and to remain nonjudgmental.

Researchers using cognitive psychology have identified a specific technique for memory retrieval. Known as the **cognitive interview**, the procedure is believed to increase the amount of correct information obtained from a wide range of eyewitnesses without producing a higher percentage of inaccurate information (Geiselman et al., 1992). This interview method involves a three-phase procedure. Rapport development, techniques for eliciting information, and finally clarification by the witness are incorporated into the structured plan to increase reported information. Originally developed for adult interviewing, the technique has been applied successfully for eliciting statements from children as well (Geiselman et al., 1992).

Interviewing the Child.   Some children are no strangers to juvenile, criminal, and family courts. As victims, perpetrators, and co-conspirators, they are routinely interviewed. Although courts are afforded wide discretion in modifying some trial practices to accommodate the special needs of children (Stearns, 1998), children's competency and credibility are usually an issue. It is not unusual for normal children to have imaginary friends, further complicating the investigation and calling into question the competence of the child to testify in court. State practice on how the judge may modify the trial varies, as does the determination of competency itself. Any interview of a child should be conducted in anticipation of future legal challenge on competency and credibility.

1. **Competency** means that a person is fit to stand trial or to take the oath to tell the truth for testimony in court. Competency is sometimes demonstrated by a child through the ability to determine the difference between a truth and a lie and to understand the morality of lying. In 1974, the revised Federal Rules of Evidence abolished the competency rule for trials in federal courts. Over one-third of states followed the federal example when it comes to the child witness and do not require a competency inquiry (Abrams & Ramsey, 2000). Thirteen states presume that children over age 10 are competent, and 18 states require a demonstration that the child understands the nature and

obligation of the oath to tell the truth. A judge conducts competency hearings in those states where no presumption exists or the age of the child dictates. Competency determination hinges in one part whether the child has the capacity to recall events, separate fact from fantasy, and maintain those memories independently without being influenced by others. The second part of the determination is that the child has a sense of moral responsibility defined as understanding the duty to speak the truth (Abrams & Ramsey, 2000).

The U.S. Supreme Court considered whether a judge could modify the procedures of a competency hearing to accommodate children for the first time in *Kentucky v. Stincer* (1987). The Court decided that a defendant being excluded from a hearing to determine competency did not violate the accused's right to confrontation. States are free to establish their own procedures based on this ruling.

2. **Credibility** refers to whether or not the child witness can be believed. Children who cannot articulate their abuse or children who have memory gaps or inconsistencies are less likely to be believed when they report abuse. For states that presume competence, juries are left to determine the credibility (believability) of the child witness. Other models decide through the competency hearing if the testimony will be allowed. Investigators must establish credibility before submitting a case for trial, and that process can be a difficult one. Because children differ from adults in their ability to remember and recount events accurately, controversy regarding child statements exists. Debate on the reliability of child statements escalated with the failed McMartin preschool case in California during the late 1980s (*People v. Buckey*, 1984). The case prompted an outpouring of research into the cognitive and communicative abilities of children and their suggestibility to provide misleading or inaccurate information. A number of suggestions for effective interviewing and specific techniques when questioning children followed, putting greater responsibility on the investigator to ensure truthful statements.

Videotaping Child Interviews.   As illustrated, videotaping can be destructive to a case. The practice itself is controversial, having both advantages and disadvantages. Many experts are in favor of videotaping because it has the potential to reduce the number of interviews, has strong visual impact, and has the potential to induce a confession when played for the offenders (Lanning, 2002). In opposition to the practice of videotaping are concerns of the artificial setting that it produces as well as potential conflicting accounts of the molestation (Lanning, 2002). The controversy considers some of the points discussed in this section.

1. Does this method provide an accurate documentation of the victim's account of the crime? It depends on the technology used as well as the skill of the interviewer. Taping only provides verification of what happens during that session. It may not record voices that are too low to be heard. Common prob-

lems result from human error, such as failure to put a tape in the machine or to recharge the batteries so that the interview is only partially recorded.

Taping will document when a child refuses to talk and serve to illustrate inconsistencies in a prior or subsequent statement. It does not guard against attacks about what was said before the interview began and how the child was prepared for the taping. Questions asked during the interview can and will be scrutinized in the future.

Alternative methods of documenting the statement are available, such as audio taping, note taking, or having the interview witnessed by a third party. Due to concerns as to the suggestibility of children, taping can be an appropriate way to demonstrate that the process was not leading or suggestive to the child witness, assuming that the professional is trained properly to interview children. The Center for Child Protection has been using videotaping in conducting interviews with suspected victims of abuse since 1983. In part, the center states, "Interviewers who are properly trained and who conduct themselves in a professionally responsible manner can benefit from this."

Professionals who routinely interview children as to suspected abuse and neglect can attest to the fact that words alone cannot adequately describe the impact of abuse to a child. While revealing the details of abuse, the body language, facial expressions, and physical demonstrations by the victim can be as illuminating as the disclosure itself. The videotaping preserves this account and freezes the abuse within the time frame of disclosure. The child who testifies is often more mature and will present differently in the years after the abuse has been documented, when the case finally comes to trial.

2. How can an investigator use a videotaped statement? Tapes are sometimes used as a training tool to sharpen interviewing skills (Lanning, 2002). Routinely used as a training method for forensic interviewers, an interview can be scrutinized to improve techniques and develop appropriate questions for future interviewing.

    Children who divulge abuse during a videotaped interview provide the investigator with an important tool for interrogation that should not be overlooked. Although this point is unexamined by research, the practice is probably more frequent than suspected. Confrontation of the perpetrator should be a routine aspect of any child abuse investigation, and the statement can be introduced in any form. Using the videotape for someone in denial breaks down barriers and may elicit confessions.

    Only one case before the U.S. Supreme Court has considered the importance of proper documenting of pretrial interviewing of children. In *Idaho v. Wright* (1990) the Court excluded the hearsay statement of a child taken in an interview with Dr. Jambura. In part the Court stated; "The questions and answers were not recorded on videotape for preservation and perusal by the defense at or before trial; and blatantly leading questions were used in the interrogation."

3. Can the prosecution use a videotaped interview of an abused child? Since it would not be uncommon for a criminal case to be conducted simultaneously with a probate or juvenile case, the videotaped interview may be an option to avoid multiple interviews and unnecessarily traumatizing the victim. Alternatively, the interviewer could testify as to the contents of the interview in the probate, family, or juvenile court. Prior to a criminal trial, a good videotaped interview may convince the defendant that a guilty plea should be entered (Lanning, 2002). Defense attorneys who witness an emotional but clear indication of abuse may advise the client against a jury trial.

Used extensively in cases that the author investigated, videotape of the victim was offered to the grand jury as evidence in support of an indictment to superior court. In this instance, no right to confrontation with the accused is expected. Use of video is not established definitively however, as no case testing the constitutionality of videotaped testimony has reached the U.S. Supreme Court.

Approximately half of the states have "general child hearsay" exception statutes that permit out of court testimony from young sexual abuse victims (Abrams & Ramsey, 2000). Some states specifically allow that hearsay be through a videotaped interview of the child victim.

The interviewer's experience and use of leading questions will be examined when the child statements are being considered for acceptance by the court (Abrams & Ramsey, 2000). The vocal inflections and facial expressions of the interviewer can mislead a child to answer inaccurately. Questions must be phrased with the age and developmental stage of the child in mind. It is useless to ask a question that the child cannot understand, so care in phrasing is an important consideration. Open-ended questions are preferred, and closed-ended questions should be avoided. Questions that suggest a yes/no answer limit the child's response and could lead the child to answer inappropriately. Leading the witness by suggestion can taint an otherwise valid disclosure. Experts agree that repeat interviews of young children are potentially harmful and should be avoided. Children can be expected to have varying degrees of memory and varying abilities to communicate their thoughts. A successful interview will depend on the skills of the interviewer, who should have realistic expectations of the child.

Interviewing the Elder Victim.   Empowering the elder victim is helpful to both the victim and the officer. Communicating respect by referring to the victim by his or her title—Miss, Mrs., Mr., or Dr., for example—can be helpful during the rapport-building portion of the interview. At all times, the dignity of the elder should be maintained. The interviewer should go slowly and use language that is easily understood but not patronizing.

According to the Police Executive Research Forum, the following guidelines are suggested for interviews with elders (Nerenberg, 1993).

- Investigations should be coordinated with adult protective services personnel or the ombudsman when possible, to avoid multiple interviews.
- Joint interviews with public health nurses or others treating medical conditions may assist agencies when appropriate.
- Interviewers should attempt to establish **rapport** with the person being interviewed.
- Whenever possible, interviewers should use audio and video technology.
- Officers should respect the confidentiality of all parties whenever possible.
- To prevent contamination or collusion, interviewers should avoid disclosure of case information to all parties involved in the alleged offense.
- Interviewers should ask general, nonleading questions.
- Officers should ask all witnesses to identify others who have relevant information and tell how those others may be contacted. Interviewers will need to identify the victim's doctor, conservator, attorney, social worker, and any agencies that provide service to the victim.

Figure 9–9 A witness may be able to identify others who will have relevant information. *(Photo courtesy of Mark C. Ide.)*

Goal 3: Provide the Basis for Successful Prosecution

This goal is satisfied when all injuries have been properly documented and evidence has been gathered. In the next chapter we explore the legally acceptable methods to satisfy this objective. Three types of evidence can be gathered: real (or tangible) evidence, documentary evidence, and testimonial evidence (Yeschke, 1997). The first form of evidence, real or tangible evidence, is physical. Things that you can acquire, such as a fingerprint or a bullet, are examples. The second type of evidence is documentary, something that is recorded, such as financial statements or 911 tapes. By themselves, these items are not evidentiary but may have significance after a crime has been committed. The third type of evidence is testimonial; both interviews and interrogations come under this heading. The majority of court-introduced evidence, approximately 80 percent, is testimonial.

CONCLUSIONS

For years, research has been gathered on what police do and how they should be doing it. This difficult task is far from complete. The role of the police officer is more complex because the job is constantly changing to meet new expectations in society. Contemporary problems call for nontraditional responses. Somewhere along the way, the definitions became too clear, too concise, too narrow. This obscured the job of policing!

Are police expected to do it all? In a way. They are expected to provide protection and service to their communities. The job requires techniques in a technical world. Preconceived notions of drama and excitement drown out the reality that domestic violence is the most frequent call for many jurisdictions, although oddly, it has rarely appeared in the profiles of what police do. Often, departments fail to validate this large portion of duty through adequate training or proper incentives.

Since the 1960s, the trend toward proactive policing for crimes of domestic status has followed other examples. The acknowledgment that the forms are varied and the victims are mixed has brought the position of policing one step closer to effective intervention. Arming police with a strategy is paramount if the goals of protection and service to all citizens are to be met. No other area of police work is this muddy. Moving from nonintervention to mediation to arrest, the criminalization of domestic violence has been achieved, and it is up to the policy makers to assure the passage of legislation that will allow legitimate police action.

The foundation for action is the successful interview. Knowing who did what, how, when, where, and why is still necessary to protect the victim and prosecute the abusers. Those questions can be answered with greater accuracy through the use of techniques meant to elicit information (Figure 9–10). The interview has changed from simply filling out a form to being a skilled art form. In some cases, the use of a professional forensic interviewer will be necessary to overcome expected court challenges.

Figure 9–10 Approximately 80 percent of an officer's investigative work consists of obtaining information through interviews. Good communication skills and a willingness to listen to people determine how successful the officer will be in obtaining a statement.

How should police respond to allegations of domestic violence? They should respond with questions, lots of them, not with preconceived ideas as to who did what based on previous experience or personal bias. Understanding the goals for public safety and the need to elicit truthful information makes clear the actual role for law enforcement: to serve and to protect.

QUESTIONS FOR REVIEW

1. Name the two most common styles used to describe policing efforts. What are the positive and negative effects of this labeling?

2. Explain the three categories of efforts to prevent domestic violence. What is the policing role within each category?

3. What is the best method to use to conduct a domestic violence interview?

4. What are the three basic phases of the interview process?

5. Why is it important to establish rapport in an interview?

6. To make a risk assessment, what questions should be asked during an interview?

7. Explain the controversy surrounding child statements. Talk about the case that prompted research into the issue.

8. Do you believe that videotape should be used in interviews with children? Why or why not?

9. Discuss some helpful hints to use when interviewing an elder.

INTERNET-BASED EXERCISES

1. Develop at least two myth and reality statements that pertain to domestic violence. Go to your favorite search engine and research the topic.

2. Are you familiar with interviewing techniques used by law enforcement? Search for the cognitive interview technique and find out how it is used in child abuse investigations. You can find this information through the National Criminal Justice Service at http://www.ncjrs.org.

REFERENCES

Abrams, D. E., and Ramsey S. H. 2000. *Children and the Law: Doctrine, Policy, and Practice.* St. Paul, MN: West Group.

Anon. 1998. "A Shelter for Battered Men." *Advocate* 764:1–8.

Anonymous. (2004, January 26). The Scandalous Secret of Family Courts. *New Statesman,* 17, 791, 6.

Baradaran-Robison, Shima. 2003. "Tipping the Balance in Favor of Justice: Due Process and the Thirteenth and Nineteenth Amendments in Child Removal From Battered Mothers." *Brigham Young University Law Review* 2003(1):227–64.

Bard, M. 1969. "Family Intervention Police Teams as a Community Mental Health Resource." *Journal of Criminal Law, Criminology and Police Science,* 60(2), 247–250.

Cassidy, Michael, Caroline G. Nicholl, and Carmen R. Ross. 2001. *Results of a Survey Conducted by the Metropolitan Police Department of Victims Who Reported Violence Against Women.* Available from the Washington, DC Metropolitan Police Department (202-727-5029).

Courvant, D., and L. Cook-Daniels. 2003. "Trans and Intersex Survivors of Domestic Violence: Defining Terms, Barriers, & Responsibilities" [Web page]. Accessed Mar 2004. Available at *http://www.survivorproject.org/defbarresp.html.*

Dickinson, Beth, Sergeant, County of Los Angeles Sheriff's Department. 1985. "Los Angeles County Sheriff's Department Preschool Investigation." February. *http://www.ieway.com/~csukbr/juslib/mcmartin.html.* 1998.

DOJ. 2003. "Enforcing the ADA: A Status Report From the Department of Justice." 1. Washington, DC: U.S. Department of Justice.

Frontline. "Other Well-Known Cases Involving Child Sexual Abuse in Day Care Settings." *http://www3.pbs.org/wgbh/pages/frontline/shows/innocence/etc/other.html.* 1998.

Geiselman, R. E., Gail Bornstein, and Karen Saywitz. 1992. *New Approach to Interviewing Children: A Test of Its Effectiveness.* National Institute of Justice Research in Brief. NCJ 135011. Washington, DC: U.S. Department of Justice.

Gillespie, Charley. 2001. "Police Training Improves Safety in Dealing With Mentally Ill" [Web page]. Accessed 2003. Available at *www.taser.com/2001/09/Akron.html*.

Goldberg, C. 1999. "Spouse Abuse Crackdown, Surprisingly, Nets Many Women." *New York Times*, November 23, p. A16.

Goldstein, Seth L., and R. P. Tyler. 1998. "Frustrations of Inquiry." *FBI Law Enforcement Bulletin* 67(7):1–6.

Hart, Timothy C. 2003. *Reporting Crime to the Police, 1992 2000*. Bureau of Justice Statistics Special Report. NCJ 195710. Washington, DC: U.S. Department of Justice.

Helfer, Ray E., and Ruth S. Kempe (eds.). 1988. *The Battered Child*, 4th ed. Chicago: University of Chicago Press.

IACP. 1999. *Police Officer Domestic Violence Concepts and Issues Paper*. April, 1999. U.S. Department of Justice.

Lanning, Kenneth. 1992. *Child Sex Rings: A Behavioral Analysis*, 2nd ed. Arlington, VA: National Center for Missing and Exploited Children.

Lanning, Kenneth. 2002. "Criminal Investigation of Sexual Victimization of Children." Pp. 329–48 in *The APSAC Handbook on Child Maltreatment*, 2nd ed., John Myers, Lucy Berliner, John Briere, C. T. Hendrix, Carole Jenny, and Theresa Reid (eds.). Thousands Oaks, CA: Sage Publication.

Levin, Amy, and Linda G. Mills. 2003. "Fighting for Child Custody When Domestic Violence Is at Issue: Survey of State Laws." *Social Work* 48(4):463–71.

Littel, K., Malefyt, M., Walker, A., Buel, S., Tucker, D., & Kuriansky, J. 1998. *Assessing Justice System Response to Violence Against Women: A Tool for Law Enforcement, Prosecution and the Courts to Use in Developing Effective Responses*. Washington, DC: U.S. Department of Justice.

Lonsway, Kim, and Pete Conis. Oct. 2003. "Officer Domestic Violence" [Web page]. Accessed 2004. Available at *www.lawandordermag.com*.

Maxwell, Christopher D., Joel H. Garner, and Jeffrey A. Fagan. 2001. *The Effects of Arrest on Intimate Partner Violence: New Evidence from the Spouse Assault Replication Program*. NCJ 188199. Washington, DC: U.S. Department of Justice.

Maxwell, Christopher D., Joel H. Garner, and Jeffrey A. Fagan. 2003. "The Preventive Effects of Arrest on Intimate Partner Violence: Research, Policy, and Theory." *Domestic Violence Report* 9(1):9–10.

Mohandie, Kris, and James Duffy. 1999. *Understanding Subjects with Paranoid Schizophrenia*. Washington, DC: Federal Bureau of Investigation.

Mouton, Charles P., Melissa Talamantes, Robert W. Parker, David V. Espino, and Toni P. Miles. 2001. "Abuse and Neglect in Older Men." *Clinical Gerontologist* 24(3–4):15–26.

NCAVP. 2003. *National Report on Lesbian, Gay, Bisexual, and Transgender Domestic Violence in 2002*. New York: National Coalition of Anti-Violence Programs.

Nerenberg, Lisa. 1993. *Improving the Police Response to Domestic Elder Abuse*. Washington, DC: Police Executive Research Forum.

Randall, Teri. 1991. "Duluth Takes Firm Stance against Domestic Violence; Mandates Abuser Arrest, Education." *Journal of the American Medical Association* 266(9):1180–84.

Rucinski, Cheryl. 1998. "Transitions: Responding to the Needs of Domestic Violence Victims." *FBI Law Enforcement Bulletin* 67(4):15–18.

Ryan, Timothy. 2002. *Why Corrections Professionals Should Be Concerned with In-Custody ADA Issues*. Large Jail Network Meeting. Longmont, Colorado: NIC.

Shepherd, Jack R. 1988. "Law Enforcement's Role in the Investigation of Family Violence." Pp. 392–400 in *The Battered Child*, 4th ed., Ray E. Helfer and Ruth S. Kempe (eds.). Chicago: University of Chicago Press.

Sherman, Lawrence W. 1997. "Policing for Crime Prevention." In *Preventing Crime: What Works, What Doesn't, What's Promising.* Report 104–378. Washington, DC: 104th Congress, 1st Session, U.S. House of Representatives.

Sherman, Lawrence W., Denise C. Gottfedson, Doris L. MacKenzie, John Eck, Peter Reuter, and Shawn D. Bushway. 1998. *Preventing Crime: What Works, What Doesn't, What's Promising.* NCJ 171676. Washington, DC: U.S. Department of Justice.

Stearns, Richard G. 1998. *The Massachusetts Criminal Law: A District Court Prosecutor's Guide.* Dedham, MA: Commonwealth of Massachusetts.

Straus, Murray A., Richard J. Gelles, and Suzanne K. Steinmetz. 1980. P. 222 in *Behind Closed Doors: Violence in the American Family.* Garden City, NY: Anchor Press/Doubleday.

Teaster, Pamela B., Karen A. Roberto, Joy O. Duke, and Myeonghwan Kim. 2000. "Sexual Abuse of Older Adults: Preliminary Findings of Cases in Virginia." *Journal of Elder Abuse & Neglect* 12(3/4):1–16.

Tyiska, C. 1998. *Working with Victims of Crime with Disabilities.* Washington, DC: Office for Victims of Crime, U.S. Department of Justice.

Wilson, James Q. 1997. "What to Do about Crime?" Pp. 14–24 in *Criminal Justice 97/98*, 21st ed., John J. Sullivan and Joseph L. Victor (eds.). Guilford, CT: Dushkin/McGraw-Hill.

Yeschke, Charles L. 1997. *The Art of Investigative Interviewing.* Boston, MA: Butterworth-Heinemann.

Zahn, M. 1991. "Wolfgang Model: Lessons for Homicide Research in the 1990's." *Journal of Crime and Justice* 14(2):17–30.

CASES

Idaho v. Wright, 116 Idaho 382, 775 P. 2D. 1224 (1990).
Kentucky v. Stincer, 482 U.S. 730 (1987).
People v. Buckey (1984).

STATUTE

Massachusetts General Laws ch. 233, § 20.

OTHER AUTHORITY

Americans with Disabilities Act, Vol. 42 U.S.C., 12132.
Lautenberg Gun Ban, H.R. 3610 (September 1996).

CHAPTER 10

LAW ENFORCEMENT RESPONSE

SIMPLY SCENARIO

Arrest Determination

Julie has been living with her lesbian partner Diane for over four years. While they both resist stereotyping of lesbian characteristics, it just so happened that Julie was the "butch" looking of the couple. Diane was petite and both dressed and acted feminine. Over time the violence in their relationship escalated. Diane begin to terrorize Julie; she killed the family cat; and she beat Julie frequently. During a particularly bad fight Julie was so frightened that she pushed Diane, who fell down the stairs. Diane called the police.

Question: Who is the dominant aggressor?

KEY TERMS

Assault
Consent search
Exigent circumstances
Mandatory arrest
Neglect
Plain-view seizure
Preferred arrest

Primary or dominant aggressor
Probable cause
Rape
Search incident to a lawful arrest
Stalking
State action doctrine

INTRODUCTION

The two emotions most readily transmitted from person to person are fear and anger. Both are present in abundance at the scene of a domestic disturbance and they will descend upon you like a demon as soon as you walk through the door. You should know ahead of time that you would feel both of these emotions profoundly. You must be ready to deal with them: "Eat your emotions" and continue to investigate calmly, systematically, and fairly (Gosselin, 2004).

Obviously missing from discussions on policing domestic violence is the fact that responding officers often feel bad when handling the call. That emotion begins when the peace officer is first dispatched. Fear and anger are present at the scene and are transmitted immediately, heightening the automatic response of the officer. Allegations of severe child abuse may invoke disbelief and often outrage. Many law enforcement officials are parents themselves. It is difficult to see children severely harmed or killed and not be affected. Determining the appropriate response requires the realization that unchecked emotions can direct behavior. Anticipating internal reactions to domestic abuse and the necessity of dealing with them will allow for fair and impartial police action.

Mike's story (see the accompanying box) illustrates the frustration officers frequently experience when they confront a complicated domestic situation. The available options include arresting or summonsing the perpetrator when a clear legal violation occurs. The case can be referred to other services if a formal arrangement has been established with local resources for occasions when a crime has not been committed. An emergency restraining order is an option in cases where the victim requires additional protections. Some states mandate that the officers stay on the scene until they are confident that the victim is safe. Information from the victim along with the analysis of the situation will help the police to make the judgment.

It is not that officers are afraid to respond to intimate disputes, and certainly no two calls are alike. Police routinely respond to life-threatening situations, and it is naive to believe that they do so without emotion. An inordinate fear, however, may be based on the mistaken belief that domestic disputes constitute the most hazardous of calls for assistance. For years, police and the public believed that intimate violence was unusually dangerous. The notion was based on statistics from the FBI showing frequent deaths for officers engaged in disturbance response. When these calls were removed statistically from other altercations, that representation was modified. It is generally accepted that the calls for domestic violence are no more lethal than other police action. To improve the inherent dangerousness of these calls, model police department initiatives work to provide higher levels of safety for both the officers and the victims. A promising approach is evidenced through the identification of high-risk cases and the tracking of repeat offenders (Littel et al., 1998).

More About It: Mike's Story

It was Christmas Eve, and I was filling in for the regular cops as a reserve officer. A woman called the station saying that she wanted her husband out of the house. I responded without out a clue about what was going on. She let me in the house and pointed to the living room, saying, "There he is: get him out of here; I can't stand him anymore." He was drunk, really drunk, sitting in a chair watching television, and he didn't even acknowledge that I was there. His nose was bleeding and the rag that he held to it was soaked with blood. "You hit him," I told the woman, "don't you know that I should arrest you?" "Get him out of here," she kept saying adding, "You won't arrest me—who will take care of our daughter!" Their 12-year-old was hooked up to all kinds of blood and tubes in an upstairs bedroom. I felt sick. What was I supposed to do? Arrest her, call an ambulance for the child, and then what about the husband? He wasn't doing anything wrong, but I didn't think he could take care of himself. Maybe I could put him in protective custody. All this on Christmas Eve! I'll never forget that night, and I still don't know if I did the right thing. No matter who I ask, the answer is always different. Soon after that, I quit the force. I don't need that kind of stuff—it just isn't for me.

TRAINING

Academies that do offer domestic violence training will frequently provide a four- to eight-hour block of time for instruction. Experts know that training is an important part of the proper implementation of domestic violence law and policy. Some state law enforcement training academies and police agencies now offer increased training and specific polices for identifying predominant aggressor training (Crager et al., 2003). Examples include the California Commission on Peace Officer Standards, the San Diego Police Department, the Washington State Criminal Justice Training Academy, and the Colorado Springs Police Department. State police academies in Delaware, Maryland, Louisiana, Tennessee, and Texas also provide specific training on the identification of a predominant domestic aggressor. Specific programs developed by law enforcement for police officers have netted some interesting results when coupled with additional training. Training for law enforcement and prosecution is the focus of nearly a quarter of the projects funded by STOP Formula Grants to Combat Violence Against Women: The Violence Against Women Act of 1994 (Burt et al., 2000). In telephone surveys and site visits on the effectiveness of the supported training, respondents indicate that victims are safer, better supported by their communities, and treated more uniformly and sensitively by first-response workers.

The Seattle Washington Police Department created a specialized domestic violence unit that provides a variety of services to victims for maximum safety as well as holding offenders accountable (Crager, Cousin, & Hardy, 2003). With each case that

---

Been There . . . Done That!

A former student dropped by my office to say hello. He was halfway through the police academy and was proud that he had been selected to tutor other recruits who were having difficulty with the academic portion of the training. Of course, I asked how much time was being dedicated to domestic disputes, since it will ultimately be the most frequent call for the graduates. Four hours, he responded, adding that the instructor tried to cram into that time frame what he had been exposed to during a semester course as my student. The academy class was told that the law requires an arrest for violation of protection orders and that it was preferred that they arrest for all disputes. Failure to make an arrest leaves the officer personally liable. Drill instructors repeatedly shouted, "What do we do at a domestic disturbance?" "We arrest everyone and let the courts sort it out," was the expected reply. They are teaching police recruits to arrest victims, I thought in horror. Why is this still happening?

---

officers respond to, they investigate as though the victim will not be available to testify at trial. To do this the patrol officers participate in specialized domestic evidence collection training on an ongoing basis. The training includes victim case studies from actual incidents responses and the specific responsibilities they have in making domestic violence arrests, treating the cases like stranger **assault**. Training includes mandatory arrest and primary aggressor decision making and detailed cased preparation. Additionally, a lethality or dangerousness assessment tool is used to identify the victims who are at the greatest risk but have not received the level of attention warranted.

Successful policing of intimate violence boils down to the requirement for enhanced personal skills broad enough to meet the contemporary paradigm shift. Police Chief Shanahan sees a need for these changes in law enforcement while urging for service delivery in a professional and competent manner (Shanahan, 1998). Moving toward that goal, training for officers has taken a new turn. Member/citizen interaction training, affectionately referred to as charm school, attempts to enlighten those with a John Wayne or Napoleonic syndrome. At least four states have such programs. Developed by the New York State Police, Massachusetts, New Hampshire, and Illinois have programs modeled after the original (Trapasso, 1998). After citizens have complained about an officer's conduct, he or she is scheduled for the 40-hour interpersonal skills training. To keep it a positive experience for the officers, only those identified for the education and the immediate supervisor is notified. Officers are assigned out on paper to other training and simply disappear to a campus setting where they attend in plain clothes. Evaluation has not yet been conducted to measure the relative success of this program.

CRIMINAL JUSTICE AMBIVALENCE

A lack of consensus on how police should respond to domestic violence in the civilian population is mirrored within the criminal justice community. Historically, police intervention has been unpredictable, criminal prosecutions rare, and victims reluctant to report to the police. Victims and their advocates charged police with failure to protect women against domestic abuses. The criminal justice community was charged with failure to respond equally to women alleging violence, researchers documented the struggle, and civil battles began in an attempt to force the system into action. The courts were accused of failing to follow through with prosecuting charges of battering. Stories of failed attempts at justice were made public; women and children were being severely injured and killed.

The police responded vehemently, blaming victims for not following through in signing complaints. Statutes that forbade officers from making an arrest for a misdemeanor not committed in their presence were offered as proof that those legal hands were tied. Legal precedent discouraged and often forbade them from entering a person's home to effect an arrest without a warrant. Further, many officers believed that arresting the perpetrator would cause more harm to the victim than good. As if that were not enough, occupational images of policing involved prosecution, and that was not occurring for the majority of domestic cases.

All sides have been openly frustrated and dissatisfied since the feminist movement opened the wounds in the 1970s. Close examination reveals that each position holds a kernel of truth. If the criminal justice community remains indecisive in its domestic violence response, a fair argument would suggest that society is also. The truth is, we just don't know yet what works best. The most telling information suggests that results are better when domestic violence is recognized as a community problem, not just a police problem. Higher arrest rates have been documented when police are part of a coordinated community response (Sampson & Scott, 1999).

THE SYSTEMS APPROACH

Why is vigorous prosecution an issue for police? Officers view themselves as an essential part of a larger group, the criminal justice system. They expect to have an impact on the other components. Therefore, even if officers are actively pursuing a **preferred arrest** policy but see that the district attorney is not prosecuting the offenders they have arrested, they are likely to stop making arrests. At the time when mandatory and pro-arrest policies were first implemented, prosecution of domestic violence was rare. Most cases resulted in a dismissal because victims were unwilling to cooperate with prosecution (Peterson, 2003). Although prosecutors routinely signed complaints for most crimes, many domestic violence victims were required to sign their own. Communities interested in the full enforcement of preferred and mandatory provisions cannot ignore the other branches of the criminal system.

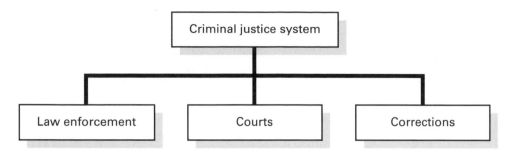

Figure 10-1   Branches of the criminal justice system.

The Courts

As the changes in police practices took hold, they were paralleled by prosecution policy changes. The movement to assure that all legally sufficient domestic cases would be prosecuted whether or not the victims were fully cooperative meant dropping the requirement that victims sign a complaint. Victim witness advocates and community volunteers are now more involved in assisting victims in filing the difficult paperwork required for a protection order. It is not uncommon for the request form to consist of five pages. With this assistance it is hoped that the victims of domestic abuse will more consistently follow through with their complaints.

Since a large number of cases resulted in dismissal, advocates pressed for criminal prosecution similar to that of other crimes. What resulted was the establishment of no-drop and evidence-based prosecution policies. This meant that prosecution would proceed regardless of the victim's participation whenever sufficient evidence exists that a crime was committed. These two distinct approaches to victimless prosecution are not mutually exclusive. Under the no-drop approach the prosecutors encourage the victim to cooperate and provide services such as counseling, housing assistance, and safety planning that will improve the situation for the victim should the case not proceed. Meanwhile attempts at gathering evidence in order to prosecute without the victim continue. The evidence-based prosecution approach assumes that the victim will not be available, and the practices include the use of "excited utterances" from 911 tapes, police testimony, medical reports, and physical evidence to build a case without the testimony of the victim. Decisions to go forward with a prosecution despite victim preference are based on the premise that victims are not failing to cooperate, just trying to stay alive. Three reasons exist for no-drop policies (Davis & Smith, 1995):

1. Such policies it remove responsibility for prosecution from victims, which makes them less likely to be targeted for intimidation attempts by batterers.
2. The state has an obligation to prosecute those who violate the law regardless of victims' wishes; to do otherwise sends the wrong message to batterers (i.e., that it is acceptable to break the law).

3. The state has a compelling interest in prosecuting potentially dangerous domestic violence defendants in the interest of public safety, just as the state has an interest in prosecuting dangerous robbers, rapists, and others who may offend.

The collection of statements and physical evidence by law enforcement will have a large impact on whether the case will result in a successful prosecution. The measure is not without its critics, however. Advocates claim that battered women are being revictimized by a system that will not be satisfied with their decisions to remain in the violent relationship. Rare attempts have been made at evaluating these presumptive prosecution policies. One study looked to determine if presumptive policies actually increase the rate of successful prosecution and conviction (Davis et al., 2001). The authors concluded that a drastic reduction in the numbers of domestic violence cases that are dismissed might be achieved through presumptive prosecution policies. They cautioned that further study was needed on the effect of the policies on victim safety and their willingness to call the police in the future. The Davis study (2001) found:

- Dismissals in one court dropped from 79 percent to 26 percent; the second court location evidenced a change from 47 percent of dismissals to 14 percent after the new policy was implemented.
- In both locations the numbers of cases that resulted in trials increased from 1 percent to over 10 percent.
- Court processing time declined by 36 percent in one court.

In another study the victim impact and the effectiveness were considered. The Smith study (2001) discovered that no-drop is not a strict policy since every domestic violence case filed was not prosecuted. Cases with prior records of the abuse were more likely to be pursued as were cases where evidence was available. Conviction rates were significantly increased from the use of the more aggressive approach, but the success depended highly on the willingness of the judges to admit hearsay (excited utterances). An important finding was that victims saw the court action as beneficial, even those who had not initially wanted any criminal justice action other than arrest.

The American Bar Association Commission on Legal Problems of the Elderly has looked at the trends in elder abuse cases in the courts and made recommendations on how to handle these cases more effectively. In its recently adopted policy, the American Bar Association (2002) urged implementation at the federal, state, territorial, and local levels of the following actions to protect elderly victims of abuse and neglect: (1) Create a nationwide structure for raising public awareness on elder abuse; (2) implement specialized training about elder abuse for all components of the justice system; (3) establish federal leadership to ensure that adult protective services and legal and other services are of sufficient quality to protect and serve victims of elder abuse; (4) create broad-based, multidisciplinary task forces or coalitions in each state to examine and develop systemic approaches to elder abuse interventions; (5) develop, fund, and implement a multidisciplinary research agenda to sustain, advance, and assess professional training and practice on elder abuse; (6) maximize and expand resources for preventing and responding to elder abuse; (7) develop adequate tools and services to enable capacity assessments and surrogate decisionmaking for victims of elder abuse; and (8) ensure that legal and other services are available to meet the immediate and crisis needs of elderly victims.

Corrections

The most common sanction for convicted batterers is mandatory treatment programs. This alternative to prison is an adequate option for domestic offenders without lengthy abuse histories, since the majority of assaults constitute a misdemeanor. Its acceptance is due to the overall goal in domestic disputes: prevention. The counseling programs that have emerged typically involve group sessions that combine anger control, stress management, and communication skills. Behavior modification and increased awareness are the goals for effective batterers programs. Recent research confirms that monitoring and treatment are appropriate sentences for domestic violence offenders since it is no less effective at deterring rearrest as jail sentences (Peterson, 2003). Current practices of jailing repeat offenders appear to be an appropriate response according to the Peterson research.

Effective in January 1997, California became the first state to require chemical castration for repeat molesters. After the second offense, molesters receive weekly injections of the drug Depo-Provera, which dampens sexual desire. Offenders could choose to be surgically castrated instead, under the law.

The Drug-Induced Rape Prevention and Punishment Act of 1996 imposes a prison sentence of up to 20 years for anyone intending to commit sexual assault by distributing illicit drugs to another person without his or her consent with the intention of committing a sexual assault. The law also requires the U.S. Drug Enforcement Administration to consider reclassifying at least one of the "date rape drugs" to provide for closer control and instructs the U.S. Attorney General to create educational materials for law enforcement.

Law Enforcement

The systems approach is illustrated through the combination of procedures and technologies to combat domestic violence. The domestic violence protocol for officers of Santa Clara County (2002) requires that the crime scene of a domestic violence incident be documented, by photograph if applicable. A check with the Automated Firearms System (AFS) and the Prohibited Armed Persons (PAP) file is conducted to determine if any involved person is prohibited from owning firearms or has registered firearms. Injuries and prior incidents to the victim or against children or pets are documented.

Preferred and Mandatory Arrest Policies.   Regardless of the debates from experts on the best course of action, the mandate to police officers is clear. Take domestic assaults seriously; treat them criminally. As most states have adopted preferred and mandated arrest policies, officer discretion is limited. Several different terms are used to express the approach of preferred arrest. Mandatory arrest laws for at least some assault and battery domestic violence cases exist in 23 states as of January 2002 (Hirschel & Buzawa, 2002).

The conditions under which departments apply the policy vary greatly. Look closely at the domestic violence statute in your state and determine how police must respond. In New York, the preference for arrest is stated in Criminal Procedure Law. Enacted in 1994, as part of the Family Protection and Domestic Violence Intervention Act, the mandatory arrest provision for New York established statutory requirements for a mandatory arrest in family offense cases under certain circumstances. Under the law, a police officer should arrest a person and should not attempt to reconcile the parties or mediate where the officer has reasonable cause to believe that

- a felony other than certain grand larceny crimes has been committed by one family or household member against the other; or
- there is a violation of the "stay away" provisions of a duly served order of protection; or
- a family offense is committed in violation of an order of protection; or
- a misdemeanor constituting a family offense is committed against another family or household member.

With respect to the misdemeanor constituting a family offense, an arrest shall be made unless the victim requests otherwise. However, the officer shall not ask the victim whether the victim seeks arrest of the assailant.

Primary Aggressor Provisions.   Arrest rates for intimate violence have increased dramatically since the preferred and **mandatory arrest** polices have been implemented. One of the unexpected consequences has been an increase in the cases in which both parties are arrested. Both the courts and the legislature discourage the practice of making mutual arrests since it fails to protect and further victimizes the individual who is not the batterer. Same-sex relationships are particularly vulnerable to dual arrests because the police may have difficulty in determining the **primary aggressor** due to the similarity in strength.

In response to increasing numbers of dual arrest in the domestic violence incidents, states began to pass "primary aggressor," "predominant aggressor," or

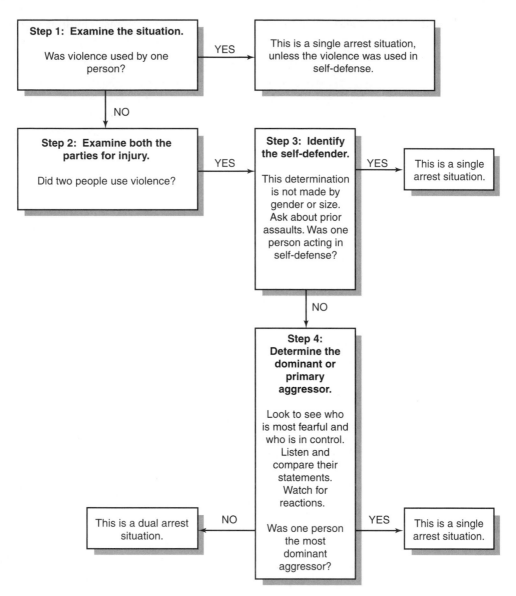

Figure 10–2   Making the dominant or primary aggressor determination.

"dominant aggressor" provisions. Currently 24 states have laws that contain a special aggressor designation (Hirschel & Buzawa, 2002). These laws offer guidance to law enforcement in making the determination on who is the victim and who is the offender, using standards other than gender or size of the individuals involved.

In situations that appear to be mutual combative, the officer can look for three elements of self-defense that may be helpful in the determination.

- The person using force had a reason to believe that he or she was at risk of bodily harm. The risk is reasonable if based on prior incidents, where a recent escalation in violence has occurred, a specific threat was made to the self-defender that caused the defense posture.

- The risk of harm was actual or imminent.

- The force used was that force reasonably necessary to prevent or stop the infliction of bodily harm. For example, a person small in stature may use a weapon to prevent the abuser from inflicting bodily harm.

Additional considerations to consider when determining who the primary aggressor is involves asking, Who in this relationship poses the most danger to the other? Who is at most risk of future harm?

HOW DO POLICE GET INVOLVED?

The ways in which the police are notified for domestic violence are as varied as the forms of violence. The three principal methods are citizen complaint, mandated report, and officer initiated.

The Citizen Complaint

The majority of calls for service are domestic dispute calls resulting from citizen complaints. These reports of domestic violence are crisis situations where the violence is still likely to be occurring. Most reports will be from telephone calls. The caller may be angry, confused, or injured at the time due to abuse. It may be a child who is frantic because a parent is being beaten up in the next room. It may also be a neighbor or someone else who is fearful of the noises from a fight next door. The dispatcher or desk officer should gather as much information as possible in order to prepare the officers who are responding. If possible, the caller should be kept on the phone until help arrives, in order to update any information on what is occurring.

Part of the reason for the fear that was discussed at the beginning of the chapter was fear of the unknown. Traditionally, officers were dispatched to domestic calls without having enough information to be prepared for what they were responding to. Knowledge is power, and in this case, knowledge of the situation can prevent anxiety and result in a better response. The following are the basic questions asked by the person taking the report and dispatching it to the officers. If the abuse is occurring at the time, any change in the level of violence is important to convey.

- Who is the caller?
- What is caller's telephone number?
- What is the location of the abuse?
- Is anyone hurt?

- Are any weapons involved (guns, knives, clubs, sticks, etc.)?
- Are there guns in the house?
- Who are the parties involved?
- What is happening?
- Is either party drunk or high on drugs?
- Is there a restraining order of protection in effect?
- Are there children in the house?

At the Scene.   Offering aid to the victim and disarming an assailant are the priorities for officers who first arrive. The officer must be aware constantly; the violence does not necessarily stop when they arrive. They must look and listen. The level of anger is likely to remain high after the officer intervenes and separates the people involved.

How the injured actually get to the hospital is dictated by police department policy. For some jurisdictions, the police and the emergency medical transportation are one and the same. In others, officers are required to transport victims to the nearest hospital in their cruiser. Some departments are forbidden by policy from transporting victims, and they would call for an ambulance. The major reason behind calling for an ambulance is that officers may not be able to render lifesaving care to a victim during transportation.

When it is safe to do so and after the victim has received emergency medical attention if needed, the officer will investigate to determine who is the perpetrator and who is the victim. This is sometimes the most difficult part of the effort to resolve any domestic dispute. Spouses and cohabiting adults talk to police the most during a dispute—that usually changes after the anger has subsided.

The next step is to assess the level of risk for injury to the victim. Questions for cohabiting couples and for dating relationships should be specific. Many states require officers to request initially that a firearm or weapon be placed temporarily in their custody. Without compliance, the officers may have the right to search for and take custody of a firearm or weapon to alleviate the threat of serious violence that it poses. The weapon might be returned after a check to determine that it is lawfully possessed. Unless the officer is required by law to return the weapon immediately, it is within his or her discretion to make the return at a later date. If the weapons cannot be seized legally, a judge may order the defendant to surrender guns, his or her license to carry, and/or his or her firearm identification (FID) card during the pending of an order or criminal prosecution.

There is no exemption for police batterers for retaining a weapon, even if they would ordinarily use the weapon in the course of their employment. Many departments have developed a policy to seize department weapons upon an allegation of abuse or a civil restraining order being issued. Anyone convicted of a domestic violence offense loses the right to carry a gun for any reason, including employment. A domestic violence conviction is an automatic disqualifier for the job as a police officer in New York; other states are following the trend.

The final step is to collect the evidence.

The Mandated Report

Police are required to file a report to the state-designated agency when they suspect abuse or neglect of elders and children. Additionally, they receive these reports to investigate after an initial substantiation. What does that mean for the police?

Reporting Requirements

1. Officers must be familiar with the conditions that require a mandated report in their jurisdiction. The circumstances under which a report is required vary from state to state. Severe abuse or neglect is usually the standard, and a suspicion—not proof—is required. Learning that a child or elder is living in a violent home is one condition that may lead to a report. If it appears that the caretaker(s) are impaired through drugs or alcohol and unable to care for dependents in the home, a reportable condition may exist. Death or severe injury due to abuse or neglect must be reported. Additional conditions that might require a report of elder abuse would be indications of coercion, intimidation, abandonment, and/or financial exploitation.

2. Police need to know where to file the report. Frequently, an initial report will go to the state's child or elder protection agency. Sometimes the district attorney's office will screen the reports for criminal violations.

3. There may be a penalty for a failure to report. The penalty itself is usually not substantial—a fine, for example—and is rarely imposed. More important, it sets up a duty to the officers. Failure to perform an expressed duty would leave the officer open to civil action. Liability is most likely to exist if a child or elder is severely harmed or killed subsequent to police knowledge of conditions ripe for abuse.

Receiving the Report.   As you can see from the sample report of abuse and neglect, the information supplied would assist in planning the investigation. Similarities exist between the elder and the child report.

1. The age and gender of the victim is helpful to determine who should conduct the interview.

2. It seems simple, but addresses for parents and guardians are not always the same addresses as those of the children. The report provides a quick and hopefully accurate way to get hold of all interested people who might have information.

3. The original reporter should be contacted to supply further facts. Rarely will a reporter put everything down on paper.

Where the interview takes place is as important as who asks the questions. To facilitate information, the setting must be safe for the victim. That means first that the perpetrator should not be anywhere around. It is unwise to question a child victim at

REPORT OF CHILD(REN) ALLEGED TO BE SUFFERING FROM SERIOUS PHYSICAL OR EMOTIONAL INJURY BY ABUSE OR NEGLECT

Massachusetts law requires an individual who is a mandated reporter to immediately report any allegation of serious physical or emotional injury resulting from abuse or neglect to the Department of Social Services by oral communication. This written report must then be completed **within 48 hours** of making the oral report and should be sent to the appropriate Department office.

Please complete all section of this form. If some data is unknown, please signify. If some data is uncertain, place a question mark after the entry.

DATA ON CHILDREN REPORTED

AGE OR

	NAME	CURRENT LOCATION/ADDRESS	SEX	DATE OF BIRTH
1)			Male / Female	
2)			Male / Female	
3)			Male / Female	
4)			Male / Female	

DATA ON MALE GUARDIAN OR PARENT

Name: _____
First   Last   Middle

Address: _____
Street and Number   City/Town State

Telephone Number: _____   Age: _____

DATA ON FEMALE GUARDIAN OR PARENT

Name: _____
First   Last   Middle

Address: _____
Street and Number   City/Town State

Telephone Number: _____   Age: _____

DATA ON REPORTER/REPORT:

_____   **Mandatory Report**   **Voluntary Report**
Date of Report

Reporter's Name: First   Last

Reporter's address: (If the reporter represents an institution, school, or facility please indicate.)

_____   _____
Street   City/Town

_____   _____
State   zip Code   Telephone Number

Has reporter informed caretaker   YES   NO
ABUSE/NEGLECT REPORT - 3

(Revised April, 1983)

Figure 10–3   Sample form for reporting abuse or neglect of children.

COMMONWEALTH OF MASSACHUSETTS - DEPARTMENT OF SOCIAL SERVICES   PAGE 2
REPORT OF CHILD(REN) ALLEGED TO BE SUFFERING FROM SERIOUS
PHYSICAL OR EMOTIONAL INJURY BY ABUSE OR NEGLECT

What is the nature and extent of the injury, abuse, maltreatment or neglect, including prior evidence of same? (Please cite the source of this information if not observed first hand.)

What are the circumstances under which the reporter became aware of the injuries, abuse, maltreatment or neglect?

What action has been taken thus far to treat, shelter or otherwise assist the child to deal with this situation?

Please give other information that you think might be helpful in establishing the cause of the injury and/or the person responsible for it. If known, please provide the name(s) of the alleged perpetrator(s).

                                                            Signature of Reporter

Figure 10–3 (cont'd)

his or her school. Even though it may be a safe place, the child will be affected in some way by the authorities speaking with him or her. Since these investigations allow for time to plan, the place where the statement is taken can be determined in advance.

The Officer-Initiated Investigation

Police can investigate a crime simultaneously with filing a report of abuse or neglect. It is not unusual for a disturbance call to involve a subsequent inquiry into abuse or neglect of a child or elder. Information may come directly to the officer through concerned people in the community or even from public appearances and during community policing efforts.

TO ARREST OR NOT TO ARREST: THAT IS THE QUESTION

Objectionable behavior does not necessarily constitute criminal conduct. Even when it does, police don't always have the power to arrest. When the power of arrest is available, they may use discretion in exercising that option. Although some accuse police officers of underenforcing the laws against domestic assault, research has shown that police have low arrest rates for nondomestic assaults as well (Feder, 1998).

How do police officers make the decision to arrest? Here are three questions that police officers consider when making the decision.

1. Does the action constitute a crime?
2. Does the officer have the power of arrest for that crime?
3. What are the alternatives?

Crimes

The following factors are taken into consideration when making the decision to arrest:

- If the violence constitutes a felony, the officer may make a warrantless arrest wherever he or she has the legal right to be present.
- A misdemeanor crime committed in the presence of an officer typically carries the power of arrest. Some misdemeanor crimes are specifically written with an authorization for an arrest. Statutes vary widely on arrest procedures for domestic violence.

Questions to consider: Does the violent act fall within the definition of a felony or a misdemeanor? Does the offense constitute a crime that carries with it the power of arrest? Is there a preferred or mandated response that would limit the discretion at the

---

Been There . . . Done That!

It is not unusual for police to make public appearances in schools to talk about good touch and bad touch. After one of these guest lectures, a teenager in the group told a friend that her stepfather was abusing her sexually. He had taken a picture of her naked when he raped her, saying that he would show it if she ever told anyone. No one would believe that she had not been willing to have sex with him, he had told her. So she had put a tape recorder under her bed one day to prove what was happening. The friend called me with that information.

I went to the victim's house when I knew her stepfather would be at work. She came to the door, and I quietly asked if she needed help. The fear in her eyes was readily apparent as she nodded. Is there a picture, a tape? Saying nothing, she again nodded, as she looked nervously into the house behind her. "I will be back," I told her.

It did not take long to prepare the affidavit for the search warrant. Armed with the warrant, three officers and I returned to the house. A lengthy search resulted in the photo—it was hidden in the garage inside a box intended for a car air filter. The audiotape was handed over as well. A social worker waited in a car outside the house until the police were finished; then she took custody of the crying teen. The stepfather came home from work and was promptly arrested for rape of a child. Additional charges were brought after an extended interview with the victim.

---

scene? In other words, officers need to know what must be done and then what can be done, in response to the violence encountered in their jurisdiction.

Assaults.   The term *domestic assault* is used to describe behavior that ranges from shoving to stabbing, from threatening to punching. Its verbal overuse in this context minimizes the seriousness of the charge. States that have codified their laws classify the assault as simple or as aggravated:

> *Simple assault:* Intentionally causing another person to fear immediate bodily harm or death or intentionally inflicting or attempting to inflict bodily harm on the person. It is usually a misdemeanor crime due to minor injury, if any.

Example: You want to go out of the house to visit friends, but your lover grabs your hair and pulls you away from the door, closing it and preventing you from leaving.

> *Aggravated (felonious) assault:* An unlawful attack by one person on another to inflict severe bodily injury. It might also be classified as assault with a dangerous weapon or assault with intent to commit murder.

Example: You fight to get the door open, and your lover pulls a knife and cuts you.

Figure 10-4   Police have the power to arrest for both misdemeanors and felonies committed in their presence. *(Photo courtesy of Mark C. Ide.)*

For other states that follow common law, there are numerous charges, each specific to a form of violence that could occur in a domestic relationship.

Assault: Any willful attempt or threat to inflict injury when coupled with an apparent present ability to do so, or any intentional display of force that would give the victim reason to fear or expect immediate bodily harm. Under this definition, an assault may be committed without actually touching, striking, or doing bodily harm to the person.

Example: Your spouse shakes his or her fist in anger while threatening to hit you. Next she or he moves in your direction as if to hit you, even if no subsequent battery (hitting) occurs. The victim must believe that the intent was to cause injury. Past experience is a good predictor.

Assault and battery: Any unlawful touching of another without justification or excuse. The battery requires a physical contact of some sort, injury or offensive touching.

Example: You slap or kick a family member, for any reason.

Assault with a dangerous or deadly weapon: An unlawful attempt or offer to do bodily harm without justification or excuse by use of any instrument calculated to do harm or cause death.

Example: You point a gun at someone and threaten to shoot him or her.

*Assault with intent to commit **rape:*** A crime of an assault, coupled with an intention to commit the crime of rape. It is the actions that lead up to a rape that does not occur. Lack of consent and force are an issue.

Example: Your date pushes you to the ground and pins your arms while unzipping his fly and ripping off your dress. You fight him off and get away.

Rape.   Sexual intercourse without consent is rape. It can be described as any intrusion into any orifice for sexual gratification. Some states include digital, oral, and anal intrusions (no matter how slight) in this definition. The use of force demonstrates a lack of consent. If there are no physical injuries, the victim must be able to demonstrate that consent was not granted. Recounting the words spoken by the perpetrator or the circumstances under which the rape occurred is one way to show lack of consent. The victim must have in some way articulated the lack of consent. Fear from threats or age (under the age of consent) may satisfy the legal requirement. All states recognize that rape can occur within a marital relationship. Victims of date rape can be adults or adolescents. Forced intercourse in lesbian and homosexual relationships can also reach the legal level of rape.

Example: Your elderly neighbor says she does not like to be alone when her son visits. Over time she confides that he puts his fingers inside her vagina, and that it hurts. You know that she suffers from dementia and lacks the ability to consent.

Stalking.   Any person who willfully, maliciously, and repeatedly follows or harasses another person and makes a credible threat with the intent to place that person in reasonable fear of death or bodily injury commits the offense of **stalking**.

Example: You receive hang-up calls each night at different intervals designed to prevent sleep. They began soon after your divorce. Getting out of work, you find a flat tire; this happens more than once. During the day, he calls and threatens you if you do not meet with him.

Review copies of the state's penal code to understand crimes explicitly intended to address domestic violence offenses. These crimes represent only a portion that may be applied in any given jurisdiction. If the call involves an elder or a child, specific legislation may offer protection in addition to the criminal codes with which the officers are more familiar. The use of protective custody may be helpful when misconduct fails to reach the level of a crime.

Domestic violence is a general term that includes a variety of offenses; think of it as many different crimes that occur within legally recognized relationships. Relationships do not change the duty of the officer to enforce the law and to arrest offenders. All pertinent criminal codes should be considered in determining the appropriate

Figure 10–5 When domestic violence occurs, and the abuser flees, he can typically be arrested on "probable cause." Additional arrest powers may come from your state's civil restraining order laws.

police response and subsequent criminal charges, in addition to offenses specific to domestic violence. Dual arrests are discouraged by most jurisdictions. Police should attempt to identify the primary aggressor, to avoid arresting both parties. Mailing a summons to domestic violence offenders who leave the scene is a feasible alternative to an arrest (Sherman et al., 1998).

Civil Protection Codes

Violation of a civil restraining order or no-contact order is an additional criminal offense apart from ongoing abuse. Usually, it is a misdemeanor, with the power of arrest given by statute. Since the violation is a separate crime, it should be considered in addition to any other criminal violations, not in lieu of them.

Mutual restraining orders exist when both parties involved in a domestic dispute have applied successfully for an order of protection against the other. The VAWA strongly discourages this practice since such restraining orders are not recognized as enforceable outside the jurisdiction in which they were filed. Law enforcement officers should not encourage application for cross complaints. The practice is considered dangerous to the one who has been victimized. State statutes may expressly forbid issuance of mutual restraining orders except in rare and extreme instances.

Mental Health Codes

In some instances it may be necessary to remove suspects and to hold them involuntarily for evaluation at a mental health facility. Emergency procedures for overnight commitment are specific to each state, with particular amounts of time allowed before a court hearing. Officers should become familiar with state mental health provisions for involuntary commitments and evaluations.

Use of Available Resources

In addition to any legal requirements that might exist for reporting abuse to another agency, response to domestic violence can be simplified by utilizing local and state resources whenever possible. Networking and developing the sources for extralegal intervention are beneficial to both the victim and the officers. If the crime involves an elderly victim, contact the local elder services or adult protection services for assistance and future follow-up. If an arrest is anticipated in a home where children would be left unattended, contact the local department of social services or child protection agency and request that they take custody. Victim witness programs exist in every state and are helpful in advising domestic violence victims of their rights and of procedures to obtain civil restraining orders. Local crisis centers are valuable in offering emergency shelter for the victim. Referrals of battered women to other agencies have been used as an avoidance tactic. That is not the suggestion here. A coordinated system approach to domestic violence response includes utilizing alternative services in addition to traditional policing.

WHAT ABOUT PROBABLE CAUSE?

Probable cause is a standard of proof that must be satisfied for any search or seizure to occur. An arrest is legally defined as a seizure and therefore falls under the same requirement for probable cause as a search. The requirement is stated in the Fourth Amendment of the U.S. Constitution and in state constitutions: "The Right of the People To Be Secure in Their Person, Houses, Papers and Effects Against Unreasonable Searches and Seizures Shall not Be Violated . . . and no warrant shall issue except for probable cause."

An officer has the task of determining if probable cause exists to believe that a crime has been committed and that an arrest is warranted. Sources for determining probable cause include

- Collective knowledge doctrine
- Knowledge about the suspect
- Suspect's behavior to police
- Reliable hearsay
- Observations of the police

The U.S. Supreme Court clearly stated the probable cause requirement in *Gerstein v. Pugh* (1975), while referring to past instances of definition: "Probable cause to arrest exists when the facts and circumstances known to the officer are sufficient to warrant a reasonably prudent person in believing that the suspect has committed or is committing a crime" (*Beck v. Ohio*, 1964). The standard is universal; both federal and state laws require meeting this level of proof to justify depriving persons of their liberty under the Fourth and Fourteenth Amendments to the Constitution. Additional states' constitutional provisions echo the sentiment. Exact requirements for the level of information to rise above mere suspicion without reaching the adjudication standard of proof beyond a reasonable doubt are clarified through both state and federal case law and legislation. "Probable cause to arrest [in Massachusetts] must exist at the moment of arrest. Facts and circumstances, which come to an officer's attention after a person has been taken into custody, may not be used retroactively to justify the arrest. However, an officer need not make the arrest as soon as probable cause arises. Unlike probable cause to search, which is of limited duration, once probable cause to arrest is formed, it will continue to exist for an indefinite period, at least if no intervening exculpatory facts come to light" (Commonwealth of Massachusetts, 1996).

A difficulty in determining probable cause in cases of domestic disputes has led some jurisdictions to conclude that the standard is met by a mere accusation of assault, regardless of any supporting evidence. Thus, when both parties accuse the other of abuse, a dual arrest is the only available option for the police. The dual arrest occurs when both parties are taken into custody. The courts have voiced a preference that police not make dual arrests in disputes, yet they may be appropriate in some circumstances.

COLLECTION OF EVIDENCE

The probable cause requirement attaches to searches as well as seizures conducted by government officials. Strict adherence to federal and state constitutional guidelines is imperative to obtain evidence that will withstand the scrutiny of the court. Therefore, it is best to conduct a search with a warrant whenever time permits. The use of searching with a valid warrant is beneficial in domestic cases and should be considered to validate the statements of victims. Its use should not be limited to fatal investigations; tangible evidence speaks louder than words.

Search without a warrant is per se unreasonable. Some exceptions to the warrant requirement do exist, however. Places that are not covered by the Fourth Amendment protection that can be searched without a warrant include common areas, entranceways, public places, semipublic places, open fields, and driveways. An open field or driveway that is posted "no trespassing" does not invoke constitutional protection. An officer may commit a trespass and be held separately accountable for that crime but still conduct the search without violating the warrant requirement.

Known as the **state action doctrine**, the Fourth Amendment and relevant state constitutions protect persons only against action by or at the direction of the state or

Figure 10-6 Proper and timely collection of evidence is critical for the successful prosecution of the family violence case. Statements as well as photographs can document the severity of the event—this evidence will diminish over time.

its agents. The Fourth Amendment is a limitation on the activities of government law enforcement officials only and not on private citizens. Constitutional protections have also been extended to control public school officials in the area of search and seizure, but they do not have to obtain a warrant or meet the standard of probable cause in the same way that police must in order to conduct a search. What that means is that police can accept evidence that has been offered by private citizens or agencies, regardless of how it was obtained, as long as the search was not conducted under the direction, encouragement, or instigation of the police. This includes medical evidence obtained during routine medical procedures not requested by police. A court order to produce medical evidence may be required if the evidence is being withheld.

It is permissible to accept drugs (evidence of date rape) from a college roommate who turned them over to school officials. A videotape or audiotape from a victim may provide evidence of child pornography or rape. Tools or instruments used in the commission of a crime, such as rope or tape discovered, or anything offered by a private citizen can be introduced as evidence. Items that have been discarded in a trash can or outside a window of a moving vehicle carry no expectation of privacy and can be seized without a warrant. It is not legally acceptable to circumvent constitutional protections by asking someone to bring evidence, however, by threat, by promise, or by any inducement whatsoever.

Some of the relevant exceptions to the warrant requirement are presented next, but this is not an exhaustive list.

Been There . . . Done That!

The investigation began as domestic but soon turned into allegations of sexual abuse to over a dozen children. The relationship between the perpetrator and some of the victims was incestual and was alleged to include digital rape as well as rape by objects. Due to the nondiscriminatory pattern of boys and girls as victims, I suspected that the man was a pedophile. Children described being given little toys and trinkets that were kept in bedroom drawers. Dolls were frequently used as objects of affection. Putting all the information into an affidavit, I applied successfully for a search warrant. The reward for these efforts was proof beyond a reasonable doubt that the perpetrator was sexually deviant and that children were the objects of his desires. When the evidence was presented at trial, John was committed to a state institution for the sexually dangerous for an indeterminate time, referred to as "a day-to-life" sentence. Should he ever be released, he will serve his sentence of over 40 years. Without the tangible evidence, it would have been the word of the children against his word, a difficult obstacle to overcome.

Exceptions to the Warrant Requirement

The courts specify the conditions under which evidence without a warrant may be collected. Conditions for making an exception are specifically outlined. Attempts to expand their meaning may result in the loss of evidence, according to Lt. Gosselin, a 32-year veteran who put together the following description of exclusions for training police recruits (Gosselin, 2004).

Consent Search. This form of exception is scrutinized more than others and must be used judiciously. Consent must be given freely and voluntarily, not a mere acquiescence to legal authority or intimidation. Although officers may mention the possibility of getting a warrant, they cannot demand, trick, or force cooperation. Consent to enter a home is not equivalent to a search consent, and even if consent is given, it may be revoked at any time. The person providing consent can do so only for areas that are commonly used. People who live together cannot give consent to search in areas that are private and used exclusively by the other person. A person who has a locked or private desk, a separate closet, or a library has an expectation of privacy and must be the one to offer consent for those areas. Since domestic violence usually occurs in a place where there is joint ownership or residence, this distinction is quite important.

Exigent Circumstance and Domestic Violence. Police routinely enter homes for domestic calls and may investigate under this exception to the warrant requirement. This allows for a sweep to be conducted to search for weapons and injured people. It does not authorize a protracted and general search of the entire home.

Been There . . . Done That!

Child protection concerns sparked an investigation by the department of social services. The single mother had had five pregnancies that resulted in two miscarriages, a stillborn, a child born with brittle bone disease, and one healthy male child. Severe neglect was the reason for an ongoing department involvement. The social worker thought that an adult incest relationship between the 25-year-old mother and her biological father had caused the multiple birth problems in what they thought to be the fifth generation of incest. Coincidentally, the father and daughter had been separated shortly after her birth and had not met until she was approximately 20 years old. Child protection services obtained DNA profiling on the mother and her father that indicated that both had parented the two living children. When the test results confirmed their suspicions, the department contacted the state police and turned the DNA reports over to me. Since there was no involvement in the department investigation by any police, the court upheld use of the DNA report in a criminal prosecution against both people. In Massachusetts, both parties are held criminally responsible for incest unless there is an indication of force (rape) or lack of consent, including that of age or incompetence.

Search Incident to a Lawful Arrest.   A person who is legally under arrest may be searched. The body and areas within the immediate control of the arrested person are included. The purpose is to allow an officer to seize weapons, and the search is used for his or her protection. It is not a general search of a house or vehicle where the person is found in order to look for evidence. The scope and intensity of the search are limited.

Plain-View Seizure.   Articles in plain view in public places or where the police have a legitimate right to be present, that are readily apparent as contraband or as the fruits or instrumentality of a crime, can be seized. This is not considered a search, and no warrant is required. To justify the **plain-view seizure**, the officer cannot move items to find identifying serial numbers to confirm that it is in fact contraband. The key point is that the contraband must be readily apparent, such as drugs, instruments of the crime, or weapons. Plain-view observation can occur where no expectation of privacy exists, such as public bathrooms (not stalls), open fields, public airspace, or a private driveway. Enhanced methods to view suspected contraband such as binoculars are acceptable. Techniques to improve hearing cannot be used where persons have a reasonable expectation of privacy, such as telephone lines in some states.

The plain-view doctrine justifies seizure of items that were not anticipated during the course of a search pursuant to a warrant. A search warrant executed for evidence of domestic violence, for example, may lead to the discovery of illegal drugs. The drugs may be seized without application for a new warrant. In some jurisdictions, the seizure must bear a relationship to the crime under investigation, however, or a new warrant is required.

Figure 10–7 Searching the perpetrator can legally take place without a warrant under special circumstances. Examples of recognized exceptions to the requirement for a warrant include the consent search, under exigent circumstances, a search incident to a lawful arrest, and when evidence is in plain view. *(Photo courtesy of Mark C. Ide.)*

What Police Look For

A checklist is helpful to remind the investigator of the responsibilities at the scene. Figure 10–8 is used for training purposes (Commonwealth of Massachusetts, 1995a). It can be adapted and changed to fit the needs and specific responsibilities in any jurisdiction.

Evidence of the crime can be seized whenever possible. This includes, but is not limited to, the following weapons:

1. When the telephone has been used as a dangerous weapon, the responding officers should seize it. Telephones are frequently used as weapons in domestic violence assaults. Sometimes used as blunt instruments, they also provide wire for strangulation attempts.

2. Knives, guns, clubs, or any other article used as a means to inflict harm or threaten the victim should be seized at the time of response.

3. Cords, ropes, or tape that was used to restrict the movements of a victim may be seized.

4. Objects that have been used for penetration of genitalia may be seized. Paper bags, not plastic bags, are the way to store properly items that may contain blood or body secretions.

DOMESTIC VIOLENCE INVESTIGATION CHECKLIST

Victim Information

Name: _____
Noted date of birth
Noted location upon arrival
Administered first aid, noted if
  medical treatment was sought
Noted time dispatched, arrived,
  and when victim spoke
Recorded excited utterances
Described demeanor
Height and weight noted
Described physical condition
Noted complaints of injuries
Described injuries in detail (size,
  location, color)
Noted relationship to suspect
Detailed description of incident
Recorded history of abuse
Recorded history of court orders
Explained rights
Provided written copy of rights
Recorded temporary address/phone
  (Do NOT include in report!)
Advised of suspect's right to bail

Does this case also involve:

Child abuse	report filed
Elder abuse	report filed
Disabled abuse	report filed

Witness Information

Identified reporting party
Interviewed reporting party
Documented names, DOBs, addresses,
  and phone numbers of all witnesses
Interviewed all witnesses, separately
Listed names and DOBs of children
  present
Recorded names of emergency
  personnel
Identified treating physician
Identified desk officer/dispatcher

Suspect Information

Name: _____
Noted date of birth
Noted location upon arrival
Administered first aid, noted if
  medical treatment was sought
Noted when suspect first spoke
Recorded excited utterances
Described demeanor
Height and weight noted
Described physical condition
Noted complaints of injury
Described injuries in detail (size,
  location, color)
Temporary address noted (if vacate
  order exists)
Noted existence of any restraining
  orders

Following Miranda, when applicable

Asked if she/he wanted to make
  a statement
Noted whether suspect knew of
  and/or understood restraining
  order
Detailed description of incident
Noted history of abuse in any
  relationship

Evidence

Photographed/described crime scene
Took full body picture of suspect
Took full body picture of victim
Photographed victim's injuries
Photographed suspect's injuries
Seized items thrown or broken
Seized firearms for safety
Seized firearms under surrender
  order
Requested medical records
Requested 911 tape

Figure 10–8   Domestic violence investigation checklist.

If the abuse allegations involve physical abuse and injury, evidence must be preserved.

1. Further evidence of the assault, such as bloodstained articles and clothes, should be secured at the scene and placed in paper bags (not plastic).

2. Photographs of the damage to property can be taken. Such damage may include smashed windows in the house or car, bullet holes, and knife slashes.

3. Photographs of the injury to the victim should also be taken, but these are normally done at the police department or hospital. Bruising on the victim may not be immediately apparent, so it is important to follow up with the victim in the days following an assault.

4. Photographs of the location can be substituted for a sketch to document where the assault took place and to portray property damage as the result of the assault.

5. If the assault took place in multiple rooms/locations, each location should be documented for damage and any evidence seized.

If the allegation involves sexual misconduct or date rape,

Figure 10–9 A victim who is choked may have bruises on the neck that resemble thumbs in the front and fingers toward the back of the neck. *(Photo courtesy of Mark C. Ide.)*

1. Evidence may include bedsheets, underwear from the victim, and any clothing that may be stained by blood or semen.

2. The victim should be taken to the hospital as soon as possible for a full medical examination. A rape kit is commonly used in emergency room protocol to collect evidence of a rape. Signs of force, such as bruising, cuts, and tissue damage, should be properly collected and preserved. It is important to explain to the victim that she or he must not smoke, drink, or eat anything prior to the examination. The victim should not shower or wash until after the evidence is collected.

3. An expert in child sexual assault should conduct the examination of a child. The amount of evidence discovered may be improved when a physician with specialty knowledge of child sexual assaults conducts the examination. Medical evidence is found in 10 to 50 percent of child sexual assault cases (Wallace, 2002).

4. The suspect should also be examined for marks, bruises, and other defense wounds inflicted by the victim. A warrant obtained for the collection of evidence and search of the perpetrator's body can yield a tremendous amount of evidence when the crime is recent. The search should include fingernail scrapings, swabbing of the mouth and genitals, and the seizure of clothing for lab analysis for body fluids. Hair combing (both pubic and head) and pulled hair samples should be taken. For convenience, the officer can obtain a rape kit, which is usually used on the victim to collect and preserve evidence.

If the allegation involves elder financial or fiduciary abuse, this investigation poses complex problems for the investigator to overcome. Two model programs, the Los Angeles FAST Program and the Bank Reporting Project, offer guidance for law enforcement in conducting joint investigations with ombudsman and adult protective services (Commonwealth of Massachusetts, 1995b).

1. The victim's bank(s) or other financial institution(s) must be notified about the investigation. Request a temporary administrative hold on all the victim's holdings, including accounts, certificates of deposit, and safe deposit boxes, pending the outcome of the investigation.

In the News: Elisa

According to the *New York Times,* her parents killed Elisa in 1996. The other five siblings watched the 6-year-old being sexually assaulted and beaten to death. Forced to drink ammonia and eat her own feces, her white bones gleamed through her brown fingers (Swarns, 1998).

2. Establish the victim's mental capacity to handle his or her affairs and obtain a written mental evaluation from the family physician.

3. Determine the extent of the estate through the conservator or other designated person in control of the estate if he or she is not suspected in the abuse. Alternative sources of information on the estate may be obtained from a relative, bank, and/or through the registry of deeds.

4. Evidence that the elder has been subjected to undue influence in financial matters is the confirmation of coercion, compulsion, or restraint. This confirmation must be documented.

If the allegation involves child neglect, the home should be searched pursuant to a warrant to document the conditions that constitute criminal neglect. Absence of available food, appropriate clothing, and adequate sleeping conditions will be noted. Severe substandard living conditions are best illustrated by photographs.

Each form of abuse and **neglect** has found its victims in death. When mistakes or oversights in evidence collection occur, they can be fatal to the case as well. Entry to a home without a warrant can be justified due to exigent circumstances, but the collection of evidence in these crimes is usually painstakingly slow. For that reason, a search warrant should be obtained as directed in *Mincey v. Arizona* (1978).

The responding officer first determines that the person is in fact deceased and calls for the medical examiner, who is responsible for the legal determination of the cause of death. The remainder of the home should be checked for other victims. It is not unusual for a domestic killer to commit suicide or to kill other members of the family as well. Once the scene has been combed for victims, it is cordoned off to prevent contamination of the area and to allow for a full investigation of the scene.

The Interrogation of Suspects

A suspect's confession presents the most injurious evidence of a crime. Properly conducted in accordance with legal requirements to ensure voluntariness, an admission provides the best evidence. Supreme Court Justice Byron White wrote, "The defendant's own confession is probably the most probative and damaging evidence that can be admitted against him" (*Bruton v. U.S.*, 1968).

Experts suggest that an interrogation with the perpetrator should always be attempted. Yet debate surrounding *Miranda v. Arizona* (1968) has caused confusion on when the officer must recite warnings. Unless someone has been deprived of his or her freedom in a significant way, and he or she is being interrogated, no warnings are legally required (Rutledge, 1994). According to Rutledge, officers should routinely interrogate suspects, despite the reluctance since *Miranda*.

When considering the decision to interrogate, the officer has options in addition to the traditional face-to-face confrontation, which can be considered custodial and/or intimidating. Obtaining statements over the telephone is one possibility. Another method is to interrogate the suspect in a nonthreatening environment such as a home

---

Been There . . . Done That!

While I routinely videotaped statements given by child victims and witnesses, my colleague preferred to tape interrogations. He always taped the entire account when a perpetrator volunteered to give a statement. With skill, he would question the assailant and elicit any incriminating statements that were offered. The majority of these amounted to confessions, which were invaluable at time of trial. Once a defense attorney viewed the tape, a plea bargain was offered. The result: Fewer young children were made to testify in a lengthy and potentially traumatic trial.

---

or restaurant. The purpose of *Miranda* is to prevent compelled statements or forced confessions through intimidation. Force, intimidation, or threats are not acceptable at any time for the purposes of obtaining a confession.

The victim becomes an agent of the police in this scenario, and caution must be taken to ensure that he or she would not be traumatized by the involvement. This method would not be considered entrapment because the offender has already committed the crime. Before using this technique, investigators should research the laws that pertain to their jurisdiction. Some states prohibit the tape recording of any phone conversations. Others allow one-party consent recording of a conversation. No warnings are required unless the perpetrator has previously been indicted or arraigned on the crimes being investigated. If the victim recorded an incriminating statement without police inducement or involvement, it is evidence that can be received by police.

William Geller suggests videotaping interrogations, noting that an estimated 2,400 police departments in the United States used the technology in 1990 (Geller, 1993). His research into the use of videotaping concluded that it led to improvements in police interrogations. The tapes, which make it easier to show that the statements were voluntary, may be used to discredit a suspect at trial.

CONCLUSIONS

Since domestic violence response can invoke fear and anger, that reaction should be anticipated. Both emotions can be met head on with the power of increased knowledge in handling the situation. Violence can involve weapons and would pose a danger to the responding officers. Domestic violence calls are not, however, more dangerous for the police than other calls involving violent situations.

As with any other case, the primary determination for the police remains, Was a crime committed? The officer must determine who committed the crime based on probable cause. Interviewing and interrogation are important tools toward this end. Truthful information gathering is the goal, and officers must take care when interviewing populations that may be influenced by misinformation. An allegation may be substantiated through the collection of evidence obtained. Since legal constraints exist that guide an officer in that task, knowledge of search and seizure law provides power for the skilled investigator to assure that fundamental fairness and decency are always maintained.

Q UESTIONS FOR R EVIEW

1. What are the preferred and mandatory arrest policies?

2. What questions should be asked during a citizen complaint?

3. What are the requirements for police when reporting abuse?

4. How do police officers make the decision to arrest? What factors influence that decision?

5. What is probable cause? How is probable cause determined?

6. What are the three types of evidence that can be gathered?

7. Explain the exceptions that allow for a warrantless search.

8. Give examples of weapons that police may seize at a domestic crime scene.

9. What evidence do police officers gather to document physical abuse and injury?

10. What evidence do police officers look for to document a claim of sexual misconduct or date rape?

11. What evidence do police officers look for to show elder financial abuse?

12. What is the purpose of *Miranda* warnings?

I NTERNET- B ASED E XERCISES

1. In December 2001, the Office for Victims of Crime updated its booklet First Response to Victims of Crime. Find this on the Internet and report on the tips for law enforcement for any of the included domestic-related topics: elderly victims, victims of sexual assault, child victims, and victims of domestic violence. Start at the Office of Justice Programs: http://www.ojp.usdoj.gov.

2. If you were to investigate a crime of rape, what evidence would you look for? What is the proper method of collecting and storing this evidence? Start your search at http://www.crime-scene-investigator.net/index.html.

REFERENCES

American Bar Association. 2002. "American Bar Association Commission on Legal Problems of the Elderly Report to the House of Delegates" [Web page]. Accessed 2004. Available at *http://www.abanet.org/aging/elder_abuse.pdf*.

Barbour, Scott (ed.). 1995. *Rape on Campus*. San Diego, CA: Greenhaven Press.

Burt, Martha, Janine Zweig, Kathryn Schlichter, Stacey Kamya, Bonnie Katz, Adele Harrell, Neil Miller, and Susan Keilitz. 2000. "Evaluation of the STOP Formula Grants to Combat Violence Against Women: The Violence Against Women Act of 1994 (2000 Report)" [Web page]. Accessed 2004. Available at *http://www.urban.org/url.cfm?ID=900041*.

Commonwealth of Massachusetts. 1995a. *Domestic Violence Investigations. In-Service Training*. Boston: The Commonwealth.

———. 1995b. *Investigation of Financial Exploitation: Skill-Building for Protective Services Caseworkers*. Boston: The Commonwealth.

———. 1996. *Police Training Program*. Middlesex County, MA: Office of the District Attorney.

Crager, Meg, Merril Cousin, and Tara Hardy. 2003. "Victim-Defendants: An Emerging Challenge in Responding to Domestic Violence in Seattle and the King County Region" [Web page]. Accessed 2004. Available at *www.mincava.umn.edu/documents/victimdefendant/victimdefendant.html#id2636079*.

Crowe, Ann H. 1996. "Stopping Terrorism at Home." Pp. 66–69 in *Criminal Justice 96/97*, 20th ed., John J. Sullivan and Joseph L. Victor (eds.). Guilford, CT: Dushkin Publishing Group.

Davis, Robert C., and Barbara Smith. 1995. "Domestic Violence Reforms: Empty Promises or Fulfilled Expectations?" *Crime and Delinquency* 41(4):541–53.

Davis, Robert, Barbara E. Smith, and Heather Davies. 2001. "No-Drop Prosecution and Domestic Violence." *Justice Research and Policy* 3(2):1–13.

Feder, L. 1998. "Police Handling of Domestic and Nondomestic Assault Calls: Is There a Case for Discrimination?" *Crime and Delinquency* 44(2):335–49.

Geller, William A. 1993. *Videotaping Interrogations and Confessions*. NCJ 139962. Washington, DC: U.S. Department of Justice.

Gosselin, Robert C. 2004. *Search and Seizure*. Massachusetts State Police Academy Course Content. Unpublished.

Hirschel, D., & E. Buzawa, 2002. "Understanding the Context of Dual Arrest with Directions for Future Research." *Violence Against Women*, 8(12):1449–1473.

Holmes, William, and Trent Headley. 1995. *Cambridge Police Department Operation Safe Home*. NIJ Grant 94IJCXK001. Boston: Executive Office of Public Safety Programs Division.

Kohl, Rhiana, Diana Brensilber, and William Holmes. 1995. *Elderly Protection Project*. Washington, DC: U.S. Department of Justice.

Littel, Kristin, Mary Malefyt, Alexandra Walker, Sarah Buel, Deborah Tucker, and Joan Kuriansky. 1998. *Assessing Justice System Response to Violence Against Women: A Tool for Law Enforcement, Prosecution and the Courts in Use in Developing Effective Responses*. Washington, DC: U.S. Department of Justice.

Peterson, Richard. 2003. *Combating Domestic Violence in New York City: A Study of DV Cases in the Criminal Courts*. New York: New York City Criminal Justice Agency.

Police Chiefs' Association of Santa Clara County. 2002. "Domestic Violence Protocol for Law Enforcement" [Web page]. Accessed 2004. Available at *www.growing.com/nonviolent/index.htm*

Rutledge, Devallis. 1994. *Criminal Interrogation: Law and Tactics*, 3rd ed. Pacerville, CA: Copperhouse Publishing Company.

Sampson, Rana, and Michael Scott. 1999. *"Tackling Crime and Other Public-Safety Problems: Case Studies in Problem-Solving."* Washington, DC: U.S. Department of Justice.

Shanahan, Michael G. 1998. "Surviving the Policing Paradigm Shift." *http://www.berettabulletin.com*. October 1998.

Sherman, Lawrence W., Denise C. Gottfedson, Doris L. MacKenzie, John Eck, Peter Reuter, and Shawn D. Bushway. 1998. *Preventing Crime: What Works, What Doesn't, What's Promising*. NCJ 171676. Washington, DC: U.S. Department of Justice.

Smith, Barbara E., Robert Davis, Laura B. Nickles, and Heather J. Davies. 2001. *Evaluation of Efforts to Implement No-Drop Policies: Two Central Values in Conflict, Final Report*. NCJ 187772. Washington, DC: American Bar Association.

Swarns, Rachel L. 1998. "3 Years After a Girl's Murder, 5 Siblings Lack Stable Homes." August 4. *http://archives.nytimes.com*. October 1998.

Trapasso, Philip. 1998. Telephone interview. October.

Wallace, Harvey. 2002. *Family Violence: Legal, Medical, and Social Perspectives*. Boston: Allyn & Bacon.

CASES

Beck v. Ohio, 379 U.S. 89 (1964).
Bruton v. U.S., 391 U.S. 123 (1968).
Gerstein v. Pugh, 420 U.S. 103 (1975).
Mincey v. Arizona, 437 U.S. 385 (1978).
Miranda v. Arizona, 384 U.S. 436 (1968).

STATUTE

Massachusetts General Laws ch. 209A, §6.

OTHER AUTHORITY

Lautenberg Gun Ban, H.R. 3610 (September 1996).

CHAPTER 11

ASSOCIATED MAJOR CRIMES: STALKING AND HOMICIDE

SIMPLY SCENARIO

Stalking and Homicide Risk

Your friend tells you in confidence that she thinks that someone is following her on campus. She describes seeing her ex-boyfriend in various places around school, but he does not attend the same college as she. Recently she has been receiving hang-up calls in the middle of the night. The whole thing is making her feel kind of creepy. She states that they had broken up at least six months before that because they didn't get along. He had an explosive temper but had never hit her.

Questions: Make suggestions to your friend on safety precautions and talk with her about threat and dangerousness assessments. Should she contact the police?

KEY TERMS

Battered women's syndrome
Clemency
Erotomania
Excusable homicide
False victimization syndrome
Familicide
Felonious homicide
Feticide
Filicide
Fratricide

Harassing
Infanticide
Justifiable homicide
Love obsessional stalker
Matricide
Parricide
Patricide
Simple obsessional stalker
Stalking
Sudden infant death syndrome

INTRODUCTION

> "Being the victim of a stalker is a hideous and insidious situation," says actress Theresa Saldana. "It never goes away. When someone is after you, it's like the proverbial bogeyman, only it's real life." (Moret, 1997)

Stalking is not a new behavior. We have referred to it as harassment, annoyance, and now know it as a domestic violence crime. Pioneering legislative action in California coined the term *stalking* and defined a set of behaviors that constitute the deviant conduct that is now prohibited by law. Unprecedented interest in all aspects of stalking has followed. Since that time, antistalking legislation has been passed in every state and in Washington, DC.

The relationship between homicide and domestic violence was assumed but not acknowledged. Statistics on homicides in the United States have been collected from police reports for many years; only recently have we documented the relationship between the perpetrator and the victim. Homicide is defined as the killing of a human being by the act, procurement, or omission of another human being (Garner, 2001). The term *homicide* is neutral and a necessary component to what most people think of as murder. Intentionally causing death to another may be homicide, but not necessarily murder.

In this chapter we explore stalking and homicide, the relationship between stalking and homicide, and their association to domestic violence.

STALKING

Celebrity accounts on the terror of being stalked heightened public awareness during the 1980s. Actresses Theresa Saldana, Jodie Foster, and Madonna are among those victimized. Mark David Chapman stalked and killed famed Beatle John Lennon. Margaret Ray, who had stalked David Letterman since 1988, committed suicide in 1998. Ms. Ray also stalked astronaut Story Musgrave for approximately four years prior to her death. Those who stalk go to great lengths to get noticed by their victims. They may do bizarre things to gain attention. Theresa Saldana's assailant, who had obtained her address through a private detective, stabbed her; John Hinkley shot President Reagan to impress Jodie Foster; Margaret Ray, claiming to be the wife of David Letterman, repeatedly broke into his house and stole his car. When her stalker killed Rebecca Shaefer in 1989, California responded as the first state to pass antistalking laws. Once thought to be a crime committed only against celebrities and politicians, stalking became known as the crime of the 1990s.

In addition to the fear generated by stalking behaviors, it is estimated that stalkers are violent toward their victims between 25 and 35 percent of the time. The group most likely to be violent are those that have had an intimate relationship with the victim (National Institute of Justice, 1998). Research on the identifying features and motivation of perpetrators and the relationships to their victims has resulted. The first national study to determine stalking's prevalence was undertaken in the National Violence Against Women (NVAW) Survey (Tjaden & Thoennes, 1998). Using a definition of stalking that requires the victim to feel a high level of fear, the NVAW survey found it was more prevalent than previously thought. Eight percent of women and 2 percent of men surveyed said they had been stalked at some time in their life. Estimating that approximately 1 million women and 371,000 men are stalked annually in the United States, the report concluded that stalking should be considered a serious criminal justice and public health concern.

Stalking may have entered the public consciousness through highly publicized cases, but it affects many people every day. It is a gender-neutral crime that is perpetrated by both men and women; it crosses all racial, social, religious, ethnic, and economic lines. Like all crimes, it can be perpetrated by strangers or by offenders known to the victim. When the victim and offender are related by marriage, intimacy, or family ties that are legally recognized as "domestic relationships," the crime is also one of domestic violence.

What Is Stalking?

Stalking is a distinctive form of criminal activity because it is a pattern of behavior that is intended to cause harm or to instill fear in a person. Following or **harassing** someone typically characterizes the offense. It is different from the majority of crimes because it consists of a series of actions rather than a single act. When the events are considered individually, they may not constitute illegal behavior. For example, sending flowers, or love notes, and telephoning someone are perfectly legal activities. When the repetitive actions of the perpetrator instill significant fear of bodily harm or cause injury to the person, it then constitutes the pattern of behavior that is legally prohibited. Intent is therefore an important element of stalking, but it is not the stalker's motives or the context in which the stalking occurs that should be considered when the crime is charged. Attempts to force the victim to comply with the desires of the offender by the use of threats or intimidation can turn the scenario into a nightmare. If the conduct of the person is seriously threatening, it should be charged as stalking, regardless of the defendant's motivations or relationship to the victim.

Stalking is a crime under the laws of all 50 states, the District of Columbia, and the federal government. Classified as a felony for the first offense in 14 states, 34 others make it a felony with aggravating circumstances or on the second offense. Since stalking is a newly created and defined criminal offense, it can be confusing. Broadly written statutes in some states have caused difficulty for criminal justice implementation and resulted in constitutional challenges. Typically, statutes define stalking as willful, malicious, and repeated following and harassment of another person. Some states further require that the perpetrator make a threat of violence that is credible. New York's laws use the terms *menacing* (Chapter 353) and *aggravated harassment* (NY Public Law Code, §240.30), yet both provisions refer to stalking behaviors.

A Boyfriend Turns to Murder

Kristin Lardner, 21, dated Michael Cartier for about 2 months before breaking up with him on April 16, 1992. Angered over her decision to end their relationship, Cartier followed her down the street, beat her, and left her lying on a curb. In the following weeks, he continued to contact and follow her. She notified the police and obtained a temporary restraining order. She also learned that he had committed inhumane acts, such as killing cats, and had a criminal record—he had beaten ex-girlfriends and had been caught injecting his own blood into a restaurant ketchup bottle. At the time he was stalking Lardner, Cartier was on probation for having attacked a previous girlfriend with scissors.

The judge who granted the temporary restraining order on May 11, however, was unaware of Cartier's criminal history and the fact that he was on probation. The judge scheduled a hearing for a permanent injunction to be held the following week. On May 19, when Lardner returned to court to obtain a permanent injunction, a different judge, who was also unaware of the man's record, treated the case routinely. He issued an order prohibiting Cartier from any contact with Lardner and requiring that he stay 200 yards away from her. Approximately two weeks later, just six weeks after he had first beaten her, Cartier shot and killed Kristin Lardner in broad daylight outside a Boston sandwich shop. Cartier later killed himself in his home. (Lardner, 1997)

It is not unusual for constitutional challenges and revision through case law to clarify some of the problems with newly established laws, and stalking is no exception. It may take years for the bugs to be worked out of the state statutes and for clarification to occur. There is a federal offense of stalking in addition to the individual state versions. These versions may vary widely. The following was used in the NVAW survey and offers a general definition of stalking that is not specific to a particular state law (Tjaden & Thoennes, 1998):

> Stalking: Course of conduct directed at a specific person that involves repeated visual or physical proximity; nonconsensual communication; verbal, written, or implied threats; or a combination thereof that would cause fear in a reasonable person (with "repeated" meaning on two or more occasions).

For NVAW, only those victims who reported being very frightened or those who feared bodily harm were counted as stalking victims. The survey used the following questions to screen for stalking victimization: Not including bill collectors, telephone solicitors, or other salespeople, has anyone, male or female, ever

- Followed or spied on you?
- Sent you unsolicited letters or written correspondence?

- Made unsolicited phone calls to you?
- Stood outside your home, school, or workplace?
- Showed up at places you were, even though he or she had no business being there?
- Left unwanted items for you to find?
- Tried to communicate in other ways against your will?
- Vandalized your property or destroyed something you loved?

Stalking Behaviors

The motivations of a stalker are varied. Offenders routinely attempt to intimidate and control their victims. Some attempt to scare the victim. Others may have a fanaticized love interest in their target. A significant factor is the stalker's desire to keep the victim within a personal relationship, since more than half of the stalkers begin before the intimate relationship has actually ended. Violence appears to occur in 30 to 50 percent of stalking cases with severe violence noted in approximately 6 percent of the cases (Rosenfeld, 2004). The most consistent indicator of violence is threats and a previous intimate relationship between the victim and the offender. Substance abuse history is predictive of an increased rate of violence among stalking offenders.

Common elements in the crime of stalking include following, harassing, and threatening the victims. The act of threatening may constitute a separate criminal offense. The actions are not only multiple events that taken together indicate a single

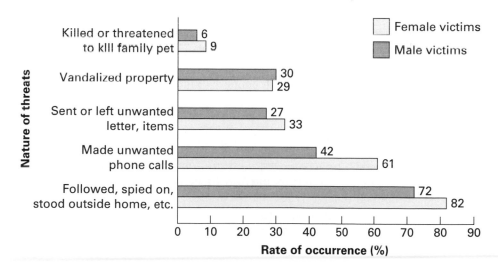

Figure 11–1   Five common stalking behaviors. *(Data from the National Institute of Justice, 1998.)*

pattern of conduct, but they must also cause fear and be intentional or willful in order to satisfy legal definitions of stalking.

Following.   The most common stalking behavior is following. Stalkers may stand outside a person's home. Still, the crime is more complex than simply following or spying on someone. It is done for a specific purpose, although each stalker is different and the range of behaviors is equally unpredictable. Achieving a victim reaction is routinely the objective of the stalker. The stalker's motivations will determine what reaction is the desired one.

Often, the offender will alert the victim to ensure that he or she is aware of the presence or intent of the perpetrator. The purpose here is to control and to intimidate the victim. For example, a note or telephone message may be sent indicating places that the victim frequents, stores that he or she shops at, and where he or she works or resides. The actions of the stalkers therefore assure that they get the victims' attention and make them aware that they are being followed or spied upon. A stalker may or may not initiate conversation if seen by the victim. Following is meant to cause fear on the part of the victim and bolster the self-esteem of the assailant.

Harassing.   It is difficult to list all forms of harassment that are possible. Harassing is generally recognized as a knowing and willful pattern of conduct or series of acts over a period of time directed at a specific person, which seriously alarms or annoys the person. A reasonable person would be expected to suffer substantial emotional distress as a result of harassment.

A coworker who consistently stands uncomfortably too close to the victim in conjunction with other acts may rise to the level of harassment. A stalker who breaks into (by key or force) the victim's home and leaves evidence that someone was in the house is also guilty of a form of harassment. Common examples of stalking behaviors include unwanted phone calls, unwanted letters, items left for the victim, and vandalized property.

Females report harassing phone calls more frequently than do male victims. The calls may be excessive, repetitive, and at odd hours of the day or night. They may be hang-up calls or heavy breathing. Depending on the pattern and type of the calling, a purpose may be determined in some instances. For example, calls may come frequently in the middle of the night to deprive the victim of sleep.

A stalker frequently attempts to contact the victim by sending or leaving unwanted items or letters. Numerous attempts at communicating with the victim routinely contain veiled threats. It is imperative that the item is looked at closely not only for its physical properties but also for its intended meaning. Flowers or a gift may be sent on an anniversary or date of significance to reaffirm the existence of a relationship that in reality no longer exists.

Threats.   The legal requirement of a credible threat against the victim can be the most difficult element to establish. Not all statutes require this ingredient, however, so it is important to know the law in your state. The threat does not need to be written or verbal to instill fear; delivering a dead animal to the doorstep or pointing a finger toward someone as if it were a gun are examples. Some states require additional conduct after a threat has been made; others specify that the threat must be one causing fear of serious harm.

This requirement might seem like an impossible obstacle to overcome since less than half of victims (male and female) are overtly threatened by their stalkers (National Institute of Justice, 1998). However, prior acts of violence against a person by the stalker may properly be admitted to prove that the threats were intended to instill fear of death or serious injury (*Commonwealth v. Martinez*, 1997). A person who had been victimized previously due to a partner relationship who then receives a veiled threat may properly react with the level of fear required to satisfy the elements of the crime, even though the "threat" at hand was not itself serious.

Thinly veiled threats are much more common than overt threats, these may rise to the level of credible threat in the face of a past or current abusive relationship. It ultimately falls on the court to determine if the action will satisfy the requirement of fear.

Threats come in unusual packages that may have meaning to the stalker and to the victim alone. Asking the victim why she or he feels threatened can enlighten others. Ripped, torn, or mutilated objects that are sent signify anger and are meant to scare the victim. They may include dolls, photographs, or broken statues, to name a few. Sending black roses or a game called "Hangman" can be threatening if the victim is afraid of the stalker or believes that the gift signifies a step closer to fulfilling an earlier threat to hurt him or her. Killing or threatening to kill a family pet indicates an extremely dangerous situation for the victim. Should this occur, safety precautions should be taken and the victim should be considered to be in imminent personal danger.

Characteristics of Stalking Perpetrators

Although stalking is described as a gender-neutral crime, the majority of perpetrators are male (Schell, 2003.) There is no single profile of a stalker; they are categorized by their relationship to the victim and within broad categories due to their behaviors. The one trait all stalkers share is that they suffer from a personality or mental disorder, if not both. Despite their demographic diversity, data show that some characteristics are more common among stalkers than others (Seymour et al., 2002):

- Eighty-seven percent are male.
- Eighty percent are white.
- Fifty percent are between the ages of 18 and 35.
- Most are of above average intelligence.
- Most earn above-average incomes.

A progression that is similar to other domestic violence crimes is also apparent in stalking. If the stalker is spurned, he or she may escalate the behavior to intimidation.

In rare instances, the contacts become a persistent pattern of behavior that turns threatening and violent. The majority of stalking does not involve offenders who are mentally ill, although the behavior is not normal or appropriate.

The relationship between the victim and the offender characterizes the first stalker category:

1. *Intimate or former intimate.* The stalker and victim may be married, divorced, or separated. They may be current or former cohabitants, serious or casual sexual partners, or former sexual partners. A history of domestic violence may exist.

2. *Acquaintance.* The stalker knows the victim casually. They may be coworkers or neighbors, or they may have dated once or twice.

3. *Stranger.* Cases involving celebrities and other public figures generally fall into this category, where the victim and stalker do not know each other at all.

Forensic psychologists refer to stalkers using this second method of characterizing stalkers; it is based on psychological and behavior profiling.

Relationship or Simple Obsessional Stalkers.   This is the most common type of stalker; it is also the best known. The perpetrator and victim typically have a previous relationship that could be marriage, friendship, or that of coworkers. Most stalkers in cases of domestic violence and dating relationships are **simple obsessional stalkers**. The use of *simple* as a descriptor refers to the fact that this is a common type of stalker, not that the issue is simple or that the victim is not at risk. Simple obsession is the most likely category of stalking to result in murder. Thirty percent of all female homicides were committed by intimate partners. Domestic violence victims run a 75 percent higher risk of being murdered by their partners (Seymour et al., 2002). "If I can't have you, nobody will" has become all too common a refrain in cases that escalate to violence. Many of these cases end with the murder of the victim followed by the suicide of the stalker.

People in this category are more frequently those who batter. It should not be a surprise that their characteristics resemble those of the domestic violence offender; they are, in general,

- Emotionally immature
- Socially incompetent
- Unable to maintain relationships
- Overly jealous
- Insecure
- Low in self-esteem

Love Obsessional Stalkers.   People in this group develop a love obsession or fixation, generally targeting celebrities and politicians. There is no personal relationship between the victim and offender; therefore, the target might also be a casual acquaintance. These stalkers tend to be persistent in their pursuit of their victims. They fantasize about the victim being their love partner and may go to drastic means to get attention. The bizarre attempts may be lethal to the victim since the stalker does not care if the attention is negative or positive.

Unlike the person suffering from **erotomania**, the **love obsessional stalker** does not believe that the target loves them. They may believe that they are destined to be with their target and only need to try harder to convince their victim. These stalkers often invent detailed fantasies of a nonexistent relationship.

Erotomania.   This term is usually associated with a stalker who has severe mental problems, including delusions. The perpetrator may actually believe that the victim knows and loves him or her. These stalkers expect the target to play the role the stalker has determined, and when threats or intimidation does not work, they may resort to violence. This stalker may continue to pursue the victim for long periods of time, up to eight or ten years. Though relatively rare (comprising fewer than 10 percent of all cases), erotomania stalking cases often draw public attention because the target is usually a public figure or celebrity (Seymour et al., 2002). Like love obsession stalkers, erotomaniacs attempt to garner self-esteem and status by associating themselves with well-known individuals who hold high social status. While the behavior of many erotomaniacs never escalates to violence, or even to threats of violence, the irrationality that accompanies their mental illness presents particularly unpredictable threats to victims.

Vengeance and Terrorism Stalker.   The fourth stalking category is very different from the others. Vengeance and terrorist stalkers seek to change the behavior of their victims without seeking a personal relationship with the victim. For the vengeance stalker he or she may only seek to punish their victims for some wrong they perceive the victim has done to them. This is typified by the person who stalks an employer after being fired. The terrorist stalker has a political agenda and uses the threat of force to keep the target from engaging in a particular activity. Prosecutions in this category have included antiabortionists who stalk doctors who perform abortions.

Stalking Victims

Anyone, male or female, can become the victim of a stalker. The person targeted for this crime has not done anything to provoke the behavior of the offender. Examining victim characteristics is part of the attempt to understand the stalker and of the phenomena that occur. According to NVAW, four of five victims of stalking are female. Men were stalked in approximately 22 percent of the total cases surveyed. Young adults are the primary targets of stalkers; over half are between the ages of 18 and 29. Many victims know their stalker. Approximately 59 percent of female victims compared with 30 percent of male victims were stalked by some type of intimate

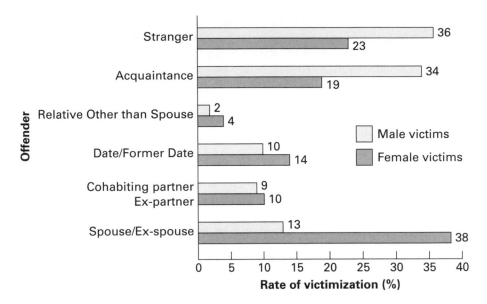

Figure 11-2   Most stalking victims are targeted by someone they know. *(Data from the National Institute of Justice, 1998.)*

partner. Stalking behaviors by former intimate partners has been closely linked as a risk factor for both murder and attempted murder. The prevalence of stalking by intimate partners has been documented as high as 67 percent for femicide victims and 71 percent for attempted femicide victims (Farlane et al., 1999). Incidence of intimate partner assault was also extremely high, 67 percent for femicide victims and 71 percent for attempted femicide victims.

Investigative Strategies

Half of all victims reported their stalking to the police, according to the NVAW survey. Some suggested that the police did not take them seriously; approximately half were satisfied with the response. We understand the importance of taking these cases seriously. Before they were killed by their stalkers, 54 percent of femicide victims reported the stalking to the police (Farlane et al., 1999). Approximately 46 percent of attempted femicide victims also had reported the stalking to the police. Here are a few key points to consider in an investigation into the complaint of stalking.

Assessing the Victim's Credibility.   Assessing the victim's credibility is accomplished by observing the conduct of the victim during the investigation. This is important since there are instances of perpetrators who report themselves as being the victim. How articulate is the victim? What are the motivations for reporting this stalking crime? What did he or she do to reach out for assistance, and was it at an appropriate time? What is the mental health and criminal background of the reporter? Determine if the statements are consistent with the injuries or documentation provided. Has this victim reported being a victim of other domestic violence crimes?

False Victimization Syndrome.   Professionals have long recognized that a small percentage of violent crimes reported appear to be false allegations. Those who suffer from Munchausen and Munchausen by proxy provide examples of recognized disorders of individuals who make false claims. **False victimization syndrome** is believed to be involved in an estimated 2 percent of stalking complaints that are encountered by law enforcement (Mohandie et al., 1998). Although this appears to be an insignificant number, even one case that involves a false complaint causes many problems for police officers who want to protect the victim from this horrible crime. It is imperative that suspected false complaints be thoroughly investigated and all attempts to find the perpetrator exhausted before concluding that it is a fantasy crime. Gently confronting the victim may be necessary at some point. Mohandie and colleagues further suggest that mental health intervention should be considered for the benefit of the person and a determination made whether charges of perjury or filing a false police report will be pursued in the future (Mohandie et al., 1998).

In a study on the characteristics of false stalking victimization, five distinct categories were investigated (Sheridan & Blaauw, 2004):

1. stalkers that claim to be victims themselves;
2. persons with severe mental disorders and persecutory or erotomanic delusions that include stalking;
3. previously stalked persons who have become hypersensitive to perfectly innocent actions of others because of fear of recurrence;
4. fictitious victims that seek gratification of dependency needs through adopting victim status;
5. and malingerers that consciously fabricate or exaggerate claims of victimization for understandable external incentives, such as financial rewards.

Their results indicated that the majority of false stalking reports are made by persons that are delusional (Sheridan & Blaauw, 2004). The next largest group of false reports was made by factitious victims, followed by reports of false revictimization.

Assessing the Offender's Conduct.   Does the offender have a mental health or criminal background? What is the employment record of the offender? Has this offender committed prior domestic violence, or are there outstanding restraining orders against him or her? The answers to these questions help the investigator to determine if the victim's perception of a threat is accurate. Some victims may tend to underestimate the potential harm in a stalking situation.

Been There . . . Done That!

For three years, the police responded to fearful complaints of a woman who was being stalked. Since stalking victims frequently endure stalking for years, this was not unusual. She produced letters that had been written to her from the unknown assailant, mailed from various locations. Often, they included graphic descriptions of his sexual prowess. He described her in detail in the accounts of bizarre sex play and professed love. She received flowers at her place of business and at her home. There were countless hang-up calls to her house. She came to the police station twice with bruises and cuts to her arms and face that were the result of confrontations with the assailant. A beautiful 25-year-old woman, she was a perfect target for this sick predator, thought the officers!

But for the police officers involved, it was a frustrating experience. They were unable to identify the perpetrator, and from the onset, they were concerned for her safety. Responding quickly to her home each time, they even put a tap on her telephone line and put surveillance on her house. Their efforts were to no avail. The only contact occurred when there were no witnesses.

As time went by, the officers began to suspect that she was fabricating the "evidence" of the crime. They noticed that she would request specific officers that she liked. Always she was freshly made-up and particularly well dressed when they arrived. Her demeanor would often change from extremely fearful to gleeful. Still, they were hesitant to ignore her complaints, especially since there had been physical assaults.

Asked to consult and offer advice to the other officers, I reviewed the evidence. The tone of the letters suggested to me that they had been written by a female rather than a male. The acts that were graphically described contained too much detail. They were literally impossible from a physical standpoint. Rather than intimidating, they were erotic stories that were meant to be so. Pictures of her injuries appeared suspicious also. The facial injuries were minor, with superficial cuts on her cheeks, but not across her nose. The bruising from being hit looked more like blush than what one might expect from an attack from an assailant. The facts did not match the evidence.

The "victim" was not pleased when she was told that the local officers would no longer respond to her calls and that a female police officer had been assigned to help her. When I met with her, my gut reaction was exactly what the other officers felt—that she was making up the whole thing. Eventually, I confronted her and she confessed that there was no stalker. She smiled broadly when I told her she had great imagination and complimented her writing ability!

It is important to document any history of problems, conflicts, and mental health problems in a suspected stalking situation. Recognizing that there is a difference between making a threat known as "venting anger" and actually "posing" a threat, law enforcement should evaluate the possibility of violent action through the suspect's past history. The task of the investigator is to gather information about the subject's thinking. Interviewing the subject may be beneficial to permit the subject's story to be related to a third party. It allows an opportunity to communicate that the subject's behavior is unwelcome, unacceptable, and must cease.

Gathering Physical Evidence.   Investigating a complaint of stalking requires full and often lengthy documentation of the actions that present an accurate portrayal of the stalking. Victims need to be aware of the need to save any form of harassment, such as photos of vandalism, injuries, answering machine messages, or notes; these are the kind of evidence necessary to form probable cause that the crime of stalking has been committed. Keeping a journal or diary is one method of gathering additional important information.

Obtain a search warrant or summons for the telephone records of the offender if the communications are by telephone. Encourage the victim to install "caller ID" to track the calls. If e-mail is the medium, trace the address to the suspect and consider intercepting all email messages designated for the victim.

Documenting Previous Law Enforcement Response.   Obtain actual reports on prior incidents of violence. Read the statements and determine whether they reflect the present situation accurately.

Interviewing Third Parties.   Talk to family members of the victim, neighbors, and coworkers to assess the level of danger that may exist. Determine the reasons the victim has come forward at that particular time. What has happened to explain the escalation or change in the behavior of the stalker? Should the police consider this an ongoing stalking that places the victim at risk to probable danger, or is the victim in imminent danger? What can be done to protect this person?

Considering Circumstantial Evidence.   Anything can be considered circumstantial evidence. Does the stalker have access to the types of messages that have been sent to the victim? For example, if the notes are sent through e-mail, does the stalker have access to a computer? Where? Do not overlook any correspondence, pattern of behavior, or gift that may have significance to the victim or the offender.

Assisting the Victim in Obtaining a Restraining or No-Contact Order.   Although the investigation is ongoing, direct the victim to obtain a restraining or no-contact order if possible. Be aware that this may give the victim a false sense of security, however. One-fourth of the women in the NVAW obtained a restraining order and the assailant later violated the vast majority of these. Victims who believe that the stalker will persist, regardless of a court order, must be taken seriously. A restraining or no-contact order does not replace day-to-day efforts to reduce vulnerability. The victim cannot let his or her guard down thinking that the piece of paper is itself full protection.

Since all states have arrest provisions for violation of restraining or stay-away orders, such orders do permit a faster police response. For the stalker who is rational and can control his or her behavior to avoid legal consequences, this is the best way to make the person accountable. Restraining orders are ineffective, however, if the stalker has little regard for the consequences of the stalking behavior and is obsessed with harming or harassing the victim.

Police officers should attempt to assess the level of threat that the perpetrator poses to the victim. Additionally, officers should suggest that victims take additional safety precautions and make contact with a local victim assistance unit. These include, but are not limited to, those suggested in the next section.

Safety Precautions for Stalking Victims

Doreen Orion, author of *I Know You Really Love Me*, suggests that stalking victims must acknowledge their being a target of this crime and take extra safety precautions (Orion, 1998). She suggests the following commonsense approaches for persons who suspect that they may be targeted by a stalker.

- To reduce the feeling of vulnerability, the author suggests getting a dog. The Los Angeles Police Department's Threat Management Unit suggests that this is one of the most effective (and least expensive) alarm systems. Installing a house alarm is an alternative.
- Never give out your telephone number or home address. Get a mail box address other than with the U.S. Post Office. List the mailbox as "apartment

Figure 11–3   Regardless of the level of threat that a stalker might pose, the victim is likely to feel vulnerable. Steps to reduce that feeling involve common safety precautions.

111" rather than "box 111." Have personal checks and business cards changed to reflect this new "address."

- If a stalker gets your telephone number, keep an answering machine on it at all times. In addition, get a new and unlisted number to give out to your friends. The stalker will believe he is still getting through to you. Get a cell phone and keep it with you at all times, even inside your home, in case a stalker cuts your telephone lines.
- Document everything. Keep all machine tapes, letters, gifts, or other correspondence. Keep a log of suspicious occurrences.
- File for confidential voter status and get a new driver's license with the mailbox "address."
- Always park your car in a well-lit area and lock your doors. While driving, keep the doors locked. Alarm your car if possible.
- If you think you are being followed while in your car, make four left- or right-hand turns in succession. If the car continues to follow you, drive to the nearest police station, never home or to a friend's house.
- Never be afraid to sound your car horn to attract attention if you are in danger.

It is important that the stalking victim attempt to assess the probability of impending danger. When emotions run high, it may be helpful to allow common sense to replace fear. Contrary to popular belief, the majority of stalking incidents begin before an intimate relationship has actually ended (National Institute of Justice, 1998). Be aware of the possibility that the violent domestic relationship may also include stalking.

Threat Assessment

The role of criminal justice has traditionally been one of response, not of prevention. This trend is changing, however, and is most notable with respect to violent crimes. Proactive policing includes advanced knowledge about the population that is most likely to commit crimes of violence. Threat assessment is a current project for stalking of public figures and has applicability to stalkers in general. The Secret Service provided findings about the histories and personal characteristics of attackers and near-lethal approachers that include the following (Fein & Vossekuil, 1998):

- Almost half had attended college or graduate school.
- They often had histories of mobility and transience.
- About two-thirds were described as socially isolated.
- Few had histories of arrests for violent crimes or for crimes that involved weapons.
- Many had histories of harassing other people.

- Most had histories of explosive, angry behavior, but only half had histories of physically violent behavior.
- Many had histories of serious depression or despair.
- Many were known to have attempted suicide or to have considered suicide at some point before their attack or near-lethal approach.

This information suggests that stalkers are generally intelligent, have violent or deviant pasts, and suffer from emotional and behavior disorders. Revenge and the need for vindication may motivate them.

DOMESTIC HOMICIDE

The loss of a family member and loved one is difficult when the causes are natural. When a person is killed, it is a tragedy not only for the victim, but also for those that are left behind to mourn. The nature of intimate relationships provides both the intensity and the opportunity for hostile aggression and even murder.

Research confirms that women, men, and children are at risk to domestic homicide. There were 1,830 murders attributed to intimate partners in 1998, approximately 11 percent of all murders nationwide (Rennison & Welchans, 2000).

In 1998, the National Center for Health Statistics listed homicide as the third leading cause of death for children ages 1 to 4 and 5 to 14, and the second leading cause for persons ages 15 to 24. Research confirms that most child murders, especially of younger children, are committed by family members or acquaintances rather than

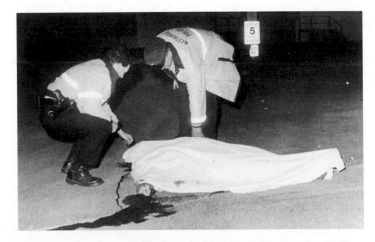

Figure 11–4 There is no statute of limitations on murder. A person can be tried at any time after the crime when sufficient proof exists to do so. *(Photo courtesy of Mark C. Ide.)*

strangers. Forty percent of children are killed by family members, 45 percent by acquaintances, and only 15 percent by strangers (Osofsky, 2001).

Three general categories are recognized to describe the forms of homicide: *justifiable, excusable*, and *felonious*.

Justifiable Homicide

Justifiable homicide is the intentional taking of another's life that is lawful, such as police officers responding to the commission of a felony with deadly force that could not be avoided. Carrying out the death sentence of an inmate and killing during combat are other examples of homicides where death is intentional but not criminal. These are killings completed as part of a person's duty. Justifiable homicide is viewed by society as appropriate behavior, even though death resulted. It is self-defense when the person committing the homicide is not at fault. In determining whether a defendant acted in self-defense, a trier of facts considers issues such as (1) whether the defendant reasonably feared that she needed to use force to defend herself; (2) whether the threat to the defendant was imminent; (3) whether the defendant met the threat with excessive force; and (4) whether the defendant had a duty to retreat.

Excusable Homicide

Excusable homicide occurs when a person kills in self-defense or in the defense of family members. A defendant who uses an excuse defense admits that the offense committed was a crime but submits that factors peculiar to the situation should prevent a judgment of criminal responsibility. Examples of an excuse defense include temporary insanity and diminished capacity. Excusable homicide is often treated as another form of justifiable homicide; they both pardon the defendant from criminal liability. A person who commits homicide that is excusable must be released from responsibility for the death through the determination of a court, after investigation by the state's prosecutor, and in rare cases through **clemency**. Excusable homicide is perceived by society to be wrong but is tolerated because of the actor's state of mind (Balos & Fellows, 2000).

Psychiatrists and psychologists frequently testify in both criminal and civil courts on the mental health of persons accused of major crimes, including murder. It is not uncommon for evidence that relates to the person's state of mind to be presented in an attempt to show a diminished responsibility for the offender who committed a crime. The best known defense is insanity. As the behavioral sciences advance, other mental health disorders, such as multiple personality disorder, postpartum psychosis, and diminished capacity, have also been recognized. One highly publicized and controversial defense specific to domestic violence is the **battered women's syndrome**.

The Battered Women's Syndrome.   An example of excusable homicide is the defense referred to as the battered women's syndrome. Proponents suggest that the continuum of violence in battering relationships excuses the woman who kills her intimate assailant. Some argue that battered women who kill their oppressors should be considered legally justified, not merely excused of the act. Opponents are divided about whether battered women's syndrome is a valid defense or a claim by someone trying to escape a murder conviction. As in any defense that is raised on behalf of the defendant, some may be legitimate applications of the concept and others are not. There is always the possibility that any defense will be used illegitimately.

The battered women's syndrome is based on the theory of learned helplessness and the cycle of abuse discussed earlier in this book. According to these theories, the battered victim begins to believe that she or he cannot influence or escape the abuser's violence. One rare reaction when faced with the "reality" is to resort to the only perceived option, that is, to kill the abuser. It is considered self-defense even though the victim may not have been in imminent danger of death or great bodily harm at the exact time that the killing occurred.

The primary source of evidence comes from expert testimony on the battered spouse syndrome. Early attempts to introduce the syndrome through psychiatrists had met with several objections, including lack of its acceptance as scientific knowledge. Expert witness testimonies explaining the psychological state of the battered woman have now been allowed in 27 states and the District of Columbia (Mangum, 2001). There are four general characteristics of the syndrome:

1. The woman believes that the violence was her fault.
2. The woman has an inability to place the responsibility for the violence elsewhere.
3. The woman fears for her life and/or her children's lives.
4. The women has an irrational belief that the abuser is omnipresent and omniscient.

In the United States, expert testimony on battering and its effects is introduced as a defense in cases where a woman has killed her assailant intimate. The battered wife syndrome has successfully been a defense in at least one same-sex partner homicide (Vickers, 1997). Robert McEwan was arrested in Perth, Western Australia and charged with the murder of his homosexual partner of 14 years. The defense was accepted and a plea of guilty to the lesser charge of manslaughter was recorded.

Clemency.   Clemency is a general term for the power of an executive to intervene in the sentencing of a criminal defendant to prevent injustice from occurring. It is a relief imparted after the justice system has run its course. Clemency provisions exist in every judicial system in the world except China. The U.S. Constitution gives the President the power to grant clemency. In 35 states, the governor can make clemency decisions directly or exercise this power in conjunction with an advisory board (Death Penalty Information Center, 2004). In five states, boards make clemency decisions, and in 16 states, the power to grant clemency is shared between the governor and an advisory board.

As the defense of battered spouse syndrome became increasingly admissible, a clemency movement began. Requests to state governors for the release of those women who had been convicted of murdering or assaulting an intimate began in the early 1990s. Ohio Governor Celeste and Governor William Donald Schaefer of Maryland granted clemency to 25 women who were incarcerated for killing or assaulting abusive husbands or boyfriends (Dalton & Schneider, 2001). Other states' governors have since followed the lead. Most of those released had been denied the opportunity to offer evidence on battered syndrome. Media attention to the clemency action fuels the controversy for this justification, which is likely to continue.

Felonious Homicide

The wrongful killing of a human being is criminal behavior; generally it is referred to as **felonious homicide**. Murder, manslaughter, or negligent homicides are categories of death with varying degrees of culpability. The term *murder* refers to the killing of any human being by another with malice aforethought. Most states provide different degrees of culpability that are designated by the criminal statute itself, often referred to as nonnegligent homicide. Murder is considered the most serious crime in our society. The penalties reflect this belief: Murder can be punished by life imprisonment or by death. There is no statute of limitations on murder; a person can be tried in a court of law at any time that sufficient proof exists to do so, regardless of how many years have elapsed since the offense.

Murder in the Family

Intense emotion, ability, and opportunity are the key ingredients common to murders committed by family members. Familiarity develops when people live together or have a close personal relationship. Often mistaken for intimacy, familiarity occurs whether the relationship is good or bad. Intimate domestic partners frequently share information about themselves during the courtship process, fulfilling the need to love and be loved; they also leave themselves vulnerable to the abusive personality. The beginning of a sexual relationship can be characterized by its intense emotions, completing the first element of intimate homicide. Individuals with poor self-concept and lacking self-control are unable to channel intense emotions, which can turn quickly from love to hate when the relationship ends or fails to be satisfying.

A second ingredient to intimate homicide is that the abuser must have the ability to carry out lethal violence. Since males commit approximately 90 percent of all murders in the United States, it is not surprising that they also commit the majority of intimate murders. Generally, men have the physical attributes to overcome their female partners if they choose to. Coupled with the psychological and social explanations for battering, there appears to be a greater willingness to engage in violent encounters in order to maintain power and control in intimate relationships. Of the

---

In the News: Police Officer Kills His Wife

On December 22, 1998, Pamela Selby, 35, was shot twice in the head while sleeping at home. On the wall was a message written in lipstick that read, "I told you I'd get you in my letter." A typewritten note was found in the home; it stated, "I'm going to kill your wife because you arrested me." Pamela and her husband, Philadelphia Police Officer Carl Selby, had a history of domestic violence. Mrs. Selby was about to leave her husband.

Several neighbors, who were interviewed by police, stated that Carl was a pleasant and quiet man. Forensic testing revealed that Officer Selby wrote the handwritten notes from the crime scene and that letters sent through the mail also originated from him. He was arrested for the murder of his wife (Sarlat, 1999). On April 30, 1999, he was found guilty of first-degree murder and sentenced to life in prison.

1,830 persons murdered by intimates in 1998, 72 percent or 1,320 were women (Rennison & Welchans, 2000).

The good news is that the homicide rate of intimates has declined over the past two decades (Fox & Zawitz, 1999). The most pronounced decline has been in the number of men killed by intimate partners. The number of men murdered by an intimate partner fell 60 percent from 1976 to 1998 (Rennison & Welchans, 2000). The number of women killed by intimates has also declined, 23 percent between 1993 and 1997. When intimate homicide was broken down by gender and race, the biggest difference was noted among blacks. Over the past two decades, the rate of homicide among black female victims fell by 46 percent and among black males by 77 percent. White females represent the only category of victims for whom intimate partner homicide has not decreased substantially since 1976. Between 1997 and 1998 the number of white females killed by an intimate partner increased 15 percent (Rennison & Welchans, 2000).

The availability of guns has been the most frequently noted factor contributing to all forms of homicide. Despite a recent decline, firearms were the weapons used in 65 percent of all intimate murders in 1996 (Greenfeld et al., 1998). More wives (95 percent) than husbands (69 percent) used a gun or knife to inflict death (Langan & Dawson, 1995). The opportunity for lethal violence is seized with the means to carry out the threat immediately with deadly force.

Spouse Murder Defendants.   Husbands and wives kill each other in a proportion that is closer to those of other intimate relationships, but the difference is growing. The number of men murdered by intimates dropped 68 percent between 1976 and 2000, from 1,357 in 1976 to 440 in 2000 (Rennison, 2003). The number of women killed by an intimate has also declined, but only by 22 percent, from 1,600 to 1,247 in 2000 (Rennison, 2003). When a husband murders his wife, it is referred to as *uxoricide*.

Femicide is a word recently come into use by scholars of domestic violence; it refers to the killing of a woman by her relative, friend, or lover. Femicide has been defined as "the misogynistic killing of women by men" (Radford & Russell, 1992, p. 11).

This welcome decline in intimate homicide has been studied, and explanations are being offered to account for this downward trend. One explanation being offered is that people are not getting married as frequently. In one study, the decline in the number of people getting married was closely related to the decline in rates of intimate homicide (Rosenfeld, 1997). Advocates claim that domestic violence hotlines, legal advocacy, and shelter interventions have been successful in lowering the rate of domestic homicide. As services to female victims of domestic violence increased between 1976 to 1996, the rate of intimate partner homicide decreased (Duggan, Nagin, & Rosenfeld, 2003).

Wife defendants are not being convicted as frequently as males, and they are receiving substantially fewer prison terms than do husbands who kill. A possible explanation is the high rate of victim provocation noted in these cases that may justify the battered women's syndrome defense. A small percentage of spouse murders are not prosecuted; typically the perpetrators are victims of domestic violence who killed their abusers in self-defense.

Risk Factors in Spousal Homicide.   Several studies have looked at the risk factors and death rituals associated with spousal homicide in an effort to understand why it happens. A recent research effort cites a combination of factors that increases the likelihood of intimate partner homicide involving an abusive man who kills his female partner, rather than one single factor (Campbell et al., 2003). The study suggests that the risk of intimate partner homicide is increased fourfold if the abuser is unemployed. A batterer's unemployment, access to guns, and threats of deadly violence are the strongest predictors of femicide. After extensive consultation and constant validity support, co-investigator Campbell developed the Danger Assessment instrument (see Figure 11–5).

The National Victim Assistance Academy outlined some major risk factors for homicide by an intimate or partner (Seymour et al., 2000):

- Prior history of violence
- Frequency and severity of violence over time
- Addiction to illegal drugs, especially crack, PCP, and methamphetamine
- The practice of threatening death rituals
- Homicidal and/or suicidal ideation
- Access to weapons, especially firearms
- Announcement of the intimate partner that she or he is leaving the relationship

In one study, an increased risk of homicide in domestic homosexual relationships was noted when there was a large disparity between the couple's ages or when the offender had an arrest history for a violent offense (Block & Christakos, 1996).

DANGER ASSESSMENT
Jacquelyn C. Campbell, Ph.D., R.N.
Copyright, 2003

Several risk factors have been associated with increased risk of homicides (murders) of women and men in violent relationships. We cannot predict what will happen in your case, but we would like you to be aware of the danger of homicide in situations of abuse and for you to see how many of the risk factors apply to your situation.

Using the calendar, please mark the approximate dates during the past year when you were abused by your partner or ex partner. Write on that date how bad the incident was according to the following scale:
1. Slapping, pushing; no injuries and/or lasting pain
2. Punching, kicking; bruises, cuts, and/or continuing pain
3. "Beating up"; severe contusions, burns, broken bones
4. Threat to use weapon; head injury, internal injury, permanent injury
5. Use of weapon; wounds from weapon

(If **any** of the descriptions for the higher number apply, use the higher number.)

Mark **Yes** or **No** for each of the following. ("He" refers to your husband, partner, ex-husband, ex-partner, or whoever is currently physically hurting you.)

_____ 1. Has the physical violence increased in severity or frequency over the past year?
_____ 2. Does he own a gun?
_____ 3. Have you left him after living together during the past year?
        3a. (If have never lived with him, check here____)
_____ 4. Is he unemployed?
_____ 5. Has he ever used a weapon against you or threatened you with a lethal weapon?
                                           (If yes, was the weapon a gun?____)

Figure 11–5   Based on several risk factors, the Campbell instrument is used to determine if an individual is at high risk of partnership murder. If you are concerned about your situation, seek professional advise. *(From Farlane, J., Campbell, J., Witt, S., Sachs, C., Ulrich, Y., & Xu, X. (1999). Stalking and Intimate Partner Femicide.* Homicide Studies, 3(4), 300–316. *www.son.jhmi.edu. Used with permission.)*

The term *death ritual* refers to the pattern of abuse that may lead to homicide. It begins when the abuser talks about weapons, then displays weapons, then brandishes weapons. This occurs while he or she is making threats to the victim. The offender may actually take the partner to a secluded area and threaten to kill him or her there if the partner ever tries to leave. The more these rituals are acted out, the more likely it is that the abuser will carry out his or her threats.

Murder-Suicide.   This is a situation that involves a homicide with the subsequent suicide of the perpetrator. Most clusters involve family members or intimates, with a husband as the most frequent perpetrator. Usually the husband kills his wife or intimate, and within minutes or hours commits suicide. Shooting is the most frequent method of killing.

_____ 6. Does he threaten to kill you?

_____ 7. Has he avoided being arrested for domestic violence?

_____ 8. Do you have a child that is not his?

_____ 9. Has he ever forced you to have sex when you did not wish to do so?

_____ 10. Does he ever try to choke you?

_____ 11. Does he use illegal drugs? By drugs, I mean "uppers" or amphetamines, speed, angel dust, cocaine, "crack", street drugs or mixtures.

_____ 12. Is he an alcoholic or problem drinker?

_____ 13. Does he control most or all of your daily activities? For instance: does he tell you who you can be friends with, when you can see your family, how much money you can use, or when you can take the car? (If he tries, but you do not let him, check here: _____)

_____ 14 Is he violently and constantly jealous of you? (For instance, does he say "If I can't have you, no one can.")

_____ 15. Have you ever been beaten by him while you were pregnant? (If you have never been pregnant by him, check here: _____)

_____ 16. Have you ever threatened or tried to commit suicide?

_____ 17. Has he ever threatened or tried to commit suicide?

_____ 18. Does he threaten to harm your children?

_____ 19. Do you believe he is capable of killing you?

_____ 20. Does he follow or spy on you, leave threatening notes or messages on answering machine, destroy your property, or call you when you don't want him to?

_____   Total "Yes" Answers

**Thank you. Please talk to your nurse, advocate or counselor about
what the Danger Assessment means in terms of your situation.**

Figure 11–5   (cont'd)

An estimated 1,500 homicide-suicides occur in the United States per year (Cohen, 2000).

Approximately 2 percent of all homicides in the United States are classified as a murder-suicide (Wellford & Cronin, 1999). In 18 percent of cases where a husband killed his wife (uxoricide), he also committed, or attempted to commit, suicide (National Institute of Justice, 1999). In Canada, the only country with a national system for collecting homicide-suicide information, approximately 10 percent of homicide offenders commit suicide (Gillespie et al., 1998). In as many as 40 percent of multiple-victim family homicide cases where a child was killed (**familicide**), the perpetrator also committed suicide (Finkelhor & Ormrod, 2001).

Cohen reports that older adults have homicide-suicide rates that are twice as high as younger adults (Cohen, 2000). Elder homicide-suicide rates represent approximately 1,000 deaths per year. Contrary to popular belief, the majority of these episodes do not represent mercy killings or acts of love, she maintains. Rather, these are acts of desperation and depression among the elderly. Physical violence, verbal

---

Case Example

The body of an adult woman was placed under a bridge abutment along a major highway. She was in her nightgown, and her hands were tied in front of her. Less than a mile away the victim's vehicle was found, out of gas. The victim was soon identified as a person reported missing from a neighboring state. She had lived with her teenage daughter in an upscale neighborhood. Signs of struggle in her bedroom indicated that she had been killed in her own home. It was an odd case; investigators sat around wondering why the body had been moved. It did not seem to make sense to the seasoned detectives. One finally remarked that the only reason to have moved the body was to move suspicion away from the house. It pointed to the daughter as the most likely perpetrator; she was the only one who would gain by the distance.

Ultimately, the daughter was charged with the crime. She had been fighting with her mother over a boyfriend of whom the mother did not approve. That disapproval cost the mother her life; it was a joint killing committed by the teenage daughter and the controversial boyfriend.

---

discord, and lawsuits were prominent in the older southeastern couples of this study. At least three types of spousal homicide-suicide involving older couples have been identified (Cohen, 2000):

1. *Dependent-protective.* These represent about half of the episodes involving elder homicide-suicide. In this category the couple has been married for a long time and is highly dependent on each other. The man fears losing control of his ability to care for or protect his wife due to a real or perceived change in his health.

Figure 11–6 Mercy killings among elderly couples are a rare occurrence. Experts tell us that the mutually dependent couple where the man murders his sick wife and then kills himself only happens in about 20 percent of elder murder-suicides. Marital conflict or domestic violence provides a more frequent explanation.

2. *Aggressive.* Occurring in about 30 percent of elder homicide-suicide cases, there is marital conflict or domestic violence within the relationship. This type is more common in young-old couples, ages 55 to 65 years. The perpetrator is usually much older than the victim. Pending or actual separation, issuance of a restraining order, and threatening behavior are common precipitants.

3. *Symbiotic.* An extreme interdependency characterizes the relationship in cases involving about 20 percent of couples where homicide-suicide occurs. One or both of the individuals are extremely sick, leading the husband to a mercy killing. The male perpetrator is often the dominant personality and the female victim is often submissive.

Familicide.   An extremely rare form of domestic lethal violence, familicide is defined as a multiple-victim homicide incident in which the killer's spouse or ex-spouse and one or more children are slain. In 1997, 6 percent of homicides of children and youth (approximately 115) were committed as part of multiple-victim family members in which a family member killed a juvenile along with other victims (Federal Bureau of Investigation, 1997).

Researchers Wilson and Daly used information from Canada, England, and Wales to examine the phenomenon of familicide (Wilson & Daly, 1996). They found that the majority (93 to 96 percent) of familicide incidents were perpetrated by men. The child victims are almost equally divided between sons and daughters. The recording of pertinent data in Chicago between 1965 and 1989 allowed analysis for familicide in that city. Of the 15 familicides during the 25-year period, one was committed by a female.

Additionally, Wilson and Daly reported that suicide is particularly prevalent in familicide cases. Interviews showed that perpetrators (some who had failed at their suicide attempt) were often despondent at the time of killing their family. Experiencing a recent devastating experience of personal and financial failure, and dwelling on the probable shame to the wife and children, are justifications for taking all their lives. Sorrow rather than anger appears to be the motivating factor for these killings.

Parricide.   **Parricide** is the killing of one's parent. When a mother is killed by one of her children, the term **matricide** is used to describe the specific form of criminal homicide. **Patricide** is the act of killing one's father. In the majority of cases where a mother or father is killed by his or her offspring, the perpetrator is an adult. Adult parricide offenders are different from juvenile offenders. They generally have a history of severe mental illness with little or no history of parental abuse. According to Weisman and Sharma, mothers are the targets more often than fathers with both sons and daughters. Sons almost exclusively commit double parricides, in which both parents are killed (Weisman & Sharma, 1997).

Compared to the other categories of lethal violence, parricide is relatively rare. Approximately 300 victims a year, and less than 2 percent of the total murder victims, are killed by their offspring (Dawson & Langan, 1994). In *Why Kids Kill Parents,* author Kathleen Heide examined the existing literature on juvenile murderers and concluded that the victim's death was perceived as a relief by the offender (Heide, 1992). This was evidenced by the apparent lack of remorse initially observed in the offender. Severe family violence was characterized in all homes where the juvenile ultimately took the life of the parent(s). Parental brutality against the youth included numerous forms of domestic violence and the witnessing of spouse abuse. Alcoholism and heavy drinking by the father were cited frequently. Heide noted that the easy availability to a gun was a critical factor in the majority of parricide cases. In a more recent review of sixty-eight parricide cases, 69 percent of the offenders had a prior inpatient psychiatric hospitalization with diagnoses of psychosis (usually schizophrenia or schizo affective disorder); 74 percent had known criminal convictions; and 64 percent had been convicted of a violent crime (Weisman & Sharma, 1997).

Infanticide.　The term **infanticide** refers to the murder or killing of an infant soon after its birth (Black, 1990). Reports on infanticide often include murdered children over the age of five, an incorrect use of the term. Children killed under the age of five are included as infanticide victims in the figures reported by the Bureau of Justice Statistics. Parents and stepparents have consistently been the most frequent killers of infants since 1976. More children 0 to 4 years of age in the United States now die from homicide than from infectious diseases or cancer. There were 593 infanticides reported in the United States in 1999 (Finkelhor & Ormrod, 2001). Almost ¾ of the infant murders are committed by family members. Male and female infants were murdered in equal numbers in 1999, typically by personal weapons (i.e., hands and feet).

　　　The felonious destruction of the fetus is called **feticide** or criminal abortion. An estimated 17 percent of adult women are battered during pregnancy; teenagers battered during pregnancy may be as high as 21 percent (Burnley et al., 1996). A pregnant woman who aborts due to injury caused by her batterer that results in the death of the fetus would be included as feticide. There is no accurate number of these deaths.

More About It: Sudden Infant Death Syndrome

Sudden infant death syndrome (SIDS) is the unexplained death of an apparently healthy infant under one year of age. It is sometimes called crib death because most of these children die in their sleep. We don't know exactly what causes these children to die, but the U.S. Department of Health and Human Services has predicted a possible 50 percent decrease in the incidence of death through precautionary measures. Known as the "Back to Sleep" campaign, the American Academy of Pediatrics in 1992 recommended that babies be placed on their backs or sides to sleep, which significantly reduces the risk of SIDS. This effort was credited with a 30 percent actual reduction in SIDS deaths between 1992 and 1995 (U.S. Department of Health and Human Services, 1996).

A large percentage of infant deaths have been attributed to natural cases, most notably **sudden infant death syndrome** (SIDS). Advanced investigation into some SIDS-related deaths has revealed criminal homicide in recent years. Mistaken identification of infanticide may be attributable to the lack of evidence generally and criminal intent specifically. Concern for the mother's loss of a child may sometimes prevent further inquiry into the death. Recent controversy surrounding SIDS death has brought an increased awareness to criminal investigation. As many as 57 percent of infant deaths ruled as accidents actually resulted from maltreatment, according to child fatality researchers (Finkelhor & Ormrod, 2001).

Many people believe that in SIDS-related deaths the infants suffocated themselves because they were found with their faces pressed into the mattress. Studies have repeatedly disproved this theory. When death is caused by suffocation, it cannot immediately be attributed to SIDS; further investigation is warranted. Petechial hemorrhages, broken blood vessels on the eyes and surrounding area, will be apparent in most cases of suffocation. Investigators should be aware that SIDS is actually quite rare, and multiple SIDS deaths in the same family or day care facility are immediately suspicious.

Figure 11-7 In the United States, approximately one woman per day is shot and killed by her intimate partner during the course of an argument.

Filicide.   **Filicide** is the killing of children by parents; it is a nonlegal term that in some studies may include victims of infanticide. Although all murder is tragic, a parent's killing of a child is a form of abuse that is difficult to understand. Children are unable to protect themselves against abuse and have no alternatives when confronted with lethal violence.

The prevailing belief is that approximately 2,000 infants and children die in the United States each year from abuse and neglect. Most deaths from known events are due to neglect. The official estimate includes only those cases that have come to the attention of authorities and were substantiated as abuse. Law enforcement officers know that abuse is not always a clear determination and that the statistics do not include those investigations where proof was lacking, or when an allegation was plea bargained to a lesser charge.

From the 29 states that provided fatality data for 1997, a trend was determined that indicated an 8 percent decrease in child fatalities. The actual number is expected to increase as information is received from the remaining states (Wang & Daro, 1998). The vast majority of the child abuse deaths in 1997 (41 percent) were from families who had prior or current contact with child protective services. Between 1995 and 1997, 44 percent died from neglect, 51 percent died from abuse, and 5 percent died as a result of multiple forms of maltreatment.

There is no one explanation that can be offered as to why parents or caretakers abuse and sometimes kill their children. In a recent clinical study, cases of victims who were killed by their mothers were recently examined (Bourget & Gagne, 2002). Most victims were less than 6 years of age, and there were several cases of the murders of multiple siblings. Of the 34 victims, 19 (55.9 percent) were male, and 15 (44.1 percent) were female. They ranged in age from approximately 4 weeks of age to 13 years. There were 27 mothers in the sample of perpetrators, and 15 of these women committed suicide after the filicide. Eighteen of the mothers had a diagnosis of schizophrenia or other psychosis.

Fratricide.   The killing of a brother or sister is called fratricide. Rarer than any other family homicide, it occurs in 1.5 percent of the total criminal deaths in the United States. It is estimated that in sibling murders, females were the perpetrators in 15 percent of the cases.

Investigative Strategies

Since 1976, more than 52,000 men and women have been murdered by those with whom they shared an intimate relationship (Greenfeld et al., 1998). The implication of a domestic relationship is far more significant for female murder victims than male murder victims, however. Males are most often the perpetrators and the victims in homicides, and they are nine times more likely than females to commit a murder; both male and female offenders are more likely to target male than female victims (Fox & Zawitz, 1999). Without obvious signs of a theft-, gang-, or drug-related murder, the investigator looks from the intimate relations outward toward the strangers.

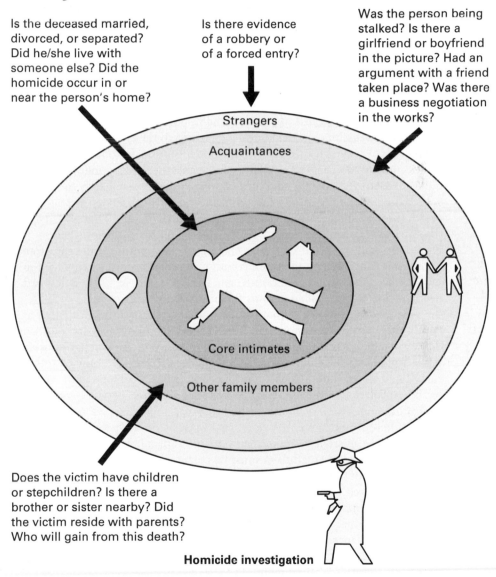

Is the deceased married, divorced, or separated? Did he/she live with someone else? Did the homicide occur in or near the person's home?

Is there evidence of a robbery or of a forced entry?

Was the person being stalked? Is there a girlfriend or boyfriend in the picture? Had an argument with a friend taken place? Was there a business negotiation in the works?

Strangers

Acquaintances

Core intimates

Other family members

Does the victim have children or stepchildren? Is there a brother or sister nearby? Did the victim reside with parents? Who will gain from this death?

Homicide investigation

Figure 11–8   The circle of death surrounds the body of the homicide victim.

The investigation of death begins with an examination of the area immediately surrounding the body. Clues within the circle of death aid in the primary first step of determining if the death is due to homicide, suicide, or attributable to natural causes. If the victim has been shot or otherwise physically wounded, cause of death may appear self-evident but cannot be considered conclusive until a forensic medical autopsy has been performed. Police officers work closely with a medical examiner, sometimes called a coroner, to determine the cause of death. If the person died under the care of a physician for a known fatal illness, an autopsy may not be necessary. For violent or sudden deaths that were not witnessed by another person, autopsy is often standard procedure. Confirmation of a sexual assault may be necessary and is considered regardless of the age or gender of the deceased. The coroner is a medical doctor who has received additional training in conducting the forensic autopsy. Officially pronouncing the victim dead and naming the cause of death are the responsibilities of the coroner.

The collection of evidence also begins within the circle and moves outward. The victim tells a story: The place where the body is found, its gender, injury, and even the positioning of the body speak to the circumstances surrounding the death. Some police departments employ specialists who are called immediately to work on evidence collection; some departments train their own police officers to do this step. Whether or not forensic specialists are called by the police depends on the severity of the crime, the apparent signs of the cause of death, and the policy in the jurisdiction of the crime. Experts in ballistics, hair and fiber analysis, DNA analysis, fingerprint analysis, and photography are among the more common forensic specialists involved in the initial murder investigation, in addition to law enforcement. As more is learned about the death, others may be called to assist the primary investigators.

Approximately half of homicide victims know their assailants, either as intimates, family members, or acquaintances. The expectation of privacy that may exist due to a domestic relationship underscores the need for a search warrant in homicide investigations. Evidence seized without a warrant may otherwise fall prey to the exclusionary rule. The rule excludes the use of evidence to prove a person's guilt when it has been seized in violation of the offender's constitutional rights.

Guidelines have been established to assist police officers and to assure that the rights inherent under the *Mincey v. Arizona* decision are protected. An example of a form that is consistent with the requirements is provided in Figure 11–9. The information contained in an affidavit must be particular to the crime committed, give the exact location of the evidence, and detail exactly what the officer seeks to seize.

The search to identify the perpetrator of the murder also begins in the circle immediately surrounding the victim. The vast majority of intimate murders occur in the victim's home. Likely suspects are considered from the core intimates outward. The core intimate refers to the husband, wife, boyfriend, or girlfriend of the victim. If the person slain is female, the probability that the suspect is someone other than a stranger is increased substantially.

The victim–offender relationship varies with the age of the victim. Of all known murders, a family member most often commits the killing of a young child. In other

* This is a Mere Evidence Search Warrant Affidavit and Application pursuant to
Mincey v. Arizona (1978) 437 U.S. 385.

A.)   Blood, semen, saliva, physiological fluids and secretions, hair fibers, fingerprints, palm prints, footprints, shoeprints, weapons and firearms including pistols, rifles, revolvers, shotguns, hatchets, axes, cutting instruments and cutting tools, blunt force instruments, projectiles, ammunition, bullet casings and fragments; dirt, dust and soil, paint samples, glass and plastic fragments, marks of tools used to gain access to locked premises or containers, and items containing traces of any of the above mentioned articles.

B.)   Constitutes evidence of an offense, or that a particular person participated in the commission of an offense, to wit: **Murder**

C.)   **Description of the location of the place to be searched goes here.**

D.)   **(The following paragraphs should be added to the wording of the Search Warrant application at the end of the Affidavit).**

1.   That the affient, _____ , is a regular member of the   Police Department and has been a member for the past _____ years. That I am presently assigned to the Detective Division's Major Crime Squad Scene processing Unit and have been so assigned for the past _____ years. That I have investigated and processed numerous serious and violent crimes, including murder, and have received specialized training and experience in the collection of physical evidence, crime scene processing and the investigation of such cases. That I have personal knowledge of the facts and circumstances hereinafter related as a result of my own investigative efforts and those of brother officers who have reported their findings to me.

(One of the two affiants should be a member of the crime scene processing unit. The second affient should be an investigator and should include his customary paragraph of introduction.)

2.   That the affiants do believe that the offense herein before stated was committed at the location to be searched in that: (Specify circumstances indicating commission of the offenses at the place to be searched: include information as to when the crime was first reported, what first officer on the scene observed, a description of the scene, etc. This information may require several paragraphs.)

3.   That the affiants have personal knowledge, based on their experience and training, that crimes of violence involve a struggle, a break, the use of weapons and other instrumentality, and/or the element of unpredictability. That the person or persons participating in the commission of a violent offense is in contact with physical surroundings in a forceful or otherwise detectable manner. That there is often an attempt to alter, destroy, remove, clean up or cover up evidence of a crime. That traces may be left in the form of blood, semen, saliva, physiological fluids and secretions, hair, fibers, fingerprints, palm prints, footprints, shoeprints, weapons and firearms including pistols, rifles, revolvers, shotguns, hatchets, axes, cutting instruments and cutting tools, blunt force instruments, projectiles, ammunition, bullet casings and fragments; dirt, dust and soil, paint samples, glass and plastic fragments, marks of tools used to gain access to locked premises or containers, and items containing traces of any of the above mentioned articles. That many of the above items are minute and microscopic, thus requiring additional specialized examination by forensic laboratory techniques.

4.   That the affiants have personal knowledge based upon their experience and training, that crime scene, such as described above, will contain physical evidence, herein before itemized, which will aid in establishing the identity of the perpetrator (s), the circumstances under which the crime was committed, and/or which in general will assist in the discovery of the pertinent facts; and that such evidence requires a systematic search to located, seize, record and process.

5.   That based on the foregoing facts and information, the affiants have probable cause to believe and do believe that evidence of the MURDER will be found within and upon (specify the place to be searched).

Figure 11–9   Sample Mincey warrant application.

More About It: The Mincey Warrant Requirement

A common misconception is that an investigation into the death of a person does not require a search warrant to seize evidence. Although many exceptions to the Fourth Amendment warrant requirement do exist, the death of a human being is not among them. Precedence for homicide investigations conducted within private homes was established in *Mincey v. Arizona* (1978) when the U.S. Supreme Court struck down the "murder scene exception" of that state. The case involved an undercover police officer who was killed during a drug buy at Mincey's apartment. Following the murder, police officers secured the scene, then conducted a four-day search of the apartment. They subsequently seized hundreds of items. The Court held that the exhaustive search of the apartment of Mincey was unreasonable and a violation of his privacy, even though the police were lawfully in the apartment.

Without a warrant, a police officer may be on the premises legally to conduct an "emergency" response, such as a search for other victims and for the killer. Hot pursuit and imminent danger to people are examples of recognized emergencies. The possibility of evidence destruction is considered an exigent circumstance. The officers may search only for evidence establishing the circumstances of death or circumstances relevant to motive, intent, or knowledge.

A person can waive his or her personal rights to Fourth Amendment protection and consent to a search of his or her property. This consent must be given prior to the commencement of the search and must be made freely and intelligently by the person or a proper third party. Consent searching is the most frequently challenged exception and should be used judicially in a homicide investigation. A search warrant is necessary, according to the *Mincey* decision, for a homicide crime scene investigation, in the absence of other recognized exceptions.

words, when a child is murdered in the United States, the most likely killer is a family member (Greenfeld, 1996). People over the age of 50 make up 12 percent of the murder victims in the United States. For victims over age 60, their children represent the most frequent killer, committing approximately 42 percent of these murders. When the murder of an elder is committed by a family member, the spouse is the perpetrator in approximately 24 percent of cases (Dawson & Langan, 1994).

Death Review Teams.   In 1978 the Los Angeles County Inter-Agency Council on Child Abuse and Neglect (ICAN) formed the first child fatality review team in the United States (Langstaff & Sleeper, 2001). The purpose of the multidisciplinary team was to share resources and information in the forensic investigation of child fatalities. Today there are child death review teams in all 50 states, Australia, and Canada. They review child deaths from various causes, often with an emphasis on reviewing child deaths involving caretaker abuse and or neglect. Benefits of the review include improved interagency case management, identification of service gaps, and systems designed to protect children. The common goal of all teams is the prevention of child death and injury. The National Center on Child Fatality Review (NCFR) provides online data sets and information on infant homicide. The searchable database online allows professionals to locate the regional resources and provides links to all 50 states. Some counties and states have extended the scope of their reviews to include fatal domestic violence deaths.

Using the same premise as the ICAN, the first elder death investigation review team (EDIRT) was formed in Sacramento, California in 2000 (Nerenberg, 2003). Its purpose was to assist in the identification and prosecution of elder abuse–related deaths and to enhance medical professionals' skill in making cause of death determinations. Forensic investigations may prove helpful in evaluating suicide-homicides and long-term care facilities. Similar teams are being formed nationwide to address the complex forensic needs of elder fatalities. Typical members of these multidisciplinary efforts include coroners, medical examiners, mental health professionals, law enforcement personnel, and prosecutors, based on the needs of the particular locality.

CONCLUSIONS

This chapter began with an introduction to the crime of stalking. It is a newly defined crime that had been linked to celebrities. The crime is called gender neutral because it affects both female and male victims, although the majority are women. A major difference between stalking and other crimes is that it consists of a series of actions rather than a single act. It may involve activities that are otherwise legal if not committed within the context of other criminal behavior. Extreme fear is often felt by those victimized in this manner.

Following or harassing constitutes a major element of the crime. The actions are purposeful, and a specific person is targeted for the unwanted attention. A stalker can be anyone: a former intimate or acquaintance, or a perfect stranger. Every report should be taken seriously, as the behavior is known to turn violent in approximately one-fourth of cases. An important note relative to the role of law enforcement is the changing role of the police officer to involve prevention in addition to crime response. This means that a threat assessment should be conducted to learn if the victim is in imminent danger.

Also included in this chapter was a discussion on domestic homicide. A substantial number of Americans have been touched by a tragic death of a close friend or family member. Although some forms of purposeful death are justified or excused in our society, this does not mean that the practice of taking a life is taken lightly or without controversy. Recent statistics suggest that the homicide rate of intimates has declined, most pronouncedly in the number of men killed by an intimate. This may be due to the increased information, services, and options that are available to victims of abuse. Another explanation is the decline in the frequency of marriage. Suicide-murder situations involving elders is a category that should be watched in the future. Since the rates for this category appear to be double compared to younger adults, we can expect this to rise with the increased aging population in the United States.

      The circle of death for both adults and children is used to illustrate the investigative strategy when a victim of homicide is discovered. The family and friends of the victim are eliminated as suspects through this method. Evidence is also located within the area surrounding the body. For these reasons, the crime scene must be protected and a search conducted that protects the legal rights of domestic killers. A search warrant should be sought whenever possible, due to the possibility of a relationship between the victim and the killer.

QUESTIONS FOR REVIEW

1. Describe the crime of stalking.

2. What are the most common behaviors of stalking?

3. What makes these behaviors illegal?

4. Why does the "threat requirement" of some statutes become a difficult obstacle to overcome?

5. Describe the three types of stalkers that were presented in this chapter. Are there any characteristics common to other forms of domestic violence offenders?

6. Although false allegations in reports of violent crime are rare, why are they significant?

7. Explain some common safety precautions for stalking victims. Why would they be necessary?

8. What is the most frequently noted factor contributing to all forms of homicide?

9. Choose one of the family relationships and describe the prevalence of murder within it.

10. What is a Mincey warrant? Why is it important?

INTERNET-BASED EXERCISES

1. How much do you know about stalking? What is the law in your state? Look to AARDVARC (Abuse, Rape & Domestic Violence Aid & Resource Collection Web site), which provides links to the stalking laws in all 50 states and other information about stalking. You can find this site at the following URL: http://www.aardvarc.org/

2. What are the victim and offender characteristics in intimate partner homicide? Find out more about this subject. Look to a report from the Bureau of Justice

Statistics, entitled *Intimate Partner Violence*, May 2000, NCJ 178247. This is one place where you can find the report online: http://www.ojp.usdoj.gov/bjs/pub/pdf/ipv.pdf.

References

Balos, Beverly, and Mary L. Fellows. 2000. *Law and Violence against Women: Cases and Materials on Systems of Oppression.* Durham, NC: Carolina Academic Press.

Black, H. C. 1990. *Black's Law Dictionary.* St. Paul, MN: West Publishing Co.

Block, Carolyn R., and Antigone Christakos. 1996. "Chicago Intimate Partner Homicide: Patterns and Trends across Three Decades." In *Lethal Violence: Proceedings of the 1995 Meeting of the Homicide Research Working Group.* Washington, DC: U.S. Department of Justice.

Bourget, Dominique, and Pierre Gagne. 2002. "Maternal Filicide in Quebec." *Journal of the American Academy of Psychiatry and the Law* 30(3):345–51.

Burnley, Jane et al. (eds.). 1996. *National Victim Assistance Academy Textbook.* Washington, DC: Office for Victims of Crime.

———. 1998. "Chapter 16 Supplement." In *Homicide: Its Impact and Consequences: Statistical Overview.* 1997–1998 Academy Text Supplement edition. Washington, DC: U.S. Department of Justice.

Campbell, Jacquelyn. 2004. "Identifying Risk Factors for Femicide in Violence Intimate Relationships" [Web page]. Accessed 2004. Available at *http://www.son.jhmi.edu/research/CNR/Homicide/default.htm.*

Campbell, Jacquelyn C., Phyllis Sharps, Kathryn Laughon, Daniel Webster, Jennifer Manganello, Janet Schollenberger, Jane Koziol-McLain, Carolyn R. Block, Doris Campbell, Mary A. Curry, Nancy Glass, Faye Gary, Judith McFarlane, Carolyn Sachs, Yvonne Ulrich, Susan A. Wilt, Xiao Xu, and Victoria A. Frye. 2003. "Risk Factors for Femicide in Abusive Relationships: Results from a Multisite Case Control Study." *American Journal of Public Health* 93(7):1089–98.

Cohen, Donna. 2000. "Homicide-Suicide in Older People." *Psychiatric Times.* January. Vol. XVII: 1.

Dalton, Clare, and Elizabeth M. Schneider. 2001. *Battered Women and the Law.* New York,: Foundation Press.

Dawson, J., and P. Langan. 1994. *Murder in Families.* NCJ 143498. Washington, DC: U.S. Department of Justice.

Death Penalty Information Center. 2004. "Clemency" [Web page]. Accessed 2004. Available at *http://www.deathpenaltyinfo.org/article.php?did=126&scid=13#process.*

Duggan, Laura, Daniel Nagin, and Richard Rosenfeld. 2003. "Do Domestic Violence Services Save Lives?" *National Institute of Justice Journal* (250):25–29.

Farlane, Judith, Jacquelyn Campbell, Susan Wilt, Carolyn Sachs, Yvonne Ulrich, and Xiao Xu. 1999. "Stalking and Intimate Partner Femicide." *Homicide Studies* 3(4):300–316.

Federal Bureau of Investigation. 1997. "Uniform Crime Reporting Program Data: U.S. Supplementary Homicide Reports 1980–1997." Computer file. Ann Arbor, MI: Inter-University Consortium for Political and Social Research. Reported by Finkelhor, David, and Richard Ormrod. 2001. *Homicides of Children and Youth.* Juvenile Justice Bulletin. NCJ 187239. Washington, DC: U.S. Department of Justice.

Fein, Robert A., and Bryan Vossekuil. 1998. *Protective Intelligence Threat Assessment Investigations: A Guide for State and Local Law Enforcement Officials.* NCJ 170612. Washington, DC: U.S. Department of Justice.

Finkelhor, David, and Richard Ormrod. 2001. *Homicides of Children and Youth.* Juvenile Justice
Bulletin. NCJ 187239. Washington, DC: U.S. Department of Justice.

Fox, James A., and Marianne W. Zawitz. 1999. *Homicide Trends in the United States.* NCJ 173956.
Washington, DC: U.S. Department of Justice.

Garner, B. (2001). *Black's Law Dictionary* (2nd ed.). St. Paul, MN: West Publishing Co.

Gillespie, M., V. Hearn, and R. A. Silverman. 1998. "Suicide Following Homicide in Canada."
Homicide Studies 2(1):46–63.

Greenfeld, Lawrence. 1996. *Child Victimizers: Violent Offenders and Their Victims.* Bureau of Justice Statistics, Executive Summary. NIJ 158625. Washington, DC: U.S. Department of
Justice.

Greenfeld, Lawrence, Michael Rand, Diane Craven, Patsy Klaus, Craig Perkins, Cheryl Ringel,
Greg Warchol, Cathy Maston, and James Fox. 1998. *Violence by Intimates: Analysis of Crimes
by Current or Former Spouses, Boyfriends, and Girlfriends.* NCJ 167237. Washington, DC: U.S.
Department of Justice.

Heide, Kathleen M. 1992. *Why Kids Kill Parents: Child Abuse and Adolescent Homicide.* Columbus,
OH: Ohio State University Press.

Langan, Patrick A., and John M. Dawson. 1995. *Spouse Murder Defendants in Large Urban Counties.* NCJ 153256. Washington, DC: U.S. Department of Justice.

Langstaff, John, and Tish Sleeper. 2001. *The National Center on Child Fatality Review.* FS-
200112. Washington, DC: Office of Juvenile Justice and Delinquency.

Lardner, George, Jr. 1997. *The Stalking of Kristin: A Father Investigates the Murder of His Daughter.* New York: Onyx.

Mangum, Paula F. 2001. "Reconceptualizing Battered Woman Syndrome Evidence: Prosecution Use of Expert Testimony on Battering." Pp. 610–613 in *Domestic Violence Law,* Nancy K.
Lemon (ed.). St. Paul, MN: West Group.

Moenssens, Andre et al. 1995. *Scientific Evidence in Civil and Criminal Cases,* 4th ed. Westbury,
NY: Foundation Press.

Mohandie, Kris, Chris Hatcher, and Douglas Raymond. 1998. "False Victimization Syndromes
in Stalking." Pp. 225–56 in *The Psychology of Stalking: Clinical and Forensic Perspectives,* Reid
Meloy (ed.). San Diego, CA: Academic Press.

Moret, Jim. 1997. "Technology Brings Stalkers One Step Closer to Celebrities." July.
http://cgi.cnn.com. January 1999.

National Center on Elder Abuse. 1998. *The National Elder Abuse Incidence Study.* Washington,
DC: The Administration for Children and Families.

National Institute of Justice. 1998. *Stalking and Domestic Violence: The Third Annual Report to
Congress under the Violence Against Women Act.* NCJ 172204. Washington, DC: U.S. Department of Justice.

National Institute of Justice. 1999. *Proceedings of the Homicide Research Working Group Meetings,
1997 and 1998.* Research Forum. NCJ 175709. Washington, DC: U.S. Department of Justice.

Nerenberg, Lisa. 2003. "Elder Abuse Prevention Teams: A New Generation." Washington,
DC: National Center on Elder Abuse. Office of the NY State Attorney. 2003. "What is a
Triad?" [Web page]. Accessed 2004. Available at *http://www.oag.state.ny.us/seniors/triad.html.*

Orion, Doreen R. 1998. *I Know You Really Love Me: A Psychiatrist's Account of Stalking and Obsessive Love.* New York: Dell Publishing Company.

Osofsky, Joy D. 2001. *Addressing Youth Victimization.* Office of Juvenile Justice and Delinquency
Prevention. NCJ 186667. Washington, DC: U.S. Department of Justice.

Radford, J., and D. E. H. Russell. 1992. *Femicide: The Politics of Woman Killing.* New York:
Twayne Publishers.

Rennison, Callie, BJS Statistician. 2003. *Intimate Partner Violence, 1993–2001.* Bureau of Justice Statistics. NCJ 197838. Washington, DC: U.S. Department of Justice.

Rennison, Callie Marie, and Sarah Welchans. 2000. *Intimate Partner Violence.* Special Report. Bureau of Justice Statistics. Washington, DC: U.S. Department of Justice.

Rosenfeld, Barry. 2004. "Violence Risk Factors in Stalking and Obsessional Harassment: A Review and Preliminary Meta-Analysis." *Criminal Justice and Behavior* 31(1):9–36.

Rosenfeld, Richard. 1997. *Changing Relationships between Men and Women and the Decline in Intimate Partner Homicide.* NCJ 166149. Washington, DC: U.S. Department of Justice.

Sarlat, Rick. 1999. "Wife of Detective Is Murdered." January 30. Philadelphia Tribune Online Edition.

Schell, Bernadette H. 2003. "Prevalence of Sexual Harassment, Stalking, and False Victimization Syndrome (FVS) Cases and Related Human Resource Management Policies in a Cross-Section of Canadian Companies From January 1995 Through January 2000." *Journal of Family Violence* 18(6):351–60.

Seymour, A., M. Murray, J. Sigmon, M. Hook, C. Edmunds, M. Gaboury, and G. Coleman (eds.). 2002. *National Victim Assistance Academy Textbook.* Washington, DC: Office for Victims of Crime.

Sheridan, L., & Blaauw, E. 2004. "Characteristics of False Stalking Reports." *Criminal Justice and Behavior,* 31(1), 55–72.

Tjaden, Patricia, & Nancy Thoennes. 1998. *Prevalence, Incidence, and Consequences of Violence Against Women: Findings from the National Violence Against Women Survey.* NCJ 172837. Washington, DC: U.S. Department of Justice.

U.S. Department of Health and Human Services. 1996. "Reduction in SIDS Deaths Helps Bring Low Infant Mortality." *Health and Human Services News.*

Vickers, Lee. 1997. "The Second Closet: Domestic Violence in Lesbian and Gay Relationships: A Western Australian Perspective" [Web page]. Accessed 2004. Available at Murdoch University Electronic Journal of Law. *http://www.murdoch.edu.au/elaw/issues/v3n4/vickers.html.*

Wang, Ching-Tung, and Deborah Daro. 1998. *Current Trends in Child Abuse Reporting and Fatalities: The Results of the 1997 Annual Fifty-State Survey.* Working Paper 808. Chicago: National Committee to Prevent Child Abuse.

Wellford, Charles, and James Cronin. 1999. *Clearing Up Homicide Clearance Rates.* NIJ Journal 243. NCJ 181728. Washington, D.C.: National Institute of Justice.

Weisman, Adam, and Kaushal Sharma. 1997. "Parricide and Attempted Parricide." In *The Nature of Homicide: Trends and Changes—Proceedings of the 1996 Meeting of the Homicide Research Working Group.* NCJ 16149. Washington, DC: U.S. Department of Justice.

Wilson, Margo, and Martin Daly. 1996. "Familicide: Uxoricide Plus Filicide?" In *Lethal Violence: Proceedings of the 1995 Meeting of the Homicide Research Working Group.* Washington, DC: U.S. Department of Justice.

Cases

Commonwealth v. Martinez, 43 Mass. App. Ct. 408, 413 (1997).
Mincey v. Arizona, 437 U.S. 385 (1978).

Statute

New York Public Law Code, §240.30.

Part Five

The Future

Chapter 12, "Research on the Internet," is the solitary chapter in Part Five. This distinction is earned because the Internet stands alone in its importance for the future of all research, and for domestic violence research in particular. Do you know how to access the valuable information that is now available there? Where do you start in searching the World Wide Web? How will you find what you want to know? Are some sites more reliable than others? What are the criteria for evaluating the information when you find it? These questions are answered in Chapter 12. In addition, many site addresses are made available for you to begin exploring. Don't get overwhelmed, but the journey to learn more about domestic violence has just begun with this final chapter.

RESEARCH ON THE INTERNET

KEY TERMS

Browsers
Dial-up connection
Directory search engines
Domain name system
E-mail address
Internet service provider
Multisearch engine
National Crime Victimization Survey

National Incident-Based Reporting System
Robot
Self-report studies
Separation abuse
Uniform Crime Reporting System
Uniform resource locator
World Wide Web

INTRODUCTION

Domestic violence is an emerging field of study that is frequently changing and being updated with new and exciting information. The Internet is an important resource on domestic violence, since all studies conducted with federal government funding are now available there. State and federal laws are often posted on the Internet along with a legal analysis. U.S. Supreme Court decisions are available more quickly on the Internet than from traditional sources. Nonprofit organizations and self-help groups are accessible and share resources over the Internet. Even job postings are listed on the Internet. Keeping up with this technology is more important than ever before. Currency in the field now demands knowledge on accessing the wealth of data available. For students who would like to know more on a specific topic and for those conducting research, get on the **World Wide Web**!

The InterNIC, developed by the National Science Foundation in 1993, maintains domain name registration through the **domain name system** (DNS). Domain names identify a location on the Internet as an address known as the **uniform**

resource locator (URL). The first part of any domain name identifies the person, place, or organization that is located at the address. The second part of the domain name identifies the group to which the address belongs. It is like having a name or street address followed by the city or state. In some instances, the second part of the domain name identifies a country other than the United States. This gives you the exact location of an address within a group. For example, the five original domain groups that were organized specified these basic categories:

Commercial sites	.com
Educational sites	.edu or .ac
Government sites	.gov
Military sites	.mil
Organizations	.org

The most popular network service on the Internet is called the World Wide Web. Born in 1991, the Web, or WWW, supports graphics, audio, and video in addition to text. Many people think of the Internet and the World Wide Web as being the same thing. This is not the case; WWW is merely one of the many services that can be accessed over the Internet. Due to its wide public use, however, it is not uncommon for people to refer to the Internet when they really mean the World Wide Web.

With the development of the World Wide Web, the superhighway of information was opened for public use through Web browsers that are used to navigate it. **Browsers** run on your personal computer and allow you to view the World Wide Web pages. The two most popular browsers are the Netscape Navigator and Microsoft Internet Explorer. There are others; Mosaic is one that is also well known.

This chapter is a peek into the World Wide Web—that service on the Internet where you can locate information, although not necessarily reliable information, on just about anything that is of interest to you. Some of the sites are animated; some contain video and audio clips. In particular, some URLs for sites that are related to domestic violence will be offered for you to explore on your own.

Before beginning, it is important to note that anyone can post information on the World Wide Web. All one needs is an **Internet service provider** (ISP), a computer that will offer access to the Internet and store that information for others to retrieve. That means that there is a lot of junk out there. Discriminating surfers understand that information obtained through the World Wide Web must be scrutinized for its credibility. Don't believe everything you see out there!

How do you find what you are looking for? How do you know that the information is reliable? More important, how do you start? All you need are the basics and a sense of adventure. The best way to learn is to "log on" and "surf." Remember: The Internet can be fun! The more you explore, the more comfortable it becomes.

GETTING ONTO THE WORLD WIDE WEB

To get onto the World Wide Web, you need a personal computer, a browser, and an Internet connection. Most computers will support a browser; any machine that is a 486 or better will do; the Pentiums will allow better performance and are preferred, however. IBM-compatible computers that come with software installed will typically have Windows ME, Windows 98, Windows XP, or Windows NT already. Microsoft Internet Explorer is the browser that comes prepackaged with the Windows software and requires that you set it up with your Internet connection through your ISP. Instructions on how to set up your browser are contained within the program. Updated copies of both Microsoft Internet Explorer and Netscape Navigator can be downloaded from their home pages if you are not running the most current version. They are also available for purchase from most computer software stores.

The next step is to connect to the Internet. Many college and university campuses have their own computer service; the local area network (LAN) is called a direct connection. You must establish an account with the school in order to access its computer network. If you are not sure, just ask someone in the computer resource office if there is a direct Internet connection available. Once you have the browser installed on your computer and you are plugged in to a direct connection, you can just log on. If you do not have your own computer, go to the university library or computer center and find out which computers are Internet connected. Some local libraries also have one or more computers that are Internet connected and available for public use.

Another way to access the Internet is through a **dial-up connection**. This requires that you have a modem connected to your computer. America Online is a popular example, although others are also available. You pay a monthly fee and in return receive Internet access, e-mail, and a variety of other online services. The alternative to a dial-up connection is an ISP. Some service providers offer unlimited use of the Internet for a monthly fee; others prorate the cost with your estimated use. If you are not sure that you will use the Internet for long periods of time, the estimated usage fee may work for you. Be careful, though; going over your allotted time may cost heavily!

The most common use of the Internet is to communicate. It is not necessary to be on the World Wide Web for this purpose, although many people use the World Wide Web to communicate with others. Communications can occur in two ways, on a personal level or the group level. Personal communication is accomplished through e-mail. Sending an electronic message requires that both people have an **e-mail address**, which is assigned by your Internet service provider, regardless of the form of connection that you have. Typically, it is your name (or some variation of your name), followed by a designation of your service provider. E-mail can be sent from within your Internet browser.

Notice that the end of the address contains the group designation. EDU refers to the education group and would be part of your e-mail address that is obtained through a university or other service provider. The second method of communication

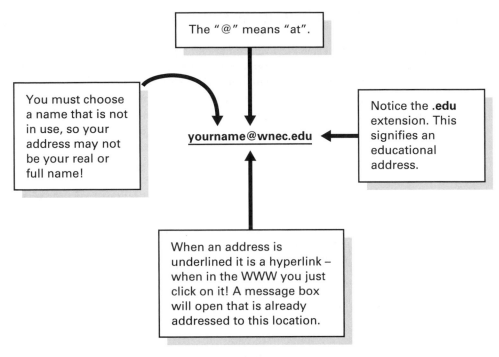

Figure 12–1   This is a *POP* (Post Office Protocol) mail address.

is on the group level. This refers to user and chat groups. Explore those on your own if you would like to "speak" with others who share your interests.

Once connected to the Internet, you are ready to browse the World Wide Web. What next? The World Wide Web is your library, literally an entrance to the world of knowledge. Open your browser and you will see an area in which to type in the URL of the site that you want to visit. The URL is a specific address on the Internet. Later in this chapter, you will be provided with the URLs of many sites that I have visited that pertain to domestic violence. Sometimes Web sites change the URL and others close down completely. If you experience difficulty in finding one of the Web sites that is listed, conduct a search using the name of the organization that had posted the original URL. Type one of these in the area marked "address" on the home page of your browser to visit these sites and press "enter." Your browser will load the page that corresponds with the URL you type in. It is important to type the URL exactly or your browser will not load the proper page. Now look at the sources that have been provided for you. Later in this chapter, you will learn how to conduct your own search.

THE BASICS OF INTERNET RESEARCH

The most basic elements of Internet research are finding information and then evaluating it for your use. Search engines help with the first element; rely on common sense and some guidelines to satisfy the second. Finally, cite the information that you use. Online citation styles provides examples of citation for different methods, including APA, MLA, Chicago style, and more. For an example of citing electronic media, go to:

http://www.cdc.gov/nchs/howto/citelec.htm

Search Engines

If you do not know the URL for the site you want to visit, you can find information by conducting a search. To do a search, you need to use a search engine. These reside on the World Wide Web ready and waiting for you to choose the one that works best for you. There are literally hundreds of search engines on the Internet. Within your Internet browser, you can type in the URL to go to a specific search engine, or you can use one that is on the home page of your browser. Whichever search engine you use, it is advisable to conduct more than one search to optimize your choices. Here is a directory of search engines that provides links to many of them: Beaucoup!

http://www.beaucoup.com/

The three major categories of search engines are the directory, the **robot**, and the multisearch. The difference between them is that robots produce indiscriminate quantity, whereas directories produce small amounts of quality information resources. Robots deal in millions of Web sites. Directories deal in perhaps thousands of Web sites.

1. **Directory search engines** are like catalogs of Web sites that have been divided into categories. Examples of this type are Google (*http://www .google.com*), Yahoo (*www.yahoo.com*), and Excite (*http://www.excite.com*). Directory search engines get the information from people who enter it into the search engine's database. A directory search is more likely to produce high-quality information, since it is more focused.

2. Robots are sometimes called worms, spiders, harvesters, or wanderers. They use a program to search, catalog, and organize information on the Internet. In the middle of the night, they go out and visit Web sites and other Internet resources and take key information from them which they act upon when you employ them in a search. Examples of robots are HotBot (*http://www.hotbot .com/*) and AltaVista (*http://www.alta-vista.net/*). The robot will give you a greater quantity of information, but the sources may be only remotely connected to the subject that you are researching.

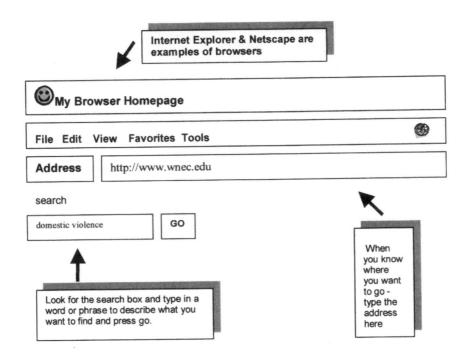

Figure 12–2   Here is an illustration of the top tool bars of your Internet browser. Note the difference between the address bar and the search box.

3. One way to overcome the dilemma of choosing the proper search engine is to use a **multisearch engine**. These search robot search engines and directory search engines and can produce different results. Some integrate the results from various search engines by eliminating the duplicate results returned. Integration takes longer to show results on your screen because the engine must process more information before producing the results. One of my favorites is DogPile (*http://www.dogpile.com*). DogPile produces the closest links to your search; it retrieves and ranks the best responses from a variety of search engines. It also "times out" your search inquiry. This means that if no results to your query are found in a specified time period, it will skip over to the next engine and conduct that search. This is helpful if you are not sure whether or not you have conducted your inquiry using the best search words possible.

Typically, you should try to use search words or words that best describe what you are looking for when conducting a search. Beginners sometimes have difficulty with choosing accurate search phrases. One way to get around that problem is to use the multisearch engine that lets you ask in question form: Ask Jeeves! (*http://aj.com/*) is an example of a multisearch engine that helps you refine your search.

Evaluating Your Source

You will need to scrutinize your resources on the Internet, if for no other reason than the volume. How do you choose the best to use? First determine your purpose: Why do you need this information? If it is to expand your knowledge and gain insight from different perspectives, the Internet is your garden! Harvest it all and don't worry. A word of caution: Don't rely on the graphics and setup of the page to make your decision on reliability; a Web page expert may not know anything about domestic violence.

On the other hand, if you are writing a paper yourself and looking for legitimate sources, you must evaluate what you find. Although some suggest that the reputation of the author is most important, this criterion is not helpful if you are new to the field of study and unfamiliar with the experts. It is more important to consider the creditability of the producer. Where does the information come from? Can you determine if the source is from a perspective that you can identify? Is this posted through a police department or other government agency? Alternatively, is the information posted by North American Man/Boy Love Association (NAMBLA)? Do you know the difference?

Another criterion used for evaluating the value of an Internet resource is the bibliography and/or references. Can you document or research the information on which the article is based? Are these legitimate sources? Consider also the date of the article and its relevance to your project. The University of Wisconsin–Eau Claire McIntyre Library posted its method of evaluating Internet resources, suggesting you look at the "Ten C's" (Richmond, 1996).

More About It: NAMBLA

The use of an acronym or other name that appears professional can be deceiving. Make sure that you know what the organization stands for before you cite it as a source! For example, NAMBLA stands for North American Man–Boy Love Association. It is a pederast organization that advocates legal reform allowing for the decriminalization of sex between adult males and boys. A sexual relationship between adults and children is child abuse. It is behavior that is prohibited by law in every state in the United States. This perspective would not be a creditable one to cite on child issues. Be careful; they, too, are located on the Internet!

THE EXTENT OF PERSONAL CRIME

Three major sources contribute to the body of knowledge that exists today on the extent of personal crime: the Uniform Crime Reports, the National Crime Victimization Surveys, and Self-Report Surveys. Measuring the characteristics of crime is the most important function of each of the major methods. They seek to determine when and where criminal acts are perpetrated; the type or severity of the crime; and how often the offenses are committed. The characteristics of the criminal, of the victim, and of the victim–criminal relationship are quantified to enhance theoretical explanations and to develop social policy. Without these contemporary methods of gathering information, our knowledge on victimization would not exist.

The Uniform Crime Reporting System

In the 1920s, the International Association of Chiefs of Police (IACP) identified the desirability of gathering information on crime and tracking national crime statistics. The Federal Bureau of Investigation (FBI) was authorized to serve as the national clearinghouse for this voluntary collection on police data in 1929. It is called the **Uniform Crime Reporting (UCR) System**. Besides being the oldest source of crime data, it is the most frequently cited source of information.

   The Uniform Crime Reports can be found by going to the home page of the FBI at

http://www.fbi.gov/ucr/ucr.htm

Monthly arrest reports from law enforcement agencies across the nation are sent to the FBI, which publishes them in an annual report, *Crime in the United States*. In addition to crime counts and trends, the report includes data on crimes cleared, persons arrested (age, gender, and race), law enforcement officers killed or assaulted, and the characteristics of homicides (including victim–offender relationships).

Drawbacks of the Uniform Crime Reporting System.   Critics cite numerous limitations in the UCR System. First, it represents only those crimes that are reported to the police. It does not reflect the actual number of crimes committed. The second limitation is the manner in which the crimes are reported to the FBI. When several crimes are committed in one event, for example, only the most serious is included in the UCR; the rest are not reported. In the past, crimes that were not indexed in the UCR could not be included. For example, *rape* was defined as forced sexual intercourse with a woman by a man who is not her husband. Spousal rape was not recognized. The report of a male raped by a domestic partner would also not be included. Another complaint about this source is the limited amount of information that has been gathered on the victim-to-offender relationship. To address these complaints, the UCR program is currently being converted to a more comprehensive and detailed one, the **National Incident-Based Reporting System**.

More About It: Evaluating Internet Resources

The Ten C's for Evaluating Internet Resources

1. *Content.* What is the intent of the content? Are the title and author identified? Is the content "juried"? Is the content "popular" or "scholarly," satiric or serious? What is the date of the document or article? Is the "edition" current? Do you have the latest version? (Is this important?) How do you know?

2. *Credibility.* Is the author identifiable and reliable? Is the content credible? Authoritative? Should it be? What is the purpose of the information, that is, is it serious, satiric, humorous? Is the URL extension .edu, .com, .gov, or .org? What does this tell you about the "publisher"?

3. *Critical thinking.* How can you apply critical-thinking skills, including previous knowledge and experience, to evaluate Internet resources? Can you identify the author, publisher, edition, and so on, as you would a "traditionally" published resource? What criteria do you use to evaluate Internet resources?

4. *Copyright.* Even if the copyright notice does not appear prominently, someone wrote, or is responsible for, the creation of a document, graphic, sound, or image, and the material falls under the copyright conventions. "Fair use" applies to short, cited excerpts, usually as an example for commentary or research. Materials are in the "public domain" if this is stated explicitly. Just as users of print media, Internet users must respect copyrights.

5. *Citation.* Internet resources should be cited to identify sources used, both to give credit to the author and to provide the reader with avenues for further research. Standard style manuals (print and online) provide some examples of how to cite Internet documents, although standards have not yet been formally established.

6. *Continuity.* Will the Internet site be maintained and updated? Is it now, and will it continue to be, free? Can you rely on this source over time to provide up-to-date information? Some good .edu sites have moved to .com, with possible cost implications. Other sites offer partial use for free, and charge fees for continued or in-depth use.

7. *Censorship.* Is your discussion list "moderated"? What does this mean? Does your search engine or index look for all words, or are some words excluded? Is this censorship? Does your institution, based on its mission, parent organization, or space limitations, apply restrictions to Internet use? Consider censorship and privacy issues when using the Internet.

(continued)

8.   *Connectivity.* If more than one user will need to access a site, consider each users' access and "functionality." How do users connect to the Internet, and what kind of connection does the assigned resource require? Does access to the resource require a graphical user interface? If it is a popular (busy) resource, will it be accessible in the time frame needed? Is it accessible by more than one Internet tool? Do users have access to the same Internet tools and applications? Are users familiar with the tools and applications? Is the site "viewable" by all Web browsers?

9.   *Comparability.* Does the Internet resource have an identified comparable print or CD-ROM data set or source? Does the Internet site contain comparable and complete information? (For example, some newspapers have partial but not full text information on the Internet.) Do you need to compare data or statistics over time? Can you identify sources for comparable earlier or later data? Comparability of data may or may not be important, depending on your project.

10. *Context.* What is the context for your research? Can you find "anything" on your topic, that is, commentary, opinion, narrative, statistics, and your quest will be satisfied? Are you looking for current or historical information? Definitions? Research studies or articles? How does Internet information fit in the overall information context of your subject? Before you start searching, define the research context and research needs and decide what sources might be best to use to fill information needs successfully without data overload.

Source: Elizabeth B. Richmond, Assistant Professor and Reference Librarian, University of Wisconsin–Eau Claire, Wisconsin. For further information or to reprint, contact Ms. Richmond at richmoeb@uwec.edu.

National Incident-Based Reporting System.   To improve the quality, quantity, and timeliness of crime statistical data collected by the law enforcement community and to improve the methodology of analyzing, auditing, and publishing the collected data, a new reporting system has been designed. Eventually, the National Incident-Based Reporting System (NIBRS) will replace the UCR. As of September 2003 the FBI has certified 22 state programs. The U.S. population covered had reached 19 percent, and 15 percent of crime was reported via NIBRS. Of the nation's law enforcement agencies, 27 percent were now reporting crime statistics via NIBRS.

The most significant difference between UCR and NIBRS is that it will report on incidents of crime in addition to arrests in a category called group A offenses. The designation as "attempted" or "completed" has also been added. Expanded victim-to-offender relationships will be reported for all crimes where a crime against a person has been committed, such as rape or assault, in addition to homicide. An increased emphasis on the circumstances of the crime, such as aggravated assaults, is another notable change. NIBRS holds great promise to increase the information on crime characteristics, in particular for domestic violence crimes.

The FBI is also authorized to collect data under NIBRS. More information about NIBRS can be found at

http://www.search.org/nibrs/default.asp

Drawbacks to National Incident-Based Reporting System.   Even with the improvements in crime statistics that are being implemented through NIBRS, one major limitation remains. The statistics will only reflect the crimes that people are willing to report to the police; therefore, they will not accurately depict crime in some categories. For example, the findings from the National Violence Against Women (NVAW) Survey found that there is a difference in the prevalence of reported rape and physical assault among women of different racial and ethnic backgrounds (Tjaden & Thoennes, 1998):

Native American/Alaska Native women	Most likely to report victimization
Asian/Pacific Islander women	Least likely to report victimization
Hispanic women	Less likely to report being raped
Non-Hispanic women	More likely to report being raped

National Crime Victimization Survey

The **National Crime Victimization Survey** (NCVS) attempts to address the problem of reporting. NCVS is the primary source of information on criminal victimization in the United States. A component of the Department of Justice, the Bureau of Justice Statistics began the NCVS program in 1973. It provides details on crime incidents, victims, and trends. A redesign of the survey was completed in 1993 to improve the questions, update the survey methods, and broaden the scope of crimes measured.

Commercial crimes and homicide are not included in this survey, which is conducted by personnel from the U.S. Census Bureau. A representative sample of approximately 45,000 households with over 94,000 persons interviewed is included to determine the extent of crime, regardless of whether or not it was reported to law enforcement. The survey includes detailed information about victims, offenders, and the nature of the criminal conduct.

Results of the National Crime Victimization Survey are compiled by the Bureau of Justice Statistics and can be accessed at the Bureau of Justice Statistics Web site:

http://www.ojp.usdoj.gov/bjs/welcome.html

Drawbacks to the National Crime Victimization Survey.   As stated earlier, the NCVS does not include all the crimes covered by the UCR. It is also criticized because it relies on people's memories of their victimization. Some people may exaggerate their victimization; others will fail to view themselves as victims at all. Incidents may have been forgotten or fabricated. There is no way to confirm the victimization reports.

Self-Report Studies

The third way to determine the extent of crime is a category of information rather than a specific source. **Self-report studies** are questionnaires or interviews given by researchers who query people on how much crime they have committed. Frequently, studies of this sort are conducted with college and high school students or in prisons. They are important because they have refuted the idea that only a small population commits crime. They suggest a large discrepancy between official statistics and the reality of criminal behavior.

On the World Wide Web, the most comprehensive source of criminal justice information to include self-report studies is the National Criminal Justice Reference Service (NCJRS). The site is a clearinghouse for research and statistics, as well as a database of criminal justice abstracts. The contributing agencies include

> Office of Justice Programs (OJP), U.S. Department of Justice
> Office of the Assistant Attorney General (OAAG)
> Corrections Program Office (CPO)
> Drug Courts Program Office (DCPO)
> Executive Office for Weed and Seed (EOWS)
> Office for Domestic Preparedness (ODP)
> Office of the Police Corps and Law Enforcement Education (OPCLEE)
> Violence Against Women Office (VAWO)
> Bureau of Justice Assistance (BJA)
> Bureau of Justice Statistics (BJS)
> National Institute of Justice (NIJ)
> Office for Victims of Crime (OVC)
> Office of Juvenile Justice and Delinquency Prevention (OJJDP)
> Office of National Drug Control Policy (ONDCP), Executive Office of the President

You can access the NCJRS Web site at

http://www.ncjrs.org/

It would probably take months to access all the documents available at the NCJRS site. You can do a search by key word, typing in words that relate to your area of interest. Another advantage of NCJRS is the abstract database, which is also searchable. This provides an abstract of documents that you can obtain in full from other sources.

NCJRS also offers JUSTINFO and JUVJUST (for free!). JUSTINFO is a bimonthly newsletter that is sent out on the 1st and 15th of each month and covers news and announcements from all NCJRS partner agencies. JUVJUST is an electronic mailing list that contains postings on a wide range of topics and resources related to juvenile justice, delinquency prevention, and child protection.

To subscribe to JUSTINFO, go to

http://virlib.ncjrs.org/JUSTINFO.asp

More About It: Bookmarks

Bookmarks are a way to keep track of the URLs that you have visited and may want to return to at a future time. In Netscape Navigator, just click on the word Bookmarks, which is located at the top left side of the monitor screen. Next, click on Add Bookmark. That's it! In Microsoft Internet Explorer, click on the icon Favorites.

There are three ways to obtain the document of your choice through NCJRS:

1. *In ASCII.* This would be a text-only, but full version of the document.
2. *In Adobe Acrobat.* This would contain all charts and graphics of the original file. Adobe Acrobat is a free download that you can obtain by clicking on the "download Adobe Acrobat now" sign and follow the directions on how to install it on your computer. It is easy and allows you to read full graphic documents. They can be printed on your personal printer exactly as they appear on the screen.
3. *In print copy.* By calling the toll-free number, you can order files that will be mailed to you. This is particularly helpful if the report is long. Some of the documents available are over 200 pages!

Drawbacks to the Self-Report Studies.   Critics cite the unreliability of offender reports as a major flaw in this kind of research. There is no way to determine if the person is exaggerating his or her participation in criminal activity to impress the researcher. Another limitation of self-report studies is that they typically investigate involvement in minor crimes, not major criminal activities. As you have noted, there are limitations to each of the different major sources of information that researchers use to determine the prevalence of crime. Together they balance each other out, offering different perspectives on similar problems. On the WWW, there is the opportunity to search for a general picture on crime or to delve deeply into specific areas. Therefore, in addition to conducting general research on crime and victimization, you may want to limit your search and focus on a particular form of domestic violence. In the next section we offer some excellent starting points for research into child abuse.

ABUSE OF PERSONS WITH DISABILITIES

The ADA Home Page has numerous links to research the rights of persons with disabilities. Also featured are stories about individuals who have been helped from the services of ADA.

http://www.usdoj.gov/crt/ada/adahom1.htm

Center for Research on Women with Disabilities (CROWD) provides information on research and training for issues such as violence against women with disabilities.

http://www.bcm.tmc.edu/crowd/

Protection from abuse and neglect for persons with a disability is featured in Chapter 13 of this online text entitled "Guidebook on laws and programs for persons with disabilities."

http://www.illinoislawhelp.org/index.cfm?fuseaction=home.dsp_content&contentID=784

The Institute on Community Integration is a component of the Department of Health and Human Services. While offering a wealth of information on issues of importance to persons with disabilities, the newsletter *Violence Against Women* is particularly good.

http://ici.umn.edu/products/impact/133/default.html

CHILD ABUSE

Wherever you see the term *clearinghouse*, you have hit a gold mine. Keep looking on that Web page until you find everything you want to know. Be sure and bookmark the home page so that you can return to it later and select another area to delve into. Otherwise, it is easy to follow a number of hotlinks off a major source and then forget how to get back to where you started.

The Children, Youth, and Family Consortium (CYFC) electronic clearinghouse was one of the first electronic libraries designed to share information about children, youth, and families. The wealth of information available via CYFC is contributed by many individuals and organizations, including the University of Minnesota and the University of Minnesota Extension Service. You can access CYFC at the following URL:

http://www.cyfc.umn.edu

A "must have" site for people interested in child abuse is the National Clearinghouse on Child Abuse and Neglect Information. Affiliated with the U.S. Department of Health and Human Services, this is a national resource for professionals seeking information on the prevention, identification, and treatment of child abuse and neglect and related child welfare issues.

http://nccanch.acf.hhs.gov/index.cfm

The Children's Bureau (CB) is the oldest federal agency for children and is located within the U.S. Department of Health and Human Services' Administration for Children and Families, Administration on Children, Youth and Families. It is

Figure 12–3 The National Clearinghouse on Child Abuse and Neglect Information is well worth visiting.

responsible for assisting states in the delivery of child welfare services—services designed to protect children and strengthen families.

http://www.acf.dhhs.gov/programs/cb/

The National Center for Missing and Exploited Children maintains a national registry on children who are reported missing. Photographs of missing children are posted on its Web page with names and descriptions. In addition to accepting tips over the Internet, the center also maintains a 24-hour hotline for reports: 1-800-THE-LOST.

http://www.missingkids.com/

The Child Abuse Prevention Network provides Internet resources for the prevention of child abuse. Special links from this home page bring the reader to information on the Military Family Resource Center, an organization whose focus is on building and strengthening child abuse prevention partnerships between military and civilian communities; Disability-Abuse.com, with a mission to prevent abuse of people with disabilities and protect others from abuses that lead to disability; and the International Society for the Prevention of Child Abuse, among others. Access to additional information for professionals who work in the field can be obtained by becoming a member of this organization.

http://child-abuse.com/

Nancy Faulkner's Pandora's Box provides links to over 200 pages on the subject of child abuse. It has links to Internet crimes, child abuse resources, child laws, and more.

http://www.prevent-abuse-now.com/

An interesting page with links on male child sexual abuse is provided by Jim Hopper. Data on prevention, prevalence, and more are available through this source.

http://www.jimhopper.com/abstats

The guardian *ad litem* is a person appointed by the court to represent the best interests of a child and to speak on his or her behalf. Information on this volunteer organization can be found at the National Association of Guardian Ad Litem (NAGAL) page.

http://www.nagalro.com/

The Centre for Research on Violence against Women and Children is an alliance of five research centers in Canada. Their research and project information is extremely helpful.

http://www.uwo.ca/violence/

The U.S. Department of Justice maintains Web sites entitled *Violence Against Women Online*. Its document library contains research regarding domestic violence, stalking, batterer intervention programs, child custody and protection, sexual assault, and economic impact.

http://www.vaw.umn.edu/

ACT—Adults and Children Together Against Violence—is a violence-prevention campaign composed of a national multimedia campaign and community-based training programs. The campaign focuses on adults who raise, care for, and teach children ages zero to eight years. It is designed to prevent violence by providing young children with positive role models and environments that teach nonviolent problem solving.

http://www.actagainstviolence.org/

Child Trends is a nonprofit, nonpartisan research organization that studies children, youth, and families through research, data collection, and data analysis.

http://www.childtrends.org/

The Office for Juvenile Justice and Delinquency (OJJDP) contains a wealth of information on all aspects of juvenile violence and crime. You can reach this site through the NCJRS page or you can go directly to

http://ojjdp.ncjrs.org/

The American Professional Society on the Abuse of Children (APSAC) self-described mission is to ensure that everyone affected by child maltreatment receives the best possible professional response. Among its resources is the *APSAC Handbook on Child Maltreatment*, 2nd edition.

http://www.apsac.org/

CHILD DEATH INVESTIGATION

The most recent survey on child death investigation is entitled *Current Trends in Child Abuse Reporting and Fatalities: The Results of the 1997 Annual Fifty-State Survey* (Wang & Daro, 1998). The report can also be obtained via postal mail by calling (312)663-3520.

The full report on child homicide in California is available at the Interagency Council on Child Abuse and Neglect site (ICAN). In addition, ICAN administers the National Center on Child Fatality Review (NCFR). Their searchable online database allows a person to type in a particular state to receive the name of a contact person who heads up the local child death review team. Child death review teams (CDRTs) have been formed in California and many other states because of concerns of professionals on the increasing number of children who were being killed by abuse and neglect. The teams, made up of professionals from many fields, look into cases of child death.

http://www.ican-ncfr.org/

Georgia's Office of Child Fatality Review home page offers information on child fatality review for Georgia with links to other states with individual pages on this topic.

http://www.childwelfare.net/CFR/cfrlinks.html#state_cfr

Figure 12–4 The "Back to Sleep" campaign is suitably named for its recommendation to place healthy babies on their backs to sleep. Placing babies on their backs to sleep reduces the risk of sudden infant death syndrome (SIDS), also known as "crib death." This campaign is sponsored by the National Institute of Child Health and Human Development, the Maternal and Child Health Bureau, the American Academy of Pediatrics, the SIDS Alliance, and the Association of SIDS and Infant Mortality Programs.

Concerned about child deaths? Learn more about the shaken baby syndrome, which was discussed in Chapter 6. This site is maintained by the Shaken Baby Alliance, a nonprofit organization dedicated to assisting shaken baby syndrome victims and their families. It is a source of education for the general public on the syndrome.

http://www.shakenbaby.com/

The American SIDS Institute conducts research and provides online information for the prevention of sudden infant death syndrome (SIDS). You can order educational materials and find referrals at this site. This is an excellent source for statistics on the annual rate of SIDS in the United States.

http://www.sids.org

CHILD MENTORING AND PREVENTION

America's Promise aims to provide every at-risk child in America with access to all five fundamental resources needed in order for them to lead happy, healthy, and productive lives. America's Promise works to mobilize national and local commitments from the private and public sectors, and more generally raise awareness of the importance of these five key resources to America's youth.

http://www.americaspromise.org/

Big Brothers/Sisters of America (BBBSA) is an organization with a universally recognized brand name and a notable absence of scandal. BBBSA, the oldest mentoring organization serving youth in the country, remains the leading expert in our field. BBBSA has provided one-to-one mentoring relationships between adult volunteers and children at risk since 1904. BBBSA currently serves over 100,000 children and youth in more than 500 agencies throughout all of the United States.

http://www.bbbsa.org/

The purpose of the Boy Scouts of America, incorporated on February 8, 1910 and chartered by Congress in 1916, is to provide an educational program for boys and young adults to build character, to train in the responsibilities of participating citizenship, and to develop personal fitness.

http://www.scouting.org/

The Boys and Girls Clubs of America seek to inspire and enable all young people, especially those from disadvantaged circumstances, to realize their full potential as productive, responsible, and caring citizens.

http://www.bgca.org/

CRIMINAL JUSTICE SITES

The National Citizens Crime Prevention Campaign was the first to air public service announcements on crime prevention. Look to see what they are doing now!

http://www.weprevent.org/

SEARCH, the National Consortium for Justice Information and Statistics, provides links to a variety of information sites. For example, you can find the Sex Offender Registry Laws for each state. Go to

http://www.search.org/

The Institute for Law and Justice is a private nonprofit company that provides research, consulting, and services in criminal justice.

http://www.ilj.org/

Personal Web pages frequently provide links to valuable resources. The Law Offices of Kim Kruglick have many criminal law links of interest.

http://www.kruglaw.com/lawlink.html

ELDER ABUSE

The Administration on Aging page, maintained by the U.S. Department of Health and Human Services, offers up-to-date information on the concerns of elders. Here you will find information on nutrition to Alzheimer's. Links are provided for caregivers, professionals, and elders on a variety of timely topics.

http://www.aoa.dhhs.gov/

Figure 12–5 Where would you go to find out about the issues of importance to the elderly? The *Administration on Aging* page.

Another great source of information on elders is the National Center on Elder Abuse (NCEA), supported by the U.S. Department of Health and Human Services. Elder law, statistics, and publications are all available from links off this Web page. The Clearinghouse on Abuse and Neglect of the Elderly (CANE), the largest computerized collection of elder abuse resources with over 3,500 holdings, is available as a searchable database.

http://www.elderabusecenter.org/

GAY AND LESBIAN DOMESTIC VIOLENCE SITES

Domestic violence in the gay and lesbian community may be as frequent as family violence in other relationships. For a bibliography on issues that affect these relationships, visit the Gay and Lesbian Domestic Violence Bibliography page.

http://www.xq.com/cuav/dvbibl.htm

The Community United Against Violence (CUAV) addresses common misconceptions about gay-battering relationships, hate violence, and other important issues regarding the gay, lesbian, bisexual, and transgender communities (GLBT).

http://www.cuav.org/

Stop Abuse for Everyone (SAFE) is a nonprofit organization that provides advocacy, information, and support for men and women who are the victims of domestic violence. It sets up and advocates for services for men and women, straight, gay, or lesbian. SAFE concentrates on domestic violence against straight men, gay men, and lesbian women, because few services exist for these groups.

http://www.safe4all.org/

DOVES Web page has a good article on the dynamics of gay and lesbian battering at

http://www.doves-stop-violence.org/gnl.htm

Founded as a nonprofit organization by a survivor of domestic violence in 1994, the Gay Men's Domestic Violence Project (GMDVP) provides community education and direct services to gay, bisexual, and transgendered male victims, and survivors of domestic violence. This project also serves the needs of heterosexual abused males, who made up approximately 20 percent of their hotline calls for help and information during 2000.

http://www.gmdvp.org/

GENERAL INFORMATION

An excellent source for information on violence against women, the safety zone was featured on CNET TV's program *The Web*, aired on the Sci-Fi channel during the week of September 27, 1997. It was also featured in *Internet Week*, September 14, 1998.

http://thesafetyzone.org/

The Family Violence Prevention Fund (FUND) is a national nonprofit organization that focuses on domestic violence education, prevention, and public policy reform. It specifically addresses domestic violence committed by athletes.

http://endabuse.org/

An electronic clearinghouse on domestic violence data appears at the Minnesota Center Against Violence and Abuse (MINCAVA).

http://www.mincava.umn.edu/

ANTISTALKING SITES

The antistalking Web site is a site for anyone interested in the crime of stalking. It is meant to be a resource not only for stalking victims, but also for law enforcement, mental health professionals, researchers, educators, legislators, and security personnel.

http://www.antistalking.com/Default.htm

Cyberstalking is explained by the Cyberangels in a site that was recently named the recipient of the 1998 President's Service Award.

http://www.cyberangels.org/

Founded in 1995, Survivors of Stalking, Inc. (S.O.S.) is a grassroots organization operated entirely by volunteers, most of which are past victims of stalking. Their goal is to educate the public and targets of stalking.

http://www.soshelp.org/

The Stalking Behavior Web site is a nonprofit, private endeavor. The Web site was created by D. T. Coon and posted on January 22, 2000. It provides information on stalking behaviors, definitions, and resources.

http://www.stalkingbehavior.com/

GOVERNMENT SITES

The Social Security Administration (SSA) announced on November 4, 1998, that it was taking additional steps to make it easier for abused, battered women to establish a new identity and obtain a new Social Security number, reducing the risk of further violence. Read about this at the SSA Web site:

http://www.ssa.gov/pressoffice/domestic_fact.html

Created in 1984 by the Justice Assistance Act, the Office of Justice Programs (OJP) works within its established partnership arrangements with federal, state, and local agencies and national and community-based organizations to develop, fund, and evaluate a wide range of criminal and juvenile justice programs. OJP's mission is to provide federal leadership in developing the nation's capacity to prevent and control crime, administer justice, and assist crime victims. Here you can search for information from specific OJP Program Offices, such as the Violence Against Women Office (VAWO); OJP bureaus, such as the Office for Victims of Crime; or OJP support bureaus, such as the Office for Civil Rights.

http://www.ojp.usdoj.gov/

The Research and Development Branch of OJP is the National Institute of Justice. Its searchable database has a wealth of information.

http://www.ojp.usdoj.gov/nij

The United States Customs Service is the primary enforcement agency protecting the nation's borders. Among its work is discovering and fighting cybercrime (which has made the U.S. Customs Service a leader in combating child pornography), money laundering, and the importation of dangerous substances. It partners with other government agencies to combat terrorism.

http://www.customs.gov/

For statistical information from various U.S. government agencies, FedStats provides many links.

http://www.fedstats.gov/

INTERNATIONAL SITES

The Australian Domestic and Family Violence Clearinghouse, established in October 1999, is a national resource on issues of domestic and family violence.

http://www.austdvclearinghouse.unsw.edu.au/Default.htm

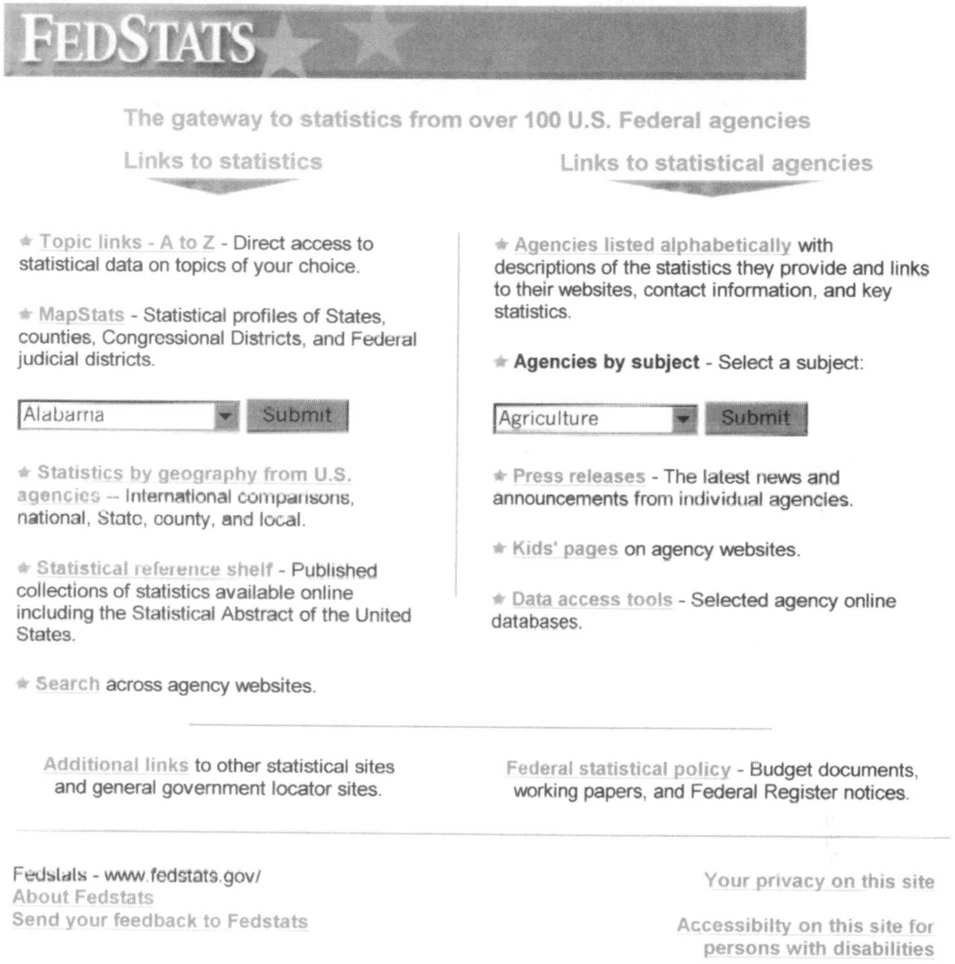

FEDSTATS ★ ★

The gateway to statistics from over 100 U.S. Federal agencies

Links to statistics	Links to statistical agencies

★ Topic links - A to Z - Direct access to statistical data on topics of your choice.

★ MapStats - Statistical profiles of States, counties, Congressional Districts, and Federal judicial districts.

| Alabama ▾ | Submit |

★ Statistics by geography from U.S. agencies -- International comparisons, national, State, county, and local.

★ Statistical reference shelf - Published collections of statistics available online including the Statistical Abstract of the United States.

★ Search across agency websites.

★ Agencies listed alphabetically with descriptions of the statistics they provide and links to their websites, contact information, and key statistics.

★ **Agencies by subject** - Select a subject:

| Agriculture ▾ | Submit |

★ Press releases - The latest news and announcements from individual agencies.

★ Kids' pages on agency websites.

★ Data access tools - Selected agency online databases.

Additional links to other statistical sites and general government locator sites.

Federal statistical policy - Budget documents, working papers, and Federal Register notices.

Fedstats - www.fedstats.gov/
About Fedstats
Send your feedback to Fedstats

Your privacy on this site

Accessibilty on this site for persons with disabilities

Figure 12–6   The gateway to statistics from over 100 U.S. federal agencies.

Project Alert is online to raise awareness and educate women in particular, and society in general, on the issue of violence against women in Nigeria.

http://prolert.kabissa.org/

WAVE is a network of European women's nongovernmental organizations working in the field of combating violence against women and children (women's refuges, counseling centers, SOS hotlines/helplines, organizations focusing on prevention and training, etc.). Currently the network focuses specifically on violence in the family and in intimate relationships.

http://www.wave-network.org/Main_frame.html

Women's Rights Center (Poland) was created to ensure that gender perspective is present during the law-making process and in the application of law and that women and men are equal before the law.

http://free.ngo.pl/temida/index.htm

Northern Ireland Women's Aid Federation (NIWAF) provides refuge and emotional support to women and their dependent children suffering from mental or physical harassment within the home.

http://www.niwaf.org/

Women's Aid—Online offers domestic violence education and resources to women in Ireland. Of particular note is an article entitled "How an abuser can discover your Internet activities."

http://www.womensaid.ie/

The Family Violence Prevention Fund provides updates on national and international domestic violence news:

http://endabuse.org/

The Human Rights Watch Global Report on Women's Human Rights is a lengthy and depressing documentation and criticism of the abuse, prostitution, forced labor, and related oppression of women in many countries.

http://cjwww.csustan.edu/cj/links.html

LAW ENFORCEMENT SITES

Crime Spider is a great link that searches for criminal justice information on the Web. Choose just about any area that you want to research and let the spider go! It crawls around hundreds of sites and finds information on criminalistics, forensic anthropology, unsolved murders, the death penalty, child abuse, domestic violence, and more.

http://crimespider.com/

Prentice Hall maintains an excellent source of internet links on domestic violence. Dr. Frank Schmalleger's Criminal Justice Cybrary of 3,109 criminal justice links provides links to information on just about any topic of interest to the profession. It can be found at

http://talkjustice.com/links.asp?453053941

Dr. Cecil Greek's criminal justice pages at Florida State University provide the most comprehensive view of resources available on the Internet that relate to the field of criminal justice. A must see!

http://cjwww.csustan.edu/cj/links.html

Police Sites

The International Association of Chiefs of Police is the world's oldest and largest non-profit membership organization of police executives, with over 19,000 members in over 100 different countries.

http://www.theiacp.org/

The Danvers, Massachusetts Police Department maintains a great source of information and links on their Domestic Violence Resource and Information Page. This site provides invaluable information about domestic law, duties of police officers, and victim rights specific to Massachusetts. It has links to some very interesting sources.

http://www.danverspolice.com/domviol.htm

The Domestic Violence Section of the Metro Nashville Police Department offers some warning signs of domestic abuse. It addresses **separation abuse** and abuse occurring after the victim has separated from the abuser, which results in a high injury rate for women.

http://www.police.nashville.org/bureaus/investigative/domestic/symptoms.htm

The Los Angeles Police Department has an enormous amount of information online regarding domestic violence indicators and the law.

http://www.lapdonline.org/

LEGAL   SITES

The State and Local Government Web Page is a Library of Congress Internet resource page. It provides links to Web, Gopher, telnet, and FTP (file transfer protocol) sites that contain the full text of state statutes, state constitutions, and other legislative resources. Unsure of the laws in your state that relate to domestic violence? Try this site!

http://www.loc.gov/global/state/stategov.html

The American Bar Association, Commission on Domestic Violence, takes a strong stand against family violence. The site offers information and resources for victims of abuse. The site contains a link to the *Model Code on Domestic and Family Violence*, the new *ABA Guide for Judges Handling Interstate Cases Involving Children and Families*, and more. Internship opportunities are available.

http://www.abanet.org/domviol/home.html

The Legal Information Institute (LII and Hermes) offers U.S. Supreme Court opinions under the auspices of Project Hermes, the court's electronic-dissemination project. This archive will soon contain all opinions of the court issued since May 1990.

http://supct.law.cornell.edu/supct/

A law browser that provides links and information on legal matters that contains a searchable database is Find Law: Internet Legal Resources.

http://www.findlaw.com/

JUDICIAL SITES

The stated purpose of the American Judges Association is to improve the effective and impartial administration of justice, to enhance the independence and status of the judiciary, to provide for continuing education of its members, and to promote the interchange of ideas of a judicial nature among judges, court organizations, and the public. Look for the online booklet "Domestic Violence and the Courtroom—Understanding The Problem . . . Knowing the Victim."

http://aja.ncsc.dni.us/

MARITAL AND DATE RAPE

The Campus Violence Project exists to prevent personal violence and to promote healthy and empowered living among college students.

http://www.ndcaws.org/projects/campusviolence/campusviolence.asp

Drugs are increasingly being associated with the crime of rape. Information on the date rape drug Rohypnol ("roofies") appears at the Drug Enforcement Administration (DEA) site, along with information on law enforcement seizure of this drug, which is often brought in from Mexico.

http://www.usdoj.gov/dea/pubs/rohypnol/rohypnol.htm

The Los Angeles Commission on Assaults Against Women (LACAAW) is a nonprofit, multicultural, feminist, community-based volunteer organization. For a nominal fee, a variety of educational materials can be ordered. The site contains tips on self-defense and violence prevention for women; a free "Rape Prevention Kit" is also available.

http://www.lacaaw.org/home.html

Wellesley Centers for Women is a collaborative, multisite project involving a comprehensive follow-up study of families in which physical and/or sexual violence has occurred. The study examines the impact of these events upon the individual, the family, and the community, thereby evaluating the efficacy of specific interventions.

http://www.wellesley.edu/WCW/projects/mrape.html

MISCELLANEOUS SITES

National American Indian Court Judges Association offers insight to domestic violence on reservations through the Violence Against Indian Women Tribal Code Project.

http://www.naicja.org/

Life Span's Police Domestic Violence Program, Spouse Abuse By Law Enforcement (S.A.B.L.E.) is a unique project that provides specialized counseling, legal, and advocacy services for victims whose abusers are police or other law enforcement personnel.

http://www.policedv.com/

As you have learned, people convicted of a domestic violence crime (misdemeanor or felony) may no longer be licensed to buy weapons or ammunition. You can find out more information at the Bureau of Alcohol, Tobacco and Firearms' Web site for state laws and ordinances relating to weapons licensing:

http://www.atf.treas.gov/firearms/statelaws/22edition.htm

TEEN DATING VIOLENCE

The American Psychological Association developed "Love Doesn't Have to Hurt," an online resource for teens in dating relationships.

http://www.apa.org/pi/pii/teen/homepage.html

If you're in a violent dating relationship, or if you're worried about a friend, this is a great site to visit. The warning signs section is excellent. It also contains an online handbook entitled "When Love Hurts," the story of Angela and Joe, a fictional teenage couple in a violent relationship. The site is developed and maintained by Liz Clayborne, Inc.

http://www.loveisnotabuse.com/intro.asp

The Teen Dating Violence site is sponsored by the City of Boulder Police Department. This simple page describes the characteristics of an unhealthy dating relationship through a set of questions. While it is aimed toward younger teens, it provides realistic situations that may be considered abusive and is applicable to all relationships.

http://www.ci.boulder.co.us/police/prevention/teen_dating.htm

Texasmalescare (TMC) is a Web site filled with useful and current information on male involvement programs and issues throughout the state of Texas. Its unique approach to social problem solving tackles tough issues by supporting and educating young men on public health and social issues. Examples of the highlighted programs include education on preventing unwanted pregnancies, sexual responsibility, and responsible fatherhood.

http://www.texasmalescare.org/

YouthInfo is a Web site created by the U.S. Department of Health and Human Services (HHS) and currently maintained by the Family and Youth Services Bureau (FYSB) within HHS. You will find, for example, a calendar of youth-related events, information on potential funding sources, data about young people, links to other sites on youth issues, and information on the positive youth development approach to supporting and partnering with young people.

http://www.acf.dhhs.gov/programs/fysb/youthinfo/index.htm

VICTIMS' ASSISTANCE

Under a grant from the U.S. Department of Justice, the National Victim Assistance Academy coordinates the activities of the following program offices and bureaus: Bureau of Justice Assistance, Bureau of Justice Statistics, National Institute of Justice, Office of Juvenile Justice and Delinquency Prevention, and the Office for Victims of Crime.

http://www.ojp.usdoj.gov/ovc/assist/nvaa2002/welcome.html

Partnerships Against Violence Network (PAVNET) is a virtual library of information about violence and youth at risk, representing data from seven federal agencies. It is a one-stop, searchable information resource to help reduce redundancy in information management and to provide clear and comprehensive access to information for states and local communities.

http://www.pavnet.org/

The National Center for Victims of Crime is recognized as the nation's leading advocate for crime victims. In addition to its toll-free number for victims of crime, it contains a virtual library of information regarding many crime categories.

http://www.ncvc.org/

WOMAN BATTERING

For publications and statistics on the associated health concerns due to family violence, visit the National Center for Health Statistics (NCHS). NCHS is the primary federal organization responsible for the collection, analysis, and dissemination of health statistics.

http://www.cdc.gov/nchswww/default.htm

A comprehensive guide to family violence is provided in the Domestic Violence Survival Kit:

http://www.dvguide.com/content.html

The National Victim Assistance Academy Textbook (2002) is an entire book online—read it chapter by chapter! Its topics include all forms of victimization, including child abuse, domestic violence, and elderly victims.

http://www.ojp.usdoj.gov/ovc/assist/nvaa2002/welcome.html

The National Coalition against Domestic Violence located in Denver, Colorado, is a grassroots nonprofit membership organization that has been working since 1978 to end violence in the lives of women and children. It provides a national network for state coalitions and local programs serving battered women and their children, public policy at the national level, technical assistance, community awareness campaigns, general information and referrals, and publications on the issue of domestic violence. It also sponsors a national conference every two years for battered women and their advocates.

http://www.ncadv.org/about.htm

The Institute on Domestic Violence in the African American Community was designed to create a community of African American scholars and practitioners working in the area of violence in the African American community and to further scholarship in the area of African American violence.

http://www.dvinstitute.org/

At the Web site of the Domestic Violence Enhanced Response Team (DIVERT), you can find information about domestic violence and teen dating violence, as well as information about the effects of domestic violence on children. This section also provides Web site links to CASA (Court Appointed Special Advocates), Legal Aid, Pro Se Clinics, and Fast Track.

http://www.dvert.org/info/

The Feminist Majority Foundation (FMF), which was founded in 1987, is a cutting-edge organization dedicated to women's equality, reproductive health, and nonviolence.

http://www.feminist.org

Formed in 1995, the Melrose Alliance Against Violence (MAAV) is a nonprofit, community-based organization that focuses on outreach, education, and community collaboration in order to raise awareness of the problems of violence.

http://www.maav.org/

JUST FOR FUN

All work and no play makes the World Wide Web a dull place to surf! When you are finished with your research, don't forget to enjoy yourself. Not only will you find neat places to visit, you will also increase your skill at navigating the World Wide Web.

Do you still prefer television? Go to TV Guide Online!

http://www.tvguide.com/

What about a night on the town? Not sure which movie you should see? Perhaps the Internet Movie Database can help you decide.

http://us.imdb.com/

For the computer shopper who is looking for a good deal, check out the auctions at Egghead.Com. Upgrade your personal computer, buy accessories or software, and do it all online.

http://www.egghead.com

CONCLUSIONS

Valuable resources for domestic violence research reside on the Internet. Knowing how to connect, what might be obtained, and how to access the information are the focus of this chapter. The electronic network that we call the Internet is described in order to note the difference between it and the World Wide Web. WWW is a service that resides on the Internet—the most popular one.

An important step in the process of Internet research is evaluation of your source. Determine your purpose, and consider the credibility of the producer of the data. Look also for a bibliography and for references, an indication that the data originate from legitimate sources. Finally, determine if the information is current and relevant to your project.

The major sources of criminal justice knowledge may sound familiar to you: the Uniform Crime Reporting (UCR) System, the National Victimization Survey, and Self-Report Surveys. These sources are accessible over the Internet, in addition to hard copies that can be found in many libraries across the country. Obtaining information from these major sources directly over the Internet may expedite your research. For those who have never examined these sources, you will be amazed at the ease with which they may be accessed! In the future, the UCR will be replaced by the National Incident-Based Reporting System, and even more data will develop from this source.

Questions for Review

1. What is a domain name?

2. What is the most popular service on the Internet?

3. Describe the three major types of search engines.

4. How do you evaluate an Internet source?

5. What are the ten C's for evaluating Internet sources?

6. What are the three major sources for information regarding the extent of personal crime?

7. Explain the NIBRS. Who is responsible for collecting data under this system? Why has the system been developed?

8. What is the most comprehensive source of criminal justice information on the World Wide Web?

9. Visit at least two sites in a category of domestic violence. What have you learned from those Web pages?

Internet-Based Exercises

1. Choose one of the Web sites that is listed in Chapter 12. Go to that site and evaluate it using the "The Ten C's for Evaluating Internet Resources." How would you rate the site that you are visiting? Is it reliable? Why or why not?

2. Write a short paper on a family violence issue you find interesting. Use only Internet sites for your research. Include a reference page that demonstrates your ability to properly cite articles found on the World Wide Web.

References

Burnley, Jane et al. (eds.). 1996. *National Victim Assistance Academy Textbook*. Washington, DC: Office for Victims of Crime.

National Center for Health Statistics. 1995. "How to Cite Electronic Media." *http://www .cdc.gov/nchswww/howto/sitelec/citelec.htm*. 2002.

National Elder Abuse Incidence Study: Final Report. 1998. Administration on Aging, U.S. Department of Health and Human Services. *http://www.aoa.dhhs.gov/abuse/report/default .htm*. 2002.

Richmond, Betsy (ed.). 1996. "Ten C's for Evaluating Internet Resources." *http://www .uwec.edu/Admin/Library/10cs.html*. 1999.

State Child Death Review Board. 1997. "Child Deaths in California." March. *http://child.cornell.edu/ncfr/calif.html*. 2002.

Tjaden, Patricia, and Nancy Thoennes. 1998. *Prevalence, Incidence, and Consequences of the Violence Against Women: Findings from the National Violence Against Women Survey.* NCJ 172837. Washington, DC: U.S. Department of Justice.

Wang, Ching-Tung, and Deborah Daro. 1998. *Current Trends in Child Abuse Reporting and Fatalities: The Results of the 1997 Annual Fifty-State Survey.* Working Paper 808. Chicago: National Committee to Prevent Child Abuse.

INDEX

Page numbers followed by *f* indicate figures; page numbers followed by *t* indicate tables.